Praise for
Make Your Business Survive and Thrive

"Every entrepreneur should add this book to their business plan. With Huff's wise guidance and practical tips, along with success secrets culled from interviews with hundreds of established business owners, it offers everything needed to build a profitable venture."

—Ellen H. Parlapiano and Patricia Cobe, Founders of MompreneursOnline.com and Authors of *Mompreneurs®: A Mother's Practical Step-by-Step Guide to Work-at-Home Success*

"This awesome book helps take the guesswork out of starting, building, and maintaining your small or home-based business. It is packed with thousands of resources and literally takes you by the hand like your own personal coach. Kudos."

—Kim Essenmacher, Marketing & Small Business Consultant, Founder of SmallBizpreneur's Network, www.smallbizpreneurs.com

"Just when you are relieved your business survived its first year and don't know where to turn to take it to the next level, Priscilla Huff is here to save the day! In *Make Your Business Survive and Thrive*, Priscilla has written a must-have marketing manual for every small business owner. With this brilliant book in hand, you no longer have to spend time on research—you can continue working in and on your business, saving you hours and hours of valuable time (and money)! I cannot wait to recommend this book to the moms in business that I work with!"

—Terilee Harrison, Entrepreneur's Coach, Speaker, Radio Show Host, and author of *The Business Mom Guide Book: More Life, Less Overwhelm for Mom Entrepreneurs*, www.TheBusinessMom.com.

"Priscilla puts it all together for us in one handy resource, all the things business owners will and do encounter along the way. A must read for anyone thinking of, or in the beginning stages of business."

—Chanin Walsh, Founder of the Bucks County Women's Business Forum, www.womensbusinessforum.org

"Whether you're getting ready to start a business or if you're in the stages of maturity or growth, *Making Your Business Survive and Thrive* is a great read. The book is chock full of anecdotes and resources from creating a brand to strategic public and client relations on a shoestring. Every entrepreneur should read this book before launching a business."

—Gina F. Rubel, Esq., President/CEO,
www.FURIARUBEL.com

"*Make Your Business Survive and Thrive!* is like having your own small business consultant, ready to tackle your most pressing problems—and able to stretch your imagination so that you can expand your ideas and success. Packed with resources, this book is the one you will refer to again and again—as your business—and you—evolve.

Priscilla Huff provides step-by-step instructions on how to set up, refocus, or build your business—and where to find additional help from a variety of media, from books to the Internet to audio classes. It's like having an immediate network of experts from which to draw. *Survive and Thrive!* is like a series of how-to business seminars in one easy-to-follow book. I was in the midst of re-creating my company when I found this treasure, so the chapter, 'Define Your Venture' proved particularly useful. With clear, effective examples and advice from those who have been there, Priscilla inspires you to move your business idea forward, removing the obstacle of 'I don't know where to go for more information. If you are researching, refocusing, or re-energizing your small or home-based business, Priscilla has packaged the information you need to succeed.'"

—Maria Evans, Principal, Maria Martino Evans Communications

"Information Central—the one-stop-shopping for resources and how-to information for growing a successful business. Priscilla Huff has done all the homework for you and packed it in between these pages so readers can get up to speed quickly on the road to success!"

—Pamela A. Carroll, President, Carroll Consulting Group,
www.carrollconsultinggroup.com

"This book will help you overcome the challenges of finding the best ways to market your business to achieve maximum success. Practical, easy-to-implement ideas and techniques you can put into action immediately."

—Jim Donovan, author, *Handbook to a Happier Life*,
www.jimdonovan.com

"After reading just a few chapters of *Make your Business Survive and Thrive*, it became apparent to me that this book should be THE guide to resources for anyone thinking of starting a new business venture!"

—David Y. Chomitzky, owner, Davlen Farms,
www.davlenfarms.com

Make Your Business Survive and Thrive!

Make Your Business Survive and Thrive!

100+ Proven Marketing Methods to Help You Beat the Odds and Build a Successful Small or Home-Based Enterprise

Priscilla Y. Huff

BICENTENNIAL
1807
WILEY
2007
BICENTENNIAL

John Wiley & Sons, Inc.

Published by John Wiley & Sons, Inc., Hoboken, New Jersey.
Published simultaneously in Canada.

For general information on our other products and services or for technical support, please contact our Customer Care Department within the United States at (800) 762-2974, outside the United States at (317) 572-3993 or fax (317) 572-4002.

Wiley also publishes its books in a variety of electronic formats. Some content that appears in print may not be available in electronic books. For more information about Wiley products, visit our web site at www.wiley.com.

Library of Congress Cataloging-in-Publication Data:

Huff, Priscilla Y.
    Make your business survive and thrive! 100+ proven marketing
  methods to help you beat the odds and build a successful small or
  home-based enterprise / Priscilla Huff.
        p.   cm.
  ISBN-13: 978-0-470-05142-9 (pbk.)
  ISBN-10: 0-470-05142-6 (pbk.)
  1. Home-based businesses—Management—Handbooks, manuals,
  etc.   2. Small business—Marketing—Handbooks, manuals, etc.
  3. Marketing—Handbooks, manuals, etc.   I. Title.
  HD62.38.H8425   2007
  658.8—dc22

                                        2006016189

Printed in the United States of America.

10 9 8 7 6 5 4 3 2 1

To entrepreneurs, self-employed individuals, and
small and home-based business owners everywhere who supply
the lifeblood and energy to the world's global economy.

And to my network of fellow writers, friends, and family for
their never-failing support and encouragement,
a special thanks.

Contents

Foreword   xi

Preface   xv

Acknowledgments   xvii

1   **Introduction: Understanding the Challenges of
    Entrepreneurship**   1

2   **Grow with a Unique Idea: Defining Your Venture**   29

3   **Grow with Effective Organization and the Right
    Tools: Time *Is* Money!**   51

4   **Grow with Planning: You Need to Know How and
    Where Your Business Is Growing**   71

5   **Grow with Financing and Money Management**   87

6   **Grow with "A Little Help from Your Friends": The
    Best People to Help Your Business Succeed**   108

7   **Grow with Innovative and Low-Cost Marketing
    Methods: Original and Fun Ways to Promote
    Your Business**   136

8   **Grow through the Media and Your Contacts:
    Leveraging Positive Press Coverage for Your Business**   148

9   **Grow with Effective Advertising Tactics: Getting
    the Best Ad for Your Money**   178

10 **Grow with Smart Customer Relationship Management**   205

**11   Grow with the Internet (It's *Still* the Wild, Wild Web):
You Can Survive and Thrive Online**   **224**

**12   Grow with Spin-Offs and New Product or Service
Developments: How Many Ways to Diversify?**   **245**

**13   Grow into the Future: How Far and Which Way Do
You Want to Go?**   **262**

**14   Ongoing Growth: Additional Practical Tips
for Maintaining and Sustaining Your Business**   **275**

Glossary   305

Additional Resources   317

About the Author   329

About the Foreword Author   331

Contributors   333

Index   337

Foreword

When I quit my job to stay home with my children, I decided to open an at-home child care business. My first marketing effort was to neatly type index cards, and then I went out one evening to post them on community bulletin boards all over town. I could not wait until I arrived home, thinking that my husband would have taken many messages for me from interested parents who saw my cards. It did not happen that way; in fact, I received no calls. Disappointed, I bemoaned the lack of response to a friend of mine, a working mother.

She suggested I make my advertising more colorful because parents of young children are attracted to bright colors, children's characters, and other items that relate to children. Following her advice, I took down my index cards, and replaced them with miniposters. Using photos of happy parents and their children engaged in fun activities that I had cut and pasted from children's catalogs, I placed them on brightly colored pieces of construction paper, along with my contact information. The response was remarkable, and my business took off.

From this experience, I learned my first marketing success lesson: Know your target customers and what gets their attention. The second marketing lesson I learned was to establish a network of people—experts, friends, business associates, and other resources—from whom you can learn tips and methods to improve your marketing skills and grow your business, no matter what stage it is at.

This book, *Make Your Business Survive and Thrive! 100+ Proven Marketing Methods to Help You Beat the Odds and Build a Successful Small or Home-Based Enterprise,* is designed to help you promote your business. It provides practical advice and methods that marketing experts, small business owners, and entrepreneurs have found effective in attracting their clients and growing their businesses. Having this book in your office library is like having a marketing consultant or a good networking friend beside you to suggest promotional ideas and resources that you can use and access whenever you face a stalemate in sales or need to find help, books, organizations, web sites, or other sources of assistance.

In my entrepreneurial ventures over the years, I also learned the value of publicity. I have been a guest on major network TV shows, have given countless radio interviews, and my family and I have been the subject of several local television news spots, and many newspaper and magazine articles. My publicity efforts even helped my mother meet Pope John Paul II. All this media coverage was the result of my learning how to get the media's attention and, consequently, potential customers—and all for a relatively small amount of time and money.

Some Free Publicity Tactics

For my first book, I planned and set off on my own book tour across the Midwest, along with three children. I stopped at various public libraries to talk about topics that were related to my book (not blatant advertising) and sent press releases ahead of my arrival to local newspapers to announce my talks. By the time I arrived at each of my stops, I had reporters and radio producers wanting to ask questions and invite me on their shows. My tour was successful, but cut short when I found I was pregnant.

To get publicity for another of my books, *Raising Happy Kids on a Budget,* I purchased beautiful outfits for my entire family at an upscale clothing thrift shop. I took a family photo of us dressed in these clothes and sent it along with my press release announcing my new book. As a result, several reporters featured us in local papers and sales of my book took off. The point is obvious: You do not need a lot of money to get your product or service noticed; you do, however, need a well-thought out market *plan.* Without a strategy or prearranged steps for marketing your business and reaching your ideal potential customers, you will just end up making a lot of media noise, while gaining few sales or leads.

When you are a small business owner or self-employed entrepreneur, it is sometimes a grind to have to do all the tasks a large company turns over to staff. You should take heart, though, that you are not alone in your entrepreneurial quests because this country has more small and home-based businesses and entrepreneurs than it does large companies. The larger movers and shakers are what you hear most about in the news or on the stock market, but it is the small business sector that keeps our economy going. Many of these business owners have tried and failed at one or more other ventures, but they did not give up and went on to have successful businesses. This book was written for them and for you, the independent entrepreneur, the microbusiness owner, the owner with a small company, and others who wish to find and live the "American Dream" of doing work you love while making enough to support your family and to have a little extra for some fun. It provides you with methods and strategies that can help your business not just survive, but thrive and more.

No one book or expert or organization is going to be the "end all" of marketing or business advice. It is up to you and your efforts to make your business a success. Those information commercials may try to persuade you that you can work an hour or two a day at a venture and make enough money to have a big house and a Caribbean vacation, but they are wrong; all they are selling you is a fantasy. If you want that dream of business success, you will have to work hard, market constantly, stay debt free, and be determined to reach your goals.

Unlike when I first started my business 20 years ago, many agencies, organizations, and other resources have been set up and are available at little or no charge just to help small business owners and entrepreneurs like you succeed. You will have to take full advantage of what is available to you and never stop learning all you can if you want to move your business to the point that you can say, "I made it!"

If you keep trying new marketing campaigns like those described in this book, your entrepreneurial journey can take you far. My previous entrepreneurial experiences helped me start a small publishing company, my business of my "team of angel" pins, and a sideline business as a professional feature speaker.

One last comment, I constantly play these axioms in my mind—my own motivational "tapes":

- "There is profit in persistence." I have told myself this since fourth grade!
- "Nothing ventured, nothing gained." My father often said this to me.
- "Expect a miracle!" I draw strength from daily prayers to God.

My hope is that you will use both the traditional and not-so-traditional business tips and marketing avenues and the resources in this book to help your business reach its full potential. I hope you will achieve the satisfaction of knowing that you overcame the challenges every small business owner faces and that your efforts enabled your business to beat the odds and become the great success you always dreamed it could be!

PATRICIA C. GALLAGHER

Preface

Starting a new business is the easy part. Having it survive and then to thrive and grow is the biggest challenge every entrepreneur faces, especially the home-based and small business owner who usually has limited resources when launching a venture. Whether a business is based in one's home or is a major corporation, certain basic principles of "getting the word out" and obtaining and keeping customers apply to every business and can be used effectively by all entrepreneurs to keep their ventures solvent and profitable. These basic principles are presented in *Make Your Business Survive and Thrive!* because they have been proven to help businesses succeed where others have often failed.

But growing a business is more than just marketing. It is managing, planning, positioning, financing, and finding the right resources, experts, paying customers, and clients, and much, much more. In this book, I provide not only important business marketing principles, but also realistic and useful suggestions that are targeted specifically for you, the small business owner and entrepreneur. I have included both proven and unique ways to grow and expand your business, as well as real-life examples from entrepreneurs for your information and encouragement.

Owners of small and home-based businesses face different challenges than larger corporations, because they have to juggle many tasks that larger companies have specialists to handle. Often new business owners start their businesses on the side while still working full-time as an employee, simultaneously balancing their finances, work, and family time. Fortunately, many successful entrepreneurs have kindly contributed marketing tips that have been effective in promoting their businesses. They have suffered growing pains firsthand in their entrepreneurial journeys and have graciously shared their experiences, both good and bad. Their advice is invaluable and they desire, as I do, to assist and encourage other business owners to succeed in their respective ventures.

Try to find other entrepreneurs to share marketing and business tips and with whom you can commiserate when business is tough and celebrate when business is good. If possible, share your business skills with others. Millions of business owners are mentors to other entrepreneurs and use their businesses in altruistic ways to help their communities and beyond. You never know how it will be returned. I was contacted by an entrepreneurial group from Ghana, Africa, and am presently gathering entrepreneurial business books they have requested to help start their own independent ventures.

My mission for *Make Your Business Survive and Thrive!* is to provide as many meaningful and practical marketing methods as possible, along with as much related information as I could find so you can take your new or established venture to the next profit level and achieve the goals of success that you have set for your business. I suggest also that you look further into the resources I have listed here, because the knowledge you seek for business success will not come from just one source, but from many web sites, books and publications, experts, and entrepreneurs with whom you may network. No two entrepreneurs' paths are exactly the same, so I invite you to implement the best of the marketing methods offered in this book and apply and modify them, as the needs of your business and your customers may dictate.

If you have additional questions or dilemmas, or want to share your own business's growth experiences or effective marketing strategies with me, please send an e-mail addressed to pyhuff@hotmail.com. Write in the subject line "Survive & Thrive," and I will be happy to respond to your query, comment, or story.

I do not promise that by reading this book, you can make your venture grow into a multimillion-dollar corporation; but it *is* my sincere desire that this book will encourage you to persist in your entrepreneurial venture(s) until you achieve the success(es) you desire for your business, and your life!

I want to wish you 100+ best wishes for entrepreneurial success!

Acknowledgments

I am especially indebted to the professionals who graciously contributed their marketing and business expertise to this book. Their advice is invaluable. I have listed their names on pages 333–336. If I have failed to mention anyone who has contributed to, or helped produce this book, I apologize and hope you will forgive my oversight.

I also wish to thank the Wiley staff and editors for their insightful editing and proofing of the content of this book for its best presentation. They are the people who work tirelessly behind the pages with the thousands of words we writers produce to turn our rough manuscripts into polished, marketable books that resonate with our readers.

Finally, a note of gratitude to my husband for his support. He has been my partner on all the wild and wonderful entrepreneurial roads we have traveled together over the years, and all of life's challenges and joys that we have mutually experienced, not the least being the raising of three wonderful sons. He is the best!

Introduction: Understanding the Challenges of Entrepreneurship

Chapter 1 presents facts and figures about the number of new businesses that fail and some of the reasons for those failures. It also describes basic marketing principles that apply to most enterprises, no matter what the size. The chapter presents 25 proven marketing essentials and methods. Numbers 1 and 2 provide detailed, basic information about marketing. The rest of the chapter describes 23 simple strategies for overcoming common hindrances to business growth.

1. Awareness of Small Business Facts and Statistics Encourages Successful Entrepreneurship

The number of men and especially women who are business owners has been steadily increasing over the past 30 or so years. Here are some facts:

Entrepreneurs Increasingly Are . . .
- *Women:* One in every 11 adult women owns a business.
  —Between 1997 and 2002, the number of women-owned firms increased by 14 percent nationwide, twice the rate of all firms in the United States.
  —Nearly half (46%) of all businesses (10.1 million) are at least 50 percent owned by a woman or women.
  —Between 1997 and 2002, the number of privately held majority or 50 percent women-owned businesses grew by 11 percent, more than 1½ times the rate of all privately held firms.

1

- *Women employers:*
  —More than 18 million workers are employed by a woman business owner.
  —One in seven workers is employed by a woman-owned business.
  —The number of women-owned employer firms grew by 37 percent between 1997 and 2002, four times the growth rate of all employer firms.
- *Women-owned businesses that contribute significantly to the nation's income:*
  —Women entrepreneurs generate nearly $2.3 trillion in sales annually to the U.S. economy (Center for Women's Business Research study, www.womensbusinessresearch.org, formerly the National Foundation for Women Business Owners, *Women-Owned Businesses in 2002* is the source for all the preceding facts.)
- *Self-employed minorities:*
  —Self-employment rates for blacks, Latinos, and women have risen sharply since 1979, according to a study released in December 2004, by the Office of Advocacy of the U.S. Small Business Administration (SBA). During the period, self-employment rates increased across ethnic groups and gender, with an overall increase of more than 5 percent (U.S. Census Bureau, March 1997 Current Population Survey).

Small businesses are vital to our economy:

- They represent 99.7 percent of all employers.
- Small businesses employ half of all private sector employees.
- They pay 44.3 percent of the total U.S. private payroll.
- They create 60 to 80 percent of all new jobs annually.
- Their share of nonfarm private gross domestic product (GDP) is more than 50 percent.
- The total value of the federal prime contracts in which they supplied goods and services in 2001 was 22.8 percent (about $50 billion).
- Small businesses produce 13 to 14 times more patents per employee than large patenting firms and are twice as likely as large patent companies to be among the 1 percent most cited.
- They have 39 percent of high-tech jobs employing computer professionals, engineers, and scientists in companies with fewer than 500 workers.
- They have 53 percent of the home-based businesses, and 3 percent own franchises.
- Owners of small businesses make up about 97 percent of all identified exporters, and producers of about 29 percent of the known export value (U.S. Census Bureau, 2001).

These findings over the past two decades suggest that small businesses will continue their entrepreneurial growth, no matter what the condition of the country's economy may be. Knowing that millions of other entrepreneurial men and women are striving to succeed is sure to encourage you to start, maintain, or grow and expand your own moneymaking enterprise(s). It should also be reassuring to know that if you were to need support or assistance in fostering your enterprise, other entrepreneurs who can mentor you are likely to live nearby. Knowledgeable professionals are only a telephone call or a mouse click away (with the vast Internet's available resources).

Why an Increasing Number of Women and Men Are Turning to Entrepreneurship

There are many reasons women and men are increasingly turning to entrepreneurship. Here are some of the most common ones. Did any of the following reasons propel or jolt you into becoming an entrepreneur?

DECREASING WAGES—DECREASING FAMILY AND PERSONAL TIME

An article entitled "The 4-Day Work Week Catches On," in an old issue of *Life* magazine (January 8, 1971), points out that the six-day week disappeared during the 1930s and that, by 1956, Vice-President Richard Nixon was discussing the possibility of a four-day work week as a goal for all Americans. It was to last approximately the same 40 hours, but workers would put in 10 hours those four days. Somewhere in the ensuing 35 years, that goal was lost. Not only are today's American workers back to the six-day work week of the 1930s, many of them work 10 hours a day and are often expected to make it a 60-hour work week, or more. And these employees include single women, mothers, and grandmothers, many of whom are widows who are forced to work well into their 80s.

It is wonderful that men and women can now pursue any career, but because wages have not kept pace with the cost of living, what used to take the average income of only one worker to support a family, today can take almost two-and-a-half incomes. It appears that employers now have two workers—the husband and wife—for what they used to pay one worker. How did that happen? Previously, if a husband or wife became sick, unable to work, or died, the other spouse could become a backup wage earner to support the family. In today's economy, there is no backup person to replace lost income because that individual is already working. Many working families are only one paycheck away from losing all that they have, and with the recent changes in the personal bankruptcy laws, they will have an even more difficult time in getting back on their feet. It is no wonder that workers and their families, especially the hard-hit middle class, are under stress.

In contrast, entrepreneurs have the potential to earn more as business owners than as employees. True, entrepreneurs typically work more than 40 hours a week, but because they are working for themselves and as their own bosses, they have the flexibility to arrange their hours around their families' schedules.

FEWER RAISES

To keep fixed costs low, more companies are giving performance bonuses instead of giving raises, and often managers have to adhere to strict guidelines for standard operation procedures, or those bonuses are unlikely. One electronics chain corporation not only demands that its managers work six days a week (what about family time?), but sends its inspectors into stores unannounced to deduct points for such minor infractions as not having all the clocks that are for sale set at the same time; or for not having all the product boxes facing the same direction. One manager said, "It's the old 'carrot on the stick,' only the stick is a mile long with the carrot dangling over a cliff."

In contrast, entrepreneurs start "at the top," as owners and CEOs of their own companies. Sure, they have all the responsibilities that go with being a business owner, but they can take their businesses in whatever direction they choose. They strive to provide benefits for their employees and their families and establish better relationships with subcontractors than they experienced when they were working for someone else. One business advocate says with a smile, "I tell all small business owners that they *are* CEOs, and equal to other heads of companies like Bill Gates of Microsoft and with whom they could have lunch, if they were invited!"

THE ECONOMY AND JOB SECURITY

Thus far, in this new century, our nation's business climate and the world's economy have been changing dramatically. Jobs, especially in manufacturing, have been discontinued or shifted overseas. Many of these jobs will never return, so unemployed workers must find new ones, often at much lower pay, or undertake training and education for new careers. Many workers' unemployment benefits run out before they can find a new occupation. In addition, many new jobs today do not include the same health care coverage or other benefits these people had in their previous positions.

Economic globalization has established a world where countries are often not in charge—corporations are. Noreena Hertz's book, *The Debt Threat,* is recommended reading for all small business owners; it explains how the world's poorest nations go further into debt at the expense of Western corporations.

In contrast, entrepreneurs are looking toward business ownership as a viable career option. Unstable economic conditions are inducing people to start ventures to secure their financial future. Rochelle Balch, says in her book, *C-E-O & M-O-M: Same Time, Same Place,* "You go to work every day. You do a good job. . . . You think you are building a future for yourself and your family. Then, one day, in a flash, it's over. 'Tough luck, but we had to cut back somewhere,' they say. 'Today is Wednesday. Friday is your last day.' All I knew," says Balch, "was I'm a single mom, in a new state, and out of work, with a mortgage to pay."

After her layoff, Balch started her own business and in several years was the owner of a multimillion dollar computer consulting business, R. B. Balch Associates (www.rbbalch.com). Balch says she now has more job security because she owns her own business and can adapt her services and products to the fluctuations of our country's ever-changing economy and markets.

Because of our sheer numbers, those of us who are entrepreneurs and small business owners can urge our country's leaders to control the policies of big business that affect our own economy and those of poorer nations. Being in control of our businesses gives us more power to band together to vote and strive for an equal global economy for all workers and entrepreneurs. We can help foster entrepreneurship worldwide.

LESS PENSION OR NO PENSION

Some large companies that have declared bankruptcy have been forced to discontinue health care and retirement benefits for their retired employees. In the *Time* magazine investigative article, "The Broken Promise," (October 31, 2005), Donald Bartlett and James B. Steele point out that many corporations are now walking away from their pledges of retirement benefits for their loyal workers, putting millions of Americans at risk for living out their "golden years" in poverty. They say our U.S. Congress has permitted this to happen by not revamping our health care system and costs and by allowing corporations to walk away from their promised employee retirement obligations while tightening bankruptcy regulations for consumers in 2005.

In contrast, entrepreneurs who want to live comfortably in their retirement years are seeking the advice of financial planners and experts. Many small business owners are progressively offering more benefits for their employees, including retirement plans, because of their concern for their employees' futures and because these benefits are an incentive for retaining highly qualified workers.

FAMILY DILEMMAS

Though many companies now offer employees flexible hours to handle family needs, there are still times when employees—especially women who are the primary caregivers of family members—face scheduling conflicts as they care for sick children or elderly relatives, or handle everyday personal concerns.

In contrast, entrepreneurs like having more control over the use of their time. Men as well as women are choosing to work from their homes to be there for their families, to attend their children's school events, or to run errands or make appointments.

HEALTH CARE CONCERNS

The U.S. Census bureau estimates than on any given day of the year about 46 million Americans have no health insurance and that 80 percent of these are working families. The AFL-CIO says working families in the United States are facing a crisis in health care, the cost of which is rising at three times the rate of inflation. Workers who *do* have health insurance are paying more for it and will pay even more as the majority of employers plan to pass health care costs to their employees.

The Kaiser Family Foundation (www.kff.org) states also that women are the major consumers of health care services and often seek coverage for their families as well. The AFL-CIO also says that women's access to care is often complicated by their disproportionately lower incomes and greater responsibilities juggling work and family (www.afl-cio.org).

In contrast, entrepreneurs have decided that if they are going to pay more for health care insurance, they are going to search for the best plans that meet their needs. As entrepreneurs, they are paying for the entire cost, but by joining business ownership organizations, they often find better coverage at lower group rates. The good news is that health care insurance coverage and costs are deductible expenses for business owners (check with your accountant or other financial experts to learn how this pertains to your individual situation).

Obtaining affordable health care will continue to be a challenge for almost *all* working Americans—employed or self-employed—until our country's leaders and legislators make it a priority.

ESCAPE FROM A JOB THEY DISLIKE OR NO LONGER FIND CHALLENGING OR FULFILLING

In the study titled "At Work 2003: Past, Present, and Future," conducted by CareerBuilder.com, it was reported, "nearly 25 percent of workers in the U.S. detest their jobs." Those workers who say they hate their jobs often feel trapped by their financial commitments of mortgages and rent, car payments, and other living expenses. Add to this, the uncertainty of job security caused by the slow economy and the fact that millions of jobs are being outsourced overseas. This same study by CareerBuilder.com revealed, "six-in-ten workers plan to quit their jobs and pursue other options in the next two years." Some may opt to go back to school (if they can afford it) to retrain for another job (some for the second time due to a second job being eliminated), while others may seek to become entrepreneurs.

In 1998, the Center for Women's Business Research, said that women business owners are more likely to have been frustrated and unchallenged in their jobs. They felt that their opinions were not being taken seriously and that they were being passed over for promotions. These women said that these were some of the reasons for starting their own businesses and that primarily they were inspired by an entrepreneurial idea.

In contrast, entrepreneurs have a sense of pride, purpose, and enjoyment in their businesses and self-employment ventures. Their enterprises are based on personal interests and passions. As entrepreneurs, women and men can start businesses they enjoy, and at any age. If they cannot afford to quit a full-time job to start a business, they can start one on the side, until their businesses' profits enable them to quit their disliked day jobs. The U.S. Small Business Administration (SBA) says that the number of part-time businesses has steadily increased since the mid-1980s and are expected to increase by about 10 percent each year.

Valerie Young quit her corporate 9-to-5 job after seven years to found the web site ChangingCourse.com that presently has 25,000 subscribers to her free electronic newsletter. She now writes and consults about changing one's direction in life and leads nationwide workshops that encourage people to tap into creative ways to make a living without a job so they can start living new lives doing work they love. Young says, "I decided a long time ago to put my money angst on hold and instead focus on finding my passion, my path, my way. Now, I work for meaning, not money."

THE DESIRE TO LEAVE LEGACIES

Like their parents before them, most women and men want their children to earn more, be better educated, and to work in whatever fields they desire. In past generations, however, few parents had businesses to transfer to their children.

In contrast, many entrepreneurs visualize their ventures providing a living for their children or at least giving them a head start in pursuing their dreams when they are adults.

Entrepreneurs inspire future entrepreneurs and become role models for the young persons who look up to them, encouraging them not to settle for anything less than what they can achieve. Statistics reveal that entrepreneurs beget entrepreneurs as numerous studies conducted over the years by business universities and government agencies have shown that many successful entrepreneurs had one (or both) parents who were self-employed. When daughters and sons see their mothers, sisters, and even grandmothers starting ventures, these children of entrepreneurs are more likely than children of employed parents to start businesses.

THE DESIRE TO GIVE BACK MORE TO THEIR COMMUNITIES

Employees sometimes feel pressured by their bosses to give to a nonprofit organization, but wish they had more time to give back to their community in other ways. Being employed full-time and trying to accomplish everyday living tasks leaves little time for volunteering. Now that it takes two-and-a-half incomes to support the average family, parents often have to squeeze out time and energy to volunteer at their children's schools or their religious institution, or to participate in additional civic activities.

In contrast, entrepreneurs are often more involved in altruistic projects with their enterprises than employed individuals. Entrepreneurs like to combine economic endeavors and social causes. They can devote time to their favorite nonprofit organizations, schools, or other neighborhood groups while garnering free publicity and community goodwill for their businesses.

Dispelling the Business Failure Rate Myth

A 2002 study conducted by the Office of Advocacy of the Small Business Administration and the U.S. Census Bureau, dispelled the ongoing myth that 9 out of 10 new businesses fail in their first year. Instead, the findings of this study revealed that three-quarters of all businesses survived two years or more, half survived more than four years, and around 40 percent survived more than six years. In addition, this study showed that one-third of all businesses closed while they were still successful. Thus, if you are a new entrepreneur or are planning to become one, you can be encouraged that the success rates for new small ventures are considerably better than you might have thought.

However, this same study concluded that approximately one-third of all businesses do close unsuccessfully. There are definite steps you can take to prevent this from happening, which is why marketing is so vital to business survival.

WHY SOME SMALL BUSINESS OWNERS ARE BEATING THE ODDS

Despite the slow economy over the past several years, many small businesses have experienced sales growth during that same downturn period. Here are the primary reasons owners of small, home-based, and micro-businesses not only stay in business but also survive and thrive:

- *They network well in their industry, communities, and beyond.* Entrepreneurs like to see one another succeed. If you do not believe this, attend a business owners' meeting or a business card exchange, observe the participants, and listen to the conversations, encouragement, and tips that these small business owners and self-employed individuals share with one another. Successful entrepreneurs will find mentors or be mentors to new business owners.
- *They are more mature.* Many people in their 50s and 60s want to try their hand at entrepreneurship, especially the 76.1 million baby boomers who generally do not want to retire to just play, but hope to work at something they enjoy. Not only do they bring a vast array of experiences and backgrounds to their ventures, but they usually have a more mature approach, are more likely to care about their employees, and treat customers with the care and respect that can foster repeat business.
- *They are not afraid to fail.* Statistics reveal that it takes an average of three business start-ups for an entrepreneur to achieve a successful enterprise. Entrepreneurs are not afraid to fail; they constantly learn from their mistakes and persist until one (or more) of their ventures succeeds. They can respond to challenges and quickly change to stay competitive and satisfy their customers.
- *They emphasize quality.* Surveys show that small business owners generally care more about the quality of their products and services than bigger

companies. They believe this is the best way for them to compete with large companies that have access to more resources but are less personal. Owners of smaller ventures strive to keep their customers satisfied to encourage their repeat business.

- *They start smaller, more manageable ventures.* Time-management issues, family responsibilities, and the desire for more money are just a few reasons that women and men tend to start a small-scale venture such as a sole proprietorship or partnership. Because their ventures are small, the owners can pay attention to the details that promote a positive image. Many business owners have gone on to expand their small ventures into multimillion-dollar enterprises, especially as venture-capital investment resources become available. Others have chosen to stay small so they can serve specialized niche markets. Thus, starting smaller and growing slowly decreases the likelihood these business owners will make hasty (and costly) decisions that can lead to failure. They can expand and adjust the growth of their business at a rate they can best handle financially and time wise.
- *They inspire loyalty.* Successful entrepreneurs value their working relationships with other business owners who partner with them on projects and develop a trust. They treat employees with respect and recognition, and offer benefits that foster loyalty, better production, and customer service creating a team atmosphere working for success.
- *They create mission statements and long-range plans.* The mission statement of core values that they create guides them in their business ethics and operations. They devise long-range plans—business, financial, and marketing—with specific goals and strategies for achieving them.

There are other reasons that small and home-based business owners are succeeding, but these are the most important and can be summed up as the three Ds—desire, discipline, and determination. Finding and keeping customers is what really keeps a business in business. Starting a venture is the easy part—staying in business is the hard task. It all has to do with successfully marketing and reaching new paying customers while satisfying loyal ones.

Suggested Resources

Books

C-E-O & M-O-M, Same Time, Same Place by Rochelle B. Balch (Glendale, AZ: RB Balch Associates, 1997).

The Debt Threat: How Debt Is Destroying the Developing World . . . and Threatening Us All by Noreena Hertz (New York: HarperCollins, 2005). www.TheDebtThreat.com. Hertz has established a debt relief fund for the world's poorest nations. To learn more, make a contribution, or send a message to our political leaders, visit her site.

Web Info

> www.emkf.org, the Ewing Marion Kauffman Foundation, provides valuable information for all entrepreneurs.
>
> www.womensbusinessresearch.org, Center for Women's Business Research, founded as the National Foundation for Women Business Owners, provides statistics and information about women who are business owners and their enterprises worldwide.

2. Learn the Definition of Marketing and Basic Marketing Principles

Business experts inform those who will be starting new businesses or ventures to expect to spend 75 percent of their time marketing their new business; and those with established businesses to expect to do some marketing on a regular daily basis. Marketing basically encompasses all the methods that bring customers to your business.

Simply put, without customers you have no business, nor can you acquire more business. Your quest is to (1) determine with market research who are your best potential (paying) customers—often called your *niche* market; (2) why they would want your product or service over that of your competitors—the unique benefits your product or service provides; and (3) if they are willing to pay prices that will enable you not only to sustain your business but also to make a profit.

Jeffrey Dobkin, direct marketing expert and author, says, "To me, the definition of marketing can be reduced to five words—if you count the 'a': Marketing is 'selling to a defined audience.' Sales are to anyone, when you pare down that number of folks you are selling to—to a more targeted group—that's marketing." To summarize, marketing is the total of all the methods business owners use to reach the best customers for their businesses.

There are many books about marketing, growing, and expanding your business, some of which are listed throughout this book. Additional ones recommended by the experts and entrepreneurs are quoted and profiled in this book. The words these marketing experts have included in defining and explaining the basis of marketing include the following (but are not limited to) P words: *product, price, promotions* (advertising), *place* (positioning), *PR* (publicity), *pass-along* (referrals, word-of-mouth), *permission, packaging, performance,* and other similar terms (see web site resources in this chapter and the Glossary on page 305).

What is even more perplexing (or you could say enlightening and challenging) is that experts such as Seth Godin in his book, *Purple Cow* (New York: Portfolio, 2003) are stating that the old marketing methods are no longer the best ways to attract customers because times have changed and you must devise a strategy to really stand out from your competitors. So where does that leave you in terms of what marketing approaches to use and not use? Traditional? Nontraditional? And how do these marketing components relate to you and your business? Do you need to know them all to make your business survive and thrive?

No and yes. Because marketing is so essential to your business's existence, experts advise you to continue to learn all you can about marketing—reading, enrolling in courses, and consulting with marketing experts so you grasp the basics and more, and can apply the most effective methods for your particular venture.

After Learning the Basics, Grow Your Business, Your Way

When you believe you have read, heard, and learned all you need or want to about marketing, then you are ready to devise and create the marketing strategy, a *market plan* that will be the most effective for your business. Your marketing methods can be as traditional or as far "outside the box" as you can manage—as long as they are ethical and effective. It is your business, and you will be responsible for deciding which methods to test and implement and which ones are the most effective.

A market plan is a vital part of your business plan. What is in a market plan? An effective plan profiles potential customers' likes, dislikes, and expectations. It defines sales strategies: pricing and sales terms, selling methods and distribution of your products or services, and your timetable of promotional advertising plans. After creating a business and market plan, the next step for you will be to test one or more of your marketing tactics and then evaluate them to see if they are worth the time and money you spent trying them. Because these plans are vital to your business, Chapter 4 focuses on them.

Suggested Resources

Books

> *Guerrilla Marketing for the Home-Based Business,* 11th ed., by Jay Conrad Levinson (Hoboken, NJ: John Wiley & Sons, 2005).
>
> *Principles of Marketing* by Philip Kotler and Gary Armstrong (Indianapolis, IN: Prentice Hall, 2005).

Web Info

> www.dobkin.com, web site of Jeffrey Dobkin, marketing books, articles.

Marketing Ethics—What Are Yours?

Every profession has a code of ethics—some written down, others unspoken. When you start a business, it will reflect your values and how you treat your peers, your employees, and existing and potential customers. Business scandals and scams taint reputable business owners. Being true to your values will guide you in your business activities and help you make decisions when you are facing difficult choices. Here are some guidelines for marketing activities:

- Be honest. Make every effort to have your service or product deliver what you promise. The rules and regulations pertaining to this and other advertising activities are discussed later in this chapter.
- If you enter into joint advertising agreements with other entrepreneurs, make sure your philosophies and businesses complement one another.
- Define your own business. You can pick up and practice excellent marketing and business tips from other business owners—but run your business in your own way, at your own pace, according to your business plans. You are your business, and this is what attracts your customers. Do not try to be someone or something you are not or your business will lose its unique qualities—what makes it stand out from competitors.
- Do not denigrate your competitors to reach new customers. Instead, emphasize the benefits that your products or services can offer clients and let them decide which one serves them best.

You do not have to like every person with whom you do business, but you do have to treat each customer with respect as a human being and strive to give full value to everyone.

Suggested Resources

Books

Born to Buy: The Commercialized Child and the New Consumer Culture by Juliet Schor (New York: Scribner, 2005).

Integrity—The Courage to Meet the Demands of Reality: How Six Essential Qualities Determine Your Success in Business by Henry Cloud (New York: HarperCollins, 2006).

Principled Profit: Marketing That Puts People First by Shel Horowitz (Hadley, MA: Accurate Writing & More, 2003). Horowitz's Ethics Pledge. www.business-ethics-pledge.org.

Web Info

www.FTC.gov, the Federal Trade Commission, see the truth-in-advertising rules that apply to advertisers under the Federal Trade Commission Act.

COMMON HINDRANCES TO BUSINESS GROWTH AND 23 STRATEGIES TO OVERCOME THEM

Entrepreneurs generally are not afraid to fail or make mistakes, but if you can avoid making mistakes as your business grows, your business is less likely to fail. You may have to overcome many obstacles to beat the odds of failing. Fortunately, with a little knowledge, you can ensure enduring success for your business. Along with the two preceding methods that have been discussed in detail, here are 23 more ways to overcome common difficulties that many entrepreneurs face.

3. Too Many Customers

Business experts caution business owners who are seeking customers to be sure they can meet the needs of any new customers. Make sure you have the time, materials, and technology; the staff, if needed; and the know-how to make your customers happy. Otherwise, you will become overwhelmed and lose business. Either say "No," to people or businesses that you cannot handle; or better yet, try to refer these individuals or businesses to other companies that can meet their needs. They will appreciate your honesty, plus the business owners who obtain new customers from your referrals are likely to reciprocate and refer potential clients to you. Another alternative is to raise your prices and have fewer customers while retaining the same profit margin.

Suggested Resource

Book

> *Discipline of Market Leaders: Choose Your Customers, Narrow Your Focus, Dominate Your Market* by Michael Treacy and Fred Wiersema (New York: Perseus Publishing, 2000).

4. Underestimating the Total Funding Needed to Finance the Growth of the Business

Business financial experts say that being unable to financially fund business growth is a leading cause of business failure. In recent years, the SBA has increased the small business loan programs available to small business owners and veterans; and several women's venture capital firms have been established to assist women in business growth.

These same experts urge entrepreneurs to explore all financial resources available to them and for which they qualify (Chapters 5 and 13 discuss financing sources and strategies in depth). When applying for a loan, carefully research the real costs of each step of your business; it is extremely important to factor in extra funds for any unexpected expenditures and also to know the status of your cash flow. Have a business-financing expert review your estimated expenses list in your business plan before you approach potential lenders.

Suggested Resource

Book

> *How to Grow When Markets Don't* by Adrian Slywotzky, Karl Weber, and Richard Wise (New York: Warner Books, 2004).

5. Lack of Knowledge and Specific Skills for the Potential Business Venture

It is important to have the skills—both basic business and those knowledge-based for your specific venture idea. How do you acquire these skills and knowledge?

Enroll in Business Management and Start-Up Courses

Contact the following in your community:

- *Local school districts and vocational-technical schools,* to see if their adult evening programs offer business start-up classes or additional instruction in the field that interests you, such as computer courses, office skills, woodworking, or marketing.
- *Four-year and community colleges* for course offerings of business and entrepreneurial studies, degree studies, and E-business ventures. Many colleges offer courses online, but beware of diploma mills that you may see on the Internet. Check with the Better Business Bureau or the attorney general's office in the state where the company is located to ensure the school is operating legally.

  Two resources for information on distance learning and online courses are the nonprofit Distance Education and Training Council (www.detc.org) or Peterson's site (www.petersons.com).

- *Local offices of the SBA* (offer free or low-cost seminars and business counseling):*
  —Service Corps of Retired Executives (SCORE, www.score.org)
  —Small Business Development Centers (SBDCs, www.sba.gov/SBDC)
  —Women's Business Development Centers (WBDCs, www.onlinewbc.gov)

Start a Business Based on Your Work Experience or Hobbies

Having a background and the necessary skills in the industry in which you start a business will provide you with greater chances to succeed. If you lack that experience, you could work full- or part-time in a job or as a volunteer in the field related to your business idea. This would provide you not only with money to help support yourself (or to accumulate start-up funds), but with insider know-how—tips, vendor contacts, and other important information. You also could get an idea whether this is really the type of business you would like to own and operate.

Expert Contacts

You cannot expect to know everything about business. As an entrepreneur, you will hear the following advice many times (and repeatedly in this book): Before you ever open your doors, have a list of experts and professionals you can consult with on every business matter. Ask for referrals from other small business owners, and make sure these experts are friendly to small business owners and are familiar with the challenges they face. A good source to meet and greet potential experts is through a local chapter of your chamber of commerce or others in your industry.

Work in the industry to get firsthand knowledge and tips and to see if this is a business in which you want to invest your time and money.

Suggested Resources

Book

Guide to Distance Learning: The Practical Alternative to Standard Classroom Education by Pat Criscito (Hauppauge, NY: Barron's Educational Series, 2002).

---

*Search the web sites to find an office located near you or call (800) U-ASK-SBA (800-827-5722)

Web Info

> www.Entrepreneur.com/howto, *Entrepreneur* magazine's free, online, how-to guide, "How to Extend Your Education."
>
> www.entrepreneur.com/topcolleges, *Entrepreneur's* "Top Colleges" listing can help you find a local school that offers entrepreneurship studies.

6. Not Staying Competitive

"A man [woman] of knowledge increaseth strength" (Proverbs 24:5, King James Version), or "knowledge is power." To stay ahead of your competitors, stay informed on the latest trends (not fads) in your industry by regularly reading business and industry publications, attending trade shows, and paying attention to trends. Study reports by respected futurists like Faith Popcorn (www.FaithPopcorn.com) and Gerald Celente (www.TrendsResearch.com) and business strategist, Chuck Martin's Net Future Institute (NFI; www.nfiresearch.com).

Obtain opinions from your faithful and potential customers—verbally, or through customer surveys or additional methods that monitor customers' feedback—to ensure, that your products or services will continue to satisfy them and accommodate their changing needs. This vital market research can help you make intelligent decisions concerning your business's objectives and future plans (see also Methods 80 and 91.)

Suggested Resource

Book

> *Tough Management: The 7 Winning Ways to Make Tough Decisions Easier, Deliver the Numbers, and Grow the Business in Good Times and Bad* (Hardcover) by Chuck Martin (New York: McGraw-Hill, 2005).

7. Unprepared for Business Growth

What if a mail-order catalog house decided to carry your home decor product? Could you (1) produce the required number of items in the specified time allotment? (2) hire competent staff in time to assist in making your products? (3) afford the extra materials required to make X amount of products to fill your orders and still make a profit?

Before you accept a large order or take on a greater number of clients, you will have to revert to your business plan to see if your business is headed in the right direction toward your set goals or if you need to modify and update it. Seek professional advice from business experts—mentors, business coaches, members of SCORE, and other specialists to help you decide whether expansion is right at this time. Perhaps you should take business growth in smaller increments that are less risky and less likely to leave you overwhelmed and poorer in time and cash.

Suggested Resource

Book

> *Profitable Growth Is Everyone's Business: 10 Tools You Can Use Monday Morning* by Ram Charan (New York: Crown Publishing Group, 2004).

8. Not Writing (or Following) a Business Plan

A business plan is a blueprint, or road map, that provides direction and increases your chances for business survival and success. To paraphrase an old adage, "How will you know where you are going, if you do not know how to get there?" Business plans can be as simple or elaborate as you want them, and need not even be written down, if you have a good memory and recall. But you *should* have a plan. If you do not know how to write one, there are many books, software programs, and experts to assist you in composing your first plan. Seek feedback about your plan from another entrepreneur, or from business experts like officers at a local chapter of SCORE.

A business plan is only effective if you apply it to the management of your business start-up. It is also vital to the success of your business to periodically monitor your plan to see if it needs revising to match your goals and present business activities (see also Chapter 4).

Suggested Resource

Book

> *Anatomy of a Business Plan*, 6th ed., by Linda Pinso (Chicago: Dearborn Trade, 2005). www.business-plan.com.

9. Inadequate Market Research and Testing

Market research is important because it provides the information you need to make business choices that can increase your profits. Without adequate market research and evaluation, you cannot implement successful marketing campaigns and identify customers' specific needs. If your products or services are not selling, you can reevaluate your marketing research methods; try some new ones; reexamine your products and services to see if they need updating or if you can appeal to different markets. Consult with a market research professional for additional advice (see also Chapter 4).

Effective market research should encompass all or most of the following features:

- The research uses more than one source on which you can base your conclusions.
- It does not abuse the trust or confidentiality of the people, businesses, or organizations that are involved.
- The research is conducted from different points of view to get a clearer picture of how products or services are perceived.
- The budget allotted for the research is adhered to, and the research stops when it reaches its answers.
- It uncovers information that is useful to you and your venture.

There are more criteria to judge whether the market research you carried out was adequate, but if your research is missing one or more of these features, you have to start over again, seek extra assistance from other business owners who are experienced in market research, or contact a marketing research professional.

Suggested Resource

Book

> *Marketing Research Essentials,* 5th ed., by Carl McDaniel and Roger Gates (Hoboken, NJ: John Wiley & Sons, 2005).

10. No Existing Marketing Plan

Just as a business plan is a blueprint for the foundation of your business, a market plan comprises all the essential tactics you need to reach the potential customers who will most want to pay for your expertise or product. It is based on your research and findings. Without a market plan, you may waste or overspend money on advertising and publicity avenues for consumers or businesses not interested in your services or product. Because a market plan includes many specific methods, an effective plan will synchronize all your marketing activities to keep your business going.

Denise O'Berry, author of *Small Business Cash Flow* (www.cashflowtruth .com), says, "Remember that business is about sales. People are not going to stampede to your business just because you put up the 'open' sign. You must have a plan for marketing your business consistently to keep those customers coming through the door."

If you need help in devising a market plan, you can ask other entrepreneurs for tips or—if they are willing to share—examples of their market plans and marketing strategies. As mentioned, you also can hire a marketing consultant or meet with other professionals (see also Chapter 4).

Suggested Resource

Book

> *Marketing Plans,* 5th ed., by Malcolm McDonald (Newton, MA: Butterworth-HeinemannButter, 2002).

11. Not Finding Effective and Affordable Advertising

Advertising is an important part of your entire market plan. The goal is to find the advertising avenue(s) that are the most effective in attracting paying customers, and also those avenues that are the most cost-effective. It is common sense to test your promotional methods and to avoid using just one way to promote your business. Even when you find the right ad combination, you should experiment from time to time with new avenues because you might just find an untapped (and lucrative) market (see also Chapter 9).

Suggested Resources

Books

> *Do It Yourself Advertising and Promotion: How to Produce Great Ads, Brochures, Catalogs, Direct Mail, Web Sites, and More!* 3rd ed., by Fred E. Hahn, Tom Davis, Bob Killian, and Ken Magill (Hoboken, NJ: John Wiley & Sons, 2003).
>
> *Guerrilla Marketing Weapons: 100 Affordable Marketing Methods for Maximizing Profits from Your Small Business* by Jay Conrad Levinson (New York: Penguin, 1996). Paperback, audio.

12. Ignoring Your Cash Flow Balance

Cash flow pertains to the revenues of your business versus its expenditures. Ignoring your cash flow balance can easily lead to insurmountable business (and personal) debt. Monitor your cash flow balance regularly to make sure your business is making money or is soon projected to do so. Keep accurate records of your spending and of money that is owed you, so you know if you should consult with your accountant for advice or to review your financial policies or projections (see Chapter 5 for more details).

Suggested Resource

Software

Up Your Cash Flow™ XT, created by Harvey A. Goldstein, CPA, www.cashplan .com; cash flow management, financial forecasting and more for small to mid-sized businesses.

13. Overspending

Overspending and overextending credit are easy to do with a business start-up, often because the new business owner cannot acquire traditional funding and has to resort to using credit cards or other high-interest loans. One of the best ways to prevent this is to have a business *budget.* Using your business plan, knowing how to operate various spreadsheet software, and consulting with financial experts will help you set reasonable limitations on business expenditures. These actions will aid you in creating a budget and a financial plan to guide you in making crucial financial decisions and constrain you from impulse spending that could bankrupt your venture.

That advice also pertains to setting up your office with expensive furniture and equipment. Better to start with good-quality used furniture and a few pieces of basic equipment and stay solvent than to impulsively buy too much and go into debt. Start modest, save money, and as your business begins to make money, invest only in the office trappings and the equipment that best serve your needs.

Suggested Resources

Books

Streetwise Finance and Accounting for Entrepreneurs: Set Budgets, Manage Costs, Keep Your Business Profitable by Suzanne Caplan (Holbrook, MA: Adams Media Corp., 2006).

Total Business Budgeting: A Step-by-Step Guide with Forms, 2nd ed., by Robert Rachlin (Hoboken, NJ: John Wiley & Sons, 1999).

14. Trying to Go It Alone

New businesses are the least likely of companies to have properly trained personnel. Savvy entrepreneurs know when and whom to ask for help when they need assistance with business concerns. They assemble their experts *before* trouble arises. Professionals most often used by business owners include lawyers, accountants, insurance brokers, and certified specialists such as computer consultants, virtual assistants, and marketing experts.

Make sure your family or loved ones are aware of the time commitment and other sacrifices that they may have to make as you start a venture. Emphasizing the positive and involving them—but not overworking them—will help gain their support, which you will need as you proceed with your start-up.

Last, join *leads groups* or business organizations to set up a referral network of reliable and honest business owners. Make sure that you feel comfortable in recommending them to your customers and that these resources, in turn, feel confident in referring you to their clients. It is like having an unpaid sales force to help your business grow. (Chapter 6 offers additional networking techniques.)

Suggested Resource

Book

Endless Referrals: Network Your Everyday Contacts into Sales by Bob Burg (New York: McGraw-Hill, 2005).

15. Not Making Full Use of Technology

Richard Henderson, publisher of *Home Business Magazine* (www .homebusinessmag.com) says, "Effective use of rapidly changing information technology will make or break your business." Learning office management technology and the latest technology related to your venture is essential. It will save you time, improve efficiency and accuracy in your business operations, and help you to keep up with competitors. To find the appropriate technology for your business, ask people in your field for their suggested software, tools, and equipment; or follow your industry association's guidelines, standards, and recommendations. If you need instruction, hire another business owner to tutor you or look for classes at local learning institutions. There is no excuse these days for not having the basic technological skills to operate your business. Handheld devices for mobile wireless technology and communications continue to become more multifunctional and affordable.

You can enroll in online courses or take advantage of free ones. Hewlett-Packard (www.hp.com) offers everything from digital photography tips to web site basics; and the SBA (www.sba.gov/training/courses.html) online has business start-up courses, including "Marketing 101: The Fundamentals."

Suggested Resources

Publication

PC Magazine, www.pcmag.com, print publication of articles, reviews of hardware, software, and other technology.

Web Info

Technology web sites (two of many) offering news and information about technology and e-zines:

http://infoworld.com, Info World

www.cnet.com, CNET

16. Lack of Customer Care

Late responses to customers' responses and inquiries warn customers, loyal or new, that you do not really care about them or about your products or services. Promptly respond to your customers when they leave messages, be on time with client meetings, and then demonstrate your thanks with a card or small gift after they have purchased your products or services. Periodically, follow up with a phone call or card to offer further assistance or just to keep in touch (see also Method 18). If you take your customers for granted, they will eventually seek out your competitors (see also Chapter 10).

Suggested Resources

Book

> *Super Service: Seven Keys to Delivering Great Customer Service . . . Even When You Don't Feel like It! . . . Even When They Don't Deserve It!* by Jeff Gee and Valerie Gee (New York: McGraw-Hill, 1999).

Web Info

> www.customercare.com, Customer Care Institute, consulting, online articles.

17. Incorrect Pricing Structure

You must determine prices that will be fair to your customers; yet they must be high enough to cover your expenses and create a good profit margin. Business experts say you should never sell your product or service by price alone, thinking that having the lowest prices is the only way to attract customers from competitors. Instead, stress the value or benefits your customers will receive by doing business with you.

The more value customers perceive and appreciate, the more they will be willing to pay. A common mistake that new entrepreneurs make is not incorporating the time it takes to produce services or products. Charge too little, and you will never get ahead or have time for anything else other than work; or worse, it may lead to the death of your business. Remember to sell value—not price, and your customers will not forget you (see also Method 43).

Suggested Resource

Book

> *Strategy and Tactics of Pricing: A Guide to Profitable Decision Making,* 3rd ed., by Thomas T. Nagle and Reed K. Holden (Upper Saddle River, NJ: Prentice-Hall PTR, 2002).

18. Not Following Up on Prospective Leads

You need to market to bring in new customers and to maintain a steady cash flow, but keeping regular customers takes less time and effort than acquiring new ones. If you fail to follow up when potential customers inquire about your products or services in response to an ad or referrals, or after they have purchased your product or service, you may not get a second chance to acquire that new client.

Response time to customers' calls, letters, or e-mails should be made the same day or, if possible, within 24 hours. Some follow-up ideas to thank clients for their patronage include sending a thank-you note or a small, appropriate gift (like the thermos that a seller of recreational vehicles sends each customer who purchases a camper or trailer); mailing postcards for special invitational sales; sending congratulatory cards for birthdays and anniversaries; or leaving a nice message on the client's phone either thanking the purchaser or asking if there are any more questions. In an impersonal world, everyone likes to feel important. Let potential and regular customers know they are and that you care.

Suggested Resource

Book

> *Customers for Life: How to Turn That One-Time Buyer into a Lifetime Customer,* rev. ed., by Carl Sewell and Paul Brown (New York: Doubleday, 2002).

19. Inadequate Marketing

As mentioned, marketing for your new business may require as much as 75 percent of your time. It bears repeating, too, that marketing must remain a daily activity of established businesses. The good news is that marketing need not be boring—you can use many traditional methods while testing some creative ones. (Patricia C. Gallagher mentioned in her Foreword that she had her new book's cover spray-painted on her minivan, along with the 800-number for placing orders, as she traveled on her book tour. Marketing *never* stops if a business is to survive and thrive. See also Chapter 7.)

If production is your strength, then hire a salesperson or barter services or products with a marketing firm.

Suggested Resource

Book

The One Minute Sales Person: The Quickest Way to Sell People on Yourself, Your Services, Products, or Ideas—at Work and in Life, rev. ed., by Spencer Johnson with Larry Wilson (New York: HarperCollins, 2002).

20. Lack of Focus

Starting, operating, and expanding a business takes a commitment of time and energy—that is a given. New business owners often go off in too many tangents or sidelines for their business, or they fail to realize how much concentrated time they are going to have to put into a business to make it succeed. Setting goals that were established in the business plan and then taking steps to achieve these goals, one by one, is the only way to accomplish them. You also must prioritize your personal activities. Instead of being the president of a community organization, opt, instead to head one yearly activity.

In her book, *Miracles Happen,** Mary Kay Ash said she placed God, her family, and then her business in that order. Going in too many directions with your life will prevent you from going forward. To stay on the road to success, focus on your marketing objectives such as programs that reach your ideal customers and strive to get your business's name and image known.

Suggested Resources

Books

Miracles Happen: The Life and Timeless Principles of the Founder of Mary Kay Inc. (New York: HarperCollins, 2003).

Six-Week Start-Up: A Step-by-Step Program for Starting Your Business, Making Money, and Achieving Your Goals! by Rhonda Abrams (Palo Alto, CA: Planning Shop, 2004). www.PlanningShop.com.

21. Failure to Protect Yourself

Be a wise business owner and heed the adage, "Hope for the best, but prepare for the worst":

---

* Ask your favorite Mary Kay consultant for a copy of this book. It has many valuable tips for entrepreneurs.

- Protect yourself, your assets, your family, and your business by having insurance: life and disability, disaster, liability, theft, health.
- Make sure you are being legal, with a registered business, licensing, best legal structure, properly worded contracts, adherence to advertising regulations, treatment of employees and independent contractors, and other legal issues.
- Other: Take precautions against security breaches; protect confidential clauses, intellectual property, unpaid invoices, and similar critical documents.

Find out all the risks you could face as a business owner and specifically with your type of business. Then consult with representatives of the agencies and experts who can best advise you about the precautions to take if a worst-case scenario should occur with little or no warning (think about Katrina).

Suggested Resource

Book

> *Small Time Operator: How to Start Your Own Business, Keep Your Books, Pay Your Taxes, and Stay Out of Trouble,* rev. ed., by Bernard B. Kamoroff (Laytonville, CA: Bell Springs, 2006).

22. Outdated Services or Products

"New and Improved!" has been the ongoing advertising campaign for most established companies since marketing began. As mentioned in Method 6, keeping up with the latest trends—not fads—in your industry is important, even to customers who are currently satisfied with your products or services. Think of the first McDonald's franchise that opened in 1955 and all the variations of sandwiches that the company has had to offer to keep its name in the news and to keep customers returning. Sure, it still has its popular Big Macs, but now there are salads, chicken sandwiches, fruit and yogurt, and other new foods. Your regular customers will expect your standard products or services, but if you find new materials to improve your present products or introduce extra services, it will pique the interest of both regular and new customers.

Then again, you may be forced to go into another sideline. My father-in-law's metal polishing business disappeared when auto and truck makers no longer made shiny metal bumpers. Instead, he purchased a new machine and offered to degrease metal parts, which turned out to be easier to do than the heavy polishing. (An old Polish proverb says, "You rest, you rust!") Do not be complacent, and always be ready to move your business forward as your markets change (see also Chapter 12).

Suggested Resource

Book

> *Think Big, Act Small: How America's Most Profitable Companies Keep the Start-Up Spirit Alive* by Jason Jennings (New York: Portfolio, 2005).

23. Not Being Current with Your Taxes

A major reason to keep good financial records is for tax-paying purposes. If you are self-employed or a business owner, you will regularly pay estimated taxes to the IRS, state taxes, and any local taxes that apply to your business. To ensure that you are keeping accurate records of the taxes you will owe (and also are setting aside that money in a separate account) and are paying on time, take advantage of accounting software like *QuickBooks* and *TurboTax*. If you get behind in paying into your tax accounts, it will be difficult to come up with the money when tax payments are due and you may end up having to pay penalties for late payments. All business owners should have an accountant or other financial professional such as an IRS Enrolled Agent (EA) with whom they can consult before they start a business, as they manage their business, and if they decide to expand their businesses. As Jan Zobel, EA, says, "While everyone is looking for a way to save taxes, often the solution is as easy as keeping better records."

Suggested Resources

Book

> *Minding Her Own Business: The Self-Employed Woman's Essential Guide to Taxes and Financial Records*, 4th ed., by Jan Jobel, EA (Naperville, IL: Sourcebooks, 2005).

Web Info

> www.IRS.gov, Internal Revenue Service's web site, can download tax forms and instructions pertaining to home and small businesses and self-employed individuals.

24. Fear of Failure or Success

It is natural to have misgivings or fear when you first start a business. That fear of failure can traumatize people and prevent them from ever going beyond the thinking stage of a business start-up. By thoroughly researching and preparing beforehand, you can decrease your odds of having your business fail. Know your weaknesses and strengths and hire or barter services with other entrepreneurs for the tasks you do not want to handle so you can concentrate on the ones you do well.

Other people actually fear their business *will* grow and succeed. They do not want to give up control of every operation. That is why it is important to know when the time is right to hire employees who can free you to carry on the operations that you prefer or are best at doing. Otherwise, you will be overwhelmed and can easily burn yourself out both physically and mentally; you may also damage your personal relationships because of all the time you spend running your business. Again, use the expertise of your professionals who can guide you through any growing "pains" (see Chapter 13).

Suggested Resource

Book

> *The 7 Habits of Highly Effective People* by Stephen Covey (Glencoe, IL: Free Press, 2004).

25. Surplus Inventory

Unsold items or out-of-date supplies and equipment may cost you money for storage and make you miss a chance to put your outlay in those items to more lucrative uses. Keeping track of your inventory is essential for the survival of your business. Inventory problems may take the following forms: Customers are complaining that your products are unavailable, lack of materials interrupts your production, your back orders are increasing, and your inventories are growing faster than your sales.

Some ways to solve these problems are to quickly sell the items you have in stock to get some needed cash. Use software to track and monitor your stock, and reduce excess inventory that is no longer of use or in demand. If you have a new product-oriented business, keep the purchase of supplies to a minimum until your sales dictate which of your items is the best seller. Do not let vendors dictate what you should buy. Establish and follow the inventory management program that works best for your business.

Suggested Resources

Software

> Quickbooks, http://quickbooks.intuit.com
>
> Microsoft Point of Sale retail management system, www.microsoft.com
>
> Peachtree Accounting, www.peachtree.com

Tags and Codes

RFID Tags (radio frequency identification tags); check your major search engines for companies.

The Barcode Software Center, www.makebarcode.com

The best way to keep your business's good health is to seek the advice of your accountant or bank as soon as a problem arises. It is better to handle it earlier than later when saving the business may be difficult or impossible. It is important early on to (1) realize there is a problem and (2) contact your business and/or financial advisor ASAP so your business does not end up being a failure statistic.

Having a positive attitude, an effective management system, and a solid business plan are also crucial in preventing your business from failing.

Suggested Resources

Books

Failproof Your Business: Beat the Odds and Be Successful by Dr. Paul E. Adams (Los Angeles: Adams-Hall Publishing, 1999).

Turning Your Business Around: How to Spot the Warning Signs and Keep Your Business Healthy by Mark Blayney (Oxford, England: How To Books, 2005).

2

Grow with a Unique Idea: Defining Your Venture

One of the questions my readers ask most often is "What is the best business for me to start?" If you are contemplating starting a venture or are just launching one, Chapter 2 can help you select the business that will best match your interests and skills and assess the profit potential of your idea, as well as explain how to showcase your venture's uniqueness to attract your target customers.

26. Choose the Best Name for Success

Naming Tips

Experts urge you to take your time in selecting a name for your business, because it will be a constant marketing tool. Here are some suggestions on choosing the best name:

- Your name should describe or relate to the products or services you provide. The name of Nancy Cleary's business, Wyatt-MacKenzie Publishing, makes it obvious to potential customers that she is a publisher. The name would not be as effective if it were "Cleary Enterprises" because it would not allow an instant understanding of the services or products that she offers. We see or hear business names everywhere, every day in our communities, on signs, billboards, the radio, and television, and in many other places. For more examples, just look at the names of businesses in the advertisement section of your local telephone directory and see all the examples of the names of the listed businesses such as "Four Persons' Plumbing & Heating," "Anytown Sheds & Fencing," or "XX Computer Consulting." See if some businesses' names do not clearly state what service or product is being offered.
- To avoid confusion or even possible lawsuits, stay away from business names that sound like well-known products and brands, publications, and famous persons. If you are an author, artist, or designer, however, using your own name can be an effective strategy to get your work recognized.

- Your business's name can designate where you do business, like "Bill's Worldwide Contracting" if you will travel around the world; or close to home with "Your Town Complete Hair Salon."
- Add a tagline—a concise statement, summarizing your company's mission for its services or products. Names with taglines ("*Extraordinary* Coach Jim Donovan, When Ordinary Results Just Won't Do" and "Trade Show Xpress, The 'How To' Specialists for Exhibit Marketing") imply that their customers will receive a little better service than that offered by competitors who just list their name with no tagline ("Smith's Professional Coaching," or "John's Trade Show Consulting" [see Sidebar: Tagline Tips]).
- Create alternative names in case someone else in your geographic region already is using the same name or has registered it.

The ideal name is the one that customers will associate with better quality and service than your competitors provide.

Legalizing Your Name

If you do not want to concern yourself with a fictitious name, you can use your legal name in the designation of your business. If your name is Bob Smith, you can title your business "Bob Smith Lawn Services." However, if your business name is "Evergreen Lawn Services," or "Executive Janitorial Services," you will have to register your name with your state's business office and county clerk's office.

This business registration requirement is also called "doing business as" (DBA) and will be printed in your local newspaper so people will know you are conducting business under another name. Your state will also let you know if that name is already registered. You can go to your local courthouse and register the name yourself or you can have your lawyer do it. If you incorporate your name, it will be protected from others using it in your state through the articles of incorporation.

There are several sources to check to see if another business already owns or has registered a name or trademark:

- Check Internet search engines.
- Thomas Register web site, www.thomasregister.com, to check for manufacturers' names.
- Network Solutions web site, www.networksolutions.com. Check their database for available domain names.
- U.S. Patent and Trademark Office web site, www.uspto.gov/main/trademarks.htm, to check for patent and trademark search information.

When in doubt, consult with a legal expert knowledgeable in business name and trademark registrations and in the formation of business legal structures.

Tagline Tips

Here are some ideas for creating more effective taglines for the name of your business. Your tagline should:

- *Specify a benefit that sets you apart from your competitors:* To stand out from competitors' taglines that only state "web design services," a computer business that offers smaller companies Internet consulting might use the tagline "executing your web strategies from start to finish." Potential customers then would know that this company offers a full package of Internet services.
- *Describe what your business does so potential customers know what you are offering:* A writer who creates custom-written poetry adds, "poetry for all occasions," and follows with a second tagline, "unique creation from your information."
- *Avoid overuse of common terms in your industry:* Professional organizers naturally tend to use *organize* or *organizing* in their names and taglines; but to differentiate from competitors, their taglines might contain unique words. Instead of "XXX Organizing: Professional Organizing & Decluttering," the business owner could try a creative name and tagline that would make the service stand out, "Home Business Makeovers, Rearranging Your Home-work Space for Success."
- *Avoid phrases frequently associated with your industry:* A telecommunications company might say, "Customizing your customer connections," instead of the common tagline, "You can count on us."

Your tagline may change as your business evolves and you find your core customers. Once you have decided on the most effective tagline for your business, be sure to place it on all your correspondence in letters, at the end of e-mail messages, on your business cards and brochures, and in other marketing communications to act as an ongoing marketing message.

Suggested Resources

Books

Trademark Basics for Naming Your Small Business. www.Nolo.com. E-book.

Trademark: Legal Care for Your Business and Product Name, 7th ed., by Stephen Elias (Berkeley, CA: Nolo Press, 2005).

Company

Named at Last, www.namedatlast.com, company that provides names and taglines for businesses; Marcia Yudkin, director, marketing expert, and author.

Web Info

> www.Entrepreneur.com/howto, *Entrepreneur* magazine's free, online, how-to guide, "How to Name Your Business."
>
> www.SBA.gov, "Selecting the Legal Structure for Your Business." pdf file.

27. Choose the Best Legal Structure for Success

How to Determine Your Legal Structure (Which Form Is Best for Your Business?)

You will need to decide under which auspices you will operate. There are several legal structures, each with guidelines, but the following three are probably the ones you will consider.

SOLE PROPRIETOR

This is the most common form of business structure for microbusinesses. You only have to choose a name and begin using it. You can use your personal name or register a fictitious one. Advantages of this legal structure are that it is the least expensive form to establish, and it is easy to control its operations and report your taxes. You retain the profits but your personal assets are liable to creditors and lawsuits.

PARTNERSHIP

This form consists of two or more owners. Advantages include sharing of ideas, operations, and resources, and it is relatively easy to set up. Disadvantages may outweigh the positives because a partnership is more costly to form, depending on the complexity of its organization; you can still be personally liable for debts, no matter which partner incurs them; and it may be difficult to dissolve.

A majority of partnerships fail, too, due to personality conflicts or disagreements as to the division of duties and direction. Two partners had been personal friends for over 25 years and joined together for a cooking-related business; but when one of the partners married, the spouse wanted the business to take different customers, and the other partner did not, so the partnership dissolved, and their friendship was permanently damaged.

CORPORATION

Because there are several forms of incorporation, you will want to discuss the matter with a lawyer who specializes in establishing corporations. Generally, a corporation is considered to be a separate entity, and only its business assets are subject to creditors, not your personal ones. However, you can still be held responsible for business liability if you have signed personal guarantees. Disadvantages include the cost of setting up this structure in your state and its complexity, which involves shareholders and a board of directors. Most states also require annual filing fees, and the IRS requires regular tax filings. A qualified accountant can advise you about these requirements.

Some Additional Legal Concerns

Your attorney or accountant should answer the following questions:

- Research to see if you need a license to operate by federal, state, or local authorities.
- Check with your accountant to see what tax ID numbers you will need—with sole proprietorships it is your Social Security number, but many business forms require a federal Employer Identification Number (EIN). Find out your responsibilities for paying local wage, income taxes, state sales taxes, and Social Security taxes.
- Have your lawyer draw up a standard contract or waivers to protect you and your business from lawsuits; and when in doubt have your lawyer review all contracts and agreements before you sign them.

It will take time to set up your business's legalities, but once these matters are established, you can operate and market your business with less worry and more confidence.

Suggested Resources

Book

> *LLC or Corporation? How to Choose the Right Form for Your Business* by Anthony Mancuso (Berkeley, CA: Nolo Press, 2005).

Web Info

> www.Business.gov/topics/business_laws, legal and regulatory information for small businesses.

> www.Entrepreneur.com/howto, *Entrepreneur* magazine's free, online, how-to guide, "How to Legally Establish Your Home-Based Business."

28. Choose a Strong Business Idea

Narrowing the Selection

So many business ideas may appeal to you that you are in a dilemma about which one(s) to pursue. Here are three questions you should ask yourself to help in your selection:

1. *Do I have the background, expertise, or experience to bring into this business?* Statistics show a better business success rate if the owner has previously worked in the industry or has the credentials to bring to a new

venture. If you do not have the credentials or experience, find out what education or training you need and if possible, work in the industry to get some hands-on knowledge.

2. *Is there an existing market—a substantial number of potential customers to make my business profitable and (very important) will they be willing to pay the price I must set to make a profit?* Take the time to write a business plan and to conduct a thorough market research to see if you will have customers for your service or product and to determine whether these customers are willing to pay the prices you need to have a profitable business. Chapter 4 discusses business plan essentials and where you can obtain assistance in writing one.

3. *Realistically, how much time and money can I afford to spend on this business at this time in my life?* Instead of working 9 A.M. to 5 P.M., you are more likely to work 5 A.M. to 9 P.M. to get your venture going. Are you and your loved ones ready to invest this much time to launch your venture? Most home businesses (and many small ventures) are started on a part-time basis. Starting this way is usually less risky financially than going full-time and allows you to test market your goods and services.

Business Matchmaker

To help you in your search, answer the following questions:

1. What are your:
   a. Strengths (What are you good at?)
   b. Interests (What do you enjoy doing? If money were no object, what would your perfect career look like?)
   c. Experience (Past jobs or military experience; volunteer positions)
   d. Accomplishments (Awards, special recognition)
   e. Education/Training (Is a degree, certification, or special training needed for any of your jobs?)

2. How much time do you have available to put into your business?
   Days a Week: ☐ 1 ☐ 2 ☐ 3 ☐ 4 ☐ 5
   Hours a Day: ☐ 1–2 ☐ 2–4 ☐ 4–6 ☐ 6–8 ☐ More than 8
   Thus, can you start your business on a part- or full-time basis?
   Is your long-range goal to have a full-time business or to keep it on the side?

3. How much money do you have to put into your business?
   ☐ $0–100   ☐ $101–500   ☐ $500–1,000
   ☐ $1,001–2,000 ☐ $2,001–$4,000 ☐ Over $4,000

4. Do you like working alone or with people?

    ☐ Alone ☐ With people

5. How much money do you want or need to earn each month?

6. What areas are you likely to need help in if any?

    ☐ Management ☐ Accounting ☐ Computer

    ☐ Sales ☐ Marketing ☐ Phones

    ☐ Clerical ☐ Delivery ☐ Other

7. Make a list of your potential customers and clients. Who are they? Where will you find them?

8. Do you know what state or province resources are available in the area where you live to assist you in finding free or low-cost business start-up and management counseling?

9. Do you own a computer, and if so, do you have access to the Internet?

10. Do you live in a rural, suburban, or urban area?

11. How will your location affect your business selection?

12. How many children do you have and what are their ages?

13. How will your business impact your family and personal life?

14. What is the principal reason you want to have a business?

15. What will you offer—product, service, Combination?

Adapted with permission from Lesley Spencer Pyle, founder of Home-Based Working Moms, www.HBWM.com.

Before you start a business or buy an existing one, you need to ask yourself and others many questions. Experts say the amount of research you do before you start your business correlates directly to your success, so take your time when searching for the ideal venture. Make a serious assessment of your own entrepreneurial skills and characteristics that will affect how you conduct your business and its marketing campaigns.

Conversing with other business owners in your industry will also give you some valuable insight and practical tips that you may not find in a text or operations manual. You can also get ideas for a product or service by reading small-business publications; brainstorming ideas from your own research or acquaintances; perusing the business book sections of public libraries, listening to or surveying others about improvements in products or services that they would welcome; and reading and researching about the latest trends in fashion, populations, and other changes taking place in our world.

What Will You Offer—Product, Service, Combination?

Basically, most businesses produce products, services, or a combination of these two. Product-based businesses sell items that are either created or invented by the owners or are produced by others for resale. These items are usually sold either retail or wholesale. With retail, you would sell your products (or another company's products) directly to the end buyer, face-to-face, through network marketing programs, or through the mail with a mail-order or online business. In selling wholesale, you are selling to distributors, agents, or retail outlets, and to catalogs that, in turn, sell directly to businesses or customers.

Service-based businesses are usually more affordable to start, and are organized based on the at-home or from-home services that the business owner can provide to individuals, groups, or other businesses. *You* are the business and are responsible for carrying out the service. You can usually start with a minimum of needed equipment, depending on your type of service.

Some businesses are a combination. The owners may start with a service-oriented business like computer consulting, but then end up selling computer equipment and supplies. It will all depend on your customers' demands.

Deciding on a business idea is only the first step in your journey to having a successful business. In marketing terms, you have to consider how much you will have to educate potential customers about your product or service, especially the new business ideas that have come into the entrepreneurial scene such as professional organizing and professional coaching, or new products that you are planning to manufacture or that are manufactured by others. You will have to explain and demonstrate to potential customers the benefits of these new products or services in a variety of marketing methods and why they need these before they will ever pay you any money.

It is essential, too, that you choose a type of business you really like. If you choose a business that you perceive only as a money-making opportunity, it will be difficult for you to sell its offerings to anyone. If buyers perceive you are an unhappy business owner, they will be reluctant to patronize your business. Many successful entrepreneurs I have interviewed over the years have expressed to me that they not only like what they are doing, they are passionate about their business; and some have said that getting paid is just an added bonus.

Suggested Resources

Books

The Best Home Businesses for the Twenty-First Century, rev. ed., by Paul and Sarah Edwards (New York: Penguin Group, 1999).

Finding Your Perfect Work: The New Career Guide to Making a Living, Creating a Life, rev. ed., by Paul and Sarah Edwards (New York: Penguin Putnam, 2002).

More 101 Best Home-Based Businesses for Women by Priscilla Y. Huff (Rocklin, CA: Prima Publishing, 1998).

101 Best Home-Based Businesses for Women, 3rd. ed., by Priscilla Y. Huff (New York: Random House, 2002).

Will It Fly? How to Know if Your New Business Idea Has Wings . . . Before You Take the Leap by Thomas K. McKnight (Upper Saddle River, NJ: Financial Times/Prentice Hall, 2003).

Web Info

www.Entrepreneur.com/howto, *Entrepreneur* magazine's free, online, how-to guides, "How to Research Your Business Idea" and "Finding the Perfect Business Idea."

29. Additional Selection Dilemmas

Several decisions that you may face in your business selection process can have a large impact on your venture(s)'s success. Your resolutions, based on the entrepreneurial direction you choose, will dictate your marketing strategies.

Part- or Full-Time?

According to the U.S. Census Bureau, an increasing number of Americans are starting successful businesses on a part-time basis and three-quarters of home-based businesses are also launched part-time. Here are the advantages to starting a venture this way:

- You can test the market response to your products or services with less financial risk. This may be the best reason to start a business part-time. With trial and error, you can take the time to test ads, sales techniques, and evaluate customers' responses to your business offerings, allowing you to find the highest-paying customers and perfect your product or service to best meet their needs.
- You can keep your debt down because part-time ventures generally cost less to launch due to lower overhead, and your profits can be reinvested into your venture.
- You may be a better candidate for a business loan because your part-time venture will have an established sales record and fewer financial liabilities.
- Your part-time business profits can help pay down your personal debt and help support you and your family. If you should be laid off, you will already have an income-producing venture that you can expand into a full-time business.

- You can take advantage of business deductions for your office (if you have a home office), equipment and supplies, utilities, and also business-related vehicle and travel expenses. Consulting with an accountant and/or tax specialist will help you stay current with tax codes and regulations.
- You will also have time to learn from your entrepreneurial mistakes and correct them as you develop your business knowledge and operational skills. You will also have a greater opportunity to acquire the necessary skills, certifications, or degrees you may need to qualify you to operate your chosen venture.

There may be a few drawbacks of operating part-time:

- You may have to sacrifice more free time to spend for yourself or family.
- You may not always be available the hours your customers need you because of your regular job's hours.
- You may become burned out with working and running a part-time business, or frustrated that you cannot take your business full time as quickly as you wish.

The advantages to starting part-time generally outweigh the disadvantages, and many enthusiastic and persistent entrepreneurs own successful businesses that were started on the side. Why not you?

One or More Businesses?

One man in my area owns 18 businesses. Now, he did not start with 18, but you, too, can own and operate more than one business at a time. Business experts generally advise against this, because one of the reasons businesses fail is that their owners are going in too many directions and never really focus long enough on the necessary tasks that will keep their businesses in the black. However, because of customers' requests or demands, an unexpected side market will open up and be just as profitable as the original or earn even more.

A woman, who originally opened an antique business in her remodeled barn, decorated the windows in imported German lace curtains. Her customers made so many requests that she became a distributor for the company and started a profitable side business, selling the curtains worldwide from the web site she created for this purpose (see Chapter 12 about spin-offs and other ways to diversify).

Sometimes entrepreneurs will operate one business to pay their bills and start another one that fulfills their passion or creativity. Most of one independent graphic artist's profits are derived from her freelance ad work for commercial clients, but she loves the design opportunities in her side business of creating high-end custom-designed wedding invitations for brides.

If your business does develop another venue or you are contemplating one or more ventures, here are some guidelines:

- It will be easier to operate and market your businesses if they evolve from one another, like the graphic artist's wedding invitations. She could use the same skills and technology that she used in her freelance work.
- Treat each business as a separate entity: Have separate banking accounts and keep careful records of each venture's financial and business activities. This is especially important for tax-reporting purposes. Consult regularly with your accountant to keep careful track of your cash flow and your financial plans.
- To give yourself more quality time, hire a mother's helper to watch young children or outsource office work you do not have time to handle with specialists like virtual assistants or professional employer organizations (PEOs) to handle employee paperwork.
- Create an individual business and marketing plan for each venture and review them regularly to stay focused on the goals you have set for each one.
- Look for opportunities for each venture to help market the other. The woman with the antique shop kept it open, even though she made more money with her profitable web site that sold her curtains. She says often out-of-town visitors would stop in for the antiques and walk out as curtain customers after seeing how they were displayed in the shop.
- Stop if you become overwhelmed (or run out of money) with the tasks of running more than one business. It makes sense to focus your energy and resources on the business that is making the most money, especially if you find yourself overextended. You can always try again, but at a later time when you have more time and your main business is running smoothly. Then, again, doing one thing, and one thing well, may be best suited to your situation and your personality. It is your call (see also Chapter 12).

For Fun or Profit?

Can you turn your hobby into a business? If you have a hobby of gardening or building furniture, you may wonder if you can turn this love or passion into a business. It is important for you to understand in business terms what differentiates a hobby from a business. In the article, "Is It a Business or Hobby?" on the IRS web site (www.IRS.gov), the IRS defines a hobby as "an activity for which you do not expect to make a profit," and goes on to say that if you do not *intend* to make a profit, there is a limit to the number and type of deductions you can take for selling as a hobby as opposed to having a business.

In the same article, the IRS lists several criteria that delineate the two, such as carrying on the activity in a businesslike manner or depending on this activity to support oneself. But the most important deciding factor that separates a hobby from a business is whether you *intend* to make a profit with this activity (also called your *profit motive*). The IRS says you *can* make money with a hobby that you should still report as income; but as a hobby, you will not be eligible for the same deductions as a business.

Keeping accurate business accounting records and files will demonstrate to authorities at all levels that you are running a business, even if some years you show a loss rather than a profit. Again, be sure to consult with your accountant or income tax specialist regularly so you can show that you do have a legitimate business.

Often, people who try turning their hobby into a business, decide not to keep it as a business. One woman who loves the music business, tried going full time, but went back to it being a hobby. She said the effort was taking the fun away from her music, so she decided to keep her day job and keep her musicians' contracting service on the side. She said this way, she would only have to deal with the people she preferred, not the ones she would have to accommodate if it were her main source of income. Hobby or business? That is your decision and will determine your marketing methods.

Businesses You Can Buy

In searching for the ideal home-based business, you might consider purchasing a business opportunity or franchise, or joining a home party or a network marketing venture with an established company such as Mary Kay or Longaberger Baskets.

An advantage that these business opportunities and franchises have over independent start-ups is that potential customers already recognize their names and related products and services. These opportunities often require their buyers to give up a certain amount of operational control. Still, many entrepreneurs invest in these turnkey ventures because they are less risky than starting a business completely on their own. You should ask whether these companies have established marketing plans and to what extent you will be asked to participate.

Some disadvantages with these businesses is that you may not have the right personality to sell these companies' goods and services; or you may not like what you are selling. If you lack enthusiasm or conviction for the company's products or services, it will come through to potential customers.

Another alternative is to buy an existing, independent company. You can hire a business broker to represent you, or you and your legal and financial experts can review the company's financial statements, existing assets, and operating procedures. You and a marketing or business consultant, lawyer, and an accountant should all conduct a company marketing analysis to see if its current activities are adequate or if they should be revised to attract more customers.

You have heard the caution before: Take the time to thoroughly investigate any business opportunities that interest you *before* investing your money and your time (see also Method 94 for turning your business into an opportunity or franchise).

Scam or Legitimate Opportunity?

Sources for you to check the background of franchises, business opportunities, or network marketing or multilevel marketing (MLMs) companies that may interest you:

- Your local consumer protection office.
- The Better Business Bureau (www.bbb.org) in the area where the company is located.
- Attorney general's office in the state where the company is located. Ask about the state's regulations regarding franchises and/or business opportunities.
- Your local postmaster. The U.S. Postal Service investigates fraudulent mail practices.
- The Federal Trade Commission (www.ftc.gov). It cannot help resolve individual disputes, but can take action if there is evidence of a pattern of deceptive or unfair practices. For registering complaints, write to: Federal Trade Commission, CRC-240, 600 Pennsylvania Avenue, NW, Washington, DC 20580.
- The National Fraud Information Center. Project of the National Consumers League; frauds and scams updates; to report a fraud, visit www.fraud.org; call (800) 876-7060 (9 A.M.– 5 P.M. Eastern, M–F).

Suggested Resources

Book

> *Home Businesses You Can Buy: The Definitive Guide to Exploring Franchises, Multi-Level Marketing, and Business Opportunities Plus: How to Avoid Scams* by Paul Edwards, Sarah Edwards, and Walter Zooi (New York: Putnam, 1997).

Publication

> *Home Business Magazine,* www.homebusinessmag.com, its annual March/April issue features a directory of home-based businesses, franchises, and opportunities; subscription or sold on newsstands.

Web Info

> www.IRS.gov, IRS, (800) 829-1040, additional information about the business use of your home, related forms, hobby or business article, and a listing of helpful IRS publications.

30. Family and Friends' Impact and Input

If your present income helps support family or friends, you will want to ask for their backing, understanding, and patience with your work schedule. Friends may offer to help or even work for you, but make a pact to agree that it is a business arrangement and to not let business interfere with your friendship.

If you operate a home-based business, you will have to set boundaries and define what is office space (and its supplies and equipment) and what is family space. That also pertains to answering phones and interacting with any clients who may come to your home. You will need some sort of child-care coverage when you are making important phone calls or need to work on a project. Sitters (in your home or theirs), family members, or participation in a neighborhood play group; or some other arrangements are all options that will ensure some uninterrupted periods when you can focus on important business tasks.

As a business owner, you are permitted to hire family members, but check with your accountant or tax specialist about employment tax requirements for them, as these taxes may be different from the taxes for other employees.

There are definite pros and cons in asking family for help, or hiring them as employees. Some will be jealous or resentful of the time you devote to a business or would just prefer not to be involved. You and your family members will have to discuss these issues openly and honestly or negative feelings and conflicts can disrupt or even destroy your business. Patricia Gallagher, marketing expert and mother of four children, says to involve your children so they feel their contributions are valuable and celebrate with them when something special occurs in your business.

On the positive side, statistics have revealed that many present entrepreneurs had one or both parents who also were entrepreneurs. Many children learn business basics in a family business and then go on to take over the business or start their own. One author invited her daughter to provide illustrations for her book. Inspired, her daughter went on to write her own book. Jill Hart of Christian Work at Home Moms (CWAHM.com) says, "Our business is truly a family affair. I try to find a task each day that my daughter (4 years) can help me with. She helps stuff envelopes, package items, count out business cards, and so on. My husband does a lot of the behind the scenes computer work for us along with many other tasks to keep our equipment and business running smoothly."

If you invite and do not force your family to assist you in business areas of their choice, they are more likely to enjoy being involved and may offer valuable insight into your business operations.

Nancy Mills, creator, "Spirited Woman's Approach to Life" (www. TheSpirited Woman.com), says there are a million marketing tips on how to grow your business, make it succeed, and generate your business. "But, the only way your business is going to zoom to the top is if *you keep your life in balance,*" says Mills. "That means taking time to smell the flowers, kiss the kids, go to the gym, dance the salsa, and read your favorite book. Most small business owners are consumed with their business in an endless cycle of stress and long hours. Pay attention to the *balance* in your life, and your marketing efforts will become much more effective—because you will want to do them, instead of having to do them," she says.

Sharing your business world with your family and friends will help them feel a part of your business world and they will be more likely to be the best backup coverage if a personal or business emergency should occur.

Suggested Resources

Books

> *The Business Mom Guide Book: More Life, Less Overwhelm for Mom Entre-preneurs* by Terilee Harrison (Deadwood, OR: Wyatt-MacKenzie Publishing, 2006).
>
> *Family Business: Key Issues* by Denise Kenyon-Rouvinez and John L. Ward (New York: Palgrave Macmillan, 2005).
>
> *Full-Time Woman, Part-Time Career: Launching a Flexible Business That Fits Your Life, Feeds Your Family, and Fuels Your Brain* by Karen Steede-Terry (Austin, TX: CMS Press, 2005).
>
> *Growing the Distance: Timeless Principles for Personal, Career, and Family Success* by Jim Clemmer (Kitchener, Ontario, Canada: The Clemmer Group, 2005).
>
> *Mom CEO (Chief Everything Officer): Having, Doing, and Surviving It All!* by Jodie Lynn (Fredonia, WI: Cedar Valley Publishing, 2006). www .parenttoparent.com.

Web Info

> www.en-parent.com, The Entrepreneurial Parent, community networking site.

31. Find a Profitable Market Niche

One of the most successful ways for a business to survive and thrive is to find and focus on a niche market—an untapped market of potential customers whose needs are not being met. Examples of successful entrepreneurs who have found their ideal niche can be seen everywhere: A computer consultant offers classes to seniors who want to learn computer basics to improve their job skills, or an independent bookkeeper finds that her most profitable niche is with the owners of seasonal contracting businesses whose spouses usually did the bookkeeping and gladly turned their business tasks over to the professional. Many inventors also find success in marketing to a niche within their industry because they already know clients who need their innovative product.

Erin Gruver, a professional organizer, discovered through experience that her best target niche was helping people pack for moving. "Once you have determined what niche you want to fill in the market and who your optimal target audience is, then you have to figure out how you can reach them," she says.

Here are some basic guidelines in finding and marketing to the ideal niche for your business:

1. *Identify your niche:* Using the results of a personal assessment, like the one in this chapter (see previous Sidebar: Business Matchmaker), correlate your preference with business ideas that interest you and make a list of those ventures that suit you best. Then research similar existing businesses to determine who their customers are and what they provide. Through market research (see also Chapter 4, Method 41), see if you can find customers in this industry who want something that no one can or wants to provide.

2. *Ask yourself these questions:*
   - Is your product or service a good candidate for a profitable niche?
   - Is there a problem that your business can solve for potential clients?
   - Have you improved on a product or service in the industry that you have worked?
   - Can you provide a product or service that is different or better than that of your competitors?
   - How much individual customization can you offer customers and still make a profit?
   - Will you have repeat customers who will need to continually purchase supplies from you?
   - Is there a market trend that your business can relate to?

Once you have defined your target niche, devise your favorite marketing strategies to this group so you get their feedback to determine if this really *is* a niche market worth pursuing.

Though you think you may have finally found a niche with great market potential, people do not always act as we expect them to, so stay ready to explore other niche possibilities if this one does not bring in the money you thought it would. Do not give up. Often, you can find opportunities for moneymaking niches within your past work or life experiences. With persistence and savvy marketing, you are sure to find a lucrative niche.

So, Have You Found Your Niche?

Joan Fisler

Who do you love to play with in your sandbox? Have you figured that out yet? As you are developing your business, pay careful attention to the client relationships that aren't just a success, but they sing. If, after an interaction, you are revved up and ready to conquer the world, you are working in your sweet spot, and quite possibly, you've identified a niche for your business. Niche marketing, in brief, is finding out the profile of your ideal clients, and then providing the services that address their needs.

You've heard the saying, "You can't be all things to all people." Niche marketing applies that wisdom to your business. Allow me to illustrate.

I knew that I enjoyed teaching and working with women. I also knew that my most prominent character trait, as observed by 15 or so of my friends and acquaintances, is compassion. I decided to work specifically with women in the process of getting a divorce as a divorce financial analyst. I tried it on and loved the educational component and the sense of empowerment I could foster at this critical juncture for these divorce clients.

Education in this area is available, and I pursued that immediately. In order to start actively attracting my ideal client, I had to research my end user. I accomplished this by interviewing not only women who had already been divorced, but also professionals such as counselors, divorce attorneys, divorce mediators, and financial divorce analysts who are outside of my geographic marketing area. The first rule of marketing is know your customers. The better you do, the better you can help them solve their problems. My research accomplished two purposes. First, I obtained valuable insight about the questions and needs of my future divorce prospects. Second, I had initiated valuable relationships with colleagues in the field, some of whom are now excellent referral sources. By narrowing my focus to divorcing women who need education and to plan for the future, I began defining my niche. I help them develop a divorce analysis that addresses their needs and provide them the hope of answering the questions that are almost always on their minds. Who is going to help you through the divorce decisions before you? You would probably be very inclined to retain my services. You would also tell your friends who get divorced next year, or in the year after.

As a business owner, you may worry about honing in on one type of client. And while there is no need to exclude more general forms of marketing, you can rest assured that if you identify your ideal clients, and figure out exactly how to supply what they need, you will be irresistible. You will have distinguished yourself from the pack and captured the attention of both the ideal client and other key players in your field. And this does not preclude you from also being a general practitioner.

While I have illustrated this concept in a divorce service business, it also translates into the manufacturing world. Think of products that have made everyday life better for you: Tupperware, travel mugs, palm pilots, garage door openers, pudding in a disposable cup.

In closing, niche marketing is an approach to business that certainly takes commitment and time to develop. However, once established, your business has been made unique in the eyes of potential clients and referral sources. You have made yourself into a professional who has specific knowledge and can problem solve for your ideal clients. So, observe whom you love to play with in the sandbox that is your business, and see if you can get to know them much better.

Joan Fisler is a certified divorce financial analyst in Wallingford, Connecticut.

Suggested Resources

Books

> *Marketing to Moms: Getting Your Share of the Trillion Dollar Industry* by Maria Bailey (New York: Crown Publishing, 2002).
>
> *Niche Selling: How to Find Your Customer in a Crowded Market* by William T. Brooks (New York: McGraw-Hill, 1991).
>
> *Trillion Dollar Moms: Marketing to a New Generation of Mothers* by Maria Bailey and Bonnie W. Ulman (Chicago: Kaplan Publishing, 2005).

32. Creating a Unique Image

A business image is how potential customers perceive you and your business. Your goal is to have an image that is easily recognizable and sets you apart from your competition. Establishing your business's unique image will help coordinate all your marketing efforts, because you will be consistent in your advertising, presentations, your professionalism, and the quality of your business offerings.

A business image includes just about every facet of your business that customers experience, from your printed materials such as business cards and brochures, your customer service and communications, to your personal image. Kimberly Kardos-Bensing, graphic artist-designer and owner of a unique conceptual design and invitation business (www.Heirloom-Occasions.com) says, "I believe the key to any successful business is a unique idea. You need to offer something no one else is able to offer, or something that hasn't been thought of. If your product is not unique, then you need to find something original about the way you offer it."

Here are suggestions for presenting an outstanding image:

- *Personally:* Dress professionally and appropriately for your industry; express an air of confidence; be courteous and use proper speech; be a good listener.
- *Communications:* Follow proper phone etiquette such as returning calls or e-mail messages; remember to express your thanks and appreciation to

the media, customers, and entrepreneurs with whom you network; be considerate; offer to help.
- *Printed materials:* Work with a graphic designer to create an outstanding identity that you can include in all your business cards, brochures, banners, and advertising items. They should be of excellent quality and be produced for a marketing purpose such as to introduce your business, to explain your products or services, or to present information. Gerry's gift basket business was home based, but she made sure her brochures describing each basket were high quality because her target market included corporate executives.

Do not be afraid to periodically update your business image to stay up with trends (not fads) or to offer a new service or line of products. Regular customers will appreciate that you are staying current and you will catch the attention of potential customers. If you need assistance in creating or improving your personal or business image, you can seek the services of image consultant specialists.

Be true to your image, though, by being yourself. You are the most important factor in your business's image, so follow through with what you promise. Do not betray your customers' trust or you will lose your credibility and business (see also Method 60).

Suggested Resources

Association

Association of Image Consultants International, www.aici.org, visit their web site to search for a consultant who can help improve your business's communications, credibility, and additional professional facets of you and your business.

Book

Priceless: Turning Ordinary Products into Extraordinary Experiences by Diana Lasalle and Terry Britton (Boston: Harvard Business School Press, 2002).

33. Branding for Business

Definition

A *brand* is a symbol, name, or other recognizable designation that differentiates your business from another. Branding suggests the intangible character of your company—what it stands for and what it represents to your customers. You have to decide what it is you want your business name and logos to represent.

How to Do It for Your Business

Here are four steps you can take to increase your business's brand as a more effective marketing tool:

1. *Share your business story.* Professional crafters and artists have better sales if they put a little about themselves and some of their history and details about their products on their hangtags or in brochures. Customers like owning something original and knowing how it was created.
2. *Originate a phrase, quote, or symbol that can be associated with your product.* One professional organizer has a passion for collecting vintage purses. She loves their design and how each one organizes the owner's contents in a different way. She worked with a graphic artist to come up with an illustration of one of her favorite purses. She exhibits it on her business cards, vehicle signs, brochures, and web site.
3. *Rank your business's position with that of its competitors.* Do you want to be known as a small but personable company? If you survey your customers to get an idea of how they see your business, you can use that to help you create a corresponding image or phrase.
4. *Consult with a professional such as a graphic artist to help you find your unique brand.* Kimberly Kardos-Bensing says, "Conceptual marketing professionals can offer that service. When you have established your special brand, then promote it with a consistent, creative message and always offer good customer service. Make your clients think they are your only client and their business is the only thing on your mind."

Even one-person business owners should brand their business to make customers notice it. Creating a brand will drive your marketing efforts and form a memory that customers will recall first whenever they need your service or products. Just be sure that you stand behind your marketing promises and deliver what your brand signifies or it will quickly be a *forgotten* memory!

> ### Look Big and You Will Be (a Marketing Tip from a One-Woman Publishing Powerhouse: How a Graphic Designer and a Little Publicity Elbow Grease Can Elevate Your Brand Equity)
>
> Nancy Cleary
>
> Did you know the first impression isn't as important as the seventh, eighth, or ninth? Marketing experts will tell you it takes seven to nine "impressions" before people will take action and buy your product, call you for

consulting, or ask you to be an expert on their TV program. So, how do you position yourself as a leader, the "go-to" person for the media, in your market? How do you build your brand's credibility and multiply those impressions and their impact?

It starts with a clear presentation of your message—verbally and visually. You must set yourself apart and make yourself memorable. Find what it is about you and your message that interests your market and the media, and communicate that quickly with words and images. Professional graphic designers can assist you once you can express your mission and your goals. They will help you put your personality, combined with your expertise, into images. Have your designer provide you with a tool kit of graphics—blazoned with your logo, name, and web site address in multiple formats (Tiff and .eps in 300 pixels per inch for printing, JPEG and gif in 72 ppi optimized for web). Be sure your business cards, letterhead, brochures, web site, and newsletters are all unmistakably yours.

Once you have these tools imbued with your branding, it's time to surround your market and increase those impressions—be everywhere your customers are. Anticipate where they will be next and be there before them; learn how to spot trends and use them to your advantage. It's easier than it sounds, and it won't cost a lot of money if you're willing to be generous with your time, energy, and ideas.

Stay on top of trends with "media alerts" from Google, Yahoo, and news outlets or subscribe to press release lead services—these PR feeds and opportunities will have the latest information to spin your own media-savvy stories, or give you the heads-up to get involved in upcoming events and publications (see also Chapter 14).

Nancy Cleary is founder and CEO of Wyatt-MacKenzie Publishing, Inc. (www.wymacpublishing.com).

Suggested Resources

Audio

Branding for Profit: Build Your Brand to Increase Sales and Customer Loyalty by James Burgin, Donald Trump, and Jon Ward, produced by Trump University, 2006.

Books

Brands That Rock: How to Win Fans and Influence Profits by Roger Blackwell and Tina Stephan (Hoboken, NJ: John Wiley & Sons, 2003).

Purple Cow: Transform Your Business by Being Remarkable by Seth Godin (New York: Portfolio, 2003).

Web Info

http://thebrandbuilder.blogspot.com, The Brand Builder Blog, informative articles and discussion.

www.Entrepreneur.com/howto, *Entrepreneur* magazine's free, online, how-to guide, "The Basics of Branding."

3

Grow with Effective Organization and the Right Tools: Time *Is* Money!

Successful entrepreneurs (and accomplished people) are skilled at time management. The old adage, "Time is money," applies to the success of your business. Chapter 3 explains how to formulate a time management plan that saves valuable revenue-generating time. Setting up and organizing efficient office and your business operations will improve your daily work schedule. This chapter presents suggestions for an economical, ergonomically comfortable, and technological office setting that will help you maintain and grow your business.

34. Learn Time Management Principles

Managing Time Is Vital to Growth

We all have the same 24 hours in a day, but some of us maximize those hours better than others, especially when it comes to managing a small business amid all the other demands on our lives. As mentioned in Chapter 1, new business owners spend as much as 75 percent of their operating time marketing their new ventures; and those with already-established businesses need to do some marketing on a daily basis. Without continued promotional activities, a business will fail. How much time you have to manage and grow your business depends on how well you manage your time through planning, setting goals, eliminating "time-wasters," organizing your work space and operations, and using technology and other aids.

Two Time Management Guidelines

WORK SMARTER, NOT HARDER

To paraphrase a saying, you can easily expand your work to fill your time. However, is it *productive* time? Are you working on the correct business tasks? How many of those tasks are potentially revenue-producing? Here are some tips to help you concentrate on the most important tasks:

- At the beginning of each week, prepare a complete list of all the tasks you have to do that week. Separate these into personal tasks and business tasks, and then list them (prioritize) in order of importance.
- Each day take this list and use it to plan your day's activities—both personal and business.
- At the end of the week, evaluate how much you have accomplished. If you did not accomplish the most important tasks, then you need to either plan fewer activities or find more time. Keep a time journal for a week listing how you spent every hour. It can provide valuable insights into how you spend your time.
- Write down in your journal everything that is normally in your scheduled work hours, personal hours, and errands. Consider eliminating or revising anything unimportant that is interfering with your work. (Instead of volunteering for another year as the president of a community organization, volunteer to help with a specific fund-raising activity.) You cannot do everything . . . well!
- Now set up a schedule, filling in all your *must* obligations and look for blocks of time to work on business proposals. Place your schedule on your favorite aid—a planner, computer program, calendar, appointments calendar, or handheld device—and refer to it regularly. Make sure that each of your business blocks of time includes marketing activities, as well as planning daily marketing tasks. Consulting with a business coach may help you determine what marketing avenues should have priority.
- Keep a short journal of each day's activities to see if you are following your to-do list. If you stick to your schedule and concentrate on your priorities in both your business and private life, you will be more likely to make the most of your time—playing harder and working smarter.

FIND BALANCE

For most of us, time is both a valued and an abused resource. The challenge is how to have time to market and grow your venture and still have a personal life. A new or expanding business can consume most of your time and may lead to burnout or neglect of your health or family relationships. However, being your own boss has advantages because it permits flexible work hours. If you can master the principles of time management, you will be much more likely to achieve your business and personal goals. Here are some suggestions for finding that perfect balance of work and your personal life:

- *Focus on what is important.* Sit down with yourself or your family and decide what goals are most important to you in work and in your family or personal life. By distinguishing what matters to you, you can create a structure for the best allocation of your time.

  Different seasons of the year can present different challenges in your work and family schedule. Janeen R. Adil, a freelance writer and author, says that her summer schedule involves some adjustments. "In the cooler early morning, I tend to find myself pulled between wanting to write and doing other activities—like gardening—that are better tended to then, rather than later, in the heat of the day," she says. "And with my daughter out of school, she and I must work to create blocks of the solitude I prefer for writing. Somehow, though, things do balance out, and everything does seem to get done," says Adil.
- *Plan your work time realistically.* Most activities take longer than our estimates; you may have to plan fewer tasks so you can complete them, instead of being frustrated because your to-do list is too long. Learn to pace yourself and do a few things well instead of many sloppily.
- *Try to set definite hours for work time and personal and family time.* Make it a habit to stick to that schedule for several weeks, and you will have trained your mind to work more productively on business matters. When it is leisure time, leave your work at your office, whether it is in your home or in another location. Your sanity and relationships will survive and thrive.

Why Do You Procrastinate?

We have all put off tackling a task. Here are some common reasons and some tips for overcoming your reluctance to start or finish a duty:

- *When a project is overwhelming:* Breaking a large project into smaller increments will help make it more manageable.
- *When you do not feel qualified (and you really are):* Self-doubts can erode your self-confidence, especially when it is the first time you are doing a project. Just get started and learn to trust your skills and abilities. If possible, have an expert look over your work. A business coach may have some strategies to help you overcome your insecurities.
- *When you do not like doing something:* For example, you may dislike cold calling. First, read some tips for succeeding at cold calling. Then reward yourself in some small way every time you make five calls.
- *When you reach an impasse:* Just as most writers occasionally have writer's block, you may run out of ideas or cannot find a solution: You

can network with others in your industry for suggestions about solving the problem. Some people find that "sleeping" on it—letting their subconscious handle their dilemmas while they sleep or take walks or breaks—helps them relax and come up with solutions.

Recognize procrastination when it happens and do not let it paralyze you so you cannot operate and market your business.

Suggested Resources

Books

Common Sense Organizing: A Step-by Step Program for Taking Control of Your Home and Your Life by Debbie Williams (Vancouver, WA: Champion Press, Ltd., 2005).

No B. S. Time Management for Entrepreneurs by Dan Kennedy (Irvine, CA: Entrepreneur Press, 2004).

Time Efficiency Makeover: Own Your Time and Your Life by Conquering Procrastination by Dorothy K. Breininger and Debby S. Bitticks (Deerfield Beach, FL: Health Communications, 2005).

Software

ACT! by Sage Software, SB, Inc., www.act.com, links your contacts, notes and history, appointments, activities, and even custom data fields to your PDA for customer contact info when you are on the road.

Personal Information Managers (PIMs) Software, sample of many, including MS Outlook, Lotus Notes, GroupWise, or host of other similar tools.

Web Info

www.thebusywoman.com, Susie Glennan's the Busy Woman's "Daily Planner," time-saving tips and products.

www.organizedtimes.com, web site of Debbie Williams, organizing coach, for articles, tips, and time management resources.

35. Identify and Eliminate Time-Wasting Activities

Work is not always fun, so we all find ways to procrastinate or waste time, even though we will not always admit that an activity is wasting time. How do you identify actions that are counterproductive to your business progress? The following tips can help you eliminate (or cut back on) and prevent frequent time-wasting pursuits:

- *Identify.* If you kept a journal of how you spent your time in all the hours of a week or more, review this time ledger to find the times you went off into tangents and the times that you actually worked on revenue-generating business activities. Make note of your most common time-wasting activities, so you can learn to avoid them.
- *Confine.* If you work from home, keep all your work in your designated office space, so you will not have to go wandering for needed paperwork. Keep only those supplies that you regularly use on your work space and take time weekly to toss out items that are trash, no longer needed, or do not work.
- *Organize.* Time wasted in searching for business items is time wasted in operating your business.
- *Time them.* Work at the times of the day when you are most productive and distractions are at a minimum. One business writer with three small children puts her children to bed, and then she sleeps until 11 P.M. She has discovered that by working from 11 P.M. to 3 A.M., she can finish a major part of her writing without interruptions. Check your journal to see the times you were most productive and schedule that time for your most difficult business tasks.
- *Condense.* Schedule errands and household duties in blocks of time, and save time by doing them all at once.
- *Enjoy them (without guilt).* Schedule time for yourself and family and friends so you (and they) can look forward to a relaxing time. Let voice mail take business messages in your "off" hours.
- *Manage mail.* Handle post office mail as soon as you receive it, and toss or file it in designated categories such as bills, catalogs, and letters for reply. Check e-mail messages daily, but do it in blocks of time to avoid Internet distractions. Use electronic e-mails to keep it separated.
- *Limit.* If you tend to wander about the Internet, limit your time in cyberspace for information, marketing, e-mail communications, and other work activities. It is easy to become addicted to being online, to the detriment of your business and your personal life.
- *Do not panic.* At times, illnesses, family emergencies, electrical storms and power outages, and other unexpected events can interrupt your business productivity and are impossible to predict. That's life!

True, life has its small, and sometimes serious, emergencies that destroy your good intentions of finishing your work. Just get back on track as soon as possible after a setback and keep going forward, controlling as many time-wasters as you can. Being aware of how you use your time can help you be more productive and organized, thus increasing the profits of your business while freeing up more time to spend with those people who are most important to you.

Suggested Resources

Books

> *Done! How to Accomplish Twice as Much in Half the Time,* 2nd ed., by Don Aslett (Holbrook, MA: Adams Media Corp., 2005).
>
> *The Time Trap: The Classic Book on Time Management,* 3rd ed., by Alec Mackenzie (New York: AMACON, 1997).

Web Info

> www.sba.gov/managing/growth/makingtime.html, "Making Time," SBA series, "Starting Your Small Business."

36. Set Up Your Ideal Office Space for Increased Productivity

Many architects and interior designers specialize in planning and designing home and small office spaces, but if you are working on a limited business budget, you can still set up an efficient and low-cost work space. Here are some major considerations.

Location

Many multimillion-dollar businesses have started in a kitchen, bedroom, or garage. The space available will dictate how your office is arranged. If you will be receiving clients in your home office, you will want a "dedicated room" and, ideally, another entrance to keep work and personal areas separate. Remodeled outbuildings, garages, and basements can often be configured to meet these criteria. If you will be using the phone often in your business, you will need a quiet place without background noise either from your home or in a building.

The type of work you do will also affect your office and work area. If your business involves creating a fine craft or uses specialized equipment that needs additional power sources or special wiring to accommodate electrical tools, you may need special zoning and safety permits. If you are producing or selling products, you will also have to think about storage for inventory and areas for packing and shipping. Are you cooking a specialty food? Only two states permit commercial cooking in a (licensed) home kitchen, so you would need to have a cooking area in another location on your property or rent a commercial kitchen.

Additional factors to consider in choosing a location include your preferences: a secluded, sunny, or scenic space; comfort and safety (especially if you have young children or pets); and space for anyone who will be working with you. Visit your public library, bookstore, or remodeling center to view examples of small offices and workspace setups.

Layout

Determine your layout and placement of office equipment and furniture for maximum efficiency. Consider your business activities and work flow just as you would a kitchen work triangle and plan to have pieces of equipment and often-used supplies easily accessible for performing simultaneous or similar tasks. Popular arrangements include the "U" shape, with three possible work surfaces, and the "L" shape, which has two work spaces and is an excellent design for setting up in corners. Before you purchase or build any office furniture, take graph paper or use design software to lay out the plan of your home office. You can use cardboard boxes to arrange a simulated office space so you can visualize the traffic pattern and how much usable space you will have. If you have carpentry skills, you could install office built-ins or, depending on your budget, purchase one of the many types of multiuse office units that can be closed when not in use.

Take a tip from all the popular cable television shows and look for creative, low-cost ways to add storage and spaces for your business paperwork and equipment. A handy person or carpenter can install adjustable shelves and extra drawers in a closet or an unused space to provide you with a place for everything related to your business and prevent your business space from becoming a disorganized wasteland. Plastic containers of every size can be labeled and neatly stacked. Having an organized work space can save you money, too, by preventing you from buying duplicate items because the originals are buried somewhere in the clutter.

Economics

In Chapter 1, Method 13 focuses on the danger of overspending, especially in purchasing office equipment and technology. Here are some suggestions for saving money on these items. The more you save, the longer you can operate and market your business:

- List the minimum office space and equipment you need to get your business running. Save on furniture and construct storage space by building or creating your own. You can build a desk and filing space for as little as $25 by using a $2' \times 6'$ sheet of laminated wood supported at either end by a two-drawer file cabinet. Purchase only the essentials and visit other home-based entrepreneurs' offices for design ideas and tips.

- Search the Internet for home office items at online communities, auction sites, and discount retailers. Some popular sites to find good deals on everything from office furniture to electronics include Bull Dog Office Products, Inc., www.shopbulldog.com; www.Overstock.com; eBay.com and its partner www.half.com; and www.Craigslist.com, a worldwide virtual community. There are many other resource sites you can investigate to compare prices, shop, and exchange information.

- To qualify for discounts, join with other home business owners to purchase office supplies in bulk. Patronize office supply stores and computer manufacturers that give reward coupons and discounts to faithful customers. Compare prices with mail-order, office products companies such as Penny-Wise (www.penny-wise.com), Quill (www.quill.com), or Viking (www.vikingop.com). These firms offer periodic specials and free home delivery if you order over a certain dollar amount, saving you time and gas money. Recycle discarded paper by cutting paper for notes and using the blank side of used copier paper for personal photocopying. Recycle whatever other supplies you can.

- Leasing equipment can be expensive, but it may be a better option than going into debt for equipment and furnishings that you may not need later on, especially if your business changes its market direction or operations. Read the terms of the lease contract carefully, especially its renewal options, cancellation penalties, and possession of the equipment after the lease is ended. If you have questions, have your lawyer review it with you. Often, you can negotiate better terms.

It is better to be thrifty when you start your venture and not overspend because you will need every dollar possible to market and operate your new business until it becomes profitable and you can afford to purchase quality equipment and technology. It is wise, too, to wait until your business has been operating awhile to determine what products and services your customers want most, and what will be the best equipment to supply their needs.

The more money you save, the more you will have to put toward marketing.

Ergonomics and Safety

No matter where your office is located, you should be concerned with its ergonomics and overall safety for you, your family, and workers. Ergonomics is an applied science that deals with the physical effects of the work you do and the most efficient and safe design for performing that work. Improper use of equipment, repetitive movements, and poorly designed chairs or desks can create work-related disorders and impede productivity. Here are some considerations:

- Your office chairs should be adjustable, comfortable, and provide adequate support for you and your back.
- Arrange the spacing between your keyboard, computer, and the height of your desk and chair to prevent wrist strain causing carpal tunnel syndrome or strains from over-reaching.
- Lighting in your workspace is crucial to eliminate glare and eyestrain.
- Safety is important to prevent accidents, falls, and hazards to you and your workers. If you have a home office, you will want to safeguard your young children from gaining access where they might swallow harmful items or be exposed to electrical danger.
- Limit pets' access to your office. Like children, pets can be harmed by eating or chewing items, especially electrical cords; and pet accidents or shedding hair could damage your equipment.

A practical analysis of the functions and requirements of your business can help you plan an affordable and optimum workspace that will allow your venture to be stable and ready to expand.

Alternative Professional Spaces

There are several reasons you may need to rent or share a professional office on a part-time basis:

- You can prevent interruptions that might occur with a home office.
- It lends credibility to you or your business.
- Your clients may find it more convenient than a home office.
- You may gain the use of equipment that you have been unable to purchase.
- Your business may appear larger than it is.

Here are alternative meeting places you can explore:

- Check with local chapters of chambers of commerce, community colleges, public libraries, small business incubators, or local financial institutions to see if they have rooms available for rent or leasing. Some provide free use of space for their members.
- Check with the Office Business Center Association International (OBCAI) to see if an office is available in your area. Their members rent rooms by the hour, day, week, or yearly (see address under Suggested Resources).
- Contact local business owners. One woman who owned the building in which her business was located, regularly rented out some of her unused office space to entrepreneurs who worked out of their homes or who were traveling on business and needed temporary space.
- Consider a work trade with another business owner who has space you can share for your meetings or project work.

- Motels and hotels often rent large rooms for conducting seminars or holding group meetings.
- Go to your clients' or customers' offices.
- Be creative. In an earlier book (*More 101 Best Home-Based Businesses for Women,* Rocklin, CA: Prima Publishing, 1998), I mentioned that I had read an article about an elementary school music teacher who had been let go because of budget constrictions. She then subcontracted with several school districts to give music lessons to their students. She had a large, carpeted van that she parked at each school and used as a classroom to give music lessons to students.
- Lease temporary office space.

What really matters is not *where* you work—it is *how* you work and satisfy your customers. Use professional office space whenever you want to enhance your business image, for meetings, or to concentrate on projects, but if you are going to rent or to lease work space on a part- or full-time basis, make sure your marketing efforts are bringing you a steady stream of new clients to meet the ongoing rental costs.

Suggested Resources

Associations/Agencies

National Business Incubation Association, www.nbia.org, assists owners of small businesses with expansion, search site for a center near you.

National Institute for Occupational Safety and Health (NIOSH), www.cdc.gov/niosh/homepage.html, federal agency provides research, recommendations concerning prevention of work-related injuries and illnesses.

Office Business Center Association International (OBCAI), www.execsuites.org, office spaces and business services.

Books

Business Leasing for Dummies by David G. Mayer and Joseph Lane (Hoboken, NJ: John Wiley & Sons, 2001).

Dr. Pascarelli's Complete Guide to Repetitive Strain Injury: What You Need to Know About RSI and Carpal Tunnel Syndrome by Emil F. Pascarelli (Hoboken, NJ: John Wiley & Sons, 2005).

The Home Office Planner by Barty Phillips (San Francisco: Chronicle Books LLC, 2001).

Organizing from the Inside Out: The Foolproof System for Organizing Your Home, Your Office and Your Life, rev. ed., by Julie Morgenstern (New York: Henry Holt & Company, 2004).

Office Furniture

Anthro Corporation, www.anthro.com, ergonomic office furniture, economical computer carts and workstations.

Business and Institutional Furniture Company, Inc., www.bi-furniture.com.

Flexy-Plan Distinctive Office Furniture, www.fyp.com.

Neutral Posture Inc., www.neutralposture.com, ergonomic chairs.

Sauder Woodworking Co., www.sauder.com, space-saving computer workstations.

Web Info

www.childproofing.com, links to companies selling childproofing safety products.

www.ergoweb.com, Ergo Web-Ergonomic products, information, and news.

www.everythingsorganized.com, Everything's Organized web site of Lisa Kanarek, organizing home office expert and author; home office tips, products.

www.soundproofing.org, Super Soundproofing, information site with soundproofing tips.

37. Business Organization

Take Charge of Your Business Time

To paraphrase a common saying, "Control your time, or something else or someone will." There are many distractions in our lives; some we can control and others we cannot. Here are some tips for managing the ones we can.

CONTROL "PEOPLE TIME"

Learn to say "No," but with tact, to those people and activities that drain your time and energy. Schedule your family time, and consult them about your business so they will not resent your business activities. Control the get-togethers or phone calls with extended friends and family, and look for altruistic opportunities to involve your business in the causes about which you want to make the most commitment.

CONTROL COMMUNICATIONS

As mentioned, set up technology to handle unexpected interruptions, telephone calls, e-mails, letters, and deliveries. State your specific reasons for contacting people when you leave voice mail messages or send e-mails so they can have the information ready when they reply. Consider hiring part-time office support help or a virtual assistant or office support person to handle and keep track of administrative duties, communications, and correspondence so you can focus on producing and marketing your core product or service.

CONTROL PAPERWORK CLUTTER

Disorganization in your office space and records can waste your work time. Create a filing system that works for your business and take a few minutes at the end of your working day to straighten your office. Hire the services of a professional organizer to help you set up efficient business operations.

Maria Gracia, professional organizer, owner of www.GetOrganizedNow .com and author of *Finally, Organized, Finally, Free,* says that when your office is so full of clutter that you can barely see over your desk or get your fingers into your overflowing filing cabinet, you may want to think about hiring a professional organizer. She also contends that most business owners are so busy with the day-to-day grind that getting organized always seems to get put on the back burner.

"What only the savvy business owners know, however, is that it's incredibly difficult, if not impossible, to get ahead when you're working in such chaotic conditions," says Gracia.

She continues, "A professional organizer can help you find appropriate storage space for your many office-related items, can assist you in getting your filing system in order, or can even work with you to streamline your hectic schedule. All of this leaves you more time for marketing and growing your business."

CONTROL YOUR FINANCES

Neglecting your record keeping and bookkeeping can lead to business failure. Monitor your cash flow frequently using the appropriate software to save time and to highlight the products or projects that are worth your investment of time and money and which ones you should eliminate. Consult with your accountant or financial expert on a regular basis.

Not all interruptions or time-consuming tasks are negative ones. Responding to new clients' inquiries or answering a reporter's questions or networking with a valued business friend who is asking for some feedback, or having a spontaneous picnic in a local park with your family on a warm, spring day are all positive interruptions with the potential for later rewards. Enjoy them and resume your schedule as soon as possible.

Improving Efficiency

Whether you are a one-person business or have employees, running your business with maximum efficiency is important to its survival. Evaluating overall performance will provide you with better insight into your business operations and the areas you need to improve. Here are questions to help you in that evaluation along with suggestions for improvement:

- Are you fulfilling the expectations of your customers and meeting their needs? Suggestions:
  —Encourage customer feedback.
  —Implement methods to respond faster to customers' inquiries or complaints.
- Can you improve the quality and delivery of your services or products? Suggestions:
  —Update your skills or that of your employees.
  —Update your equipment and technology for faster, more accurate, and improved production.
  —Use better quality materials.
  —Look for ways to work more efficiently with suppliers.
- What experts or networking contacts in your industry can give you some efficiency ideas? Suggestions:
  —Hire a professional to evaluate your business's performance.
  —Attend trade shows, industry conferences, or meetings with other entrepreneurs for their ideas.
- What marketing methods can you streamline, combine, or eliminate? Suggestions:
  —Assess your old methods and see if you can deliver them at a lower cost or in conjunction with one another.
  —Try new promotions, ads, and publicity approaches, one at a time and monitor the responses for their effectiveness.
- Hire a professional organizer or time management specialist to review your business's daily operations.

Once you have a better awareness of your business, decide on the steps you need to improve your business's use of its time and operations. Review your business efficiency periodically to stay competitive and make the profits you need.

Suggested Resources

Association

National Association of Professional Organizers, www.napo.net, networking, referrals.

Books

The 80/20 Principle: The Secret to Success by Achieving More with Less by Richard Koch (New York: Doubleday, 2005).

Organizing from the Right Side of the Brain: A Creative Approach to Getting Organized by Lee Silber (New York: St. Martin's Griffin, 2004).

Web Info

> www.getorganizednow.com, organizing tips for home and office; *Finally, Organized, Finally, Free,* by Maria Gracia, book or electronic version.

Software, Organization

> If you have fewer than 10 staff, you can track your business efforts using software with simple database or spreadsheet capabilities. Check for software reviews in the Review section at www.CNET.com.

38. Technology

Advancements of affordable technology and Internet connections, plus an increase in trade relations among countries are helping small businesses find markets the world over. Just because computers, printers, and other technology are within your means, however, does not mean they will be the best for your business. Smart research and planning will help you buy equipment that will improve your business operation today and help you adapt to any business changes and growth.

The type of business you have will dictate the specific tools and technology your venture requires, in addition to general office equipment. Starting with only the essential equipment will give you time to test your business operations and customer responses before you make major technological investments.

Essentials

HARDWARE AND OTHER EQUIPMENT

Look for the computer packages offered by companies like Hewlett-Packard or Dell because their packages have compatible major hardware, and these companies offer warranties, service contracts, and easy ordering of supplies. You can save money by purchasing multifunctional equipment such as all-in-one printers, scanners, copiers, and fax machines. As your business grows, you can always invest in more expensive equipment.

SOFTWARE

Most computer packages come with already-installed software such as home office suites of word processing, database management, accounting, and spreadsheets. For your specific business and its operations, follow your industry's recommendations for software programs. Just as you keep your office in order, keep your computer files organized, saving files to designated folders and using shortcuts to your programs, databases, and the Internet.

CONNECTIONS

For a small business, you will want to have a client/service-based network operating system that has file and printer services with backup. You will need dedicated Internet access preferably (over dial-up) through cable, DSL, or more complex Internet solutions such as a T1 line that can handle more users. Look for a service agreement offering fast service if your Internet connection should go offline. You will want to be sure to have enough broadband bandwidth for your use now, and for any employees you hire in the future.

PROTECTION

Unexpected storms, power outages, computer virus attacks, and security breaches frequently affect Internet connections and operations. Here are some major problems that you will want to prevent using available technology (companies mentioned do not constitute an endorsement).

Use uninterruptible power supply (UPS) devices to keep your PC running during a power failure. They will give you time to save your work and shut safely down. Use surge suppressors for power brownouts. Company: American Power Conversion (APC) West Kingston, RI 02892, www.apc.com.

No computer is safe from viruses. Even Apple computers, once thought safe, now can be attacked by a virus. Use virus protection software to protect against computer viruses, and download regular updates. Some virus companies include Norton AntiVirus (www.symantec.com, which also makes "Norton SystemWorks," combining virus protection, disk repairs, and other functions) and McAfee antivirus (http://www.mcafee.com/us).

PROTECTING DATA

Install software that schedules automatic data backups like Backup Exec made by SeaGate Software; and use external zip (hard) drives like Imation SuperDisk, because all hard drives will eventually crash. Some companies include SeaGate Technology (www.seagate.com) and Imation Corp (www.imation.com).

Other backup options include using an offsite company or if your company is larger, having a network-attached storage system installed at your business's location.

While traveling, safeguard your laptop computer against theft or loss; protect its contents along with that of any desktop computers, computer peripherals, and other assets such as LCD projectors and video equipment. PC Guardian Anti-Theft Products, Inc. (www.pcguardian.com), Securtech Co. (www.securtech.com), and a number of other firms provide these safeguards; or you can check in the volumes of the *Thomas Register of Manufacturers* or search online at www.Thomasnet.com for manufacturers of these devices.

Technology for Growth

Working from a home office, you can now "meet" with clients and connect with associates within your home, office building, or across the country or world.

Here are some additional technological options you may want to consider as you maintain and grow your business:

- Videoconferencing is an exchange of sound and video images among two or more distant individuals. High-speed Internet access, sound cards, speakers, microphones, Web camera, and software enable videoconferencing. All people who are involved in the conferencing can hear and see in the real-time mode over the Internet. Images that can be transmitted include data from graphics, applications, or files; video streams; and immovable images of objects.

  Both parties must have a similar equipment setup for the videoconference to be successful. Some conference centers and office centers like Kinko's rent videoconferencing meeting rooms.
- Computer networks for the home and small business can be built using either wired or wireless technology. Wired *Ethernet* has been the traditional choice in homes, but *Wi-Fi* wireless technologies are gaining ground fast. Both wired and wireless can claim advantages over the other; both represent viable options for home and other *local area networks (LANs)*.
- Teleconferencing and virtual meetings are other ways to talk to multiple computer users from a home office. They involve using PC and dial-up connections, or using a phone unit that can handle two or more calls coming in on separate phone lines.

Another virtual meeting option is paying to use a Web conferencing service like the services of Cisco MeetingPlace (www.meetingplace.net). The only technology you need is a telephone and a Web browser to communicate with others in real time. Holding teleclasses has become a profitable sideline for many business experts.

Two additional examples of technology that entrepreneurs are using to sell information products directly to customers are (1) podcasting, using personal audio players for downloading information; and (2) electronic publishing of e-books and articles that customers can purchase online and download. Business owners can sell information directly to customers.

If you need assistance with your computer or information technology at any time, consult with a computer technologist or specialist. Get referrals from business owners or industry associations. Technology is evolving everyday and will provide you with new ways to inform regular customers and entice new ones.

Technology for Entrepreneurs with Disabilities

According to the U.S. Department of Census, people with disabilities are almost twice as likely to start a business as nondisabled individuals; and 14 percent of people with disabilities are self-employed, compared with 8 percent of nondisabled persons. Advancements in technology and adapted equipment—

hardware, software, home office furniture—have enabled many persons to overcome disabilities and operate a home-based or small business.

If you have a disability or want to help a disabled person start a business, see Disability Resources on page 68 to obtain further information and assistance.

All persons with disabilities can join others interested in starting a business or owning an established business. They can receive free or low-cost business counseling services at the following centers, which are located all over the United States and its territories (call the SBA number or search the web sites for locations near you):

- Small Business Development Centers (SBDCs), www.sba.gov/SBDC.
- Women's Business Development Centers, www.onlinewbc.gov.
- Service Corps of Retired Executives (SCORE), www.SCORE.org.
- Veterans' Assistance SBA's Office of Veterans Business Development (OVBD), www.sba.gov/VETS.
- Several regional OVBD offices for veterans assist in entrepreneurship including the "Procurement Program for Service-Disabled Veteran-Owned Small Business Concerns." Visit web site or call: (202) 205-6773.
- States: Contact the offices of your local state representative or senator to see what technical, financial, and rehabilitation services are available for persons with disabilities.

Postage Technology

To save time and money mailing packages and business correspondence, you can take advantage of equipment and online sources such as a mail meter or an electronic postage system. In addition to enhancing your business image, metered mail enables you to assign the exact postage and in different classes, get feedback on responses to direct mailing campaigns, and eliminate trips to the post office.

How it works: You need a postage meter that you rent, along with a base and a scale that you can buy if you want. Or you can print either postage or shipping labels with postage from your computer with the U.S. Postal Service® or one of their approved vendors. Visit www.usps.com/onlinepostage for more information. Costs range from a few hundred dollars to several thousand dollars. If you only send out a few pieces of mail a day, the investment may not be worth it for you. However, if you launch a direct mail campaign, you can save time and money while reaching potential customers. Compare prices and services to find the best company for your postal demands.

Suggested Resources

Associations

Independent Computer Consultants Association, www.icca.org, nonprofit member support organization, consultants' search capability.

The National Association of Computer Consultant Businesses (NACCB), www.naccb.org, a national trade association of professional computer information specialists.

Computer and Technology Publications

PC World, www.pcworld.com, web site of a computer and business magazine, latest technology reviews.

Smart Computing, www.smartcomputing.com, web site of print publication that puts technology into "plain English" for computer users.

Look for others in your local bookstore, news stand, or large library.

DISABILITY RESOURCES

Association

Disabled Businessperson Association, www.disabledbusiness.com.

Book

Unlikely Entrepreneurs: A Complete Guide to Business Start-Ups for People with Disabilities and Chronic Health Conditions by Roseanne Herzog (Traverse City: North Peak Publishing, 1999).

Federal Government

U.S. Small Business Administration (SBA), (800) 827-5722 (SBA INFO LOCATOR).

Web Info

www.abilitiesexpo.com, Abilities EXPO, many assisted living products, and technology.

www.blvd.com, the Boulevard is a web site containing information on products, resources, publications, employment opportunities for persons with disabilities, and more.

www.wcdexpo.com/, World Congress and Exposition on Disabilities (see also Additional Resources in the back of the book).

POSTAL RESOURCES

Companies

Postage companies for price/service comparisons of mailing shipping for businesses: Pitney Bowe's PitneyWorks, www.pitneyworks.com; Stamps .com, www.stamps.com.

Federal Government

U.S. Postal Service, www.usps.gov, general and shipping and confirmation information. Publications online include business tips and how to save time on mailings, www.usps.com/grow/manageyourbusiness/welcome.htm.

Web Info

www.informationweek.com, online technology information.

www.techweb.com, online technology information and portal, and other technology links such as informationweek.com, Internetweek.cmp.com, and others.

39. Keep in Touch with Customers While on the Road

Whether you frequently travel short or long distances or both, mobile technology will keep you connected and online. Most likely you own one or more devices that can help you be a productive "road warrior," no matter where you go. These products include, but are not limited to, pagers; cellular phones with text messaging, photo, and Internet access capabilities; contact manager software; adapters for connecting to alternative power sources (backup batteries); fax software; personal digital devices and other handheld devices; and any additional technology that enables you to communicate with others.

One writer uses software installed onto her laptop (and cords) to connect her cell phone to the Internet when she has free minutes. The drawbacks with this technology are that she can only use it where her cell phone has a signal and with this software it is a slow connection; but she can still access the Internet, and more importantly receive her e-mail messages.

Typical mobile technology includes laptop computers, remote access software, personal organizers, pagers, cellular phones, national Internet Service provider addresses like Hotmail.com or AOL, contact managers, adapters to hook up your equipment, fax software (or use a fax service like eFax, www.efax.com), and any other equipment that you can pack up and take with you for accessing people, files, or the Internet.

Mobile Business Tips

Here are some additional mobile business tips:

- Before leaving on your trip, check to see what cyberservices are available at your hotel or motel, public or college libraries, cyber cafés (www.netcafes.com) or nearby office supply or printer centers that cater to out-of-town business travelers. With this information, you can cut down on the devices you have to lug around. You also can send documents for copying to some office supply centers via e-mail and have them printed and ready when you arrive at your destination.

- With laptop wireless capabilities, you can find free wireless access in many public places and some chain stores. For availability, visit WiFi Free Spot (www.wififreespot.com).
- Consider using automatic follow-me services that for a fee will try to find you by relaying incoming messages to your pager, handheld, or cell phone.
- Check with your Internet service to see how to connect to your e-mail while on the road or use a free Web-based e-mail account with one of the major free e-mail services like those with Excite, Yahoo, Hotmail, and others.
- When traveling overseas, carry assorted couplers, connectors, adaptors, and jacks for your laptop as well as jacks for converting local phone systems. Ask a computer consultant for recommendations. Make sure to take a fully charged battery pack with you.

Additional technology can help you do business while traveling, but you will want to find what works best for your purposes and to purchase it as you can afford it and need it. Technological devices will continue to improve in capability and affordability, but the key to success for you is to use them to help maintain and grow your business and not because they are cool pieces to own. Before purchasing, ask yourself, how is this piece of technology going to help market and grow my business?

Suggested Resouces

Books

Going Wireless: Transform Your Business with Mobile Technology by Jaclyn Easton (Chino Hills, CA: Collins, 2002).

I Only Have ROIs for You: A Strategy Guide for Using Mobile and Wireless Technology to Make Money, Save Money and Run a Better Business by Craig Settles (Poughkeepsie, NY: Hudson House Publishing, 2004).

Publications

Handheld Computing Magazine, www.hhcmag.com, information about handheld devices.

Smartphone and Pocket PC magazine, www.pocketpcmag.com; Thaddeus Computing Inc., www.thaddeus.com; publications and catalogs for mobile computing users.

Software

TimeReporter, www.iambic.com, for on-the-road business tracking.

Grow with Planning: You Need to Know How and Where Your Business Is Growing

Chapter 4 provides guidelines for writing and implementing a business plan and marketing plan, conducting simple market research to find the best potential customers, creating a realistic marketing plan, deciding on a pricing structure, and setting achievable goals for the growth of your business.

40. Creating a Business Plan

Business Plan Basics

A mistake often made by business owners is their failure to plan. Although you should write a business plan *before* you launch a business, many entrepreneurs start up without one. Then they realize that they need one to show potential lenders or to help them decide the direction their business should take. Business plans can be simple or complex, are modified according to the type of business, and can be revised as business goals or markets change. Some compare a business plan to a blueprint that provides you with a solid framework for your business. What is most important is that you use it and refer to it often to help you monitor your business operations, marketing activities, and growth.

Here are the major components of most business plans, each of which can be written briefly or expansively:

- *Cover page:* Include the business name, address, telephone and fax numbers, e-mail address, and web site.
- *Executive summary:* Explain the entire concept and purpose of the business.

71

- *Table of contents:* This shows the organization of your business plan.
- *Statement of purpose:* Describe your plan's purpose: for use as a guide? for a loan? to attract investors?
- *Mission statement:* Give the reason(s) for your business's existence and its customer benefits.
- *Business description:* Specify your business operations, products, and services; the legal structure; your goals, objectives, and any key success factors.
- *Competitor analysis:* List your competitors—their operations, strengths, and weaknesses—and profile their customers. Describe the unique products or services that will make your business stand out from your competitors.
- *Market plan:* Profile your potential customers' likes, dislikes, and expectations. Explain sales strategies: pricing and sales terms, selling methods of products or services, and advertising plans. This is the time, too, to consider how much money you will set aside to launch or expand your business.

    Kathy J. Kobliski, author of *Advertising without an Agency Made Easy* (www.silentpartneradvertising.com) advises:

    > You must set up an advertising budget as a line item in your business plan, right along with money for rent, payroll, inventory, office equipment, and so on. One of the biggest mistakes business owners make is underestimating the importance of connecting their business with their potential customers—they fail to advertise. When you're new, you have no customers, only potential customers, and they won't come just because you open the doors and turn on the lights. People need to become familiar with your business name and they need to be given a really good reason to show up. So advertise consistently.

- *Your qualifications:* What qualifies you to operate this business successfully: education, training, experience?
- *Business operations:* You need to describe the products or services you will be selling, their unique features, your capability to meet customers' demands, your necessary equipment, and your business hours.
- *Financial information:* This is the most critical section of your business plan, so consult with a professional if you need assistance. This section includes start-up costs, a cash flow statement, a profit and loss statement, and a breakeven analysis.
- *Sales projections:* Show sales figures based on market analysis and test marketing to potential customers.
- *Summation:* Briefly tabulate your goals (short- and long-term) and objectives, and state your commitment to the success of your business.
- *Appendixes:* These would be any supporting documents, quotes, estimates, articles, market research data, and other related information.

Sometimes, writing a business plan can save you both time and money. It may reveal that the business idea you have chosen is beyond your financial reach or capability, or that not enough (paying) potential customers exist to make it profitable, or that this venture is not what you thought it was going to be. It is better to find that out now, than later.

Creating a business plan will provide your business with a path and course to follow to achieve those objectives. Review it periodically to make adjustments to it as your business growth dictates. This planning process will focus your business on its future growth and stability. Remember, "Businesses don't plan to fail, they just fail to plan." A business plan is the most important step you can take toward making your dream of owning a successful business a reality.

Experts Can Help You Write a Business Plan

You can hire professional business plan writers who may charge you thousands of dollars, write one yourself with related books and software, or look into other possible resources. Here some additional places to look for assistance in writing a business plan:

- *Federal government:* The following have local offices across the United States, and its territories and offer free or low-cost seminars and counseling for business start-ups and management.
- *Local offices of Women's Business Center (www.onlinewbc.gov) or a Small Business Development Center (www.sba.gov/SBDC):* The SBA's Service Corps of Retired Executives (SCORE, www.score.org). Visit these sites to find offices nearest to you.
- *Business incubators:* They help established businesses grow by taking them to the next level of operation. Search the web site of the National Business Incubation Association (www.nbia.org) for a member location.
- *Community or business colleges, chambers of commerce:* Other business organizations may offer business plan writing courses or one-day workshops.
- *Other experts:* You may also want to consult a lawyer for legal issues, an accountant for help with the financial parts of your plan, or a professional business plan writer.

After Your Business Plan, What Comes Next?

Congratulations! You have a completed business plan. Now what are the next steps (see also "Marketing Calendar" in Chapter 14)? Here are some suggestions:

- Draw up a schedule of the steps you will take to implement your business plan: apply for a loan; write a marketing plan (discussed later in this chapter); handle legal concerns of establishing your business; set up accounts; purchase business supplies and equipment; take courses or attend trade shows; and perform any other tasks that are necessary to get your business under way.

- Continue your market research to look for any missed market niches and to stay current with economic trends and coordinate that research with your market plan.
- Consult with your financial advisor to develop a budget and set up your record keeping for monitoring your cash flow and reporting business taxes.
- Set specific business goals and deadlines to achieve those goals.
- Keep personal and business debts low. Borrowing on high-interest credit cards could ruin your business and your credit. Staying solvent longer will enable you to survive until your business becomes profitable.
- When in doubt or reach dilemmas that could be costly, ask for help from your experts and other business owners.

Review your business plan on a regular basis to stay focused, and it will keep you from failing.

Suggested Resources

Books

Anatomy of a Business Plan, 6th ed., by Linda Pinson (Chicago, IL: Kaplan Business, 2005). See also software.

Business Plan for Dummies, rev. ed., by Paul Tiffany and Steven D. Peterson (Hoboken, NJ: John Wiley & Sons, 2004).

CD

Creating a Successful Business Plan, order through Entrepreneur.com's www.SmallBizBooks.com.

Software

Automate Your Business Plan, www.business-plan.com, companion software to Linda Pinson's book.

Business Plan Pro, www.paloalto.com, www.bplans.com, software, including 500 sample business plans.

Web Info

www.Entrepreneur.com/howto, *Entrepreneur* magazine's free, online, how-to guide, "How to Build a Business Plan."

www.sba.gov, the SBA has free online information such as, "Business Plan Basics: Elements, Writing, Using the Plan," key word search for "business plan."

www.score.org, SCORE's 60-second guide "Writing a Business Plan" and SCORE web site (www.score.org/business_toolbox.html) has helpful "Templates for Your Business" that you can download for your use: "Business Plan for an Established Business" and "Competitive Analysis."

41. Implementing Market Research

What *Is* Market Research?

One of the most important components of a business plan is the preliminary market research and its results. Market research is the broad collection and analysis of information pertaining to potential customers' preferences for services or products. It is not, however, a once-and-done task. For you to stay competitive, market research must be an ongoing process. It becomes marketing research whenever you are investigating a specific population or potential customers for a particular product or service.

The question often asked by hopeful or new business owners is "How do I go about performing market research?" But I respond by asking, "What information do you want?" and "What or who can provide you with that information?" Keep these two questions in mind whenever you look for facts, figures, or people in your quest for ideal customers.

What Information?

You need to ask the right questions to obtain information you can use to define your marketing planning and the delivery of your products or services. Here are questions to determine your target customers:

- Potential customers
    —Consumers: Where do they live, work, play; what are their families like, their culture, income level, clothing, marital status; what do they read, watch, listen to, other?
    —Companies: Size, location, services or products; their customers; other?
- What benefits does my business offer?
- What problems does it solve?
- How much are potential customers willing to pay?
- Who are my primary competitors and how many exist?
- Are there smaller niche markets whose needs are not being met by a larger company?

These are but a few of the many questions you may ask. Look to marketing experts, books, magazines, and web sites for more recommended queries to zero in on your ideal customer. Your goal with market research is to discover who is most likely to buy your product and how many such potential customers exist.

What Resources?

Market research can be your *direct* efforts, or it can be your *indirect* analysis of data and reports gathered by government, industry, media, or other research firms. Depending on your budget, you can hire marketing research firms or consultants to assist you or you can use the following free or low-cost resources to gather the market data you need.

YOUR NEIGHBORHOOD

- *College or public libraries:* Look for listings of manufacturers in the volumes of *Thomas Register of American Manufacturers* (www .thomasregister.com); suppliers, business, and telephone directories (to find competitors); local government agencies and associations; local newspapers; U.S. Census reports, which give the local demographics and details of defined populations in your areas and around the country; and specific and general how-to business start-up and management books. Also look in the volumes of the *Encyclopedia of Associations* because many trade associations have research findings from their own industries.
- *Business owners' organizations:* Local chapters of chambers of commerce, women's organizations like the National Association of Women Business Owners, and other entrepreneur groups have listings of area businesses, profiles of members and area residents, plus additional relevant community demographics that may influence residents' buying decisions.
- *Colleges and universities:* Contact these institutions for any recent reports and studies by staff and professors.
- *State legislators and local officials:* Information should be available on state, county, and municipal statistics, contract possibilities, and business support programs.
- *Industry suppliers, salespersons, agents:* These can be sources of information on potential customers' preferences, buying trends. Ask for referrals from other business owners or by attending trade shows and conferences.
- *Community residents:* Survey or question relatives, friends, members of organizations, and other residents for feedback or form your own informal focus group. Ask what improvements or added benefits they would like to have in services or products like yours.
- *Media sources:* Local cable and national television channels, and newspaper and publication advertising directors have data of their viewers and readers that you can request.

ADDITIONAL MARKET RESEARCH RESOURCES

- *Online*
  - —www.Fedstats.gov, Databanks of more than 100 U.S. statistic databases.
  - —www.Ask.com (formerly Ask Jeeves), provides listings and hits from major search engines.

—www.researchinfo.com, ResearchInfo.com, free marketing research resources including a Web survey tutorial.

—www.thomasregister.com, *Thomas Register of American Manufacturers,* look for listings of manufacturers.

—"You.com," through your own Web site feedback or e-mail responses
from potential customers.

COMPETITORS

Analyze their marketing methods, their businesses' offerings, and customers'
responses you hear (directly or indirectly), and their methods of delivery. A better understanding of what they offer can give you an advantage in advertising
the added benefits your business provides over theirs. On a positive note, your
competitors may be looking for others in their industry to network with or may
give you leads to customers who need things those competitors cannot or prefer
not to produce, thus opening the possibility of a niche market for you. For
example, three desktop publishers who live in the same area refer potential
clients to one another for work they do not handle. Each owner specializes in
her own services.

Remember that there are responsibilities when you conduct market research. Polling or questioning people for purposes other than nonobjective
feedback is wrong and may hurt your reputation as well as the reputation of
honest market or opinion researchers. (Visit the Market Research Association's
web site for information about research abuses such as *sugging,* and *frugging.*)

OTHER ENTREPRENEURS

Talk to other entrepreneurs and those with whom you network for leads and information, especially those who have been in business for some time. Ask what
research sources were most helpful to them.

How to Analyze?

When you feel you have collected an adequate amount of research, stop and analyze it. Your next question should be, "Now that I have this information, how
should I use it?" Look at what you have and see if your data can answer your
questions or goals for this specific marketing activity or for your overall business
or market plan. In making your analysis, use a basic spreadsheet program or an-
alytic software packages to produce charts and statistics. If your research was not
fruitful, you might want to consult with a research firm or marketing consultant
who can interpret your findings or make further recommendations for more
productive research (see also Method 9 for some tips on market research).

Without satisfactory market research and evaluation, you cannot employ
successful marketing campaigns or identify customers' specific wants and
needs. Comprehensive market research is crucial in forming your marketing
plan and directing your advertising and marketing resources.

Suggested Resources

Association

Marketing Research Association, www.mra-net.org, glossary of terms and professional member benefits.

Books

How Customers Think by Gerald Zaltman (Boston: Harvard Business School Press, 2002).

The Market Research Toolbox: A Concise Guide for Beginners by Edward F. McQuarrie (Newton, NH: Sage Publications, 2005).

Software

The Survey System, Creative Research Systems, www.surveysystem.com, software for telephone, online, and printed questionnaires.

JMP, www.jmp.com, desktop statistical discovery software.

Web Info

www.marketresearchworld.net, the Market Research Portal, a free market research resource.

www.ResearchInfo.com, search for free marketing research resources.

www.sba.gov/training/courses.html, "Conduct a Marketing Analysis," a free online SBA course.

42. Creating a Market Plan and Market*ing* Plans

A market plan is an essential tool for business maintenance and growth. It encompasses *all* the results of your market research, your target customers, the unique features of your product or services, your pricing, and the promotions you plan to use to reach your market. Developing one will help you think about what makes your business unique and how to get the message out to desired audiences.

Your market plan covers all the promotional methods you want to use. Once in place, it can be the source of countless, individual market*ing* plans that you target toward a specific activity, to be met by a specific date, such as writing a press release or scheduling a direct mailing campaign for a new product or service.

Components

If your business is newly started or you want to revise an old plan to increase sales, here are some important market plan components:

- *Your objectives:* How will your business use varied promotions to reach an ideal market of customers and deliver these as a unique product or service at a competitive price?
- *Satisfying customers:* How will you use your market research to satisfy the needs of your target customers with optimum products and service and monitor their responses to maintain the best quality possible?
- *Specifics:* What mix of low-cost and fee-based promotions will you use, how will you evaluate their effectiveness, and how many can you do within your business's budget?

Take your written plan and review it. Make sure it is concise, considers your mission, accentuates what your business brings to your customers, and focuses on your ideal customer.

A successful marketing plan balances your current endeavors with goals that you can adjust for future growth and develops your business's unique entity to attract a steady flow of paying customers.

What Is Your Mission?

A market plan, like your business plan, is a guide that will keep you organized and on a revenue-generating track. You can space your marketing activities so that you have sufficient time and money to carry them out: You can accomplish more marketing goals with a system and dateline than with haphazard efforts. One way to keep focused is to review the *mission statement* in your business plan. A mission statement declares your business's purpose and the reason for its presence. It is the focus toward which all your marketing plans and programs should be directed. A mission statement can be your mainstay for a decade or more. It should be brief but memorable.

Before you start to market a product, service, or idea, work up a mission statement. It will help you refine your business objectives. Mission statements are important for every enterprise—whether it be a one-person business, an agency, a corporation, an industry trade group, or a nonprofit organization. The American Marketing Association (www.marketingpower.com) has three principles in its mission statement, one being: "Improving—Advancing marketing competencies, practice, and thought leadership."

A mission statement is important to your business in the following ways:

It can . . .

- Activate your marketing plan in setting your future goals and objectives.
- Set an accurate and consistent tone for all your business communications.
- Define the customers your business will be most likely serving.
- Focus on the benefits you promise your customers.
- Help you understand the purpose of your business and give you the inspiration and nerve to withstand the rigors that a business owner often experiences.

A well-written statement can be an effective marketing tool to capture the attention of prospective customers. You should be able to explain your business's fundamental nature, merit, and its undertaking in one or two well-articulated sentences that you can readily pronounce to anyone who asks, "What is your business?"

When you have finally decided on your mission statement, review it daily to maintain a clear vision of your purpose and keep you connected to the customers you most want to reach.

What Is Your Strategy?

Your market plan is a strategic course of action to bring in new customers, to keep their loyalty so they will return often for repeat purchases, and to add value to your product or service for pricing purposes. Your market plan helps you achieve your objectives through strategies to accomplish your end goals (see more in Method 43).

With your plan in place, you can use it as a strategic base from which you can form each marketing activity. You will want to undertake an all-encompassing strategy that blends successful marketing and sales tactics to bring in a steady and consistent income. These tactics will include all your marketing efforts and activities as well as the management and operation of your business. Your marketing mix includes how you promote, price, sell, and select your system of distribution and sales follow-up.

Professionals generally agree that the marketing mix of every marketing effort consists of the Four Ps—Product, Price, Placement, and Promotion. *You* control these Ps:

- *Product:* You pick the products, services, or expertise your business is going to offer and add the value that will benefit your customers.
- *Price:* Pricing is based on an ongoing evaluation of the cost and time involved in running your business and meeting your customers' expectations.
- *Placement:* This refers to distribution or how you will deliver your services or get your products to your customers. It has also been referred to as the *Place,* the location of your store or other end-of-sales setting.
- *Promotion:* It includes everything you do to promote sales of your service or product. Its main purpose is to get the attention of potential customers and have them buy from you instead of your competitors.

Some marketers include another P—Positioning. Your *position* is the actual perception of your business in the minds of your potential customers or target market.

A well-executed market plan is crucial to the survival of your business and will enable you to attract and hang on to customers by fulfilling their needs.

Suggested Resources

Books

Creating a Mission That Makes a Difference, Vol. 6, by John Carver (Hoboken, NJ: John Wiley & Sons, 1996).

Make Your Mission Statement Work, 2nd ed., by Marianne Talbot (Oxford, England: How To Books, 2003).

The Market Planning Guide: Creating a Plan to Successfully Market Your Business, Products, or Service, 6th ed., by David H. Bangs (Chicago: Kaplan Business, 2002).

Marketing Strategy and Competitive Positioning, 3rd ed., by Graham J. Hooley, John A. Saunders, and Nigel Piercy (Upper Saddle River, NJ: Financial Times/Prentice Hall, 2003).

Software

Marketing Plan Pro, Palo Alto Software, www.MarketingPlanPro.com, Many sample marketing plans you can view online for free; package includes book, *On Target: The Book on Marketing Plans*.

Web Info

www.Entrepreneur.com/howto, *Entrepreneur* magazine's free, online, how-to guide, "How to Create a Marketing Plan."

www.score.org/guides.html, SCORE's 60-second guide, "Creating a Market Plan."

43. Setting Marketing Goals and Pricing Considerations

Objectives, Goals, and Strategies

Where do you go from here? Consider the marketing ideas you would like to attempt, the potential market you would like to reach, and how you would like to do this. List the ones that you can realistically afford to do in terms of your money and capability. Use your market plan and your calendar to set some realistic marketing objectives and goals and then work backward, writing down the strategies—your marketing mix—that you will need to apply to reach those goals.

You can break down each marketing campaign as follows:

- *Marketing objectives:* Write brief statements that answer questions like "What am I trying to achieve?" For example, your objective could be, "I want to introduce a new service for my errand business."

- *Marketing goals:* Then you can set several goals to accomplish this: "To test-market this new service for one month with my regular customers"; and "To offer this service as a stand-alone offering or as a package."
- *Marketing strategies:* "I will send a photo and press release to the newspapers in my target area, and add a striking magnetic banner to my business vehicle announcing this new service."

Synchronize the deadlines of your business objectives, goals, and strategies with your personal calendar, so you can progress smoothly and productively with your business marketing plan, while still having room for personal time.

Assess and review both your long- and short-range objectives and their goals on a regular basis. Your long-range objectives help decide a marketing plan. Some goals could be to have your business reach a certain profit level, or produce X number of products, or diversify into sideline services or products, or leave a legacy to your children. Whatever your purpose, remember these goals are yours and use them to choose the best marketing strategies to achieve the success you desire. If you need help in setting business objectives and goals, consult with a professional business coach.

Pricing Matters

Pricing is more than simply coming up with a price tag. Pricing poses a dilemma for every new business owner. If your prices are too high, customers will not buy, and if your prices are too low, you chance not making the profit margin needed to sustain your business. Plus, your customers may think your products and services are inferior compared with those of your competitors.

Here are some pricing strategies:

- Make it a primary strategy to convince your customers that your product or service is of more value to them than your competitors' offerings. Value can be perceived as something that enhances your customers' enjoyment or saves them time or money, or both. Identify your customers' problems and discover how much it is worth to them for you to provide a solution. Customers purchase results, so market the *benefits* of your services. Base your prices on your customers' *needs,* not just your expenses.
- Use your breakeven analysis (sales equal expenses) to know the *least* you must charge to make a profit (see Method 50), but allow a margin of error and do not cut yourself too short. Get to know your industry and professional associations' pricing guidelines. Many, like the Graphic Artists Guild (www.gag.org) and other professional and trade associations, sell manuals and handbooks with helpful price-setting guidelines for members. Their publications and Web sites also offer frequent articles and tips for determining rates, as well as online discussion boards for members to discuss pricing and billing issues.

Some experts recommend you start with low-end pricing, but business owners tend to underprice their services or products. It may be better to charge higher than lower rates because it will give you room for unexpected costs and negotiations. Expand your services to include some higher-paying clients and try to find a balance between your expertise, the market prices, and the profits you desire to make.

Know the purpose behind your pricing strategies. Besides ensuring that your business will be profitable, decide how your rates will benefit your business. Is it to attract a wealthier market? To entice customers from competitors? To establish you as a professional? Your pricing will make a statement about your business to the world, so be careful what it says.

Learn to turndown unprofitable work. You may find you have more than enough business to handle, but the question is, "Are you making money?" It is better to work for fewer clients at your calculated higher rates and make your projected income than to work for many clients at lower rates. The quality of your work will be better with fewer hassles.

Track your work hours. Take advantage of technology capabilities to track your schedule, time, billing, and rates. These figures will assist you with your accounting and bid estimations. Use this same data to conclude which projects and clients are the most profitable.

Trial and error is a good pricing strategy if you are unsure just who your best customers are, or if you are offering an unfamiliar product or service to your target market. Track customers' reactions and sales and adjust your pricing to what the market will bear and ensure profits.

Pricing is an ongoing, variable process and it may take some time before you arrive at rates that please your customers and satisfy your bottom line. Keep accurate records of your time and expenses and schedule regular meetings with your bookkeeper or accountant, especially in your start-up years. Knowing what you must charge for your services will help your business survive and thrive while enabling you to pace your workload and live comfortably. (See also Method 47, "Profitable Pricing.")

Suggested Resources

Books

Marketing Strategies for Competitive Advantage by Dennis Adcock (Hoboken, NJ: John Wiley & Sons, 2000).

Pricing for Profitability: Activity-Based Pricing for Competitive Advantage by John L. Daly (Hoboken, NJ: John Wiley & Sons, 2001).

The Strategy and Tactics of Pricing: A Guide to Growing More Profitably, 4th ed., by Thomas T. Nagle and John Hogan (Upper Saddle River, NJ: Prentice Hall, 2005).

Software

> Time-Tracking Technology:
>
> QuickBooks Pro, Intuit, Inc., www.intuit.com, accounting and time-tracking.
>
> TimeSlips, Sage U.S., Inc., www.timeslips.com, time and billing program.

Web Info

> www.lowe.org, Edward Lowe Foundation's Entrepreneur's Resource, search for "Marketing."

44. Testing and Evaluating Your Marketing Steps

Affordable Test-Marketing Methods

Before forming a plan for a particular marketing activity, you should do some basic test-marketing, as discussed in Method 41, to avoid hit-and-miss tactics and a waste of your resources. Here are just a few (of many) affordable test-marketing methods:

- Give or provide samples of your products to family, friends, or acquaintances and encourage them to give you their honest feedback. If you have a service business, ask these same people if they would be willing to try it for the same honest feedback.
- Send out a questionnaire with a quarterly promotional newsletter or e-zine to get feedback on a new sideline business or product or service.
- Ask a high school or business college class if they would be willing to do some market research for you as a class project.
- Team up with other business owners to regularly test one another's new business offerings.
- Evaluate these and additional test-marketing results to decide if and where you will plan your next marketing activity.

Conducting thorough test marketing will guide you in making strategic business decisions and in becoming a successful entrepreneur.

Evaluating a Marketing Plan

Business owners often find it difficult to know whether their marketing tactics are working. This can be especially tricky when you use a combination of marketing activities simultaneously or are using personal-contact tactics such as networking.

Richard Hoy, who co-owns BookLocker (www.booklocker.com) and Writers-Weekly (www.writersweekly.com) with his wife, Angela, says that many small business owners throw money at various promotional strategies without understanding which ones are making them a profit and which are just costing them money. He advises that you should always try to measure your promotional efforts in some meaningful way.

"It makes sense," says Hoy, "if you take an ad for $100; you need to make more than $100 in profit (not just in sales) for your promotion to be considered successful. Otherwise, you are just wasting money. And that is the one resource small business owners cannot afford to waste."

Hoy continues, "If your promotion drives people to a web site, there are dozens of inexpensive tools one can use for measuring site traffic and campaign response. If your promotion drives people to call on the telephone, try to use a unique phone number so you can count the number of incoming calls. And as a last resort, you can simply ask customers how they heard about you and make a note of it."

He adds that once you have a good understanding which promotional efforts bring you the best customers, you can put more money into them and cut back on all the others.

All marketing plans, no matter how well thought out, should be evaluated for their effectiveness. It can be difficult, especially if you are using several marketing efforts at the same time. Here are some ways to determine whether the marketing plan you used was worth your time or money:

- Look to see if your marketing activity increased your sales and revenue.
- Ask those potential customers who responded to your marketing activity and those customers who purchased your business offerings how they learned about your business.
- Look to see how often potential customers tried to contact you with the means you made available (return postcards, phone queries, e-mail messages), or sought more information about your business in other ways.
- Do a cash flow analysis after the marketing activity to see if the financial investment was worth it.

Evaluating the plan gives you the opportunity to investigate other options that might be more successful or to accept that no plan is needed or should be carried out.

Many factors are involved in assessing the results of a particular marketing method, but its main objective is to attract potential customers who then decide to go ahead and buy from your business over a competitor's. Successful marketing plans focus on customers' needs and the benefit(s) your offerings can bring to them. When you find an effective marketing plan, it is fine to repeat it, but continue testing and evaluating other plans to keep your business profitable and to reach new potential customers and untapped markets.

Suggested Resources

Books

Bringing Your Product to Market: Fast-Track Approaches to Cashing in on Your Great Idea, 2nd ed., by Don Debelak (Hoboken, NJ: John Wiley & Sons, 2005).

Hitting the Sweet Spot: How Consumer Insights Can Inspire Better Marketing and Advertising, rev. ed., by Lisa Fortini-Campbell (Chicago: The Copy Workshop, 2001).

5

Grow with Financing and Money Management

One of the biggest problems an entrepreneur faces in starting, maintaining, and growing a business is financing. Chapter 5 provides viable options for both start-up and ongoing ventures. Many entrepreneurs underprice their products and services, so pricing guidelines are included for the best pricing to produce maximum profits. Managing the cash flow of a business is crucial to its solvency, so this chapter suggests ways to scrutinize and monitor it as a business develops.

"It's all about money!" That is a statement you are certain to hear about both your personal and business life. Whether you start and operate your business on a shoestring or invest a lump sum of money, finance experts will tell you that what counts is how wisely you use it to achieve your objectives and goals.

45. Business Financing

Preliminary Considerations

If you are a business owner, there never seems to be enough money. Where you get money and from whom will depend on your answers to the following questions:

- How much money do you need?
- How many years has your business been in operation?
- What are your personal and business credit ratings?
- Do you have collateral to guarantee the loan?
- How long have you been in business and what are your profits?
- What is your projected financial forecast?
- What types of financing you are seeking?

Before searching for funds, you need to know how much money you will need, your likely funding sources, and how to prepare loan proposals and financial statements. Here are some suggestions:

- Make an estimate of the amount of money you will need. If you have not already done so, draw up a business plan (see Method 40). If you have a plan, it should show you how much money you need and how you will use it. Your business plan is almost always required when seeking out a bank loan or funding from other established lenders. Make sure you include a cash flow statement as well as all your projected business and personal expenses for the next 6 to 12 months. If this seems daunting, ask your accountant or financial expert to help you work out the figures for your own use and for applying for a loan.

- If you have a start-up or a part-time business and intend to expand to full time, experts recommend that you save enough money to cover your living expenses for six months to two years. You also are more likely to receive a loan from lenders or investors if you have invested a good sum of your own money into your business.

- Many entrepreneurs choose to operate their businesses on a part-time basis, thereby having a financial cushion through their employment. Because these entrepreneurs are not pressured to make money for support, they have time to identify their ideal customers by trying various marketing campaigns and test-marketing their products and services.

SBA Loans and Other Government Sources

GOVERNMENT SOURCES—FEDERAL

These offices have loan information or can direct you to other resources that handle financial lending:

- *U.S. Small Business Administration (SBA, 800-827-5722, www.sba.gov):* Call for the telephone number of SBA offices nearest you for information on the current SBA loan programs or visit the web site. Click on "Financing Your Business" to learn if you qualify for such loans as the basic SBA 7(a) loan program, the Prequalification Loan Program, Certified Development Company/504 Program (CDC), The Microloan Program and others. For most of these loans, you have to show proof that you own a for-profit business, that you can repay the loan based on your cash flow, and that you meet other set standards. If you plan to apply for such a loan, call banks that are certified by the SBA in your area (guaranteed by the SBA) and talk to the loan officers to learn how to qualify your business.

- *Small Business Development Centers (www.sba.gov/SBDC):* These offices are usually located at universities. They offer all kinds of business counseling, seminars, and sometimes business conferences. They do not have access to funds, but can refer you to further contacts and resources in your community.

- *Small Business Investment Companies (SBIC, www.sba.gov/INV):* They offer services and investments for and in small businesses. Your SBA district office can give you contact information for office locations in your state.
- *The SBA's Office of Women's Business Ownership (OWBO, www .sba.gov/women and www.onlinewbc.gov):* This is the only office in the federal government specifically targeted to facilitate the growth and development of businesses owned by women. It *does not* provide direct funding or loan guarantees to women business owners, but *does* help them achieve financial success through prebusiness workshops, management/technical information, and guidance on how to access capital. It also has a listing of Women Business Development Centers across the United States.
- *Women Business Development Centers (www.onlinewbc.gov):* These centers provide workshops and programs for women entrepreneurs and established women-owned businesses.
- *Service Corps of Retired Executives (SCORE, www.score.org):* This Is a volunteer management assistance program of the SBA that provides one-on-one counseling, workshops, and seminars. SCORE chapters exist throughout the country. Many work in conjunction with local chambers of commerce. Search the web site for offices near to you.
- *Internal Revenue Service (IRS, www.irs.gov, 800-829-1040):* Call for a listing of helpful publications such as *Business Use of Your Home; Your Business Tax Kit: Starting a Business and Keeping Records*, and others.
- *U.S. Department of Agriculture (USDA, www.usda.gov):* Rural Business-Cooperative Service. The USDA provides information about federal rural development programs (see also your local USDA Cooperative Extension Office in your county [usually affiliated with a state university, with an office in every U.S. county]).

GOVERNMENT SOURCES—STATE

There is a primary state government agency, office, or state office of economic development *in each state* that provides one-stop guidance on financial programs, contracts, and services that the state offers to small businesses including minority and women's opportunities. Contact the office of your state senator or state representative for referrals and information. Most of these state legislator offices have manuals for small business owners as well as directories of state agencies.

GOVERNMENT SOURCES—LOCAL AND STATE

- SBA's Certified Development Company/504 Loan Program: CDCs are nonprofit corporations set up to help the economic development of their communities. CDCs work with private lenders and the SBA to finance small businesses. There are about 270 CDCs nationwide. Search the www.SBA.gov site for a CDC in your area.

- In addition to the federal, state, and national offices in your area, contact your local business groups and associations for any existing entrepreneurship support programs. Some community development centers have money to lend.
- Check also to see if your local or county government has any funding programs.
- Foundations, colleges, and local schools may have various programs and continuing education programs to help entrepreneurs with start-up and funding information.
- Specialty loans for women are available from some banks. They offer qualified business owners a one-page application that can land you an unsecured credit line or loans. Check with banks in your area or seek referrals from other women who are business owners.

The Truth about Grants

The U.S. Small Business Administration does *not* offer grants to *individuals* to start or expand a small business. The SBA only offers a limited number of grant programs to state economic development agencies, nonprofit organizations, and universities that, in turn, give funds to business owners whose companies contribute to their communities' development, job potential or education. The SBA's grant program to Women's Business Development Centers (WBDCs— over 200 in the United States) has been essential in assisting many women all across the United States and its territories to start new businesses and expand current ones. These centers provide business training, counseling, and other assistance (not funding, but *how* to get funding) to women business owners and women who want to start businesses.

Apart from government sources, private organizations, industry groups, and associations sometimes offer grants to entrepreneurs. Check with business owners' organizations for more information and referrals.

Credit Cards*

One study conducted by a major credit card company revealed that over three-quarters of small business owners used credit or charge cards for various business expenses such as purchases for technology equipment and supplies, travel,

---

* Visit Dr. Robert D. Manning's informative web site about credit card use in the United States. He is the professor of finance and past Caroline Werner Gannett chair of the Humanities, Rochester Institute of Technology, Rochester, New York. www .CreditCardNation.com.

and entertainment, and to purchase business and professional services. They can help build your business's credit rating; they are convenient; and they are good for emergency purchases if you are short on cash.

New laws about bankruptcy and ever-increasing higher rates and penalties for late payments, however, should make you consider other alternatives. At one time, credit cards were one of the primary sources women had to fund their ventures. Today, women have many more funding options available. If you must use credit cards, look for the ones with the lowest interest rates and pay off the balance at the end of each month before your business gets too deeply in debt.

Using debit cards is a good way for you to avoid going over your spending limit. If you do not have it in the bank, you cannot spend it. Though numerous successful small start-ups have been financed with credit cards, use restraint to prevent their overuse and to ensure your business stays solvent.

Bank Loans

When considering a bank loan for your business, talk first to loan officers at your own financial institution. They are familiar with you and may make some recommendations. Ask them what they require for a business loan application and also if they are participants in the SBA's loan programs.

Make sure you also survey other entrepreneurs and ask them to recommend a small business-friendly bank or institution. Shop around for the best loan packages, understand the terms, and review them thoroughly with your accountant or financial expert.

If you do not need a loan right away, but think you may need business financing in the future, consider paying down personal debt, and actively save to invest in your business. It will increase your chances for outside funding, and enable your business to weather the ups and downs of economic cycles.

Information (and Financial Experts) You Can Take to the Bank

If your business already exists, you will have to produce more paperwork than for a start-up loan. The information you must submit will vary with each lending institution, but most of them will want to see the following:

- A report explaining why you need the loan and how it will help start or enhance your business.
- Your business plan with an earnings forecast.
- Business and personal tax returns. The lender will inform you how many years of records are required.
- Credit histories, business and personal.
- Your personal financial statement showing your liabilities (bills, debts, living expenses) and assets (items of value).

- Proof of any collateral (assets you are going to use to back your loan) or the promise of a creditworthy person to be a cosigner. If you do not have collateral or are turned down, consider applying for an SBA guaranteed loan.
- Your experience in your business's industry and as an entrepreneur.
- How much money you plan to invest in your venture or have already invested. Banks require you to invest a certain percentage of your own money.
- A plan for how and approximately when you will pay back the loan.
- What type of loan you need short-term (for a turnaround project) or long-term (for purchasing a major piece of equipment).

If this is the first time you have applied for a loan, consult with your accountant to help you review your financial statements and understand and prepare the needed information for your loan application. Some entrepreneurs even take their financial experts with them to meet with a bank's loan officer. The more information you have, the more likely you will be to get the loan.

Suggested Resources

Books

> *Credit Card Nation: The Consequences of America's Addiction to Credit* by Robert D. Manning, PhD (New York: Basic Books, 2002).

> *Free Money from the Federal Government for Small Business and Entrepreneurs,* 2nd ed., by Laurie Blum (Hoboken, NJ: John Wiley & Sons, 1996).

> *How to Get a Small Business Loan: A Banker Shows You Exactly What to Do to Get a Loan,* 2nd ed., by Bryan E. Milling (Naperville, IL: Sourcebooks, 1998).

> *Launching Your Home-Based Business: How to Successfully Plan, Finance and Grow Your New Venture* by David H. Bangs and Andi Axman (Chicago: Dearborn Trade, 1997).

> *The SBA Loan Book: Get a Small Business Loan—Even with Poor Credit, Weak Collateral, and No Experience* by Charles H. Green (Holbrook, MA: Adams Media Corp., 2005).

> *Starting and Operating a Business in the U.S.* by Michael D. Jenkins and Rhonda Abrams, Introduction (Palo Alto, CA: The Planning Shop, 1999). Book and CD-ROM.

Credit Bureaus (Personal and Business)

The following credit bureaus provide a free personal credit report once a year:*

---

*The Fair Credit Reporting Act (FCRA) requires each of the nationwide consumer reporting companies—Equifax, Experian, and TransUnion—to provide you with a free copy of your credit report, at your request, once every 12 months. The Federal Trade

Dun and Bradstreet, Business; www.dnb.com/us, for business credit checking and other services such as obtaining a "Duns" number for your business.

Equifax, www.equifax.com.

Experian, www.experian.com.

TransUnion, www.transunion.com.

Grants

Ask reference librarians for available CDs or directories of available listings of grant sources.

"The Catalog of Federal Domestic Assistance" (annual), www.gsa.gov/fdac, lists annually awarded federal grants for each year.

Federal grant resources, http://www.sba.gov/financing/basics/grants.html.

U.S. State & Local Gateway Competitive Grants, www.firstgov.gov/Government /State_Local/Grants.shtml, links to community, state grants, microloans.

SBA Loan Information

Basic financing topics and grant information, www.sba.gov/financing.

SBA "Snap Shot" of SBA loans, www.sba.gov/financing/sbaloan/snapshot .html.

Web Info

www.BankRate.com, national banks' comparison rates.

www.bbb.org, Consumer/Business Tips: "Applying for Business Credit?" synopsis of your borrowing rights.

www.Entrepreneur.com/howto, *Entrepreneur* magazine's free, online, how-to guide, "How to Raise Money for Your Business."

www.microenterpriseworks.org, Association for Enterprise Opportunity, advocates Microenterprise development.

www.score.org/guides.html, SCORE's 60-second guide, "Financing Your Start-Up Business."

www.score.org/guides.html, SCORE's 60-second guide, "Getting a Loan"; also available at the site are helpful "Templates for Your Business" that you can download for your use: "Bank Loan Request for Small Business," "Loan Amortization Schedule," and "Personal Financial Statement."

Commission (FTC), the nation's consumer protection agency, has prepared a brochure, "Your Access to Free Credit Reports," explaining your rights under the FCRA and how to order a free annual credit report. Visit www.FTC.gov for more information.

46. Creative Financing

Definition

John D. Rockefeller said, "I have ways of making money that you know nothing of." So it is with creative financing in that it refers to alternative, sometimes ingenious, methods to raise money for a home, college, or in, this case to start, maintain, or expand a small business. The following sections give some suggestions.

Ideas

Many self-employed entrepreneurs have stated that raising capital for their start-up, for a new marketing campaign, or for expansion has been one of their biggest business challenges. Self-employed individuals and small business owners use many alternative (but legal) methods to get the money they need. Here are a few of the most common ones:

- *Personal resources:* Make an inventory of any valuables and assets you have that you can turn into cash—antiques, coins, and other valuables; stocks and securities; or insurance policies, IRAs, or pension plans. Before borrowing on any of these plans, though, make sure you are aware of the payback terms and any resulting penalties.
- *Part-time employee or venture:* Besides allowing you to "test" your business offerings with your customers, moonlighting, or working at a sideline job, allows you to pay down personal debt or put the money earned toward equipment upgrades. A part-time venture can also give you entrepreneurial experience in the industry that your business will be or is presently in, practice in time management skills, and an opportunity to work out ways to balance a venture with your family and personal needs.
- *Income of one venture for funding another:* Numerous individuals who started selling specialty items on online auctions have discovered narrow, but profitable business niches.

    One musician taught private music lessons in her home, but used part of her teaching income to fund her designer business of creating specially designed handbags to sell to small clothing and accessories stores and at craft shows. Another entrepreneur, who has a cleaning business that helps finance her jewelry-making venture, says, "One pays the bills, and the other is the outlet for my creativity."
- *Budgeting and cost-cutting:* Look for ways to spend less. List your expenses, and seek ways to economize by comparing banks' services, ordering supplies in bulk or with other entrepreneurs, or renting or purchasing used equipment.
- *Awards, contests:* Industries, foundations, associations, or companies sometimes sponsor annual awards with cash or will award money for busi-

ness research. Keep alert to what is available through networking sources, your reading, and media announcements. Check in a public or college library to see if they have a copy of the latest edition of Gale Research's *Awards, Honors, Prizes,* an international directory of awards given out that describes thousands of awards for achievements in many fields (see also Method 67 about awards).

- *Family, friends:* This is one of the most-often used ways to raise money for business purposes, but it can lead to hard feelings and misunderstandings if a formal agreement was not drawn up and signed by both parties. The company Circle Lending says on its web site that $89 billion in outstanding debt exists between family and private parties, with the likelihood that $12 billion of that money will never be repaid.

  If you have a signed agreement, with regular payment schedules, you are more likely to repay the loan, just as if you had received the loan from an established lender. You and your friend or family member might want to meet with a financial expert to help you work out terms that are agreeable to both of you and financially manageable for you. Some entrepreneurs will also ask for gifting, based on inheritances. Check with your accountant as to the amount that you can receive without having to pay taxes.

- *Corporate sponsors:* If you have some experience or recognition in your field or industry and are creating new products and technology, you may be able to find a larger company that offers money or access to a distribution network in exchange for licensing rights to new products. Patricia Gallagher started an at-home child care business, self-published a how-to manual on the subject, and through the publicity from marketing her book, she was asked to be a spokesperson for several kid-related products. She used that money to help finance other of her ongoing business promotions.

- *Factoring:* In this method, your account receivables (your invoices for work completed or products that have been ordered from you) are sold to a third party, called a *factor,* a company that pays you a percentage of your invoices. This type of financing occurs more often with manufacturing-type businesses than with service businesses and helps continue your business's cash flow until your invoices are paid.

- *Supplier-vendor-customer:* In this type of financing, you ask your suppliers or vendors if they will agree to accept payment for a longer time period (e.g., 90 days instead of 30 days). If customers make advance payments, you can use their advance cash for your business. With both, be sure to make your payments as agreed and fulfill the delivery of your customers' goods or services. Some customers or companies will participate in the funding of the research and development of a product.

- *Partner financing:* If you participate in joint ventures with other business owners or partner with one or more individuals formally for a business arrangement, you can pool your financial resources. Again, have signed legal contracts with all those involved to designate responsibilities and payments.

- *Internet:* Entrepreneurs are now using the Internet to seek information about venture capital funding and investors (see also Method 99).
- *Bartering:* See Method 49.
- *National associations, foundations:* Business organizations and foundations supporting entrepreneurs may have funding programs available in your area. Count-Me-In for Women's Economic Independence (www .count-me-in.org) is a nonprofit organization that raises money from individuals and organizations to make small business loans to women across the country.

Thoroughly research all possible financing resources available to you and then decide which ones will best help your business get the backing it needs to start, grow, and succeed.

Once you have financed your business, concentrate on your marketing to keep it growing and increasing in profits. Draw up a business budget and examine every purchase carefully, and you may never need to borrow money again.

Suggested Resources

Books

How to Raise Capital: Techniques and Strategies for Financing and Valuing Your Small Business by Jeffrey Timmons, Andrew Zacharakis, and Stephen Spinelli (New York: McGraw-Hill, 2004).

Instant Profit: Successful Strategies to Boost Your Margin and Increase the Profitability of Your Business by Bradley J. Sugars (New York: McGraw-Hill, 2005).

65 Ways to Finance a Small Business: A Creative Financing Guide by Lawrence Shirey (Scottsdale, AZ: Webmark Publishing, 2005), http://65ways .com.

Web Info

www.circlelending.com, CircleLending, specializing in managing financial transactions between private parties such as *friends and family members;* web site has free loan guides available for downloading.

47. Profitable Pricing

One new entrepreneur wrote on a business message board "Help! I am meeting with my first client tomorrow and I have no idea what to charge for my services!" You should not set prices in haste, because determining how much to charge for your services or products involves a thorough assessment of several factors. Trying to decide how much to charge for your products or services is a difficult challenge for every business owner. You want to cover your costs for materials, overhead, distribution, and the time it took to make or complete your business's offerings; and you must include your profit margin. At the same time, you want your prices to be competitive. Here are guidelines to assist you in configuring the ideal price for your business.

Comparisons with Competitors and Your Industry

Compare your prices with your competitors' prices, and take special note of exactly what their pricing packages include. This is crucial so you can highlight to potential customers or market niches what quality differences or uniqueness they can get by patronizing your business instead of your competitors. Let your industry's pricing recommendations also help you set prices. The Graphic Artists Guild (www.gag.org) has price-setting publications for its members, and the annual *Writer's Market,* published by Writer's Digest Books, includes a section, "The Business of Writing," that cites current fees paid to professional writers for their work.

What Price the Market Will Bear

If you have a new business, review your market research that focuses on who your target customers are, how they value your offerings and their expectations, and what they are willing to pay. The better you know your clients, their expectations, and their perceived value of your services, the better you will know how much they are able (and willing) to pay you. Assess, too, your surrounding areas. What potential customers' are willing to pay in one town may be much higher (or lower) in a nearby city or location. Identify your customers' problems and discover how much it is worth to them for you to provide a solution. Customers purchase results, so market the *benefits* of your services.

Base your prices on your customers' *needs,* not just your expenses. Covering *all* your business expenses is the just the start of where you will base your prices. Your customers' responses to your pricing will determine how high you can go.

Pricing Components and Formula

To figure your price, you have to know all your costs. These include the following:

- *Fixed costs:* These are expenses that stay constant and are not affected by the sales you make or do not make—rent or mortgage, property taxes, insurances, retirement plan contributions, depreciation and interest on loans, and others.

- *Variable costs:* These are expenses that change based on how much you sell, your materials, your time and labor, office supplies, utilities, postage, and unexpected costs.
- *Breakeven point:* This is the dollar amount your business must make to break even; that is, sales income must equal costs. To stay in business, you must make a profit, so the price you charge must be higher than the cost of providing your service or making and distributing your product.
- *Pricing formula:* Then you have to work out your own pricing formula. For a service-type business, your business would be based on billable hours, the realistic estimate of hours you can bill (work in a year); your target salary (what you wish to make a year); and your profit margin, the amount or percentage of profit you add onto your hourly rate to keep above your breakeven point or for payment of employees' wages. For a product-based business, you have to calculate your cost per unit. It is important to your business's survival to work with your accountant or financial expert to develop a formula that is best for your business and financial situation.

Recognizing Signs to Adjust Your Prices

Be careful if you jump-start your business or add a new product or added service by offering lower prices than your competition. If you do not make it just an introductory offer for say, new customers only, you may not meet your costs and will exhaust yourself trying to keep up with the demand. Here are some other signs that it may be time to raise your prices:

- If your expenses surpass your gross income, either look for ways to cut costs (but not quality) or raise your prices. Start with raising prices for new customers and then slowly with the rest of your clients. Try to stay within mid-range pricing compared with your competitors, unless your target market is an exclusive one.
- If you cannot keep up with the demand for your product or service, raise your prices. You will work less, but make more.
- Raise your prices if the economy is good or your industry is recommending that action.
- If you are rated one of the best in your area or in your expertise, people will be willing to pay more for your product or advice.
- If you have purchased items or added services that add to the quality of your business, you can raise your prices.

Too many new business owners tend to underprice, so make sure you charge what you are worth and continue to monitor and adjust your prices to keep your business solvent and in demand.

Pricing Strategies and Tips

- *Create a rate sheet.* For your convenience, create a rate sheet of charges for your services or products that you can quote to customers, including setting minimum rates for which you will work, percentages for added costs of services, late payments, and estimation costs.
- *Identify the reasons for setting your prices.* The primary goal should be obvious: to set prices that will ensure that your business will meet its expenses and make a profit. You could also price your business' products or services to set yourself apart from your competition's pricing, to establish yourself as a professional, and as part of your overall marketing strategy.
- *Consult financial experts* to help you estimate all the possible costs involved and the projected number of hours for completion when submitting a proposal bid for projects or to produce specified quantities of your products. Have your lawyer create contracts for payment schedules, including clauses that will permit you to charge more for change requests requiring you to work extra hours.
- *Take advantage of your industry's recommended software and tools* to help you streamline your business' billing and bookkeeping, plan presentations for project bids, and to project and monitor your ongoing cash flow. Take note of venues that make the most money for your time invested.
- *Put it in writing.* With your business lawyer, create a standard contract for your use.

You will discover that setting the best prices for your business' products or services will be a continuous and challenging effort to please your customers and make money. Review your pricing on a regular basis to adjust your prices according to variations in the economy, increased value to your product or services, your customers' preferences, and your competition's offerings. If this seems complicated, talk to your accountant, who can advise you what you need to charge based on all the factors involved with your venture.

As one business owner said, "When I went to my accountant for pricing advice, he told me he did not know how I even stayed in business. His suggestions and recommendations saved my business and increased my profits." Knowing what you must charge for your services will help your business survive and thrive while enabling you to pace your workload to please your customers and live comfortably. (See also Method 43, "Pricing Matters.")

Suggested Resources

Books

> *The Art of Pricing: How to Find the Hidden Profits to Grow Your Business* by Rafi Mohammed (New York: Crown Business, 2005).
>
> *How to Sell at Margins Higher Than Your Competitors: Winning Every Sale at Full Price, Rate or Fee* by Lawrence L. Steinmetz and William T. Brooks (Hoboken, NJ: John Wiley & Sons, 2006).
>
> *Strategy and Tactics of Pricing: A Guide to Growing More Profitably,* 4th ed., by Thomas T. Nagle and John Hogan (Upper Saddle River, NJ: Pearson Education, 2005).

Web Info

> www.BizOffice.com, "Pricing Your Products," *The Small and Home-Based Business Library.*
>
> www.score.org/guides.html, SCORE's 60-second guide, "Developing a Pricing Strategy."

48. Establishing Payment Options

Installment and Financing Plans

In the 1920s, along with the sale of automobiles, came the first installment and financing plans for customers who could not afford the entire cost of a new vehicle. Since then, it has been common for business owners to offer their customers various financing plans to pay for goods and services, because many people like to buy first and pay (later) in installments. If you are thinking about offering your customers these options, first check with an attorney who specializes in business for contracts and advice about any interest regulations and related laws you must follow.

Payments

You should have several ways customers can pay you, the easier the better, but you also want to protect yourself from check or credit card fraud. Here are common ways to accept customers' payments.

CREDIT CARDS

Statistics show that people with credit cards generally make more purchases and more often than those who pay by cash. If you want to accept credit cards, you need a credit card merchant account, a bank account, and a card processor. Get referrals from other business owners who have vendor status for recommendations.

Contact the banks or card companies to compare their requirements, transaction fees, equipment rental, and liability responsibilities. Ask how they handle problems that might occur, and how and what technology they use to verify legitimate card users. Use updated credit card processing machines because many have Address Verification Software (AVS) built into them that automatically verifies that a person's billing name and address match.

If you are turned down for vendor status, ask your bank to recommend an independent service organization (ISO) that can match you with a bank meeting your needs. The disadvantage is that it may cost you much more to go through an ISO than to deal with your local bank. Check also with the bank with which any ISO claims that it does business to make sure it is legitimate. Some industry and business associations also offer credit card vendor status as part of their members' benefits.

CHECKS

Many customers who do not wish to use credit cards or to give these numbers online or over the phone, may prefer to pay by check. The plus for this method is that banks do not charge a transaction fee. The minuses, though, are that checks can bounce, signatures and check amounts can be easily forged, or those signing the checks could be unauthorized to do so. If you accept checks as payment, take precautions such as waiting to send items until checks clear, or calling banks to verify purchasers' accounts can cover their check amounts.

Some business owners also use services like ECHO, ChekFaxx, Telecheck, PayByCheck, and others that offer several ways for customers to pay by electronic checking, and may even send follow-up reminders to your customers via e-mail. Your costs involve the transaction fees and check-processing software. These services are convenient for your check-paying customers, offer screening for fraud, and assist you in collecting on returned checks.

ONLINE PAYMENT SERVICES

Companies like Microsoft Commerce Manager, LaGarde, or PayPal and others that provide secure shopping cart software and online payment services are good for you and customers who are purchasing items online, whether it is on your e-commerce site or through an online auction, or directly buying and selling on your own. Even if you have a merchant account, these online payment options will protect your customers' sensitive information, and will save you time and work if you have online catalogs, or other e-commerce ventures.

MONEY ORDERS

Some customers still prefer to use paper money orders for payments. These are almost as good as cash, but the risk of forgery and fraud is still there. They can also send paper money orders to you through the U.S. Postal Service.

If you need assistance in establishing the best payments and credit policies for your business, contact your small business experts or those at offices like SCORE (www.score.org).

Rewarding Loyal Customers

Here are several ways you can thank your customers financially that will encourage their repeat business and spread the word about your generosity:

- *Have special sales.* A small, family-owned appliance dealer in our area offers loyal customers periodic sales by invitation only.
- *Extend a warranty or service.* This appliance dealer extends the service agreement one year beyond the manufacturer's coverage period. One woman who owns a consulting business says she sometimes offers to assist her regular clients on a limited basis with presentations after a project is completed. "This is both helpful to the client and gives me additional exposure to potential customers."
- *Offer discounts to customers who purchase large quantities or hire you for large projects.* Monitor your cash flow to see that such offers do not cut into your revenue or take away time from your ongoing marketing activities.
- *Send customers a monthly postcard or newsletter.* Your message can include helpful money-saving tips related to your product or service.
- *Reward referrals.* Send a little gift to a customer who refers you to a new paying one.
- *Reward prompt payers.* Offer discounts to customers who pay their bills rapidly.

Collection Tips and Guidelines

Whether you are owed money (accounts receivable) for items from your customers, other companies, retailers, or from those to whom you have provided services, your primary goal is to get paid ASAP. The following tips will help you get your money:

- Send an invoice along with your order or as soon as you have completed your project (see Sidebar).
- Have an established payment policy and make it known to your customer or client.
- Make sure you send or give the invoice to the bookkeeper or person who writes the checks.
- Be wary to whom you extend credit. Be suspicious about anyone who makes large orders of items with no concern about costs. If it is a service project, have a signed contract with payment installments due at the completion of each stage. Research the credibility of new customers.

- Call, send an e-mail message, or write a letter as soon as an account is past due. See if your invoice was lost or went to the wrong person, or if there is any other legitimate reason that your customer did not yet pay.
- Keep a record and all copies of dates, happenings, and correspondence for future reference in the event you need to go to a mediator or court.

Invoice Basics

Some business transactions are verbal, but having a standard business contract or payment policy drawn up by an attorney can eliminate confusion and communication problems. Even if your agreement is verbal, experts advise that you might want to have a simple contract that states in writing what you and the other party agreed to; it will make it much easier to bill with an invoice.

Here are some of the possible items to include in your invoices:

- Invoice number
- Date
- Purchase order number
- Item description
- Quantity
- Bill to and ship to address
- Sales rep name
- Terms of payment
- Shipping method
- Tax ID number
- Discount percentage
- Miscellaneous

Many computer software bundles that come already installed on many computers have basic invoices you can modify to fit your needs. Depending on how you prefer to keep your business organized, you can file both paper and electronic invoices for each customer.

49. Bartering

Bartering, sometimes referred to as work-trade or work-for-trade, is an exchange of goods and services without the use of money. Bartering was probably the first form of commerce, before any paper money or coins were ever created. One graphic artist has traded her design services with writers, Web designers, professional organizers, and other microbusiness owners. If you and other entrepreneurs are short of cash and have compatible services or products, it is an excellent way to get items or services you cannot afford. Bartering transactions can take place between two people who agree to an exchange of services or products of approximately equal value.

There are also barter exchanges or groups in which club members trade, save, or spend their credits (cash value given) for one or more members' items or services, usually for a small transaction fee.

Not all bartering agreements or exchanges are equal, however. Here are some pros and cons:

Pros

- It can save your business money.
- You can get goods or services that might not have been affordable otherwise.
- Bartering can provide you with exposure to reach potential customers.

Cons

- Not all barter exchanges are stable, and if an exchange should dissolve, you may lose the credits you have saved. Ask for referrals from trusted business owners for reputable clubs that have been in business at least five years.
- Unless two independent business owners sign a contract with specifics, it can be difficult to prove who did not live up to the agreement if a bartering deal goes bad. One small business owner, Mary, provided her services in good faith, but the other party, Mae, with whom she bartered a business service, took eight months to complete her exchange and then decided to charge Mary in cash (because now she needs money) for the extra hours it took her to finish Mary's project. They had to seek a mediator to resolve their dispute.

Bartering is not for everyone or for every business situation. If it interests you as a low-cost method to benefit your business, try it on a temporary basis and afterward analyze it truthfully to see if it is worth it.

Although no money is exchanged, the IRS still considers services or goods obtained or given through a bartering agreement as taxable sales or income. Be sure to keep accurate records of any bartering transactions in which you participate. For more information, visit the IRS web site (www.IRS.gov) and read its page, "Bartering Income."

Bartering can help market your business while getting goods and services you need for your business now instead of later.

50. Cash Flow Basics

Cash flow refers to the amount of money coming *into* your business from sales and the amount of money going *out* to pay your business expenditures. Your cash flow can predict your business' future costs and income and can help you create marketing and budget plans to bring in more sales and control your costs.

Determining Cash Flow

To find your current cash flow,* you can use a cash flow worksheet from Microsoft Excel or another spreadsheet software, plug in your income and expenses totals and compare the balance with your projected income.

Monitoring

With your cash flow budget sheet, you can make a cash flow projection of the next month, six months, or year. It can help you keep an eye on your inventory, the number of paying customers you have, how many more you should strive to obtain, and the marketing activities you can afford to attract new customers. It can also alert you that you need to cut back on expenses.

Boost your positive cash flow by offering incentives to customers to pay sooner, looking for ways to cut costs (but not your quality), trying new low-cost publicity activities, or finding ways to enhance the value of your business offerings and raise your prices.

"Cash Is (Still) King"

You may be making big profits on the products or services you sell, but that does not mean your business is in good shape. Small business expert, Denise O'Berry, author of *Small Business Cash Flow: Strategies for Making Your Business a Financial Success* (www.cashflowtruth.com) says though small business owners may negotiate the best deals for huge profits, they may have no cash to show for it.

"It is a good thing to have profit in your business, but the key to business success is having cash. Profits do not equal cash. At any given time your profits can be tied up in inventory or accounts receivable and could be completely inaccessible to you. What really counts in your business is having cash on hand so you can take advantage of opportunities to expand your business and deal with emergencies as they arise. Cash is king for a small business," says O'Berry.

Regularly review the essential components of your cash flow alone or with a financial expert to ensure the stability and steady growth of your business.

---

* Business Owner's Toolkit (www.toolkit.cch.com) has a section, "Cash Flow Budget," and a free cash flow budget sheet that you can download for your use.

Suggested Resources*

Associations

International Reciprocal Trade Association (IRTA), www.irta.com, a nonprofit organization promoting barter as a responsible form of commerce.

National Association of Trade Exchanges, www.nate.org, a nonprofit organization serving barter groups and members.

Books

The Complete Guide to Getting and Keeping Visa/Master Card Status by Larry Schwartz and Pearl Sax (Boynton Beach, FL: Fraud & Theft Information Bureau™, 2000).

How to Collect Debts and Still Keep Your Customers by David Sher and Martin Sher (New York: AMACOM, 1999).

Make Sure You Get Paid and Other Business Basics by Bonnie Huval (Tamarac, FL: Llumina Press, 2005).

Small Business Cash Flow: Strategies for Making Your Business a Financial Success by Denise O' Berry (Hoboken, NJ: John Wiley & Sons, 2006).

Payment Processing Services (Just a Few of Many That Exist)†

Americart, www.cartserver.com/americart, Internet storefront, contact for setup, monthly fees, and other terms.

Charge.Com, www.charge.com, a company that provides e-commerce services to businesses, including small and home-based operations that do business online.

Electronic Clearing House, www.echo-inc.com, a company that provides businesses with electronic payment processing and financial service solutions.

Software

Cash flow: Up Your Cash Flow™ XT created by Harvey A. Goldstein, CPA, www.upyourcashflow.com.

Invoices: Microsoft Small Business Accounting 2006, www.microsoft.com, accounting basics including invoices.

---

*Companies listed are solely for information purposes and do not constitute an endorsement. Seek legal counsel before signing any business agreements or contracts.

† Does not constitute an endorsement. Check with your financial experts to decide on the one that best suits your venture.

Web Info

www.BizOffice.com, "Pricing Your Products," "Bartering Your Expertise and Services," and other topics. *The Small and Home-Based Business Library.*

www.cashflowtruth.com, cash flow articles by small business expert and author Denise O'Berry.

www.MyMoney.gov, topics about staying financially fit offered by the federal government including starting a small business, budgeting and taxes, and other related financial matters that impact your life.

www.score.org/guides.html, SCORE's 60-second guides, "Collecting Payment" and "Managing Cash Flow."

6

Grow with "A Little Help from Your Friends": The Best People to Help Your Business Succeed

Chapter 6 presents networking, choosing the best business experts, and the process of hiring. Joint venture options are also discussed.

51. Your Neighborhood

Organizing a Marketing Support Group

The CEOs of large businesses periodically get together at conferences or fly to a resort to confer with associates about the latest business news. On your scale, you can simply meet with other self-employed individuals or small business owners on a regular basis to exchange marketing ideas and other helpful information. One small business owner discovered that her local bank had a community room available for group meetings. She reserved it for a certain date and then placed a press release in her community newspapers inviting other self-employed individuals to come to introduce themselves.

She had a good turnout and after that meeting, the group would get together several times a year to brainstorm marketing ideas and tips. They never formalized their group, nor did they charge membership fees. She said, as busy as all their lives were, the group liked the informality of it. What was valuable, she added, was the rapport they developed. The group members could call one another or exchange e-mail messages whenever they needed some help or feedback on handling a problem or on an idea they were contemplating.

Many business owners never meet with one another in person, but participate in Internet message boards or list groups, or online communities. Some are offshoots of major web sites like www.iVillage.com with message boards for specific businesses. Like all business communications, posting on boards has rules and guidelines. Most do not permit spamming, but you can leave a sig file (signature file) with your URL. The more you are there to help others, the more respect you will gain—in person with your group or online (see more in Method 88). You can easily form your own networking group, no matter where you are.

The Value of Business Owners' Associations and Organizations

Joining an established business ownership group provides numerous benefits. Here are just a few:

- You can receive membership discounts on office supplies, equipment, travel (car rental, lodging), books and industry publications, business stationery, merchant accounts, telephone services including toll-free numbers, member-to-member discounts, and more.
- There are publicity opportunities in publications and media.
- Referrals to customers often come from other members and from a business listing in membership directories (print form or on the association's web site).
- Members have access to experts who can answer business-related questions.
- Subscriptions to the periodic publications of an association's industry include updated news about current industry trends and important marketing tips.
- Seminars, conventions, and meetings are held so members can hear national speakers and attend workshops together.
- Prepaid legal services are available.
- Members can join health insurance group plans at lower rates.
- Financial start-up advice and cash grants are available with some associations' benefits.
- Members have access to associations' online sites that provide ideas, leads, links, message boards, chats, and additional information.

Do some preliminary research before you join. Meeting locations, membership fees and benefits, and the members themselves will all be factors in whether an association or group will be mutually beneficial for your business and for the organization. You may need to join one or more for a trial period. Remember, too, that being an active member can give you that personal contact you may crave while helping to increase your business knowledge and management skills.

Meet to Eat

Sharing food and drink seems to make it easier to talk with someone else. It gives a sense of well-being whether you are eating with family or friends or for business. Having "power lunches" or dinner meetings fosters good feelings and can help you market your business. You may not have the funds to eat at five-star restaurants, but many nice local eating establishments are affordable and work as well, sometimes even better because the atmosphere is more relaxed.

One active business owners' networking group met monthly at a local coffee shop when they first started. They met at the shop in the evenings, usually on nights when the shop was not crowded. The owner of the coffee shop was pleased to offer the space because the group's referrals brought in sales and other customers. The group was so well attended that another larger group incorporated it into theirs, and they finally found a permanent home for their membership in a nearby town. Many of the original members still go back to that coffee shop to meet one-on-one with clients, though, because of its nice atmosphere.

In another instance, the women members of several adjoining chambers of commerce, hold bimonthly luncheon meetings with all their members. Each meeting is held at a different restaurant or institution and is sponsored by one of the members, who is the speaker or schedules one. This gives her the opportunity to highlight her business or the organization's offerings. Meal prices are discounted for members, and they are encouraged to bring guests.

After the meal, each woman is invited to introduce her business with a brief statement. Not all the attendees are business owners. Some of the women work for banks, institutions, or local media that have membership. The luncheons are well attended and are a great way to network and meet new people. As one woman said, "The men do golf. We do lunch!"

Promotions to Organizations' Members

Most business ownership and organizational groups have periodic business card exchanges open to the public. You can attend these functions to introduce yourself and your business and to evaluate whether this group is a good match with your business's mission and goals. Even if your customer market is national or worldwide instead of local, you never know whom you will meet and what opportunities may result.

After losing two major clients who accounted for over a hundred thousand dollars in billable hours, Mike Ference developed a new way of networking that he called *Microwaveable Marketing*. It produced quick results and helped him successfully rebuild his home-based enterprise. He describes his system in the following sidebar:

Microwaveable Marketing

Mike Ference

"Sure, those old textbooks say that effective marketing requires long-term commitment, that a brand or message must appear many times in different media before it sinks in—but you want *instant* results for your marketing efforts, right? Well, for relatively instant and *effective* marketing, you can't beat joining your local chamber of commerce or one of the business networking groups in your area.

Think about it—these local groups give business and professional folks a chance to shine in front of dozens of active members under ideal networking conditions. Many groups meet weekly, bimonthly, or around a special calendar of events and allow members to announce any new developments or activities going on in their business or professional lives. And some organizations have publications or web sites that offer even more opportunities to publicize your company's success story.

Here are a few guidelines to follow when joining an organization that's designed to help you network your way into new business and new business relationships:

- Be just as concerned about doing business with other members as you are about other members doing business with you.
- Attend as many functions as you can. If you're not able to attend an event, try sending someone from your staff as a substitute.
- Provide a door prize at every event you attend. Include some promotional products with your logo, as well as a gift certificate, or a discount on your products or services. Include catalogs, brochures, or any other materials that help to promote your business or profession.
- If the organization has a newsletter, volunteer to write an article on your area of expertise. Make copies of the article and send them out with your invoices, or make a flier and let people read them while they are waiting in your office.
- Often, if an organization has a newsletter, it's looking for news about members. Volunteer to be interviewed. This type of publicity can be priceless, especially if it's followed up by sending copies of the article to your key customers, or anyone you want to do business with. Always remember to send a little note or make a personal call to thank the writer. As one of the few who do, you'll always stand out in the writer's mind and become a quotable source in future articles.

- Be the first to welcome a new member. Do it with sincerity and not with a business card or order pad in hand.
- All organizations need to raise funds to meet their financial obligations. Help out where you can, even if it just means returning a call to let an event organizer know you're not able to participate.
- If you're unable to provide financial support to the organization over and above the cost of membership, volunteer your services for their fund-raising activities and other events. Many organizations have golf outings, luncheons, or other activities where able bodies can play an important role.
- Donate cocktail napkins and other disposable items imprinted with your logo or company message. When these items are used at organizational events, your message will be inches away from everyone's eyes, often for hours at a time.
- When you join the chamber, you'll meet the cream of the crop in the community—people accustomed to giving much more than they expect to receive in return. Don't be someone who takes unfair advantage of that generosity; be one of the generous ones. Trust is a valuable resource, and it can be squandered in one or two careless or selfish acts. Always be on your best behavior. The goal of joining these organizations is to build relationships that will last a lifetime.

Follow this lead and you can expect results that quickly turn into new business and, more importantly, new business relationships. Try it for the next 12 months—you'll be glad you did."

Mike Ference is the owner of Ference Marketing & Communications, a full service advertising agency (www.ferencemarketing.com).

Political Service

Though politics and business conjure up headlines of kickbacks, abuse, and corruption, it can be a good relationship if handled with ethics and proper protocol. You can become a spokesperson for a particular group of business owners or entrepreneurs. Maybe, there is zoning that needs to be revised to accommodate home-based businesses in your area; or some aspect of small business needs more support from your state's or region's legislators.

Writing letters, and then publishing them in your local papers' "Letters to the Editor" sections; meeting with politicians; visiting their offices to get more information about existing programs benefiting small businesses; or volunteering to do nonpartisan political service can help establish your image as an advocate for entrepreneurs and keep you current with any pending legislation affecting small business.

Sponsoring and Participating in Seasonal Parties or Festivals

Whenever a church organization travels to a nearby mental health institution to hold seasonal parties for the residents, they can always count on a local grocery store to provide them with beverages and other goodies. When a local National Guard unit was deployed to Iraq, many businesses participated in hosting a community appreciation event for the unit's members and their families.

Every region has its seasonal celebrations of festivals, fairs, and shows. With sponsorships, or through donated time and service, your business can gain much exposure with the publicity for the event. Calendars, programs, and media announcements list participating organizations and businesses, providing multiple opportunities for potential and faithful customers to notice your business and your community goodwill. Many sponsors also have their own booths or stands to make additional contacts. Anyone who has been involved in putting on a party or community event will tell you how he or she developed better relationships and friendships. As one business owner said, "When you meet someone, you learn their name and maybe a little about them; but when you *work* with someone, you really get to *know* them! It really is a win-win for you, your business's marketing, and your community" (see more in Method 70).

Open Houses

If you have a "brick-and-mortar," store, holding an open house for your customers is a great way to let new people see your merchandise. If you do not have a storefront, you might approach a business owner who does and ask if you can help her organize and hold one. One woman with a home-based antique business has an annual open house the first weekend in December, inviting her customers to come for refreshments and see her decorations. Each person attending receives a free ornament. This same entrepreneur is invited by a local historical society to decorate a room in one of their landmark buildings, providing her with additional opportunities to showcase her antiques and specialty lace curtains. Offering refreshments, live entertainment from local musicians, or even artwork from local students will help make your open house even more special.

Networking for Business

Networking involves assembling and sustaining relationships with other business owners or individuals to exchange useful information in the pursuit of a business or personal goal. You accomplish this by attending meetings, events, trade shows, talks, and other places where you can meet people in person. In virtual networking, you do the same, but over the Internet.

Marketing experts agree that the key to successful business networking is to focus on how you can help your fellow networkers with information; and they, in kind, will think of you in relaying information and referrals. These experts also recommend that you know *why* you are networking: To learn more? To develop more media contacts? To find new markets? Then seek to build a network that will help you achieve those objectives.

Here are some additional networking tips:

- *Be pleasant, self-confident and do not dwell on your own problems.*
- *Be ready with your 30-second pitch (elevator pitch) that will get a new person's attention.* See Method 79.
- *Be a good listener.* One college student did a social experiment by not talking for a year. He said he wanted to become a better listener! You do not have to go to that extreme, but people in a social situation will tend to go to that person who wants to listen rather than to the one who never stops talking.
- *Follow up with new contacts.* Trade shows or conferences present great opportunities to meet potential networking friends. To cement those new relationships, send notes or cards afterward expressing your pleasure in meeting them. One entrepreneur uses the business cards other entrepreneurs give her to jot down the information they are seeking. Then she sends them all letters with leads or sources they may find helpful.
- *Keep in touch.* Whether you do it at planned meetings, through lead-generating clubs or informally, be sure you attend and/or communicate through other means on a regular basis within your network so you will think of one another when you hear beneficial news or leads.
- *Be genuine and try to avoid jealousy for someone else's success.* Help others, and they will remember you—they really will!

You cannot be a homebody and survive in business. Being out there in your community and the world will provide you with countless opportunities to promote your business and make wonderful new friends of all ages and backgrounds (see also Method 62).

The U.S. Small Business Administration says that differently abled individuals are starting businesses at twice the rate of people who do not have mental or physical challenges. Many persons with disabilities or chronic health problems often do not have as easy an access to get around as abled persons; but with ongoing advancements in technology and biomedical engineering and adapted equipment and vehicles, many persons with disabilities are able to run productive enterprises independently. Cell phones, wireless computers, voice-activated software, and other devices are helping these individuals to connect to customers and associates around the world using the Internet and other communicative equipment.

The U.S. Department of Labor's Office of Disability Employment Policy (www.dol.gov/odep) has among its programs services for those wishing to start their own businesses. You can visit www.DisabilityInfo.gov, "An Online Resource for Americans with Disabilities" and contact the nearest Small Business Development Center (www.sba.gov/SBDC), as well as your state senators and representatives for more information about availability of training and business counseling for those with disabilities.°

Suggested Resources

Books

> *Encyclopedia of Associations,* Gale Research. Lists thousands of professional and interest-related associations in all areas.

> *Never Eat Alone: And Other Secrets to Success, One Relationship at a Time* by Keith Ferrazzi and Tahl Raz (New York: Doubleday Publishing, 2005).

> *Smart Networking: How to Turn Contacts into Cash, Clients, and Career Success* by Anne Barber and Lynee Waymon (New York: American Management Association, 1997).

> *Unlikely Entrepreneurs: A Complete Guide to Business Start-Ups for People with Disabilities and Chronic Health Conditions* by Roseanne Herzog (Traverse City: North Peak Publishing, 1999).

52. Assistance from States (United States) or Provinces (Canada)

Local, State, and Federal Resources

Your local, state, and federal taxes help fund entrepreneurial programs that assist men, women, and minorities, people with disabilities, veterans, and others in starting and managing small businesses. It is up to you to take full advantage of them.

LOCAL

In addition to your local business organizations, check with the offices of your city, township, regions, and at the local offices of state and federal agencies (see listings in this section) for any classes or programs they offer to foster small business development.

Public and college libraries can supply a wealth of business-related information. In addition to the volumes of the *Thomas Register of American Manufacturers* (www.thomasregister.com), you will find other directories such as *Ward's*

° See also Additional Resources at the back of the book.

Business Directory of U.S. Private and Public Companies; Industry Surveys (Standard & Poor's) that includes details of U.S. industries and trends; and additional resources of industry and business.

Large libraries may have CDs with millions of business listings like the *American Business Disc* or have access to the Internet and may subscribe to various online databases like *ReferenceUSA*. Library systems now have their holdings online, so you can check to see if a book or other resource is available anywhere in the entire system. If the library is designated a depository for SBA documents, it will have pamphlets detailing governmental programs and information for start-up businesses and loans.

Many libraries have community rooms where various speakers and organizations conduct presentations and meetings. Chapters of SCORE may hold business start-up sessions. If you can talk about a subject related to your business, you might offer to do a presentation or demonstration that the media may cover, just as it did with Patricia Gallagher's book tour. Your presentation cannot be a blatant sales talk, and you cannot charge a speaker's fee if it is a public library.

Depending on the library's funding, some have entire sections in separate rooms or areas designated to business and commerce. Libraries are not just for bookworms any more.

STATE

Check with your local business organizations and offices of your state senators and representatives for the programs they have for businesses, including women and minorities, veterans, and those with disabilities. Most states have business start-up manuals that include information concerning the state agencies that deal with safety, taxes, licensing, regulations, legalities, and employees. Inquire about how your business can qualify and bid for contracts. If you run into bureaucracy problems, state legislators or their staff can assist you in resolving many such difficulties.

For more states' business information, you can check in your local library or bookstore for the latest edition of *Starting and Operating a Business in the U.S.* by Michael D. Jenkins and Rhonda Abrams. A companion CD-ROM details state laws applicable to businesses in all 50 states. You can also access much of your state's information online: Start with this site: http://dir.yahoo.com /Government—Yahoo's portal into federal and state government web sites.

FEDERAL

Many offices are sponsored by the U.S. Small Business Administration (SBA, www.SBA.gov; www.business.gov; see also Resources in the back of the book). You can call the SBA INFO LOCATOR (800-827-5722 or 202-205-7333, TDD), for the hearing impaired or search for centers, online courses, and other business information: www.sba.gov/asksba. Just a few of the vast SBA resources:

- *SBA Library:* www.sba.gov/training/library.html, The library of the Small Business Training Network houses hundreds of SBA publications and links to thousands of outside small business resources including over 200 free SBA business publications; eBiz Portal; Online Universities and Colleges and links to free online courses; free start-up business guide; and online courses—Marketing Basics, Research, Competitive Analysis, Marketing Plan, Ads & PR, Trade Shows, e-Marketing, Signage, and a free online Marketing Course.

- *U.S. Small Business Development Centers:* www.sba.gov/SBDC, The U.S. Small Business Administration (SBA) administers the Small Business Development Center Program to provide management assistance to current and prospective small business owners. There are now 63 Lead Small Business Development Centers (SBDCs)—one in every state, the District of Columbia, Guam, Puerto Rico, Samoa, and the U.S. Virgin Islands, with a network of more than 1,100 service locations. Subcenters are located at colleges, universities, community colleges, vocational schools, chambers of commerce, and economic development corporations. Each center develops services in cooperation with local SBA district offices to ensure statewide coordination with other available resources.

  These centers work in conjunction with the business departments of universities and also offer ongoing free or low-cost business counseling and seminars. Some SBDCs are designated U.S. Export Assistance Centers (USEACs; www.sba.gov/gopher/Local-Information/Useacs/) that assist business owners in venturing into international trade and most SBDCs offer seminars for inventors; and provide free or low-cost business startup courses and counseling services for entrepreneurs and small business owners. Ask also for information about Tribal Business Information Centers (TBICs, www.sba.gov/naa/tribes) for Native Americans; and U.S. Export Assistance Centers.

- *Service Corps of Retired Executives (SCORE):* www.SCORE.org, SCORE is a nonprofit organization and a resource partner with the SBA and also offers free counseling and low-cost seminars. It comprises over 10,500 volunteers—women and men, working and retired successful business owners, executives, and corporate leaders—who volunteer to help entrepreneurs start and grow enterprises. Go to their site to find the office nearest you. The SCORE web site offers online counseling, how-to guides, and business templates. The site also has links for Women, Minority and Hispanic Entrepreneurs, Veterans, National Guard and Reservists, Young Entrepreneurs, and Manufacturers.

- *Office of Women's Business Ownership:* www.onlinewbc.gov, Women's Business Centers (WBCs) represent a national network of more than 100 educational resource centers that are partially funded by the U.S. Small

Business Administration (SBA) and whose mission is to assist women start and grow small businesses. They can refer you to lawyers, business insurance companies, and other helpful professionals.

The web site www.onlinewbc.gov/resources.html offers links to partners and resources; and the site "MyBiz for Women," www.sba.gov/women, offers links to other federal programs.

OTHER SBA RESOURCES

- Business information centers, www.sba.gov, technology, on-site business counseling.
- Minority business development agency, www.mbda.gov.
- Office of technology, www.sba.gov/sbir.
- U.S. Equal Employment Opportunity Commission, www.eeoc.gov.
- Cooperative extension services, www.csrees.usda.gov/Extension, are located in every county and are part of the U.S. Department of Agriculture (USDA.gov). These offices work in affiliation with state universities, and in some states, they sponsor courses and programs for home business owners. Contact your local office (in the white or blue pages of your telephone directory), or visit the USDA web site that provides links to cooperative extension offices.
- Internal Revenue Service, www.IRS.gov, tax forms, information and an online workshop, "Small Business Self-Employed Online Classroom."

Canadian Government

- The Canada Business Service Centres (CBSCs), www.cbsc.org, provide a wide range of information on government services, programs, and regulations and answer questions about starting a new business or improving an existing one. Web site also provides contact information for each province and territory (see also Additional Resources in the back of the book).

Governmental Contracts

Government agencies at all levels purchase goods and services from many small businesses. It may be a lucrative market for your venture.

LOCAL

Municipalities, cities, towns and townships, school districts and provinces and territories all put out bids for work and products that their employees cannot handle. They publish these contracts in local newspapers for bids from business owners. Talk to the directors of contracts at these offices to see how your business can apply and what licenses, insurances, and other requirements you must have to be eligible.

STATES, TERRITORIES

For contract procurement information and to learn what is available in your state or territory, these resources should prove helpful: legislators' offices; Departments of Commerce; Women's Development Bureaus: your chamber of commerce office; Department of Revenue (Taxes); and the local offices of your Small Business Development Centers (SBDCs) and Women's Business Centers (WBCs).

SBDCs and WBCs can also lead business owners through the process of certifying a business. Certification programs also exist for women, minority, and disadvantaged business owners to help them obtain government contracts at the state and federal level.

FEDERAL

Small business expert Dr. Robert Sullivan, author of *United States Government—New Customer*, says on his website, "The United States Government is the world's largest purchaser of goods and services to the tune of over $225 BILLION . . . , and . . . the majority of purchases are for $5,000 or less."

The federal government helps disadvantaged, small and women-owned businesses qualify for a percentage of these contracts. Here are some of the best places for contract information:

- Business Matchmaking, www.businessmatchmaking.com, SBA program to match corporations with small businesses.
- WomenBiz.gov, www.womenbiz.gov, information for women business owners' selling to the government. Also see the FAQs at this site: www.sba.gov/GC/indexprograms-cawbo.html.
- PRO-Net, http://pro-net.sba.gov/pro-net/register.html, business registration information about registering for contractor databases: PRO-Net, Central Contractor Registration (CCR) and Electronic Posting System (EPS).
- GovCommerce.net, a government-to-business e-purchasing system developed by Fedmarket.com, http://www.sba.gov/GC/indexprograms-cawbo .html, another web site for federal contracting.
- You can also contact nearby Small Business Development Centers and ask for the person in charge of the "Government Marketing Assistance Program." This person can assist you in certifying your business (minority, women-owned) and contracting procedures.

These offices may provide your business with a steady income stream and market that you never thought of before. Once you are registered, you can sign up to receive e-mail notifications of possible contracts that may be suitable for your business offerings. Contracting with local governments may take some time until you learn about all the procedures, but the profit potential in contracting is worth the effort.

Suggested Resources

Books

Building a Dream: A Canadian Guide to Starting Your Own Business, 6th ed., by Walter S. Good (Whitby, Ontario, Canada: McGraw-Hill Ryerson, 2005).

Internet Law and Business Handbook by Dianne Brinson and Mark F. Radcliffe (Chicago: Independent Publishers Group, 2000). Book and disk. Includes information about Canadian e-commerce laws.

The Small Business Start-Up Guide: Practical Advice on Selecting, Starting and Operating a Small Business, 3rd ed., rev., by Robert Sullivan (Great Falls, VA: Information International, 2000). www.isquare.com. Contains a section, "State Specific Information."

Starting and Operating a Business in the U.S. by Michael D. Jenkins and Rhonda Abrams, Introduction (Palo Alto, CA: The Planning Shop, 1999). Book and CD-ROM.

United States Government—New Customer! A Step-by-Step Guide for Selling Your Product or Service to Uncle Sam by Robert Sullivan (Great Falls, VA: Information International, 1997). www.isquare.com. Out of print; copies may still be available in bookstores or libraries.

Organization

Women's Business Enterprise National Council (WBENC), www.wbenc.org, provides information on certified women's businesses.

Publication

Commerce Business Daily, http://cbdnet.gpo.gov, lists federal contracts.

Web Info

http://web.sba.gov/list, SBA Free Newsletter and Publication Subscription Center, electronic newsletters from the SBA.

www.ipl.org, Internet Public Library, University of Michigan's web site of business and other information.

www.isquare.com, Dr. Robert Sullivan's web site, business start-up and management resource site, also has additional information about state and federal contracts.

www.libraryspot.com, Library Spot's extensive web site of research resources.

53. National and Global Contacts

Joining a National or International Industry Association or Organization

Many of the benefits of joining a national or international group are similar to those if joining a local business ownership group; however, national and international business-related organizations offer some additional advantages that business owners can use to maintain and grow their businesses.

National and international groups can . . .

- Promote standards and ethics of your particular industry.
- Have representatives that act as political and industry advocates for business owners or professionals. For example, the National Writer's Union (www.nwu.org) assists their members in handling grievance issues.
- Offer publications with specific industry management tips for members.
- Publish periodicals, newsletters, and journals.
- Set ethical conduct and pricing suggestions.
- Hold national and regional conferences, with great opportunities to increase networking contacts and promote one another's businesses.
- Provide mentors for new members.
- Help promote members' services and products through their web sites.
- List members contact information in their directories and online so potential customers, media, and fellow members can reach them.
- Offer cash grants or financial start-up advice available with some associations' benefits.
- Keep you updated on industry trends.
- Sponsor annual awards that can bring you national recognition.

Many industries have their own professional organizations like the Promotional Products Association, International (www.ppa.org/default), the National Writer's Union (www.nwu.org), or the Greeting Card Association (www.greetingcard.org); others focus on specific business populations like the National Association of Women Business Owners (www.NAWBO.org); or general business ownership like the National Association for the Self-Employed (www.NASE.org).

As with the local or statewide business groups, you cannot join all the national or international organizations, so look carefully for the ones that match your business and your objectives. After you join, explore all the marketing opportunities and support that association membership can provide to reach across the country and around the world for new customers and networking.

Conference Attendance Tips

Whether you attend an entrepreneur conference or a national event or expo related to your business and self-employment ventures, think of it as an investment of your time and money. You should know *why* you are attending. What are your objectives? To expand your network? To learn more about marketing or management? To hear about new innovations in your industry? Make sure you bring plenty of business cards to exchange, and follow up with any leads or new contacts you made during the sessions.

There are no guarantees that by attending a business conference your entrepreneurial skills will improve or your profits will increase, but at the very least it's a day out and an opportunity to make new friends. It may be the energizing factor you need to achieve the success you've always wanted.

Suggested Resources

Book

> *Encyclopedia of Associations.* Look for these volumes and others that list associations from around the world (see also Resources in the back of the book).

Web Info

> www.allconferences.com, AllConferences.com, an online directory of conferences, conventions, trade shows, events, business meetings and other such gatherings.

54. Experts

Survive and Thrive with the Right Business Experts

One of the best characteristics of successful entrepreneurs is that they are not afraid to ask questions until they find answers. They are also not afraid to ask for help. There will be many times when you face challenges in your business that need an expert's advice, opinion, and service. It is important to have a list of experts (lawyer, accountant, and marketing specialist) on hand *before* you even start your business. Call it a kind of insurance in the event something happens (and it will if you stay in business for any length of time). You may never need all the experts you have lined up, but it will save you time and trouble if you find your experts now.

In interviewing experts, ask about their qualifications, experience with businesses like yours, references, rates, memberships in professional or trade associations, licenses, fees, and any other information that will help you choose the best one for your business.

To save time and money, and free up more personal and business time, you can also hire other small business owners to walk your dog, clean your house, plan your meals, run your errands, and perform any other task that takes you away from concentrating on marketing and revenue-generating activities.

Expert Sources

Here are places to find the experts you need:

- Telephone directories, including specialty ones such as women's business directories or some other designated group of business owners. Many specialty directories can be picked up for free at libraries or grocery stores.
- Professional and trade organizations like the National Association of Professional Organizers (www.napo.net), the Financial Planning Association (www.fpanet.org), or referral directories for professionals like lawyers or nurses.
- Referrals, recommendations from other business owners and business owners organizations.
- Media sources.
- Internet searches.

Incorporate the expenses of hiring experts into your business plan and budget. Then you will have the funds to pay one *when* you need one.

Additional Experts You May Need

When it comes to succeeding and growing your business, you may want to consider consulting and hiring the following two experts:

1. *Business coach:* Many entrepreneurs tend to try to take their business in too many directions at once. They are not sure which market is the best one, so they haphazardly try too many marketing campaigns and never get the response they want from customers. Business coaches are professionals who help entrepreneurs and business owners decide what their primary business objectives are and then focus on steps to accomplish them. Most business coaches specialize in certain industries or professions and see or call their clients on a regular basis to monitor their progress.

   A business coach can help you identify areas you need to further research; write or revise a business plan; explore new income streams from international trade; determine your eligibility for government contracts; assist you in handling specific problems (or refer you to another expert); and be someone with whom you can discuss new ideas.

Erin Gruver, a professional organizer, says, "Coaching has helped me to step back, define what goals I have, and how to develop a plan to achieve them. Having a coach has also helped me be accountable for what I want to do, and in the process, I have learned quite a bit about myself and how I work."

It is important to find a coach with whom you feel comfortable and has some understanding and experience of who you are, where you've been, and where you would like to go with your business.

2. *Marketing consultant:* Many entrepreneurs do not realize what a marketing consultant can do for them. Bert, an owner of a home decor business, said that hiring a marketing consultant gave her promotional ideas that were original, affordable, and showed immediate results. Marketing experts can provide you with a new perspective or attitude toward your business while guiding and encouraging you to try new marketing strategies. They can also save you money by reviewing your market plan and marketing strategies and making sure your advertising and promotional dollars produce results. Be careful to choose a marketing expert who is familiar with your industry. Many marketing specialists hold seminars or give talks or workshops to promote their services. Try to attend a few of these by different individuals. Observing them and hearing what they have to say will help you decide which one to contact.

Business Mentor: Find One, Be One

Mentors are individuals who have worked or operated a business or have been through life events that you are experiencing. They can be valuable resources for business owners who are starting or managing a business. Your mentor might be your husband, wife, or other relative; or it could be a speaker you have met and heard at a business meeting or conference. They can provide you with new marketing ideas and ways to tackle current business problems. Teachers, nurses, and other professionals are pairing experienced staff with younger ones and finding it is helping the younger ones learn and giving the mentors a new enthusiasm for their profession.

A good mentor relationship has a good "fit" for you: strong in skills where you are weak. Your mentor does not have to be in the same field as you, but needs to have business and marketing expertise. You will want to choose a mentor who is successful, is active in a business network, and is patient but will challenge and motivate you—and celebrate your successes with you. Mentors should also evaluate your business's problems and give you specific solutions to solve them, or have a personal network that they can tap into for you.

If you admire the way someone is managing and marketing his or her business, you might ask if you could meet on a regular basis for a time, in person or even through e-mail messages. If the person cannot do it, ask for referrals of others you can contact. Some people do not like to reveal their success secrets, but many entrepreneurs enjoy sharing and are pleased when their advice has helped others succeed. Meetings and conferences or even groups on the Internet are places to find mentors or to become one for someone else.

Many entrepreneurs become mentors for others. They pass along their business wisdom to the next generation. Mentors offer insights and advice that you do not always find in books and can encourage you to keep striving to achieve your business goals.

Do not hesitate to tap into the knowledge of all these experts—it can make the difference between success and failure.

Suggested Resources

Associations

American Marketing Association, www.marketingpower.com, search for marketing experts; also articles, publications, and marketing handbooks.

Worldwide Association of Business Coaches, www.wabccoaches.com, search for business coaches.

Books

Power Mentoring: How Successful Mentors and Protégés Get the Most out of Their Relationships by Ellen A. Ensher and Susan E. Murphy (Hoboken, NJ: Wiley, 2005).

Your Lawyer: An Owner's Manual—A Business Owner's Guide to Managing Your Lawyer by Henry C. Krasnow, JD (Chicago: Agate Publishing, 2005).

Web Info

www.comprehensivecoachingu.com, site for those wanting to become a business coach.

www.Entrepreneur.com/howto, *Entrepreneur* magazine's free, online, how-to guide, "Hire an Attorney."

www.score.org/guides.html, SCORE's 60-second guide, "Finding a Business Mentor" and "Finding the Right Business Coach."

55. Establishing Your Own Board of Directors

From participating in networking groups, or mentor relationships, some business owners form their own advisory "board of directors." Your board could consist of three to eight people who help you brainstorm ideas and solutions for your business. For guidance with her new homeowners' referral business, Home Remedies® of NY, Inc. (www.homeownersreferral.com), Debra Cohen established a board of advisors and asked two contractors to be her members. "Their opinion is invaluable to me especially since I launched this business with no contracting experience whatsoever," she says.

Corporations pay their board members but you could treat your members to lunch or some other small way to repay them for their assistance. Who should you ask? People who are business savvy, professionals, maybe a lawyer, or an accountant, or a financial expert, and others who respect you and want to see you succeed. Having a diverse group is the best. Their personalities should be different, also. You want planners, strategists, problem solvers, those who will challenge you, and those who are positive thinkers and possess a good sense of humor.

You can offer to be on their "boards" also, in essence a group board of members who meet regularly or as needed, to provide feedback and brainstorm ideas for each other. Used successfully, your board can help you achieve your business objectives.

Suggested Resources

Article

"How Advisory Boards Can Keep Your Business on Track: Why Every Small Business Needs a Board of Directors" (Cover Story). In *Do-It-Yourself Retailing* by Shelly Bucksot (Indianapolis, IN: National Retail Hardware Association, November 2004, available on Amazon.com).

Book

The Small Business Bible: Everything You Need to Know to Succeed in Your Small Business by Steven D. Strauss (Hoboken, NJ: John Wiley & Sons, 2004).

56. Employees

When to Hire

You may be able to handle all your business tasks at first, but when you find yourself overwhelmed with orders or working on weekends or late at night, you need to hire or contract extra help. Besides wondering whom you are going to hire or subcontract, you will also have to give up a certain amount of control and trust someone else to do what you did before. As one entrepreneur asked when she needed to hire someone to assist her in making sales calls, "How can I expect someone else to have as much enthusiasm as I do about my business?" The answer many successful business owners give is that they finally realized they could not do everything well, so they decided to concentrate on what they did best and oversee others to do the rest. It makes obvious sense, because if the quality of your business offerings suffers because you can no longer keep up with customers' demand, then your image will suffer permanent damage.

Before you take that first step in hiring someone, ask yourself the following:

- Why do I need help—for permanent or seasonal work or for a particular project?
- Can I afford to hire someone and will hiring help make my business more productive or bring in new customers?
- How much time will hiring someone free up for me?

The answers to these questions will help you determine whether the time is right for you to get extra help and in what forms: full or part-time employee, independent contractors, leased workers, temporary help, or other options. Consulting with your accountant and lawyer will help you make this decision because they can work out the financials and advise you about IRS tax requirements and employee regulations concerning minimum hourly wages, employee benefits, OSHA, workers' compensation, and other issues.

Searching and Hiring the Right People

When one woman, a mother of two active girls, was asked how she managed her property management business and promoted her husband's art, she said, "I hire the right people."

Clarify the specific tasks you want someone to do. Small business owners usually look first for workers to handle the clerical and office duties, ordering of supplies, and other time-consuming activities. This gives owners more time to concentrate on marketing and to focus on the creation of their product or services.

Advertising for help in classified ads or through Internet job sites is one way to find help, but there are other creative ways to find the right persons for your tasks. People whom you have had some experience with in classes, volunteer activities, former interns or referrals from other business owners may provide you with excellent candidates. You will also want to thoroughly check their background and references for your own protection. There are procedures you must follow in hiring and firing, so know what you are doing or go to a human resources consultant or use a staffing agency to handle this instead.

Employee Incentives and Feedback (Including Marketing Ideas)

A woman who owns a successful computer consulting business recently flew her small staff of valued employees to an island resort for a brainstorming meeting. She said it was a great way to motivate them, get some great new marketing ideas, and foster good publicity for her business as her employees spread the word about their fun trip. Few small business owners can afford to reward employees to this extent, but there are many ways to recognize your employees' contributions.

Employees who are happy will be loyal, do high-quality work, and treat your customers and clients with courtesy and respect. Be enthusiastic, communicate clearly, and reward hard work with unexpected gift certificates and recognition. Treat your employees with respect and remember that they have personal lives and concerns. An important consideration is to listen to their suggestions and ideas. A laboratory assistant who works for a small pharmaceutical research company said she liked the way the owner encouraged them to express their ideas for improving procedures at monthly meetings and actually tested suggestions and put some of them into practice.

Alternative Options

If you cannot afford to hire an employee or are not ready to enter into all the regulations and requirements that hiring employees involves, you may want to consider other options for getting help.

FAMILY AND FRIENDS

Whether on farms or in the family store, millions of people in our country have worked in family businesses. If you hire family, you could be eligible for certain tax breaks, and child labor restrictions generally do not apply to having your children work for you (except for mining, manufacturing, or hazardous jobs).*

There are pros and cons about having family or friends work for you. It can be difficult to separate business from family issues, and strained relations can result. Some children grow up resenting that they were forced to work with their parents, siblings, or other relatives. Others say that working in their family businesses gave them a good work ethic and understanding of financial matters. As mentioned previously in Chapter 1, many studies conducted by universities and agencies around the world have shown that many entrepreneurs who had one or both parents who were self-employed were inspired to start businesses.

If you plan to hire your family members, discuss frankly any problems you could foresee. Talk to each other about your mutual expectations and agree to discuss openly any concerns about the business. If possible, agree to keep the working relationship on a professional level and refrain from asking for personal favors that you would not request from a nonrelated employee.

Allen Hart, CWAHD.com, Christian Work at Home Dads (www.cwahd .com), says, "Depending on your business, there may be work that you can handle for your spouse. For example, with my wife's web site, Christian Work at Home Moms (www.cwahm.com), Jill will often need someone to write a script,

---

* Check with state and federal departments of labor to be sure you are not violating any labor laws.

set up an e-mail account, or proofread a document. Some of the tasks aren't going to be the most glamorous but five minutes could save your partner hours of time and added stress."

Many successful businesses started as family ventures and were passed on from generation to generation. Working with relatives can be beneficial, but only if mutual respect and standard business operations are followed.

FURTHER OPTIONS FOR HELP

- *Professional employer organizations (PEO):* PEOs help businesses of all sizes grow by freeing up the principals to concentrate on their core product or service and not office administration. You hire your employees and set their wages, but PEOs handle the human resources tasks of payroll, insurance, workers' compensation, taxes, benefits, legalities, applicant background checks, and other employee-related matters.
- *Employee leasing companies:* You contract with the leasing agency to provide workers for a specific period of time.
- *Interns:* Check with high schools and colleges to see if they have intern programs for students who wish to work part-time in the industry of the professions and careers that they plan to pursue after graduation. College students majoring in business and marketing can bring new promotional insights that are being taught.
- *Business and office support services:* These companies handle a wide range of clerical and word processing services. Some specialize in certain professions and industries.
- *Virtual assistants (VA):* VAs are microbusiness owners who provide administrative and personal support to clients in long-term and deeply collaborative relationships. VAs free a client up to do more of what their client loves and does best.
- *Special populations:* Many senior citizens like to continue to work at part-time positions and their maturity and experience can give a boost to your business. You might also contact country workshop programs or businesses with employees with special needs to see what services or products they can provide.

No matter which option(s) you choose to get help, your business will fare better with the best persons you can find to help you.

Put a Virtual Assistant to Work for You

Kelly Poelker

Small business owner + Virtual assistant = Bigger Business Image

For years now, many small business owners have recognized the advantages of partnering with a virtual assistant to start, maintain, and grow their businesses at a fraction of the cost to hire an employee. Why? There are too many advantages to list here, so let me just focus on one in particular that you might not be aware of—big company image.

A virtual assistant empowers you to market your business as a team, not just "you" as the business owner. By having a virtual assistant in another part of the country, or world for that matter, you can even market multiple office locations. It's not unusual for customer service or order fulfillment to be handled outside of the company "headquarters."

Utilizing unified messaging services like FreedomVoice that offer a toll-free number with multiple extensions (among other benefits) enables the team to appear much bigger to callers when you can offer a menu of departments they can reach—even if it's just you and your VA taking the calls. Always use plural pronouns like "we" and "us" when referring to the company in your marketing materials, conversations, and correspondence. As a trusted and vital member of the team, your virtual assistant can easily become an extension of your business and allow you the room to grow while not getting bogged down with details. And, you can do it all while saving hundreds (and thousands) of dollars a year on office rental, employee taxes, benefits, vacations, and such that you would incur if hiring an employee.

Kelly Poelker is a master virtual assistant and president of Another 8 Hours, Inc. (www.Another8Hours.com).

Suggested Resources

Associations

International Virtual Assistants Association, www.ivaa.org, networking, directory of VAs.

National Association of Professional Employer Organizations, www.napeo.org, networking, referrals.

Book

American Bar Association Legal Guide for Small Business: Everything a Small-Business Person Must Know, from Start-up to Employment Laws to Financing and Selling a Business by American Bar Association (ABA) (New York: Random House Information Group, 2000).

Web Info

www.Entrepreneur.com/howto, *Entrepreneur* magazine's free, online, how-to guide, "How to Hire and Orient a New Employee" and other human resource guides.

www.score.org/guides.html, SCORE's 60-second guides, "Employee Recruiting," "Hiring the Right People," and "Training Your First (or 50th) Employee."

57. Subcontracting

When Is an Employee *Not* an Employee?

The IRS (www.IRS.gov) says in its online page, "Self-Employed Individuals or Independent Contractors (ICs)," "If you are in business for yourself, carry on a trade or business as a sole proprietor or an independent contractor, you generally would consider yourself as a self-employed individual. You are an independent contractor if the person for whom you perform services for has only the right to control or direct the result of your work, not what will be done, or how it will be done." The key word here is *control.*

As an IC *you* are in control of your work and with whom you do business. It also applies to you when you hire or subcontract a self-employed individual or a service to help you. If you dictate to workers when, where, and how they work, they will be more likely to be considered as employees according to IRS criteria and you will have to cover salary, payroll taxes, unemployment, workers' compensation insurance, and other benefits.

True independent contractors, however, are *not* your employees and are responsible for reporting their own taxes and insurances; they will usually work at their own locations, use their own tools, and use a written agreement or contract for their work. If you are unsure whether you are an IC or the work arrangement you have with those you hire fits IC criteria, consult with your accountant and a lawyer familiar with worker and independent contractor issues.

CONSULTANTS

There will be times when you reach roadblocks in your business's progress: Your sales may be dropping; you need someone with specialized skills that you lack to help you complete a large project; or you just need a different perspective from someone experienced in your industry. That is when you can consider hiring a consultant. Some specialize in general business management, and others work in designated fields like marketing, human resources, or other specific areas of business.

You can find consultants through professional organizations, your experts, business directories, colleges and universities, or government agencies such as the ones mentioned in Method 52. Choose two or more to interview: You need to learn (1) whether they have experience handling the need you have, (2) what their fees are, and (3) whether they can provide an estimate or proposal stating how they will address your problem. Then have your lawyer draw up a contract clearly stating their and your responsibilities; the results you expect in a designated time period; and payment arrangements.

As mentioned, a contract will help keep the independent contractor status straight between the two of you.

After using a consultant, assess the value the person brought to your business so you can modify any future contracts or arrangement details.

Negotiating Contracts

Legal experts advise you to have a contract, verbal or written (preferred), whenever hiring or being hired for jobs. Even if you make a verbal agreement, you should write up the terms and both sign it to prevent future misunderstandings. When presenting a contract to the parties involved, however, never feel you or the person to whom you are offering a contract have to accept all the provisions. As one expert told a business owner, "Everything's negotiable."

Before you sign a contract or want to have one created, educate yourself with some of the common boilerplate language so you will better understand the basic provisions offered you or vice versa, such as disclaimers, noncompete clauses, and waivers that will cover unforeseen circumstances should either of you be delayed or unable to complete a project.

Knowing what you want in a contract will save you and your lawyer time in creating the one you want written or reviewed. You might want your lawyer to put the following terms into contracts you are presenting or add them to any contracts that a business gives you—the stages of a project when either of you can be paid or pay; and the conditions that permit either of you to terminate the contract before the work is completed.

When it doubt, follow your legal advisor's advice and do not allow yourself to be rushed into signing a contract you do not like.

Suggested Resources

Books

> *Consultant and Independent Contractor Agreements,* 5th ed., by Stephen Fishman (Berkeley, CA: Nolo Press, 2000). Book and CD-ROM.
>
> *Working for Yourself: Law and Taxes for Independent Contractors, Freelancers and Consultants,* 6th ed., by Stephen Fishman (Berkeley, CA: Nolo Press, 2000).

E-Form Kit

> "How to Safely and Legally Hire Independent Contractors," forms and instructions to use to hire independent contractors, order through Nolo Press www.nolo.com (company has other publications dealing with the legal aspects of having employees).

Web Info

> www.Entrepreneur.com/howto, *Entrepreneur* magazine's free, online, how-to guides, "How to Hire Subcontractors to Reduce Your Load" and "How to Hire Professional Service Providers."

www.IRS.gov, IRS publication number 1779: "Independent Contractor or Employee?"

www.toolkit.cch.com, "Business Owner's Toolkit", search "Business Tools" for a free independent contractor agreement to download.

58. Partnering

To Be or Not to Be a Partner

You may be best (personal) friends with someone, but that does not guarantee you and that friend or even a third person will get along in a business arrangement. Statistics show that a large percentage of partnerships fail due to lack of communication about each partner's duties and responsibilities, money issues, marketing focus (which directions to take their business), and even jealousy over who gets credit for the success of the business.

Two women who were friends for over 25 years entered a specialty food and catering business. When one of the women married, however, she wanted to include her husband and the other partner did not, so the partnership and the friendship ended on a sour note.

Before forming a partnership business structure, frankly discuss among all parties what strengths and maybe negatives you would bring to such a business relationship; your expectations; how you will handle disagreements; and what would happen if any of you should die or decide to leave. You may decide that it would be better if you work together, not as a formal partnership, but as a team of self-employed individuals.

Partnerships always sound good at first, but the dissolving of a formal one can be costly. Lawyer fees and court costs could prevent you from financially continuing the business, even if you should decide to buy out your partners' interests.

Joining Forces with Other Entrepreneurs

Another way to get assistance to grow your business is to collaborate with other entrepreneurs and business owners in efforts that will be beneficial to each other's ventures. The craft and artist business magazine, *The Crafts Report* (www .craftsreport.com) often features skilled artisans who work together to form one piece. For example, a woman who created custom footstools buys another woman's hand-painted buttons to decorate her stools. The woman with the buttons signs each one, so her product is individualized from the other woman's product.

The next section discusses some ways you might collaborate with other business owners.

MARKETING EFFORTS

Join together for cooperative marketing efforts. A group of antique shop owners located in a historic county, created brochures together that they placed in their shops for customers. The brochures included a description of each store and a map showing the locations. One of the shop owners said it encouraged customers who like to go antiquing to visit all the shops.

Additional ways to market together include sharing co-op advertising, jointly sponsoring fund-raising events for nonprofit organizations, networking marketing information, doing joint mailings, and teaming up on projects. With Internet access, many home business owners are forming virtual alliances by posting reciprocal links, articles, and tips, and by writing columns. They invite one another to be Internet radio guests or chat hosts and offer affiliate programs. If you are a distributor for a larger company, sometimes it will contribute money for your co-op advertising.

Make sure the entrepreneurs' skills and products and services with which you participate in joint ventures complement one another and that you share like business ethics and goals.

Joint ventures can save you money, increase the public awareness of your business, and form a strong networking chain and friendships.

How Your Competitors Can Assist You

Competitors can help promote your business. Here are some ways:

- *Like businesses, but different customers:* One lawn and garden center may specialize in providing shrubs and trees for consumers and another may sell annual and perennial flowers. They can carry one another's cards, give referrals, or place in their ads that their flowers or trees are from XYZ garden centers.
- *What is missing?* In conducting market research, survey potential customers for feedback about what is lacking in other businesses like yours and what would they like to see added in services or products?
- *Sincerest form of flattery:* Examine closely the successful competitors in your neighborhood or when you attend industry conferences to see if you can incorporate some of their marketing strategies into your own marketing plans, but with your own twist to attract new customers.

Using the wealth of knowledge from your network of experts, business friends, and others in combination with your own enthusiasm and hard work can help your business grow richer in profits and in strong business relationships that will help you when you need help.

Suggested Resources

Books

The Complete Partnership Book by Edward A. Haman (Naperville, IL: Sourcebooks, 2004).

The Partnership Book: How to Write a Partnership Agreement, 6th ed., by Denis Clifford and Ralph Warner (Berkeley CA: Nolo Press, 2001). Book and CD-ROM.

7

Grow with Innovative and Low-Cost Marketing Methods: Original and Fun Ways to Promote Your Business

Efforts to grow one's business need not be expensive or boring. Chapter 7 presents unique and economical ways to make your business stand out from its competitors. These suggestions will encourage you to evaluate your venture so you can originate your own creative marketing strategies.

Although some business owners would rather do anything but marketing and prefer, instead, to work on the production of their business offerings, other entrepreneurs love it. They seem to have a special knack at originating unusual but effective marketing activities within their business budget. Creativity is the process of generating new ideas or methods or of looking at old ways differently to solve problems. Vadim Kotelnikov, inventor, author, and founder of Ten3 Business e-Coach (www.1000ventures.com) gives this definition of entrepreneurship combined with ingenuity: "Entrepreneurial creativity is coming up with innovative ideas and turning them into value-creating profitable business activities."

Entrepreneurial creativity can be used to find business niches, solve problems and, in marketing terms, to attract new or regular customers in unusual or unique ways that make you and your business stand out from the competition. Here are some ideas and resources that may spark your own entrepreneurial creativity.

59. Market Creatively

Marketing Innovation Guidelines

No matter whether you are a fan of pro football, many businesspersons like to watch the Super Bowl for the commercials as much as for the game. In fact, these television commercials and their cost make almost as much news as the event in itself. The following day, TV stations usually have advertising experts analyze these costly ads and rate them as the best and the "worst." The consensus of these experts is that no matter how humorous or poignant these commercials are, if they do not fix in the viewers' minds *who* the advertisers are and *what* benefits they were trying to sell, then the ads were not worth even a few dollars, let alone the millions these companies spent per minute. The marketing moral here is that creativity and originality are worthwhile techniques only if your message leads to company recognition or moves people to purchase your products or services and increase your profits.

Here are guidelines to help make your creative marketing more effective:

- Know your target market. Review the findings of your market research and get current feedback from potential customers, especially if you are launching new offerings or thinking of revising your present ones.
- Update yourself on your industry's current trends, competitors' recent activities, and the media's perception of your industry.
- Once you know these current specifics, you can begin to search for an idea that will generate excitement for your product or service. A woman who had a toy shop sponsored a kite-flying event that took place at a local park in the windy month of March. She had experts demonstrate how to make your own kite and fly it, set up a showcase of vintage kites, and held a kite-flying contest. She had great press coverage, and of course, she had lots of kites for sale, along with books and materials for making kites.
- If you have decided to include the excitement factor in an ad or a publicity event, then also make sure to incorporate the benefits of your product or service to potential customers. You want them to remember your business and what it can do for them as well as the "Wow" factor that attracted them. The owner of the toy shop emphasized that the commercial kites she sold were easier to fly and less likely to be damaged if they crashed.
- Once you have the idea, the excitement factor, and the reason people should buy from you, you must decide what action you wish your customer to do. As funny as the famous Geico (with the green gecko) car insurance commercials are, the announcer ends every commercial urging television viewers to call or go online for free insurance quote comparisons. And the owner of the toy shop gave out plenty of discount coupons at the event to encourage people to visit her shop.
- Always analyze your creative marketing campaign afterward to see how effective it was. Like the Super Bowl commercials or movie trailers, even if your effort made the news, unless it translated into making more money for your business, then all it did was entertain. Unless you are in the entertainment business, you should scrap that method and start again. Do not be discouraged, though; creative thoughts seem to generate more creativity. Maybe you will come up with an original advertising tactic that

scores better profits than any of your big competitors who are spending far more with much poorer results.

Creative Marketing Principles

You may think all creativity is spontaneous and chaotic but innovative marketers follow similar, basic marketing principles:

- *Do something that no one else will do.* Kathy, a lawyer specializing in wills and estates, says she prefers to personally answer clients' phone calls. She says they are usually surprised at first because they expect an office assistant to answer her phones. Kathy says it saves time for her and her clients because they can immediately tell her their reasons for calling and not have to leave any messages. If she is in court or with a client, when clients call, she gets back to them the same day.
- *Try a new method of delivery.* One touring company in the Southwest drives tourists around in pink jeeps.
- *Offer coupons or discounts.* Lesley Spencer Pyle, author of the *Work-at-Home Workbook* (www.hbwm.com) says that offering a "sample" to let people try your product or service before purchasing can be advantageous. As a writer, you could offer one free hour to attract their business or free consultation to get people to call. You also could offer discounts to regular customers or those with large orders.
- *Put ads in alternative publications.* Stores or institutions frequented by the public often have free pickup publications that charge less for advertising than newspapers or magazines. A local free classified penny paper charges little for classified ads, and the papers are mailed to people in over four counties.
- *Use exceptional attention-getters.* The owner of a novelty light business, wears his flashing logo on a baseball cap and hands out business cards when people inquire about his lights. Another woman whose company makes canvas awnings had a tailor make her a business suit using her striped awning material. People not only noticed her unusual suit, they could examine the quality of the material.
- *Try tips from other industries.* See what has worked in other industries and try it with your own industry. You probably do not have a "Jumbo, the Elephant," that can walk through town like the one that advertised P. T. Barnum's circus, but maybe something related to your business can catch the eye of those who drive or walk by your storefront. An example is the life-size statue of a chef that stands outside a local restaurant. Many stores hire people to dress up in costumes and point to their sales signs as drivers go by. Car dealers have those huge inflatable characters or balloons. For prices usually less than typical billboard advertising, you could hire a professional window painter like Jeannie Papadopou-

los, aka "The Window Jeannie" (http://windowjeannie.ca). She is a Canadian artist who has developed a thriving venture, painting business owners' windows to attract potential customers from drive by and walk by traffic with colorful visual information announcing the owners' sales and other specials.

- *Attend live events.* One of the draws of a popular Renaissance fair is the jousting on horseback. The event is often featured in local television news reports. At a fudge shop on a resort town boardwalk, two employees stir the fudge in a huge copper kettle behind their storefront window. Many strollers pause to observe the fudge-making process and then walk inside to buy some candy.

- *Do the unexpected.* Rewarding customers with an unexpected thank-you note or a little gift of appreciation helps make an impression that you care about them and not just the sales.

- *Start the talk.* A unique feature or offer can create a "buzz" or a word-of-mouth curiosity about your service or product. In the late 1960s, a small airline company had its flight attendants change into different colorful outfits throughout the entire flight. Because of passengers' talk, people booked flights just to see the attendants' fashion show.

One caveat: Be careful your creative marketing strategies do not backfire. Think of the original movie of *King Kong* when he breaks out of his chains while he is on stage for a paid exhibition. You are unlikely to use a gorilla or elephant to grab people's attention, but make sure that your promotions are safe, are in good taste, and stay within your marketing budget.

Plan your marketing strategy carefully, so though it may appear spontaneous, you are in control. These are just a few of some of the basic ways you can implement innovative strategies. With a creative eye, analyze commercials in the media and take note of some unusual ways that people get attention for their name or for their businesses. Then have fun and try your own.

Suggested Resources

Books

Big Moo: Stop Trying to Be Perfect and Start Being Remarkable edited by Seth Godin, "The Group of 33" (New York: Penguin Group, 2005).

Off the Wall Marketing Ideas: Jumpstart Your Sales without Busting Your Budget by Nancy Michaels and Debbi J. Karpowicz (Holbrook, MA: Adams Media Corporation, 1999).

There's No Business That's Not Show Business: Marketing in an Experience Culture by Bernd H. Schmitt, David L. Rogers, and Karen Vrotsos (Upper Saddle River, NJ: Financial Times/Prentice Hall, 2003).

Software

Business E-Coaching, www.1000ventures.com, motivational programs including "Entrepreneurial Creativity."

Web Info

www.gmarketing.com, site of Jay Levinson, "Guerrilla Marketing" expert and author of many marketing books; site has articles, daily tips, and more.

60. Establishing an Unforgettable Business Image

The primary point in Method 32 was that once you had an established image for your business, it would be your marketing guide to help you stay consistent in all your marketing efforts. Here are several additional tips for marketing your business image to potential customers.

Marketing Your Image

All the following factors should work together to create a unique image that sets your business apart: price, style, quality, service, a variety of products or services, appearance, placement of your business. Review each of these components to see if one or more needs some readjusting (if your products are sold to outdoor sports enthusiasts, then your printed materials, products, photo or illustrations, should reflect ruggedness and outdoor scenes):

- Using your market research, review the profile of your ideal target customers and make sure your business image is part of what they want or need. Your research should have revealed the following about your prospective buyers—ages, hobbies, occupations, cultural background, jobs, education, family and marital status, and other characteristics. If you are targeting young persons who like to hike, ski, and snowmobile, then advertising should have scenes of young men and women participating in these sports, and the related products, or services that these customers will need to participate in their activities.
- Develop a visual representation or logo that your customers can connect to your offerings, products, and services that will benefit them. Think of the Nike "swoosh," or McDonald's Golden Arches.
- Always operate with professionalism. That includes how you treat your customers and employees, how you deliver your products, and whether you present your business as an efficient and well-run operation.
- Always be on the lookout for original, efficient, and effective ways to remind prospective customers of your business image. If you need assis-

tance, consult with a conceptual marketing expert who can help you focus your marketing activities to satisfy the needs of your targeted customers (see also Method 32).

Suggested Resources

Books

Before the Brand: Creating the Unique DNA of an Enduring Brand Identity by Alycia Perry, David Wisnom, and David Wisnom III (New York: McGraw-Hill, 2002).

Off the Wall Marketing Ideas: Jumpstart Your Sales without Busting Your Budget by Nancy Michaels and Debbi J. Karpowicz (Holbrook, MA: Adams Media, 2000). www.impressionimpact.com.

61. Budget Marketing

Making every dollar count is important when your market plan is on a tight budget. With some business savvy and strategies, you can use effective ways to find new customers that will be as good as, if not better than, businesses that pay more for advertising and promotions.

Highlighting the Benefits of Your Business

Whether your marketing budget is large or small, the way to get the most impact from your marketing plans is to emphasize the benefits your customers will receive from patronizing your business. Method 59 stressed that potential customers perceive the value of a product or service in terms of how it will improve their lives or solve a problem, and experts say that should be the main focus of your marketing strategies.

There are many car and truck manufacturers and they all produce vehicles with different features, but you choose one because you perceive it has benefits that will help you. You might buy a luxury car to enhance your professional image, or an all-wheel drive car if you need a vehicle that can take you safely through ice and snow to reach clients who are homebound, or a truck if you need to carry tools or tow a utility trailer.

To identify the benefits of your business, make a list of its features. Then, beside each feature, list the benefit your customers will receive from it. Debra M. Cohen (www.homereferralbiz.com) is the president of Home Remedies™ of New York, Inc., a homeowner's referral business. After finding reputable contractors in her own area for various remodeling jobs at her home, Cohen came up with the idea of her business and how it would benefit both home owners and contractors. She says, "I figured homeowners in my community could benefit from a service which would prescreen contractors, and reliable contractors could benefit from a service which would help them to promote their businesses."

When a customer calls, Cohen arranges an appointment with the appropriate contractor; once a contractor has been hired, Cohen is available to answer questions, address concerns, and ensure that the job is completed to the homeowner's satisfaction. There is no charge to homeowners for using Cohen's Home Remedies, but each contractor in her network pays a prenegotiated commission on all new business secured. Cohen's best marketing methods are word-of-mouth referrals and direct mailings to targeted homeowners that she says generate a 10 percent response rate each month. Cohen's service *benefits* both her homeowner clients and the contractors in her network.

The same pertains to a product. An electrical drill for a woodworking hobbyist will have different features from the ones found on an electrical drill that serves a full-time carpenter. Based on their features, the maker of each drill will then advertise its benefits for the targeted buyer.

Make a total count of your business's benefits and combine them into a statement that summarizes them all. Place this statement on all your promotional materials and web site, and from it you can develop your tagline, slogans, and overall marketing position.

Assemble an Outstanding Portfolio

Carol, from Chicago was one of the first professional organizers in her area. To help educate the public and reach potential customers, she sent press releases to the media and had a number of newspaper features written about her and her new type of (at the time) business and consumer service. Carol also included before-and-after photos of her clients' homes and offices that she had organized, along with testimonials. She then went to a local office supply store and had all the newspaper clippings, photos, and clients' comments bound into packets to hand out to prospective new customers and selected media who requested them. She also compiled a portfolio for display at trade shows and business meetings and expanded it as she tackled new projects. Carol said the packets and her portfolio were a big reason that her business took off before many other organizers succeeded in her area.

Many professionals—from photographers, web site designers, and graphic artists to skilled artisans and crafters, balloon decorators, and garden designers—develop work portfolios. But like Carol, business owners who provide services also can compile a portfolio. Besides photos and media clippings, you could include awards and other recognition certificates, samples of your work, your bio and resume, and anything else that shows off your expertise.

Before making a portfolio, try to look at portfolios that others have made. Then decide on the format and presentation that you prefer and that will be the most effective showcase of what you have to offer. Have a logical order of your items and a representative cross-section of your best work. Keep it simple, label each page, and use quality paper and binders to enhance your professional image. Update it periodically as your business grows. It may take a little effort in assembling your portfolio, but a good one can differentiate you from your competitors and persuade customers to hire you first.

Using Marketing Interns

Some business owners participate in master of business administration (MBA) Internship programs, paying for their help, while the students get credit for their experience in helping business owners with marketing strategies or projects. If you are interested in having marketing interns, contact your insurance agent to see if you and they are covered by liability and accident insurance. Experts advise you to plan the activities that you will have the intern become involved in, but remember you are training this student, too. Also check the regulations about using interns as volunteers and not as substitutes for paying positions.

One of the benefits of having interns is that they can keep you updated about the current marketing trends and the latest technology, as well as bring you new ideas and assist in your ongoing projects. In turn, you can provide them with hands-on experience and feel pride in enabling young persons to gain experience that can help them in their future careers.

Learn Low-Cost Marketing and Advertising Methods

Study and learn low-cost marketing approaches to jump-start a new business or to give a boost to an existing one:

- Be your own copywriter. If you cannot afford to hire an advertising agency or marketing consultant, you can learn basic copywriting skills from books, software, or courses to help you compose your own ads.
- Do not ignore traditional marketing methods. The Internet is a great medium to reach potential customers, but not everyone has access to the Internet and it is not always the best way to target a market.
- Apply often, if not daily, inexpensive marketing methods like networking and word-of-mouth advertising. The more you do these, the more proficient you will become and the greater exposure you and your business will get.
- Keep your eye on changes in your industry and your existing customers' preferences so you can change your offers or approaches to meet their needs. You have an advantage because you can make changes in your offerings much more quickly than larger competitors.

Stay the (marketing) course. Do not give up. Successful entrepreneurs are persistent. Build on your successes and pledge to use a mix of creative and traditional marketing tools every day, so your business will survive and thrive (see also Method 74).

Suggested Resources

Books

Advertising without an Agency Made Easy 3rd ed., by Kathy Kobliski (Irvine, CA: Entrepreneur Press, 2005). www.silentpartneradvertising.com.

Big Business Marketing for Small Business Budgets by Jeanette Maw McMurtry (New York: McGraw-Hill, 2003).

Guerrilla Marketing for Free: Dozens of No-Cost Tactics to Promote Your Business and Energize Your Profits by Jay Conrad Levinson (Boston, MA: Houghton-Mifflin, 2003).

Web Info

www.ducttapemarketing.com, John Jantsch's web site of small business ideas, strategies, and resources.

www.Entrepreneur.com/marketing/, *Entrepreneur* magazine's online article, "Promoting for Pennies," by Gwen Moran, 20 creative ways to promote your business.

www.internships.com, sells the "National Internships Guide 2006."

www.internshipprograms.com, internship programs.

www.score.org/guides.html, SCORE's 60-second guide, "Marketing on a Limited Budget."

www.silentpartneradvertising.com, Kathy J. Kobliski, advertising specialist, articles.

62. Networking Partners

As mentioned in Chapter 6, establishing a strong network of contacts can be one of the best ways to market your business. Effective networking costs little in dollars and cents, but it requires you to invest time in finding the best people to include in your network and in fostering relationships that will be beneficial to all involved. It is good to have a mix of people in your network, from local politicians and entrepreneurs, to bankers, media representatives, and marketing experts.

Peter Bowerman, author of *The Well-Fed Writer* and *The Well-Fed Writer: Back for Seconds* (www.wellfedwriter.com) says, "Make it easy for someone to help you." Bowerman continues with these tips:

- Always look at things through the eyes of your target audience. When I'm asking someone to help me out, if I make it easy for them to do it, chances are, it'll happen. For example, as a self-publishing author.
- If I want someone to post a review on Amazon (after they wrote a 'Great book!' e-mail), I send them the actual link to my book on Amazon. I don't expect them to find it themselves. Result: 100+ reviews with an average of close to five stars.
- When I send out review copies (and the e-mails announcing their arrival), I include a link to my "Media Resources" section (www.wellfedwriter.com/media .shtml): everything a reviewer needs to put a review together (including 'news pegs'). I don't count on them to figure out the angles; I spell them out.
- If I want some 'key influencer' to promote an event of mine to their communities, I send a ready-to-go promo blurb, as if written by them, so that it's just a simple cut-'n'-paste to get it handled.

"In each of these cases, I'm thinking about them, their reality, their pressures, and the fact that I'm not a high priority in their world. And because I'm not, I need to make it as easy as humanly possible for them to do what I'm asking them to do," says Bowerman.

Networking relationships are only as good as the people who are involved make them. Designate a file for each person in your network and when you come across a new lead or information that might be beneficial to your partners, list it in their file and periodically send it to them. Whenever you ask for assistance, remind them that you are always ready to return the favor in the form of endorsements, contacts, or referrals.

A networking group is never static. You should constantly be on the outlook for new contacts. Some members of your group will drift away or go into other fields, but the best ones are those that encourage and help each other to achieve profitable success (see also Methods 14 and 51).

Suggested Resources

Books

Make Your Contacts Count: Networking Know-How for Cash, Clients, and Career Success by Anne Baber and Lynne Waymon (New York: American Management Association, 2001).

One Phone Call Away: Secrets of a Master Networker by Jeffrey W. Meshel and Douglas Garr (New York: Portfolio, 2005).

Power Networking Second Edition: 59 Secrets for Personal and Professional Success, 2nd ed., by Donna Fisher (Austin, TX: Bard Press, 2000).

63. Word-of-Mouth Advertising

Studies conducted by major research companies over the past two decades reveal that a majority of people are influenced by the opinions of family and friends when deciding what car, appliance, music, movies, or other items to buy; where to shop or eat or visit; and what professionals and businesses they can rely on. That is why word-of-mouth (WOM) should be part of your ongoing market plan.

Maria T. Bailey, CEO of BSM Media (www.bsmmedia.com) and an expert on marketing to mothers, says, "Distribution is King when it comes to marketing a product or business or even yourself. You have to get the word out. Distribution includes creating a buzz about your business, generating impressions online, scattering your name all over the place and expanding your reach/services as far as your next customer."

The following sections offer ways you can get the buzz going about your business and keep the referrals coming.

Getting Referrals

Raleigh Pinskey, author of *101 Ways to Promote Yourself,* says, "Don't leave money on the table or throw an opportunity out the window . . . just because you wouldn't ask for what you wanted." In this case, get in the habit of asking customers or clients after a sale or a completed service if they know anyone else who could use your business offerings. You can remind them of this through customer satisfaction surveys or follow-up phone calls.

Share referrals with other business owners whose target market is the same as yours. A computer consultant who makes house repair calls to home-based business owners might refer them to professional organizers if his clients' offices need to be more efficient and clutter-free; or an accountant can refer clients to independent bookkeepers or tax specialists. Lawn maintenance contractors that prefer to keep up the grounds of large companies' or apartment owners' can refer homeowners to lawn care services that specialize in the care of smaller properties of homeowners.

Periodically, get in touch with customers who have made purchases or used your services. Your call, letter, or e-mail may remind them that they could make another purchase or use your services again. Something as simple as a refrigerator magnet with your logo and phone number can prompt current customers to recommend you to their family or friends who have a problem similar to the one that you solved for the customer.

Never stop looking for other ways to encourage referrals.

Rewarding Referrals

Reward those who have brought you new customers with thank-you cards, entertainment tickets, gift baskets and food gifts, a free session, or discounts toward their next purchase of your products or your services; or find some other way to show your appreciation.

Successful marketing methods need not be expensive, and can even be fun. There are many more economical and innovative methods you can try to get your business noticed. The challenge for you is to find the ones that help you establish a steady stream of customers to keep your cash flow positive and profitable.

Suggested Resources

Association

Word of Mouth Marketing Association, www.womma.org, trade association advocating ethics and standards, teleclasses.

Audio

Target Your Referrals Expert Roundtable, CD with referral ideas by small business expert, Denise O'Berry, www.targetreferrals.com.

Books

Buzz: Harness the Power of Influence and Create Demand by Marian Salzman, Ira Matathia, and Ann O'Reilly (Hoboken, NJ: John Wiley & Sons, 2003).

Buzzmarketing: Get People to Talk about Your Stuff by Mark Hughes (New York: Portfolio, 2005).

Instant Referrals: How to Turn Existing Customers into Your #1 Promoters by Bradley J. Sugars (New York: McGraw-Hill, 2005).

The Secrets of Word-of-Mouth Marketing: How to Trigger Exponential Sales through Runaway Word of Mouth by George Silverman (New York: AMACON, 2000).

E-Book

Buzz Marketing: 10 Easy Ways to Get Word of Mouth by Ilise Benun. www.marketing-mentor-store.com.

Web Info

www.buzzoodle.com, Buzzoodle is a web site with resources, articles, an e-zine, and a book about buzz and word-of-mouth marketing.

8

Grow through the Media and Your Contacts: Leveraging Positive Press Coverage for Your Business

Getting potential customers to notice your business is the most important goal in enabling your business to grow, expand, and succeed. Using the media and other public relations (PR) tactics is an excellent way to get many people to notice your business at little or no cost. However, there is a difference between advertising and PR, and every entrepreneur should understand this to get media coverage. Chapter 8 presents ideas for getting publicity for your business, tips for approaching media contacts, and some secondary products you can create for additional profits.

64. Attracting and Producing Publicity for Your Business

Publicity is getting coverage in the media. You generally do not have control over what is written or said about you or your business or other matters related to you as you do in ads or other paid promotions. Some business owners or self-employed persons have a knack for attracting publicity, good and bad. Though it is said that even "bad" publicity is "good" publicity, it is better to learn how to generate good coverage and build credibility among your customers.

Public Relations Tips

As part of your business's market plan, map out a PR strategy with objectives and specific goals to help increase your visibility and profitable leads. Remember, you have to communicate who *you* are. Let people get to know you, your business's mission, and why they should buy from you. Here are some additional tips:

- Learn which media will be most likely to reach your target customers: Consumer publications or newspapers? Business journals? Network or cable TV? Radio stations (which ones?); Professional or trade journals? Other?
- Send news that will be of specific interest to your potential customers. If you are a computer consultant whose customers are small business owners, send your information to the editors of business journals or a newspaper's business editor.
- Keep an updated database of those media contacts who have accepted your press releases, letters, and tips.

Just like all plans, review your PR plan periodically to evaluate if these venues are helping you achieve your goals and meet your objectives.

Grabbing Media Attention

When Debra M. Cohen launched her Home Owner Referral Network (www .homeownersreferral.com) on a shoestring budget, she challenged herself to find inexpensive ways to market her business. Cohen says, "By far, the most effective promotional tool I've discovered is press attention. Once my business was successfully up and running, I decided to approach local papers with my story. After only a few weeks a newspaper editor contacted me regarding my business and ran a half-page article about my company in the business section of the paper. My phone didn't stop ringing—I must have received more than 100 calls from homeowners and contractors in the area who were interested in my services. The third-party endorsement of my business and the exposure were invaluable!"

It is "free" advertising when your name and business get into publications, and like Cohen's example, it can have far-reaching, positive effects for your business launch and growth. Editors and reporters receive calls everyday from people who want coverage, but not everyone's story or request is news, especially when it comes to business. Here are more tips for gaining publicity:

- You have to have news to report. Starting a new business, opening new headquarters, sponsoring a public event or contest, receiving an award, are all items that an editor will see as something to cover.
- Look for an interesting angle or "hook" that makes you or your business different from others. The fact that two women owned a music lesson business was not newsworthy, nor was the fact that they subcontracted with local school districts whose budgets could not fund individual music instruction for students; what *was* newsworthy was that they were able to

teach out of their specially equipped van that they parked at each elementary school. That hook got them a mention in a story about self-employed women.

- Springboard from a current news story. If a newspaper or television covers a story or announces that it is going to do a series that relates to your business, send them some tips or another point of view based on your own experience.

Think in terms of headlines. If your story lead is not interesting or worthy of attention, then rethink how to present it or look for another angle that will grab the media's attention.

Media's Likes and Dislikes

The care and feeding of media is not that difficult. There is an unwritten protocol in developing a lasting relationship with your media contacts. Here are some common likes and dislikes:

- *Dislike:* The first and foremost is not to hassle media contacts by constantly calling them for coverage. Wait until you have real news.
- *Like:* They like information that they can use for their research like statistics and persons they can interview (besides yourself).
- *Dislike:* They do not like being called when they have a tight deadline.
- *Like:* They want you to be immediately available for a quick quote when they are on a tight deadline. If they leave a message, get back to them ASAP.
- *Dislike:* You have too many words in your press release or information, or you have too large a press kit.
- *Like:* They want clearly labeled, high-quality photos.
- *Dislike:* Avoid sending material that is not appropriate to media's audience; do not send it to the wrong contact person (editor, reporter, writer); and do not misspell their names and titles.
- *Like:* They want sources they can depend on and who act with professionalism.
- *Like:* They appreciate thank-you notes for including you, with some of your comments about how their audience responded to their coverage.

If possible, ask editors and media contacts how they prefer to be contacted, their pet peeves, the best times to be reached, and what they specifically like in the terms of news and subjects.

Finding Key Editors and Reporters

In planning your public relations strategy, the first step is to thoroughly research and make a list of the best editors and reporters for covering your business and reaching the most receptive audience. You can find these on the mastheads of newspapers' editorial pages; or call the media's main switchboards or see the contacts listed on the media's online site for e-mail or phone numbers; or visit your public library and look in directories like *Bacon's Newspapers/Magazines Directory, The Working Press of the Nation,* or *Gale Directory of Publications and Broadcast Media, Gebbie Press' All-in-One Media Directory* (can search online at www.gebbieinc.com). You can also subscribe to industry publications like *Editor and Publisher* (www.editorandpublisher.com) and others for other media contacts. If you can get your story picked up by a wire service like the Associated Press (www.ap.org) or United Press International (UPI) (www .upi.com), or news syndicates such as the Los Angeles Times Syndicate, N.Y. Times News Service, or King Features (www.kingfeatures.com), your news could possibly reach newspapers and radio stations around the country.

Joan Stewart, a publicity expert who publishes an e-zine, *The Publicity Hound's Tips of the Week* (www.PublicityHound.com), offers these PR tips:

- Don't buy expensive paid advertising unless you absolutely have to. Rely instead on free publicity in newspapers, magazines, radio and TV stations, and in print and electronic newsletters and blogs.
- Spend the time to get to know journalists who cover stories that your target audience needs and wants. Here are ways to build relationships:
- Never pitch a journalist unless you have read their publication, or seen their news show, or you are familiar with their work.
- When you have identified a journalist you want to contact, a good way to make an introduction is to call or e-mail them and comment on their work. It could be a story you thought missed a key angle. Or a TV show you found entertaining.
- Suggest other sources for the story you are pitching. Don't expect them to quote you exclusively.
- Ask "How can I help you?"
- Stay on their radar screen every three or four months by providing what they need.

Always double-check to see if your media contacts are still working for the media and if their contact information is still current before you send off your news. You can also find media contacts by asking for referrals from your networking partners, attending business owners' meetings and events, and going through Internet List groups.

Getting Media Kits

To acquaint yourself with media audiences, you can request their media kits. These kits are compiled for their advertisers and contain important information on their audience. Armed with data, you can slant your advertising and articles or publicity news to appeal to them. Typical kits include specific statistics and characteristics (the demographics) of their audiences: their education, occupation, marital status, family members, hobbies, their buying habits, and additional information gathered from the media surveys. These kits sometimes include important industry statistics that are good openings for your press releases or articles.

You might also request an editorial calendar so you can prepare article queries or plan to coincide one of your special events. Try to read sample issues and back issues from six months to a year, so you know what has been covered and can get an idea of the tone of the writing. Check the media's web site because they often have this information available online, usually under "advertisers," as well as their writer's guidelines if they accept articles. These kits, guidelines, and back issues are free market research that can help you in your public relations strategy.

In turn, in Method 66, there are essentials for putting together your own press kit, an important marketing tool in your public relations plan.

Suggested Resources

Audio

Media Madness: Effective Ways to Capture the Ongoing Interest of the Press by Nancy Michaels. Audio program, resource guide. www.impressionimpact .com.

Books

Guerrilla Publicity: Hundreds of Sure-Fire Tactics to Get Maximum Sales for Minimum Dollars by Jay Conrad Levinson, Rick Frishman, Jill Lublin, and Mark Steisel (Holbrook, MA: Adams Media Corporation, 2002).

The Publicity Handbook, New Edition: The Inside Scoop from More than 100 Journalists and PR Pros on how to Get Great Publicity Coverage by David R. Yale and Andrew J. Carothers (New York: McGraw-Hill, 2001).

Web Info

http://newsdirectory.com, newspapers listing.

www.101publicrelations.com, books and information about generating free publicity.

Publicity E-zines for Professionals, Organizations, Companies, Entrepreneurs, and Small Business Owners

www.publicityhound.com, *Publicity Hound,* published by Joan Stewart, publicity expert; excellent articles, e-books, e-zine

www.publicityinsider.com/freezine.asp, *Publicity Insider*, published by Bill Stoller.

www.score.org/guides.html, SCORE's 60-second guide, "Generating Publicity for Your Business."

65. Write a Newsworthy Press Release

Tips for Getting Your Press Release Published

A successful businesswoman told another woman who was seeking some tips on how to boost her present business, "There are tons of free ways to get great publicity. I would start with press releases to all your local papers, big and little. Look for a news story to tie in with or holidays or any other special event." Peggi Clauhs and her mother, Winnie McClennan attribute the successful launch of their home-based Pennsylvania cooking school, "The Cooking Cottage at Cedar Spring Farms" (www.thecookingcottage.org) to their press release that was published in a nearby city's newspaper. "Start (your business) off with a great press release," says Clauhs. Their press release brought customers from all over the readership area and their business has now expanded into hosting cooking and gourmet one-day trips to New York City and Philadelphia as well as European culinary tours.

What components make it most likely that your press release will be published? Here are some questions to help you:

- Does your press release announce real news or is it beneficial to the media's audience?
- Does the lead sentence have a *hook*—an interesting statistic or fact or story? If you send an electronic press release, your subject line should have the topic and a short hook, such as "Baby Boomers Need Organizing," which a professional organizer used for a press release.
- Is your press release in the format that the editor prefers? Is it double-spaced, and does it answer the five "Ws"—Who? What? Where? When? Why? Does your release have your contact information? Do not include your business or personal e-mail address in the body of your press release or you risk receiving spam mail. If you send virtual press releases, they will be deleted if they are sent as attachments. If you are not sure of the format, ask.
- Is your most important information included in the beginning paragraphs of your news release? Editors cut from the bottom up.
- Does it sound like an ad for your business or (better) does it include experts' quotes, statistics, and other comments by individuals?
- Have you concentrated on a main point?
- Have you proofread it for typos, grammar, and clarity?

- Did you mention in your release additional items such as free samples, pamphlets, or tip sheets that are available on request?
- Do you have high-quality photos (or ones available should an editor request one) to accompany your press release?
- Do you plan to follow up and contact the persons who received your press releases to see if they have any questions or need additional information?

Once you have a successful press release template, you can easily modify it to fit each media's slant and target audience. If you need assistance in writing press releases, contact a freelance business writer or a public relations firm.

Who Gets Your Releases? (Is Your List Current?)

With virtual or print press releases, you will save time and money and develop stronger media relationships if you submit your releases and information to the people designated to receive them, and the audiences who will be interested in your information. You can damage your credibility if you send mass press releases, either through "snail mail" or over the Internet, to editors or writers who never cover your topic or to unknown e-mail address recipients. In the latter case, these mailings can be designated as spam and you risk having your e-mail account shut down.

If you care enough about getting good press coverage for your business, then you have to show equal respect for the media by ensuring your releases are formatted correctly, are worthy to be published, and are sent to the correct persons. It is just common sense! Keep your list of contacts current, so your press releases do not end up in trash cans, metal or virtual. You can prevent sending out doubles of your press releases to the same persons if you keep up-to-date records of all your mailings. In a computer file or on paper create a chart that includes the following:

- Media's name, address, web site, main switchboard number
- Contact person's name, title, phone, e-mail
- Title of press release and the date sent
- Published or not
- Response to published release from audience, others
- Follow-ups of thank-you calls or notes, comments, or corrections

How Often to Send out Releases

Public relations specialists say you can send out a press release to your media sources as often as once or twice a month. Your release should announce something interesting such as a new product or service you are introducing, an anniversary you are celebrating, awards or recognition you have received from your industry, a workshop you are conducting, a speaking engagement you have coming up, a free service or product you are donating, or a notable person you are hiring or partnering with.

If you read a daily newspaper or newswire online and note the releases and the topics being submitted, you will get some ideas about what is important to the media and what is not. If you repeatedly send out dull or nothing-is-really happening news releases, you will lose your credibility among your media sources and even your "happening" releases may get rejected.

One author uses some "off the wall" tactics when she sends press releases in the postal mail. Depending on the publication and editors, she will send out her press releases in envelopes of different colors, will personally type or handwrite the editors' addresses for a more personal note, or will write "requested material" on some of her press release packages. These may be creative ways to catch editors' attention, but your press release still has to be written in the expected format and contain content that is newsworthy to have a chance at being published. See the sidebar sample of a press release from Wyatt-MacKenzie Publishing, Inc.:

Wyatt-MacKenzie Publishing, Inc.

"I think I can. I think I can. I think I can. I can! I can! I can!"

The Little Co-Op that Could—The One-Year Anniversary of the Mom-Writers Publishing Cooperative has 18 mom authors and their inde publisher chanting this mantra about publishing their books and competing in the big leagues. Although six thousand miles separate them collectively, three thousand pages bind them—as does a share in each other's royalties, publicity leads, book promotion costs, and both publishing and parenting advice. In Year One, the Co-Op has . . .

- Garnered six book award finalist nods including *ForeWord* magazine's Book-of-the-Year.
- Appeared in over a dozen print magazines individually and as a Co-Op including a 3-page feature in a total of 180! magazine issues recently featured on *Good Morning America*.
- Appeared in over twenty newspapers nationwide including a feature in the *Chicago Tribune* and a full-page story in the *Boston Herald Parents & Kids*.
- Authors who were interviewed on over 40 terrestrial and Internet radio shows.
- Authors who had four major TV appearances including *Weekend Today*.
- Members who have launched three noteworthy industry resources: The Mom-Writers Literary Magazine, Mom-Writers Talk Radio, and The Author's Companion: A Self-Guided Course on Book Promotion CD-ROM.

This unique group is the brainchild of publisher and designer Nancy Cleary. "For seven years we put out one mainstream title a year and realized the difficulty of one new author trying to get big enough publicity to move books out the front of bookstores instead of the back."

To attract a hearty brood of publicity-savvy authors for her Co-Op, Cleary offered her own version of a five-digit advance package including author branding, promotion, and career-building. Membership dues help Cleary to keep her small press in the black. "I am providing an unparalleled publishing experience, and positioning these authors for career success that is bigger than their books."

If you miss us at the 2006 BEA, watch for us in 2007 for the prerelease party of the Co-Op's collaborative project documenting their journey, "A Book Is Born" (Wyatt-MacKenzie, NOV 2007).

Wyatt-MacKenzie Publishing, Inc.
Mom-Writers Publishing Cooperative
Elevating the brand equity of mom authors with excellence
in design, packaging, publishing and promotions

541-964-3314 FAX: 541-964-3315
15115 Highway 36, Deadwood, OR 97430

Celebrating our EIGHTH YEAR of publishing moms
http://www.wymacpublishing.com

Happenings and Your Press Release (Timing)

Nancy Collamer, a career counselor and founder of Jobs and Moms (www.jobsandmoms.com) shares this favorite trick for getting free publicity for her web site: "I send a well-crafted e-mail to syndicated career columnists that either offers them 'hot tips' or provides insight on a recent news story related to 'Jobs and Moms.' Columnists are always looking for new story angles so they really appreciate getting input from experts. This strategy costs me nothing other than the time spent writing the e-mail and compiling the list of e-mail addresses. Since almost all the major media outlets have career columnists, I can get widespread PR coverage with just one e-mail," says Collamer.

Make it a point to read, watch, and listen daily to major media sources. Without actually getting a direct quote, you can mention a famous person's comment and its source in a press release if it pertains to your topic. It lends more authority to you as an expert and to the topic of your news.

Suggested Resources

Book

Effective Public Relations (Essential Managers Series) edited by Moi Ali and Adele Hayward (New York: DK Publishing, 2001).

Web Info

Press Release Distribution Services°

http://www.24-7pressrelease.com, Press Release Newswire, paid and free press release distribution services; pdf file of press release writing tips. www.prweb.com/pressreleasetips.php, press release tips and sample from PRWeb a press release distribution company.

www.press-release-writing.com, press release writing, distribution service, products, articles.

66. Press Kit Essentials

Designing a Low-Cost Promotional/Press Kit

Press (media) kits are ready packages of promotional information about you and your business that you can hand out to the media. Ask other business owners for samples of their press kits to get an idea of the format and what is typically included. Here are the most common components:

- Business name.
- Owner/contact person's name.
- Contact information: Address, phone, and fax numbers, e-mail address(es).
- Description of your business's services or products.
- Web site URL.
- Business profile (see Chapter 14, "Write a Dynamic Company Profile"). Be sure to include your own credentials and background.
- Business identity materials: Include business cards, catalogs, brochures, and small promotional products like pens, pencils, letter openers, and such.
- Your current press release. You can exchange old releases for new or revised ones depending on who is receiving your press kit.
- Photos: Good sizes are 5-inch by 7-inch or 8-inch by 10-inch; or postcards with your business's logo, and products or services highlighted on it. To save money, you can use color photocopies or black and white photos (some magazines like them).
- Press clippings of features about you and your business, but not too many. Include the most recent.
- Sample interview questions (see Chapter 14, "Radio Interview Tips").

You could also put all this information, including photos, on a CD and mail it; some media prefer this method of transfer.

° Listed here for their press release writing tips, not an endorsement.

Put all these materials into regular-sized folders. The cover is up to you. Just be sure to have your name and the business's name on the front. Visit your local office supply store to see which folders you prefer. Make sure the kit looks polished and professional and fits your business image. Get several opinions from friends or business associates or possibly an editor or marketing consultant who has seen or examined press kits.

When they are assembled, have them ready on request or send them to the media when you are involved in an event or are sending press releases around to receive publicity for another reason. Always have some with you when you are attending business meetings, conferences, or trade shows to give out to writers or reporters you may meet. Contact them later to see if they have any further questions.

Update your press kit as needed and maximize the opportunities it can provide.

Photos

Whether you are camera shy or love to have your photo taken, you will need photos for many purposes in your business: your web site, reporters, press kits, articles, brochures, book covers, and many other times. Customers like having a face with your name. Besides the usual head shots, have photos taken of you in action—when you are speaking or leading a workshop, demonstrating your products, or performing a service. Have several copies of each pose to give the media or editors when they request them, or to send along in your press kit or with press releases.

A professional printer can have color and black and white copies of your photos made up for you to distribute and also create photo postcards for you to give out or send.

DIGITAL IMAGES

With digital cameras' instant shots, you can take some inexpensive and excellent shots of your work or other pictures of you in different settings. These are easily downloaded into a file and can be sent as an attachment to recipients around the world. You can also take the disk or photo card to a department store or photo outlet and have the photos that you select printed out.

Read your digital camera's manual and some digital photography books and have fun experimenting with your camera at different settings and lighting. The results can enhance your presentations and printed materials that feature your work and your business.

PROFESSIONAL PHOTOGRAPHERS

There will be times you need a commercial photographer for your business. You may be putting together a catalog or planning other promotional projects. Before you contact a photographer, consider the setting of the proposed photos: indoor or outside, people or buildings, close-ups or action shots, color or black and white.

To find a photographer, check with your local business ownership organization for referrals. Ask how it was to work with these photographers. Talk to one or more photographers to compare pricing and their experience and ask to see some of their samples. Tell them what you need and request that they visit the setting for the photo shoot before actually taking the photos. Meet them and the photographers to get an idea of the conditions under which they will be taking the photos. Make sure you have signed photo releases from any of the persons featured in the photos. You might discuss who will own the copyright of the photos if you want to use them again in the future.

High-quality photos can enhance your business image and make your business appear larger than it really is.

Suggested Resources

Books

Digital Photography Pocket Guide, 3rd ed., by Derrick Story (Sebastopol, CA: O'Reilly Media, 2005).

New Publicity Kit by Jeanette Smith (Hoboken, NJ: John Wiley & Sons, 1995).

67. Maximizing Publicity with Contests and Awards

If you want to create some excitement for your business, you can enter one of the hundreds of small-business contests, ranging from local business awards to national events. Rochelle Balch, owner of a successful computer consulting business, encourages readers of her book, *Brag Your Way to Success,* to enter contests or try to be nominated for awards to boost their self-confidence and to gain recognition in their field and community. In her book, Balch illustrates her personal example of entering a contest for an award based on a business owner's community involvement and business success. Balch did not win, but was a finalist. As a finalist, Balch was featured on a televised segment and in a newspaper article (with photo) about the contest. She also said she met some new journalists and made media contacts that she has kept current, leading to additional public appearances.

Nominating Others

As part of fostering your networking relationships, if you see a contest or award nominations being accepted that would be appropriate for your business associates, contact them. If they are interested, offer to write promotion letters for them or assist in preparing their nominations. In the future, they may do the same for you. Volunteering on awards committees in your field will also raise your image of expertise and provide more opportunities for networking contacts.

Nominating Yourself

You know yourself; you know your business and what you have achieved. Most contest or award regulations permit self-nominations, usually with additional personal references. If you believe you are qualified and fit the criteria, then why not? Many people, especially women, believe it is wrong to brag, but when you are entering a contest or filling out an award application, it is not the time to be modest.

Research what awards are given out in your community, your industry, or your organization, and decide which ones you might qualify for. Find out whom to contact and review the application process. Have an updated biography, or "bio," or a resume ready to use for candidate interviews and as a general part of your publicity strategy. Make sure it lists your accomplishments to date.

A win will help your business gain respect and recognition, as the contest directors will list your name among the winners when notifying the press. You may not always win, but as in Balch's example, you can receive media attention just by entering or being a finalist. Even being a finalist is newsworthy enough to send out a press release. If you do win, make sure you notify all the media contacts on your list for more publicity potential.

If you do not win, try again. Balch says that she enters the same contest every year and will keep on doing so until she wins or they tell her to stop. When you win, you will really have something to brag about!

Suggested Resources

Books

Awards, Honors and Prizes (2 Vols.) edited by Kristin B. Mallegg (Farmington Hills, MI: Thomson Gale, 2005). Usually found in libraries' reference sections.

Brag Your Way to Success: The Guidebook to Self-Promotion by Rochelle Balch (Gendale, AZ: RB Balch & Associates, 2001). www.rbbalch.com.

68. Writing Pieces for Promotion

Writing is an effective method to publicize your business and become established as an expert in business or industry. You say you are not a writer? Well, if you have solved a problem, saved time or money, made *more* money, or developed a new material or technique, you definitely have something of interest to readers.

Before proposing to write for any market, you should (1) be familiar with the publication where you plan to submit an article or column, and (2) get a copy of the writer's guidelines or ask the editor what style and length of writing is preferred. There are many venues for your writing. Here (and in Method 71) are some tips for getting published.

Writing Columns

Most of us have a favorite columnist that we read every day in newspapers, magazines, or online in blogs or web sites. To even be considered as a columnist, you should have experience and credentials in business or your industry or some other special subject. You should also have had articles, books, or e-books published or formerly worked as a columnist in another publication. Many experts start out by being guest columnists, by providing "op-ed" essays that reflect their views on a specific topic, or by simply offering to answer subscribers' questions in a question-and-answer format.

Before you approach an editor, you should have several sample columns, published or unpublished, so the editor can review your style of writing.

Do your market research beforehand to see if there are existing columns like yours and if the publication uses freelance pieces or columns. The competition is stiff to become a regular columnist. Jodie Lynn, who writes the syndicated column, "Parent to Parent" (www.parenttoparent.com) shares some of her publicity tips and encouragement:

1. Spread the word yourself by contacting everyone you know about your endeavor. If you send out a press release, follow up by telephone.
2. Try to stay within a reasonable budget for press releases. By building a rapport with others in your area, you can ask them directly to help promote your business.
3. Offer your time in writing articles for web sites, magazines, and newspapers that could utilize your materials online or in print, for free. This, in turn, offers you free exposure and incredible advertising.
4. Turn negative remarks into positive ones.
5. Never give up on your dream.

Article Basics

There are general consumer and business (print) magazines like *Money* (*http://money.cnn.com/magazines/moneymag*), *Entrepreneur* (www.Entrepreneur .com), *Home Business Magazine* (www.homebusinessmag), and many trade publications like *Editor and Publisher* (www.editorandpublisher.com) for the newspaper industry, *Advertising Age* (http://adage.com) for the advertising industry; or *The Crafts Report* (www.craftsreport.com), for professional craftspersons and artists; and many professional journals, newsletters, print and electronic (e-zines);

and organizations' publications, that all need articles for their print and for their online versions.

Maria T. Bailey, author of several books on business and marketing, and editor and founder of BlueSuitMom.com, says, "There are several ways to establish your credibility. Get quoted which takes a good PR plan. Write articles and of course, distribute them. Many online resources and web sites are happy to take on free content. Find the right fit for your articles and make sure to include your byline with a link to your company web site."

Generally, trade and smaller publications are easier to break into and can build your reputation as a writer and expert, while providing you with some publishing clips (published articles, columns) that can lead to your being published in larger and higher-paying markets.

Writing gives you tremendous exposure because many published articles are also posted on the publications' web sites. As mentioned, know the publication you are writing for, and get a copy of its writer's guidelines. Ideally, the industry publications you read regularly are the ones you should first approach because you are already familiar with their content, their style, and more important, their audience.

If possible, only sell "first rights" to your article and retain the others, so you can offer reprints or revisions in noncompeting publications. Business books for writers, like the *Writer's Market,* explain the different types of rights and provide guidelines for approaching editors and publishers.

To maximize exposure, you should look for different aspects on one topic and write about those subjects for other publications. If you are a professional speaker writing about how speaking in public will help publicize your business, you could write on the different types of software and multimedia technology that workshop leaders and presenters could use to make their presentations more dynamic, some effective speaking tips and mannerisms to avoid, or how to make a living as a professional speaker.

If you compile columns or articles, you may discover a profitable writing niche that leads to self-publishing or in a publisher offering you a book contract.

Article Marketing

Diana Ennen

Writing articles is an excellent way to get exposure for your books, products, or web site. Naturally you want to write articles that have great content and that you have expertise in and also that you offer tips that others might not know. However, sometimes it is even more important is that you send the articles to the right places. The best article won't do much good if it won't get read. That's why I recommend personalized article submissions. Hire a VA [virtual assistant] or assistant to search for places on the Internet that have articles related to your topic. Make sure to follow those sites' guidelines for article submissions. Each [web] site is slightly different so spend the time to do it right. Look for places [web sites] with good page rankings from Google as you want to know that those articles will get read when you spend the time to place them.

Then comes follow-up. Sign up for Google Alerts under your name and topic and then the keywords for the article you just submitted. People use these Google Alerts today to find what they are looking for and this applies to not only the media. Potential buyers definitely do as well. They find this an easy way to get information on their topic of interest.

Now once you notice that your article or press release has been included in the Google Alert, you can write a brief letter of thanks to the people at the article submission place. Get personal. I think it helps for them to see that there's a "real person" behind that article. Also, submit more articles to them. They should go into your main database for the first ones to submit to when you write the next article and subsequent articles after that. Also, if you have a links page on your site, provide a reciprocal link. It is nice to give that site exposure as well.

For article writing, we know the importance of having them keyword driven, but many don't know why. One client commented to me once that she went to one of the places that I submitted to, which was an excellent place, however, it had thousands of articles. She was curious how her article could get recognized. I quickly showed her that once I typed in her topic and keyword in Google, her article pulled up and because that site was such an excellent site with great Google ratings, and because we took the time to use our keywords wisely, when someone was looking for her topic, they found her article.

By making article submissions a part of your regular marketing, you will see increased profits and also gain status as an expert in your Industry.

Diana Ennen is the author of *Virtual Assistant—The Series: Become a Highly Successful, Sought After VA, and Words from Home* (www.virtualwordpublishing.com) and publisher of *Sledgehammer* (www.pauloreyes.com).

Letters to Editors

If you are an effective letter writer, you can gain exposure for you and your business by writing a response agreeing or disagreeing with, or adding information to, a previous issue of a publication or a specific article in it. At the close of your letter, most editors permit you to list your brief contact information, which will allow unexpected leads or potential customers to contact you. Editorial pages will usually list their specifications and to whom you should address your letter.

As with other writing, here are some tips to get your letter published:

- Keep it brief, not more than 150 words, and try to respond within a few days of the publication's issuance.
- Mention the article you are responding to and why you are writing.
- Back up your stand with facts, figures, or quotes.
- Have someone proofread your letter for errors and clarity.
- Be professional in the tone of your letter. Write with feeling about something that matters to you. In this type of letter, you can and should express your opinion.
- End with a short summary of your position and do not forget to include your name and the credit or contact information the editor permits you to list for potential leads.

Authors enjoy getting feedback, and they may include your quote or comment in a future book. Send your e-mails via their web site or through their publisher.

Placement of "Tips" Articles or Tip Sheets

Online electronic newsletters and other small publications like *fillers*—extra little tidbits of business tips or statistics, brief news comments or statistics, checklists and quizzes, or troubleshooting Q&As. You can collect these as you operate your business. Some publications pay for fillers, while others do not. If they do not offer compensation, you can offer them nonexclusive, one-time publishing rights, and then you can submit these same tips to other, noncompeting online or print publications, also on a nonexclusive basis.

If you have doubts about your writing capabilities, enroll in some local how-to writing courses and then write and revise. The more you write, the better your skills will become, and the more opportunities will open up for publicizing your business with your words.

Suggested Resources

Books

> *2006 Writers Market* edited by Katie Brogan, Robert Lee Brewer, and Joanna Masterson (Cincinnati, OH: F & W Publications, 2005). Annual directory of thousands of market listings for book publishers, consumer magazines, trade journals, and contests and awards; and literary agents.

> *Syndication Secrets: What No One Will Tell You!* by Jodie Lynn (Fredonia, WI: Cedar Valley Publishing, 2006).

Electronic Book

> *How to Be a Syndicated Newspaper Columnist* by Angela Adair-Hoy. www.writersweekly.com.

Magazine

Writer's Digest, www.writersdigest.com, print magazine that covers the basics and all genres of the writing industry.

69. Learn Basic Media Training

The more you garner contact with the media, the better your chances will be of receiving invitations to be a speaker, to give radio interviews, or to be a television guest. Some people enjoy being in front of the public, while others freeze. If you do not feel confident in presenting yourself, you can contact professionals such as image consultants, speech specialists, or media trainers to help you with your wardrobe or public speaking skills or to help you be a better communicator for all possible media opportunities.

Some media trainers specialize in certain professions or industries, so ask for referrals from business associates, professional speakers, or local radio or television producers. Having this training will help increase your self-confidence, but you will have to practice often to perfect your skills. Start with smaller speaking engagements and workshops to build your confidence. Be well prepared and just be yourself: Talk about what you know—you and your business.

How to Get on Radio, TV, or in Films

As mentioned, if you want coverage from the media, research the best ones for you and your business. Find out whom to contact for your business story: the persons, editors, or producers who are assigned to cover certain subjects such as entertainment, community events, education, and other areas. Find out the best way to approach those reporters, writers, or producers. Then when you need media to cover your story, send in your press release and stage an event that will highlight your product or service.

Have that kite contest if you operate a toy store, or stage a fashion show for pets if you are launching a new line of pet accessories. The media likes unusual headline stories. If you hear of a national story that relates to your business, your book, or your product, contact local media who may want a local "angle" about this story.

Jeanette R. Benway, inventor of the stroller blanket, the "Cozy Rosie" (www .CozyRosie.com) says the best marketing strategy is to let a lot of people know about your product at no cost to you.

"This happens," says Benway, "when an article featuring your product appears on TV or in a magazine or newspaper. Reporters learn about your product by reading your press release. A press release is a fun or very interesting article that you write about your product to get their attention. This press release should be specific to the reporter or magazine that you are trying to reach."

She continues, "Recently we sent a press release to a television reporter whose segment is called 'Does it work?' challenging her to test Cozy Rosie, the blanket that stays on your stroller. She took the challenge, aired the test, and announced that Cozy Rosie Does Work! Nothing better than that!"

Have your press kit ready to give out and include a fact sheet about your industry and sample questions for the interviewer to ask you. Yes, it is contrived, but media hosts like to sound knowledgeable and with these sheets and questions, they will; and of course, you will *know* the answers.

Remember to thank your host and producers for having you as a guest. Stay in contact with any media that you meet and offer to supply them in the future with information or tips or leads to sources if they need someone to interview. They will appreciate your offer as a networking source. Offer, too, to be available for last-minute interviews on local radio and cable television shows as a "fill-in" guest to replace unexpected cancellations. Ask for a tape of your shows that you can show as demonstrations of your work when you talk or conduct workshops.

Three Professional Secrets to Make Your Radio Interview a Classic

Susan Harrow

1. *Personalize your presentation.* Listen to the host for cues as to how he addresses his audience. He may tell you about the weather, mention what has happened in their town, allude to a recent guest, or refer to a past show. When you link your information to what is personal and relevant to your audience, they will connect with you as one of them. While this is a more subtle way to relate to your host and audience, it often makes the difference between having people feel like you understand them or not.

2. *Create vivid word pictures using all the senses.* The Dean of the Graduate School of Journalism, University of California, Berkeley, and Chinese scholar Orville Schell told this resonant story on the radio. "In 1926, when a protest against Japan reached the gate of Heavenly Peace, the War Lord then in power fired in the crowd killing 50 people, wounding 100 and the square was bathed in blood. China's most famous writer Lu Hsun said a striking line: 'Lies written in ink will never disguise truth written in blood.'" In less than 25 seconds Schell has given you a picture of a political climate visually, auditorily, and emotionally.

3. *Tell stories, stories, stories.* People remember stories. If there is one thing and one thing only you learn from being on radio it is to tell stories. They touch the heart, and people respond quickly to you.

Susan Harrow is a media coach and marketing strategist (www.prsecrets.com, www.prsecrets.com/publicityblog.html, www.bookedonoprah.com).

Start Your Own TV or Radio Program

If you are an expert in your area, see if there are any opportunities at your local cable television station to host a show related to your business. Again, see what trends are popular on the national channels. If your business involves something your target customer can view on television, you may want to consider this promotional avenue. If you are a dog trainer, you might host a show helping local dog owners solve their pets' bad habits. Gardening and birding are two of the biggest hobbies in the United States. If you have a background in these areas, you could offer a proposal to the show's producers.

A woman who owned a health food store, hosted a weekly radio question and answer show; as did a lawyer who answered listeners' questions. You will have to supply some demonstration tapes and a tentative outline of your proposed programs.

Just because you are on television or radio, does not mean you can forget other marketing methods. There are no guarantees for instant success or profits. One author was on a nationwide talk show twice for her books, but few sales developed from those appearances. Almost all her sales were the result of her own media efforts to a local audience that she knew was interested in her book. However, being on television shows—whether local or national—looks good on your credit sheet and will improve your status as an expert. In the case described here, the woman had photos, audiotapes, and videotapes of her appearances that she could use for promotional purposes.

Additional PR Opportunities

Television, radio, and personal appearances are three ways to reach a large number of potential customers. The media search through membership lists of organizations like Home-Based Working Moms (www.hbwm.com) and other business owners' organizations to find likely interview candidates among women entrepreneurs or other business owners. Additional fun and interesting PR opportunities are presented in Method 70.

Tips for Getting on TV Talk Shows

Patricia C. Gallagher

- Send a one-page proposal for a show with a short bio.
- Try to tie the proposed show in with some current news or with a national special day or week.
- Give a title for the topic of the proposed show. Think like the show's producer—a little sensationalism/controversy (in good taste) in a subject attracts viewers. If it's on the negative side, offer a positive solution from you, the "expert."

- Establish why you are the "expert" on this topic—books or articles you wrote about this topic as well as your own experiences.
- Suggest three questions you can just "picture" the show's host asking on this topic.
- Offer to help get other panelists to be on this show.
- Offer to be available on short notice should another show have to be postponed.
- Be flexible for the producers. It's their show.

If you follow these tips, you will have made the work easier for the TV show's producers. It is still no guarantee you will get on their show, but it will help increase your chances. Plus, they may remember you when you approach them with a topic for your second appearance or even ask you to help them find panelists for another show.

Patricia C. Gallagher has been on more than 100 radio and television shows including Oprah Winfrey, Sally Jessy Raphael, CNN, FNN, Hour Magazine, Maury Povich, and other shows (www.teamofangels.com).

Suggested Resources

Books

Free Publicity: A TV Reporter Shares the Secrets for Getting Covered on the News by Jeff Crilley (Dallas, TX: Brown Books Publishing, 2003).

Public Relations Kit for Dummies book and CD-ROM, rev. ed., by Eric Yaverbaum and Bob Bly (Hoboken, NJ: John Wiley & Sons, 2006).

Directory (Pay to Be Listed)

Radio-TV Interview Report, www.rtir.com, trade publication for producers.

Web Info

http://syndication.net, web site of Chris Witting, founder, president of Creative Broadcast Consulting; syndication consulting; free database of syndicated radio programming on the Web that you can search.

www.mediapost.com, listing of radio stations.

www.PRSecrets.com, Susan Harrow, publicity and media training expert; articles, e-zine, media training teleclasses; www.prsecretstore.com, e-books, books about getting media appearances, promoting your book, yourself, other.

http://www.silentpartneradvertising.com/which_media.htm, "Which Media Will Work?" by Kathy J. Kobliski, author of *Advertising without an Agency Made Easy.*

70. Special Events and Outreach Ideas

There are many other special events and activities that can garner you publicity. One woman who had a child care referral business said some of her best marketing strategies included conducting free parent workshops at hospitals with birthing centers. She put together a workbook for parents that included evaluation checklists and state regulations concerning both at-home child care businesses and company-run centers that parents could use when deciding which child care facility to use.

This woman used her experience to help parents select quality child care programs. Of course, all these parents were potential customers, knowing that they could come to her for a referral if they needed to find a program that met their needs. Showing people that you are helping others promotes goodwill and helps make your regular customers more loyal because they are contributing to worthy causes. Just be sure to include business cards and have your business's name and logo visible on all donated products or materials, displays, or on your clothing for "silent" advertising. Like the owner of the child care referral business, offer your services or products to groups or events that relate to your business and industry. The next sections include other possibilities to get you and your business noticed.

Sponsoring Special Events with Nonprofit Organizations

Holidays, seasonal parties, sports teams' tournaments, religious groups, and art festivals offer endless publicity opportunities for you to volunteer your time and money to sponsor the music, refreshments, prizes, team uniforms, and many other needs of nonprofit groups on a local, state, or national level.

Sponsoring Benefit Contests or Sweepstakes

These events can be fun and rewarding if you choose to dedicate the proceeds toward a local or national nonprofit organization. You may even end up becoming a spokesperson for an organization's chapter or region. If you can relate or support the contest to the nature of your business, it will attract more customers to your venture. If you are a garden consultant, you could sponsor the prizes for a neighborhood garden contest; or if you sell or make costumes, you could hold a Halloween decorating contest. If you are originating a contest or event, check with legal experts to make sure you adhere to any regulations about the type of contest you sponsor and other such considerations.

Charity Auctions and Donations*

Public radio and television stations often hold auctions to raise money. Donations of your products or services are a good way to have your name heard and your products seen on TV by the public. Holiday dinners of organizations often look for donations of table gifts to give away to members. Lesley Spencer Pyle of Home-Based Working Moms (www.hbwm.com) says, "This is a good way to receive publicity that goes with the event or charity."

Presentations at Local Organizations and Institutions

Offering to do presentations or talks at business organizations' meetings and community groups is an excellent way to have people meet you on a personal basis. Your talks should be informative and helpful to your audience. A lawyer could talk to a business major college class on the legalities involved in setting up a business; or an independent tutor could talk to parent groups with tips for helping their children with homework. Keep talks short, focus on one topic, make eye contact, and know to whom you are speaking, so you can talk to their needs and concerns. Offer free tips or resource sheets and have your name and contact numbers at the end of the sheet (see also Method 90).

Establishing Scholarships

For as little as $100 a year, you can sponsor scholarships that high schools, private learning centers, vocational-technical schools, and other institutions award annually to students. Your business name will be listed as a scholarship donor in the programs and directories distributed to attendees of the graduation and awards ceremonies.

Teaching Classes, Directing Seminars, and Giving Demonstrations

Colleges, high school, and vocational-technical schools and learning centers hold adult evening school classes, women's and business conferences, and other learning sessions that are wonderful opportunities for you to teach a class or workshop based on your expertise and business skills. Here are some examples: A woman who sells herbs and herbal plants teaches a class on how to set up a backyard herb garden; a lawyer holds an estate-planning workshop; a personal fitness instructor teaches classes at a senior citizens center; a professional storyteller holds a seasonal storytelling session for children at local libraries. The possibilities for exposure and publicity are endless when sharing and teaching

---

* Author's note: My personal thanks to the Bill and Melinda Gates Foundation (www.gatesfoundation.org) for donating $72,000 to purchase new computers for my county's public branch and community libraries.

others. Have a course syllabus or outline of your program, references and your credentials, and your media information when you approach the persons responsible for scheduling and hiring teachers and demonstrators.

Community Volunteer Opportunities

Participating in volunteer activities is an excellent way to make contacts and share your expertise and skills with those who need them. "You are likely to meet people who you don't know and who could be future customers or clients," says Lesley Spencer Pyle, president of Home-Based Working Moms (www.hbwm.com). "Volunteering doesn't have to mean cleaning up litter or other community activities; it also can be volunteering to do something related to your business. If you are a caterer, you could volunteer to help with a conference or to make food for the needy. And if you are a desktop publisher, you could volunteer to work on a community publication. As a bonus, the local paper may publicize your kind effort if it is made aware of it."

Professional Panels

Businesses and organizations often hold panel discussions for members or for the public to review problems or present information. Usually each panel member has an opportunity to express an opinion, followed by a question-and-answer session for the attending audience. Let organizations and institutions know that you are available for these panels. You have the opportunity for potential customers to meet you and for you to meet them and other experts for possible leads or networking.

Establishing Yourself as an Expert

All the previously mentioned community activities, speaking, writing, and appearing on local networks help establish you as an expert in your field. Offering free workshops and seminars will also garner more free publicity and potential customers. It takes time to build your credentials, but the more you share your knowledge, the more you will be recognized as someone of note; and you will be contacted often for quotes, feedback, or as a guest on talk shows. Whenever you are invited to give your advice in public, avoid sales pitches and concentrate, instead, on providing helpful suggestions and answering the questions you are asked.

Patricia C. Gallagher, author of two books on child care businesses, says, "Besides the possibility of getting on talk shows, you might just end up with some lucrative side benefits like I did as a products spokesperson for two child-related products. That would never have happened if I did not get myself known as an author and 'expert' on children."

Maria T. Bailey, author of *Trillion Dollar Moms: Marketing to a New Generation of Mothers* (www.bsmmedia.com) says, "One way to gain distribution is to become an expert in your field. Establish yourself as the very best in some way. It may be to identify a new niche or focus for your industry or to become so good at solving a problem that you become the 'go-to' person for answers. An expert is often quoted, which means others will be distributing your word for you. It saves you time and gets others to help you do your job."

Bailey continues, "Promote yourself on an ongoing basis as an expert in your field. Not only will others begin to recognize you as such, but your confidence and productivity will exhibit that of an expert almost subconsciously."

Designate a Special "Day"

Debbie Williams, owner of Organized Times (www.organizedtimes.com), an Internet-based home-organizing business and John Riddle, an author of 34 books, both created special days related to their business and profession. Several years ago, Williams founded "National Organize Your Home Day," to be held annually on the second Monday of January; and Riddle established "I Love to Write Day" (www.ilovetowriteday.org) to be held every November 15, where people of all ages across the country practice their writing skills. These events guarantee that Williams and Riddle will receive calls at least once a year from media all over the country and will have their names and web sites mentioned in articles and news—all free publicity.

Perhaps you can't choose a national day (but maybe you can if you create an original one), but you can pick up on an already-designated day or holiday or a national event that relates to your business and stage a sale, an event, or a happening. Another possibility is to offer an article on the topic, all to create news for the media and publicity for you and your business. An owner of a web site selling items and gifts for left-handed people celebrates every August 13, National Left-Handers Day, by sending out press releases and a little story about famous left-handers.

Sponsoring special events and supporting nonprofit groups and organizations is good for your soul and well-being while helping to further community causes. But if you also focus your altruistic efforts toward your potential customers, you can generate more publicity and sales while helping others. Entrepreneurs who donate their time and money will tell you they are well rewarded in more ways than money.

Suggested Resources

Books

> *Chase's Calendar of Events 2004: The Day-to-Day Directory to Special Days, Weeks, and Months*, 47th ed., by the Editors of Chase's (New York: McGraw-Hill, 2003).

> *Promotional Feats: The Role of Planned Events in the Marketing Communications Mix* by Eric J. Soares (Westport, CT: Greenwood Publishing Group, 1991).

Directory

Yearbook of Experts, www.Expertclick.com, listing of experts (you pay to be included) that media can contact.

71. Selling What You Know

If you are already an established expert or are on the way to becoming one, you can sell your knowledge and hands-on experience by writing booklets, e-books, books, and articles, or by creating audio and visual products with CDs, videos, and other supplementary by-products. The advantage here is that you do the work once and then sell it many times, often to a niche market.

Jim Donavan, professional coach and speaker (www.jimdonovan.com), self-published a little motivational book, *This Is Your Life, Not a Dress Rehearsal,* based on his talks and work. He approached a network marketing company that purchased thousands of copies for their representatives. These products all help identify you as an expert and enhance your image.

Writing Basics for "How-to" Publications, E-Books, or Articles

As mentioned, how-to information is always in demand from people who want to learn how to do something for the first time, better, faster, cheaper, prettier, and any other way. If you achieved success in your business or used a new method or procedure, editors, publishers, and potential customers will be interested.

In writing how-to articles, books, and publications, start with a careful outline to provide a logical order of tasks. Write an introduction stating who you are, what qualifies you to write this book, and your reason for writing it. Then write following these general steps: Introduce your topic or chapter; present the problem, challenge, or demonstration you will be writing about; describe each step in detail, and then describe your finished accomplishment. Add resources at the end for readers who want to pursue more information, and do not forget to add your contact and ordering information. If you are self-publishing these products, hire a professional copy editor or proofreader to look over your information for correct grammar and spelling.

Many of the marketing and business experts quoted and listed in this book have written e-books and e-reports that visitors to their sites can purchase and download onto their handheld tech devices. Nancy Collamer, founder of Jobs and Moms (www.jobsandmoms.com), sells some e-reports from her site. Several years ago, she wrote an e-book, *Layoff Survival Guide: The Ultimate Guide to Managing the Transition from Pink-Slip to Paycheck,* that continues to be a good seller for her. E-books can run in length from 30 to 100 pages and target niche markets. Using software like that from Adobe (www.adobe.com),

Software995 (www.software995.com) and other like companies, you can convert your e-book into a downloadable package, and sell these from your web site or other sites that will take a commission to sell your product.

Production of CDs and Videos

Vicki Payne (www.foryourhome.com), a well-known stained glass artist and instructor, has a successful television instructional shows. She once taught stained glass classes and hired a photographer to videotape the classes for her students who missed classes. Those instructional tapes eventually led a PBS station to invite her to do a show that continues to be popular. Payne branched out into selling books, tools, and instructional DVDs.

Jeannie Papadopoulos, was in the window-painting business for almost three decades. She said so many people wanted to learn how to start and develop this business, that she and her husband put together a workshop. The workshops were sold out, and seeing that there was little in the way of books or instructional manuals, Papadopoulos turned her workshops into DVDs and is selling from her web site (http://windowjeannie.ca) and through her publicity activities.

Instructional and demonstration videos can be important sales tools. Hire professional video specialists and include biographical material along with your lessons. You can use these same videos at trade shows, for presentations, and as demo videos for TV station producers.

Book Publishing: Publishers versus Self-Publishing

If you have more material than can be written in an e-book or you wish to expand on that format, then you can consider approaching a publisher with a book proposal. Generally, you will need a thorough outline and several sample chapters. Look at publishers who produce books about your topic, and then visit their web site or write for a copy of their author's guidelines. Look in current editions of reference books like the *Writer's Market* or the *Literary Market Place* for the names of agents and publishers and the names of their editors and acquisitions editors.

Penny C. Sansevieri, CEO of Author Marketing Experts, Inc. (www .amaketingexpert.com) says, "Books are a terrific way to build a business for a variety of reasons. First, books are credibility builders. In an age where credentials and credibility are important, buyers want to know what makes you better than your competitor. A book can really help set you apart. Not only does it help leverage your expertise but it gives your prospective customers a sense of who you are before they even engage your services. More and more buyers want to 'sample' before they buy and a book is a great way to help facilitate this sampling process. Also, books are 24/7 sales tools that can give you exposure far beyond the reach of an ad."

"Books can also be used as promotional tools to help garner media interest or speaking engagements. It's much easier to get into the media spotlight when you have a book and most speaking venues won't consider you unless you're an author. Keep in mind that these days, it's easier than ever to get published and most business owners have their books already finished in the form of articles they've written and published in professional journals or online," says Sansevieri.

With technology today, many people self-publish their books. Think of the market that you are writing for and create a book-marketing plan to target those readers. Peter Bowerman successfully self-published his first book, *The Well-Fed Writer* (www.wellfedwriter.com) based on his years as a professional copywriter. He wrote many articles to publicize his book and it was picked up by book clubs. He was so successful that he wrote a sequel, *The Well-Fed Writer: Back for Seconds,* and plans to soon release his third book, *The Well-Fed Self-Publisher.* If you have proven sales with your self-published or produced items, larger companies or publishers may approach you to sell them or to obtain licensing rights (see Chapter 12).

Consider trying one or more of these products to increase your publicity and profits.

Suggested Resources

Association

Small Publishers Association of North America (SPAN), www.spannet.org, for self-publishers and small publishers, FAQ section about self-publishing.

Books

The Complete Guide to Self-Publishing: Everything You Need to Know to Write, Publish, Promote and Sell Your Own Book, 4th ed. by Tom and Marilyn Ross (Cincinnati, OH: Writer's Digest Books, 2002).

Get Published Today! No More Rejections by Penny C. Sansevieri (West Conshohocken, PA: Infinity Publishing.com, 2002).

How to Publish and Promote Online by M. J. Rose and Angela J. Adair-Hoy (New York: St. Martin's Press, 2000).

Sams Teach Yourself DVD Authoring in 24 Hours by Jeff Sengstack (Upper Saddle River, NJ: Pearson Education, 2003).

The Well-Fed Self-Publisher: How to Turn One Book into a Full-Time Living by Peter Bowerman (Atlanta, GA: Fanove Publishing, 2006).

Writing Short Stories and Articles: How to Get Your Work Published in Newspapers and Magazines, 3rd rev. ed., by Adele Ramet (Oxford, England: How To Books, 2005).

Book Club—Writing

Writer's Digest Book Club, www.writersdigestbookclub.com, writing how-to books in all genres.

Web Info

www.bizwaremagic.com/Steps.htm, "10 Steps for Producing a Professional E-zine" by BizWareMagic.

72. Trade Shows

The SBA says on its Web page, "Trade Show," that trade shows are an excellent and relatively, affordable opportunity for business owners and "entrepreneurs to meet many potential customers face-to-face in a brief period of time inexpensively."

Finding the Best Ones to Attend

Most industries and organizations will hold annual meetings, business conferences, and trade shows for their members. Some are open to the public, while others are only for industry participants. Ask for recommendations, feedback, and opinions of those entrepreneurs and business owners from your networking partners and business associates who have attended and participated at some shows.

Check your business owners' organization for the events they might hold. Then attend some to get an idea of the show's participants and people who attend. If you decide that this is one in which you would like to exhibit, request an exhibitor packet for pricing and other information.

Tips for Maximizing Your Attendance

Once you have decided to attend a show, devise a marketing plan and goals for it so you can make the most of your time and market potential. Here are some considerations:

As an Exhibitor

Prepare all your materials and equipment in advance. Set up a portable file with all the paperwork for the show. Set up a mock booth to see if you have everything you need and to evaluate its appearance. Read the show's manual and prepare accordingly. Enter early to receive discounts. If it is a consumer show, send out press releases and mailings to regular customers or potential buyers. On the day of the show, work your booth, but have another representative to relieve you and give you time to walk the show. Have plenty of handouts about your business and a system for taking interested persons' contact information.

As an Attendee

Plan which booths and persons you wish to meet. Take advantage and attend any in-show demonstrations or workshops, and listen to special speakers. Carry your business cards and samples to hand out.

Promptly follow up contact leads you make with thank-you notes for visiting your booth or sending materials that were requested. Evaluate the experience. If you need some professional advice, find a trade show consultant who can guide you through your first show or provide you with additional marketing tips and ideas.

Suggested Resources

Books

> *How to Get the Most Out of Trade Shows* by Steve Miller (New York: McGraw-Hill, 2000).
>
> *The Trade Show Marketing Handbook* by Ruth P. Stevens (New York: South-Western Educational & Professional, 2004).

Publication

> *Trade Show Week*, www.tradeshowweek.com, print and online.

Web Info

> www.Entrepreneur.com/howto, *Entrepreneur* magazine's free, online, how-to guide, "How to Work a Trade Show."
>
> www.sba.gov, type in "Trade Show" in search box; article and information.
>
> www.tsnn.com, trade show resources.

9

Grow with Effective Advertising Tactics: Getting the Best Ad for Your Money

Most entrepreneurs advertise their businesses in some way, but every business owner faces the dilemma of finding advertising methods that are both cost-effective and the most effective in attracting new customers. Chapter 9 lists advertising avenues you can explore and implement. There also are tips for evaluating the ones that best fit your venture.

An important marketing principle is to choose the media in which you can afford to advertise most often, with the best response. Advertising is a paid-for public form of communication, to promote your products or services. Your advertising challenge is to get the attention of prospective customers and then have them pay. The following sections present options that can attract paying prospects.

73. Direct Mail Advertising

Direct mail to potential customers can deliver a sales message to your target market, but it generally has only a 2 percent to 4 percent response rate. Here are some suggestions for improving the number of responses to your mailings (see also Method 78).

Direct Mail Considerations

Direct mail can consist of letters, postcards, self-mailers, a combination of these items, or other pieces that are sent directly to potential customers. Just as in every marketing campaign, you should create a direct mail program that is well written and consistent in its delivery. Direct mail involves more than a one-time mailing. Marketing experts say it may take a many as seven sales contacts before a potential customer responds, and some may not contact you for months or longer.

Some essentials of a direct mailing campaign include compiling a list of likely prospects; planning a logical, regular, mail schedule; crafting the right mailing piece; telling your recipients what actions to take; following up on responses; seeking ways to keep costs down with alternative delivery methods; and taking advantage of postal and other discounts. A typical direct mail package usually contains a sales letter, a pamphlet or flier, and a reply card.

Mail-order marketers, Internet companies, and other companies whose products are profitable to send through the mail or delivery services, prefer direct mail. The challenge for you is to determine whether direct mail will be a profitable way to reach customers and how to do it economically.

Direct mail can also promote your business. Bert, who owned an antique and home decor business, built up a mailing list at home shows. She sent these persons invitations to come to a seasonal open house, and many who attended became regular customers. You can also promote consumer services such as bookkeeping, cleaning, home repairs, and consulting this way.

Before starting a direct mail program, read all you can on the topic; talk to entrepreneurs who use it; or meet with direct marketing consultants referred to you by networking contacts or through trade associations for help in devising a mailing program. If you do not know what you are doing, you could waste money in mailing to people who do not want or need your product or service.

Compiling a Direct Mail List

To increase the odds of having a mailing list with good responses, you should know what you want to accomplish with this mailing: Reach new customers? Offer specials to regular customers? Sell products? Schedule appointments to meet potential customers? You should also know the makeup of the people to whom you are mailing—their preferences, hobbies, income, and where they are located.

If you have a business-to-business service like bookkeeping, accounting, janitorial, or others, you can start by mailing a brochure to members of organizations to which you belong. Because direct mailing can be expensive, decide how much time and money you are willing to invest in this strategy. Will it be worth it to you or would you rather concentrate on publicity tactics and word of mouth?

You can rent mailing lists from brokers and companies specializing in this area, but with our transient society, lists quickly become obsolete. Check in the business section of your phone directory or look in your library for trade directories or in larger libraries for the *Standard Rate and Data: Direct Mail Lists* (http://srds.com). If you use a list broker, ask whether the firm has had experience in working with business owners like yourself.

The best lists are those that you put together yourself. You can do this in several ways: Garner names and contact information from people who attend trade shows, business or consumer conferences, and referrals; from your web site; and other direct sources. Using a combination of this personal database and lists you rent, you can start out your mailing slowly and as you can afford to do so.

Jeffrey Dobkin, direct marketing specialist and author (www.dobkin.com) says, "Direct marketing *only* works when you can tightly define your very, very best prospects. List selection is most important; it's also the worst job in the whole direct marketing process. It's tedious, unglamorous, fraught with wrong turns yet remains your most critical decision. Alas, in the end, you'll never be sure if it's correct until mailing."

Test Mailings

Once you have compiled (or purchased) a list, the next step is to conduct some test mailings to see what parts of your direct mail campaign succeed and what parts do not. You need feedback on the look of your mailings such as the graphics and envelopes, and on the best times to do a mailing.

More important, your testing should reveal potential customers' reactions to your pricing: Are there enough customers in this area to sustain your venture, and can they be reached through mailings? You do not have to do thousands of mailings, but make sure you send out sufficient pieces to receive enough responses to assess the mailings. Test mailing will allow you to measure the pace of your customer responses, providing you some idea how many pieces you should mail in your designated time period. Testing will be meaningless unless you thoroughly evaluate your results (see Method 75). Direct mailers never stop testing and trying new direct mailing strategies, because it helps bring in new business and keep them in touch with faithful customers.

Attention-Grabbing Creativity

Depending on your finances and ingenuity and the image you want your business to portray, you might try some creativity with your mailings. You could try different colors or sizes of envelopes, colorful graphics, or scented paper, or add a free gift to highlight your mailing. Check with a postal employee to make sure your mailings comply with regulations and that you will not be charged too much extra for special handling of your envelopes.

You can have some fun with this and make your envelope stand out from all the other pieces people receive daily in their mailboxes. Some commercial printers specialize in direct mail and can be a good source of ideas and also show you samples of creative mailings.

Direct Response Wording (Copywriting)

If you have read books by Bob Bly and Peter Bowerman, you realize the impact of the right *copy* or wording on all your direct mail pieces. You can hire a free-lance advertising copywriter, or you can study books and try writing your own promotional pieces. Your advertising messages should be clear, concise, and businesslike. Use familiar persuasive words like *you, new, save, results, guarantee, easy,* and *money* to communicate your message. Offers for free trials and samples encourage customer response, but be careful not to overuse this strategy in your copy, or you will sound false.

Avoid capital letters, too, because they are difficult to read. Also if you use e-mail messages, you know that capitalized words are synonymous with "shouting," and no one likes to be yelled at.

Emphasize how the benefits of your business can help your customers, and encourage the recipient to *act.* Prompt prospects to respond in some way. One printer's direct mail piece says, "Our company has everything you need in a print partner as well as the personal touch you deserve. Give us the opportunity. . . . Get a jump on your competition! Give us a challenge and we'll meet it!"

This business also asks customers to let them "Be Your Marketing Partner" and offers a free report for anyone contacting them.

Answer all queries or responses to your offers as soon as possible to reinforce customers' exposure to your business and to demonstrate your promise to customer service.

Look at promotional pieces of like businesses for tips, read books on the topic, and study marketing publications like *Direct Marketing* magazine for additional copywriting success tips.

Cooperative Marketing

Many small business owners form marketing cooperatives to reduce the cost of direct mail campaigns and other advertising and multiply their lead possibilities and coverage. You can include one another's fliers or coupons in each other's mailings. You can also place larger print ads together by splitting the costs with co-op advertising. Several home business owners did this by taking out a sizable display ad in their local paper's annual business section and received excellent responses. You might consider jointly sponsoring fund-raisers for nonprofit organizations. You will receive free publicity for your businesses and help foster goodwill in your community as you work together to contribute to worthy causes.

Not all partnerships work, so before joining with someone else, be frank with one another and assess whether your businesses complement one another, that the marketing strategies equally benefit both businesses, and that you both have similar business experience. Good co-op promotional strategies can double your marketing power and multiply the profits for all the businesses involved.

Direct mail may not work as well for one business as it can for others, but with persistence and a willingness to learn its basics, it can be an excellent opportunity to energize an existing business or launch a new one (see also Chapter 14, "How to Increase Back-End Sales").

Suggested Resources

Association

Direct Mail Association, www.the-dma.org, National trade association of business and nonprofit groups using and supporting direct marketing methods.

Books

The Art of Partnering: How to Increase Your Profits and Enjoyment in Business through Alliance Relationships by Edwin Richard Rigsbee (Dubuque, IA: Kendall/Hunt Publishing, 1994).

Directory of Mailing List Companies: A Guide to Mailing List Sources (Directory of Mailing List Companies) by Barry Klein (Ed.) (Austin, TX: Todd Publications, 2006).

Do-It-Yourself Advertising and Promotion: How to Produce Great Ads, Brochures, Catalogs, Direct Mail, Web Sites, and More! by Fred E. Hahn, Tom Davis, Bob Killian, and Ken Magill (Hoboken, NJ: John Wiley & Sons, 2003).

The Elements of Copywriting: The Essential Guide to Creating Copy That Gets the Results You Want by Gary Blake and Robert W. Bly (New York: Longman, 1998).

Well-Fed Writer: Financial Self-Sufficiency as a Freelance Writer in Six Months or Less by Peter Bowerman (Atlanta, GA: Fanove Publishing, 2000).

Publication

DIRECT magazine, www.directmag.com, Industry publication.

Web Info

www.dobkin.com, web site of Jeffrey Dobkin, marketing expert; direct marketing books, articles, and more.

www.Entrepreneur.com/howto, *Entrepreneur* magazine's free, online, how-to guide, "How to Create a Direct-Marketing Campaign."

74. Ad Tips

Along with all the publicity tactics, you should try advertising to help grow your name recognition. The more people see your name, the more they will remember you and then your business. Repetition is an important function of advertising. You cannot expect one expensive display ad to bring in sales or promote your business. In fact, you may not get any response at all. Potential customers will become increasingly aware of your business, the more you advertise. Try advertising for at least a year to determine the best marketing mix for you and your business. But you generally pay for advertising, so you have to budget advertising dollars into your marketing plans. Fortunately, there are many affordable advertising avenues you can try.

Here are some things to consider when choosing a publication or media for advertising purposes:

- Make sure the publication has an existing audience who read it on a regular basis.
- Do the market research to see how much of that audience consists of your target market, or potential customers.
- How often does the media get published or reach its audience?

Whereas you generally do not control what is printed or said about you (publicity), with advertising you have a say in the wording and where it is placed, even if you hire a professional or agency to help you. Publications and other media usually have staff to assist you in composing an ad, but be careful that it does not sound like all the others in that media.

Ad Structure Basics

Most advertisements consist of these basics:

- *Headlines:* These words grab the attention of readers and tell them what to expect. The wording should consist of action verbs, but not be too forceful or demand that readers "Buy Now!" Headlines can provide audiences with news, advice, promises, mystery, humor, and direction. They can be short or long, depending on the intent of the ad.
- *Graphics, photos, illustrations:* Pictures or photos or sounds (radio, Internet) create interest and often convey the purpose of your product or service. You can use clip art, original illustrations or graphics, or commercial or digital photos. Children, animals, and attractive models are all attention-getters. Cost and availability may decide what you can and cannot include. Use your logo in all your ads, printed materials, signs, vehicles, and products. It enhances your business image and increases how often potential customers see it and connect it with your business.

- *Fees, charges, costs:* These influence whether potential customers patronize your business so the costs should be included in your ads.
- *Other factors:* Lettering and typeface, color, and size are also important factors when placing an ad.

Experiment and test variations of these ad basics to see which ones get the best responses.

Federal Trade Commission Rules

The Federal Trade Commission (FTC) has rules and regulations regarding the wording, claims, and fulfillment of advertising and mail order. To learn about these laws, go to the FTC's site, www.FTC.gov, and click on "Business" and then, "Advertising Guidance," or write Federal Trade Commission, CRC-240, 600 Pennsylvania Avenue, NW, Washington, DC 20580.

Peak Seasons for Advertising

Advertising for major holidays, especially Christmas, starts earlier every year. That is because most purchases for gift items are done at this time. If you make handcrafted seasonal gifts, your wholesale market may start as soon as February. The best advertising seasons vary with the type of business you have. Florists have Mother's Day and Valentine's Day; accountants have the tax season; real estate agents have their peak selling times—and so it is with just about every business.

What is important to know is that most publications and media have editorial and advertising deadlines set months ahead, so make sure you know the dates by which you must have your ads ready or reserved to match the times that your target market is ready to buy. Prepare customers for a new season by sending postcards for preseason sales or discounts and follow up at the end of the season in clearance sales. To cover off-season sales, think of spin-off products or services related to your main business. A garden center sells all sorts of dried flowers and wreath-making supplies in the winter. The owner of a lawn maintenance service clears driveways of snow in the winter (see also Chapter 12).

Specialty Directories

There are many other venues to place your ads. Again, follow your target market—what they read, what they do for fun or work, where they go, what web sites they frequent—all provide alternative placements for your ads. If you own a rental condominium on the beach in a resort area with a warm climate, you could place ads not only in national, state, and regional newspapers, but also in area guide books; rental and accommodations guides; surfing and fishing publications; specialty publications like *AAA World* or *AARP The Magazine,* and regional and top web sites.

Do not overlook "evergreen" phone directories like the *Yellow Pages* and *Women's Yellow Pages.* Some niche business owners put out their own business directories according to their cultural or religious background. If you have a restaurant or outdoor-related business, regional travel guides are good places for your ads. The opportunities for advertising are numerous and often more affordable than standard media. Talk with your local chamber of commerce and visit your public library to find samples of these directories.

Multilingual-Global Ads

You can live just about anywhere in this world and still conduct business. The Internet, new technology and availability of transportation even to remote regions have helped to create a global economy, permitting people to buy and sell worldwide. If you have a successful business in your country, you may want to consider branching out into international markets.

International business is the same in that you will want to find a target niche. As mentioned in Chapter 6, some U.S. Small Business Development Centers (www.sba.gov/SBDC) have staff that specialize in export and import counseling for entrepreneurs and small businesses. They can help you analyze your business to see if it is a good candidate for an international market.

If you have contacts in other countries and are familiar with the cultures, then you have an advantage of knowing whether they might respond differently to your products. If you are not multilingual, nor familiar with the customs and preferences of a country that may have potential customers, you can hire such experts as an international marketing specialist, translator, and cultural specialist to help you take your business to an international level (see also Method 89).

The Benefits of Classified Ads

Although classified ads are not as pretty as display or color ads (other than some of the publications' typeface print), they deserve consideration in your marketing toolbox. You can sell directly to the buyer, or you can advertise a product or service and then offer readers more information if they write or send an e-mail. Either way, you will have found some hot prospects, not cold prospects who have never heard about your business and did not ask for any information from you. You can add these hot prospects to your database mailing list and follow up periodically with them, even if they do not purchase anything the first time you send them sales literature (see Chapter 11 for online classified ads).

Writing good copy for a winning classified ad is much the same as writing any ad. Your ad should start with a bold headline and follow with a description of your product or service, your offer, including prices, and contact information for ordering or calling. For a few dollars more, publications often offer to box your ad with a heavy line, making it easier to spot. Be sure to include wording that encourages the reader to act now on your offer.

Two women who had a wicker shop discovered that their weekly ads in a classified paper distributed free to area residents, with an occasional display ad in the same newspaper to announce specials, brought in more business than larger, more expensive ads in other local publications. "They may be small, but they are mighty profitable," said the one partner.

How to Get Your Advertising at a Discount

John D. Schulte

There are four key points that are important to all advertising: Reaching the right audience, having a good ad created, paying the lowest possible rate for the advertising space, and tracking the effectiveness of the advertisement. This article is about buying your advertising at the best possible price.

No matter what an advertising sales rep may say to you, not everyone pays the same advertising rates. There are ways to get discounts on the published rates, but to get the discounts you have to know about them. If you do, you can almost always negotiate the price you pay for advertising. Here are the most common discounts you should know about:

Mail Order Rate: Many magazines and some newspapers have a special rate for mail order or direct marketing advertisers. When you order a media kit, ask them to include the mail order rate card if they have one. In today's world, almost everyone can be considered a direct marketer, or create an advertisement that would qualify as a direct marketing/mail order ad. Experts also suggest, if you use an online buying service, and you're asked what kind of company you are at registration, always register under direct marketer/mail order if the option is given, there is no downside, and there are extra possibilities of getting better rates.

Agency Discount: When you create your own ads for a magazine, according to its specifications, you should be able to get an agency discount of 15 percent to 20 percent. If the agency discount is not printed on the magazine's rate card (usually in small print) ask the sales rep. In the old days you needed to really be an agency, but now, if you're creating your own ad, you are the agency, so this discount should be available to you.

Remnant Space: It's rare that any media sells 100 percent of the available advertising space (or *time* for broadcast advertising) before publication date. Whatever space, or time, is left over (not sold) at deadline is called *remnant space,* and is made available at a big discount. It goes fast and you have to be ready for it; you have to be ready to commit *now* and you have about 24 hours to get the ad in.

This means your ads have to be completed beforehand and ready to go. Most magazines have very similar advertising sizes, known as Mechanical Dimensions. They may fluctuate a little bit, but in general you can expect and prepare for something like this. Then only minor size changes need to be made, but the look, feel, and content will remain the same. Here are some common magazine and newspaper advertising sizes so you can get ready:

Full Page: 7 $''$ × 10$''$

⅔ page: (Vertical) 4⅝$''$ × 9¾$''$

½ Page: (Vertical) 3⅜ $''$ × 10$''$

½ Page: (Horizontal) 7$''$ × 4¾$''$

⅓ Page: (Vertical) 2¼ $''$ × 10$''$

⅓ Page: (Horizontal) 3⅜$''$ × 7$''$

⅓ Page: (Square) 4½$''$ × 4⅞$''$

⅙ Page: (Vertical) 2¼ $''$ × 4¾$''$

¼ Page: (Vertical) 3½$''$ × 4¾$''$

⅙ Page: (Horizontal) 4⅝$''$ × 2¼$''$

So if you're going to be using space ads, always try to get remnant space in the publication first, especially when you are first testing a new publication. Two publications that have regular remnant space are, *USA Weekend,* and *Parade* magazine. Both are delivered through Sunday newspapers.

Early Payment: Most media offer a small discount, around 3 percent or so, when paying upfront or within 15 to 30 days. Look for it or ask about it.

Buy Multiple Insertions: All media give price breaks for running multiple ads during a year. This is detailed on their rate card, and in most cases you don't have to run them consecutively if you don't want to. Many times you have a full year to place the ads. Ask the sales representative. Then you will have time to cancel future ads if the first ad does not work. (If you buy at a multiple rate and then cancel, expect them to bill you extra for the difference between your multiple rate discount and what you actually used.) You can also try asking the sales representative to give you the next-level discount on an ad you want to run.

Buy Ads through a Buying Service: Media Buying Specialists buy large amounts of advertising space in the certain media they work with and offer it to their clients at a discount. You can find some good ones listed in the reference section of the Direct Marketing Toolkit book from the NMOA [National Mail Order Association].

You can also sometimes trade for advertising. Some people write articles for magazines, newspapers or newsletters, and instead of getting paid in cash they trade for advertising space. The editor of the magazine gets editorial content, helping get their job done (meeting deadlines), and the writers get advertising to promote what they sell. Some writers write just to get a byline at the end of the article. Here is another example of why it's good to know a lot about what you sell. Be the expert! A list of media buying services are listed in the NMOA Industry Contact Directory.

Buy Ads through an Advertising Auction: This is one of the greatest new ways to buy advertising at a discount. The best one I know about is Media-Bids.com (http://www.mediabids.com). It works like this; you register on the site (it's completely free to use), and then enter details of the ads you want to run, and in what type of magazine or newspaper you want and the geographic location, and how much you want to spend, then publications bid to get your adverting. You can get some great deals doing this, so I highly recommend signing up, even if you just want to watch what others are paying. MediaBids also has a direct marketing and mail order classification you can choose when you register, so when you sign up, make sure you classify yourself as such to get even deeper discount offers.

Recommended Reading: Every person that needs to create advertising for their company should also read Creating Successful Small Business Advertising by Jerry Fisher (http://www.nmoa.org/catalog/fisher.htm) and other books by history's great advertising practitioners: Max Sackheim, John Caples, Claude Hopkins, John E. Kennedy, and David Ogilvy.

John D. Schulte is president of the National Mail Order Association (NMOA). Visit www.nmoa.org for more tips and information on advertising and direct marketing and a free newsletter. This sidebar is from his book *Direct Marketing Toolkit*.

With any mailing and advertising, make sure you have adequate staff and inventory, and a system in place for processing orders, should you be lucky enough to get a rush of orders.

Suggested Resources

Books

Advertising without an Agency Made Easy, 3rd ed., by Kathy Kobliski (Irvine, CA: Entrepreneur Press, 2005).

Communicating with Customers around the World: A Practical Guide to Effective Cross-Cultural Business Communication by K. C. Chan-Herur (San Francisco: AuMonde International Publishing, 1994).

Direct Marketing Toolkit by John D. Schulte (Minneapolis: National Mail Order Association, 2006). Book and CD-ROM.

A Short Course in International Marketing: Approaching and Penetrating the Global Marketplace by Jeffrey E. Curry (Novato, CA: World Trade Press, 1998).

Think like Your Customer: A Winning Strategy to Maximize Sales by Understanding and Influencing How and Why Your Customers Buy by Bill Stinnett (New York: McGraw-Hill, 2004).

The 33 Ruthless Rules of Local Advertising, rev. ed., by Michael Corbett (New York: Pinnacle Books, 1999).

Web Info

> www.48hourprint.com/ink-spot/index.html, online print center with articles and templates; magazine, *Ink Spot*.

75. Tracking Ad (and Marketing) Responses

For one reason or another, many small business owners do not track their advertisements, or marketing efforts, preferring to ignore it and hope that their methods are working. But it is crucial to your finances and future growth to follow up and evaluate every advertising and marketing effort you implement. There are several methods that you can use to measure responses. Some entrepreneurs will set up separate phone number extensions that are listed in their ads; others will put a code in the address or a coupon to clip and redeem; and others will simply ask anyone who contacts them, "How did you hear about us?"

It does not matter how you track your ads as long as the system provides the data to evaluate whether the ads and endeavors were worth your expenditures.

Tracking System

Whether you use a manual system or management software to analyze your paid advertising efforts, you should have a system that can provide you with an accurate accounting, that you are comfortable using, and that is consistent in the data you are assessing.

Try not to track too many ads at once or too many aspects of any one ad. Set a goal for each ad you place and calculate its worth. If it did not pay for itself, then decide if it is worth it to try it again at another time, to reword or redesign it, or to move on and try another method.

Tracking Response and Measuring Your Advertising

John D. Schulte

The "key code" is the secret weapon used by smart advertisers to measure the effectiveness of their advertisements. It lets you know what advertisement is working, what mailing list is working, what magazine is working, what web site or banner ad is working, what offer or "appeal" is working, and so forth.

The key code is tied to the response device someone uses to contact you after reading your ad. Response device simply means what method is used when contacting you, by mail, by phone, by fax, by e-mail, by special web page, and so on. The key code itself can be a department number in an address people mail to, a unique phone number people dial, or the special extension they would ask for when they call, or the name of a special person they would ask for, or it can simply be a special "secret code" someone has to mention to get a special deal. When using the web it can be a special web page people get to when they click on a banner (these are called landing pages.)

The important thing is that the response device of each advertisement has its own "unique" code so you can precisely track where orders came from and to what ad they responded.

Many times you will see this as a "Department" number in an ad. For example, Mail this coupon to "ABC Company, *Dept. 1001*, Anytown, United States." Other times the order form, or return envelope, has the code printed on it. The important thing is to have something in place so you know exactly where the order came from, which advertisement or what mailing, or what mailing list produced it.

When placing ads that run from month to month in the same magazine, make sure you use a different code for each month so you can track which month is best for generating the most orders. For example, if you were running an advertisement in *Good Housekeeping* for the months of January, February and March of 2007, your key codes may look something like this: Dept. GH17 for the January ad, Dept. GH27 for the February ad, Dept. GH37 for the March ad. The GH stands for Good Housekeeping, the first number stands for the month, and the last number stands for the year.

You then create an advertising chart that has all the ads you are running listed on it with the key codes, and each time an order comes in, or someone calls, you associate that key code with that customer. At the end of each month you tally it up and see what ads resulted in the most closed sales and/or profit.

There are many order management software packages that have this feature if you don't want to do it by hand. You can also set up a spreadsheet or database yourself if you want.

By using key codes in all your advertisements, over time you will be able to make more money with your advertising dollars. You will know where to advertise, when to advertise, and what your advertisements should say to get the best results.

John D. Schulte is president of the National Mail Order Association (NMOA, www.nmoa.org).

Evaluating What Works Best

Measuring results is what you want to do to assess your ads and also your other marketing campaigns. Analyze the data, responses, and most important how much the ad cost and how many measurable responses it brought in terms of sales. It is all about the money! You will want to crunch the numbers to evaluate your *return on investment* (ROI), as this sales figure is called. Simply put, it is a cost/benefit assessment where you scrutinize how much it cost you in actual dollars spent and in the "soft costs" you invested (the time and effort you put into this campaign). The ROI assessment will reveal if a particular effort cost you more than was spent or expended.

If ads or other efforts did not bring in a response or lead to the actual sales you expected or hoped for, look it over and see if it needs a makeover in wording, appearance, lettering, or its overall message. Here are some questions for evaluating each public relations promotion, ad, or other marketing effort:

- Which potential customers responded?
- Did any unexpected groups respond?
- Was the campaign worth the effort in terms of money and energy expended?
- Was there a time period or season when there was a better response?
- Did cooperative advertising and joint efforts work well for all involved?
- What was the response to pricing? To discounts or free introductory offers?
- Overall, what marketing effort(s) worked the best?

Use the results of your ad purchasing decisions, and all marketing methods, including direct mail and publicity efforts to see if you met your goals, and to measure which ones increased your sales and expanded your customer database. Assess often because you never know which effort will succeed or how long it will work. Once you discover the most effective ads or methods, repeat often, but do not depend on just one method too heavily. You never know when a buying trend will phase out, or the economy will dip. Keep your business alive and sustain its future by always trying new marketing tools, so that you will have a continuous moneymaking stream, no matter what happens in your industry or the business world.

Suggested Resources

Books

> *Marketing ROI: How to Plan, Measure, and Optimize Strategies for Profit* by James Lenskold (New York: McGraw-Hill, 2003).
>
> *Precision Marketing: The New Rules for Attracting, Retaining, and Leveraging Profitable Customers* by Jeff Zabin, Philip Kotler, and Gresh Brebach (Hoboken, NJ: John Wiley & Sons, 2004).

Web Info

> www.marketingsurvivalkit.com, "Marketing Survival Kit," small business marketing tips, tools, books, and templates and many articles.

76. Promotional Products

Advertising Specialties

Choosing gifts and novelties to carry your business name, logo, and contact information should involve research and planning. Know what objectives you want to accomplish by giving out these products. Start with a limited amount to help stay within your marketing budget and to test customers' responses. Finding a promotional products consultant is one of the best ways to do this. These experts can help you align these items with your business in keeping with your image and brand. Authors can have bookmarks with photos of their book; bookstores can offer tote bags; professional organizers can give calendars with organizing tips for each month. There are endless other possibilities for this type of "silent advertising."

With your promotional products, you can also work cooperatively in direct mailings. You could offer your products as free bonuses for other business owners to include in their direct mailings. It improves their customer response rates and provides your business with more exposure. You might also share costs with these entrepreneurs or with your suppliers.

Another possibility is to consider whether one of *your* products could be used as a promotional product and licensed to other companies (see also Method 93 and Chapter 14, "Choosing the Best Promotional Product for Your Business").

Cards and Stickers

Many businesses send out seasonal cards at the end of the year, but you can send cards at other holidays or commemorative events or as a special thank-you to your best customers. Janet Crenshaw Smith, of Ivy Planning Group (IVY; www.ivygroupllc.com) says that instead of doing the usual Christmas and December marketing campaigns such as sending cards with gift baskets, her company decided to select a less common holiday. They reached out to their customers with a special Valentine message.

"We've been sending Ivy V-Day gifts for years, so each year we're challenged to do something even better," says Smith. "2006 was fabulous. We sent beautifully packaged boxes of fortune cookies, with customized messages in the cookies. The messages included 'Happy Valentine's Day from Ivy Planning Group' of course, but also messages that subtly promoted our products + the web site of the product." Smith continues, "Most people don't get a lot of 'marketing mail' for this holiday, perhaps because they're hesitant to associate *love* with their customers? Well, we don't because we absolutely love ours! (maybe because we're woman-owned, who knows?)."

Depending on your advertising budget, you can have a graphic designer incorporate your business's identity and the season or occasion to create a one-of-a-kind card, or you can meet with your printer for ideas. You can also create your own using desktop publishing software and special embossed or metallic paper that you can buy at office supply stores.

Stickers are no longer just lick and press. Stickers can be fun, and attention-getting items. To promote her children's activity book, Patricia C. Gallagher had colorful stickers made that said, "Ask my mommy about her book." She placed these stickers on every letter she mailed to media and other correspondents. Again, if you plan to use stickers, consider how and where you will hand them out—at trade shows? applied on promotional items or sales letters? Other?

Make them more effective with color, paper, and in the wording with strong headlines as well as your business name and contact information.

Aliza Sherman Risdahl, Web pioneer and author of Internet books, says her business cards and postcards were among her best marketing tools when she started her Internet company, Media Egg (www.mediaegg.com). Risdahl says, "When I first started my Internet company, I had a miniscule budget for marketing so I had to get creative. Two things I made were hot pink business cards that I copied and had cut at Kinko's and canary yellow glossy postcards with the company logo, name (Cybergrrl!) and web site URL printed boldly on the front that I had printed."

Risdahl continues, "People constantly told me that they never had trouble finding my business card on their desk because the color stood out. And the postcard—people not only sent it to friends and colleagues, but they'd tack one on their office wall. Talk about constant branding!"

These items can go a long way in promoting your business. Research the possibilities and then do some trials to test their effectiveness.

Suggested Resources

Association

Promotional Products Association International, www.ppa.org, industry association and membership referrals.

Book

Power of Promotional Products by David Blaise and Maria Carlton (Wyomissing, PA: Blaise Drake & Company, 2003).

77. More Visual Tactics

Phone Views*

Phone numbers, ground line or cell phones, are important for communication between customers and you. Getting toll-free numbers makes sense, especially

---

* A note about fax solicitations: In a recent ruling by the Federal Communications Commission (FCC, www.fcc.gov) concerning its Junk Fax Prevention Act of 2005, the FCC has issued regulations about sending fax advertising to recipients, requiring direct permission; identification of senders; and "opt out," provisions. For more information, visit the FCC web site.

if your target marketing encompasses an area outside your local calling area. Include it on all your marketing materials and in ads and publicity campaigns because it encourages customer inquiries and responses and helps your customer service (see also Method 79). If you get a toll-free vanity number like (800) MY-BIZNAM(E), it will help customers remember your number and business. Vanity numbers work best, when they look familiar, and use easy-to-spell words. Be sure to put the numerical telephone equivalent for the letters, for people who have difficulty in dialing the "letters."

There are many beneficial options with an 800-number. If you combine it with an automated voice mail system, you can leave advertising messages, set up voice mailboxes to answer frequently asked questions or do simple surveys; offer fax-on-demand information, and have messages sent to you almost anywhere on your cell phone or Internet e-mail (see also Methods 79 and 86 for phone and Internet message tips).

Today more companies are using cell phones for interactive advertising. As people pass by billboards or posters they can get ring tones, coupons, or even videos, and technologists are saying it will not be long until people can actually purchase items through billboards. Though your business may be small, technology provides and will continue to provide new ways for you to advertise and conduct business with customers. That is why it is so important to follow the latest business news in your industry (see also Chapter 14, "Reading for Business and Marketing Success").

Nontraditional Visual Tactics

Look for nontraditional visual opportunities to get your message or business recognized. Here are six suggestions using sight and a combination of your other senses:

1. *Action:* You see it in the malls all the time at the kiosks selling action toys. The vendor will operate a remote control car in front of you. It is very hard to resist trying a "test" drive.
2. *Scent:* A coffee shop vents its coffee aroma out the door. It is almost irresistible to coffee connoisseurs who walk by.
3. *Music:* Marketing to baby boomers? Show posters of the Beatles or the Beach Boys and play their hits of the 1960s and early 1970s, and you will have people stopping by just to sing along.
4. *Touch:* A specialty shop selling spun Alpaca wool has sample garments on display and encourages customers to feel its soft texture.
5. *Taste:* Grocery stores often have samples from vendors or at their deli department for you to taste and enjoy.
6. *Sight:* How about the crazy blown-up characters often seen at car dealers, or someone who is dressed up in a costume and waves at you as you drive by? As mentioned previously, some store owners have found that

hiring a professional window painter like Jeannie Papadopoulos to decorate their windows, advertising their holiday specials, has been an excellent draw for people walking or driving by. Papadopoulos says, "Window
painting provides instant visibility. If you don't do something to make you
more noticeable, you are overlooked. Over 50 percent of shopping is
spontaneous buying for everything. Our customers' windows get noticed!
Potential customers are curious and want to see what is on sale or they
are attracted to the business by the signage and graphics! It definitely
gives the client an advantage to have billboard size advertising for a better cost than radio, TV or newspapers. Signage is read by all, whether
they want to or not! It still is the best value for the 24/7 coverage it gives!"

As long as the visuals you use are tasteful and do not hurt your business
image, what you try is limited only by your creativity.

Vehicle Signage

Patricia C. Gallagher had her minivan painted with her book's cover plus the
800-number for ordering the book. Gallagher says, "All in all, it was a great trip.
I did sell some books and received valuable recognition and some great publicity along the way."

You may not go to that extreme, but vehicle lettering, vanity license plates,
bumper stickers, and magnetic signs are all fun and attention-getting visuals
you might explore for "free" advertising. Two women who partnered together
in their clowning business, had clown bumper stickers with their images and
phone numbers. Take notice of all the vehicle signs you see the next time you
drive or are stuck in a traffic jam.

What's Your "Sign"?

Portable or permanent signs are traditional in their purpose, but can be made
modern with new graphics and materials. Those simple wire signs, often used
by political candidates and real estate agents, are relatively inexpensive and can
be placed with minimum damage to the ground. Two women who opened a
women's fitness center in a shopping mall, placed a number of these signs with
their name, logo, and store location for drivers to see as they drove in and
around the mall parking lots. These signs are easily moved and the coverings
just slip on and off, so specials and announcements can easily be changed as
needed.

Sandwich board signs are sturdy and larger, and entrepreneurs often set
them at intersections where drivers who are waiting for lights can read them.
Permanent signs with lights, interchangeable letters, and those that you can
program with your latest offers, prices, and information are excellent for brick-
and-mortar store locations. Many contractors will place their lawn signs at their

job locations for drivers who walk by. Your sign may be the first contact your customer has with you, so think of signs as part of your identity package.

Some businesses distribute door hangers that slip over home owners' doorknobs. For signs, door hangers, and other visuals that are not located on your property or in your store window, check policies and regulations about solicitations, permits, and permission requirements for the placement of your signs.

Logos and More

Logos are the recognizable, exclusive images that are identified with and owned by an organization or business (see also Method 60). As mentioned, use a logo whenever possible on your business stationery and other promotional materials. A well-designed logo will reinforce your business image and make it memorable. A logo should be simple, represent your business and what it does, have a unique look, and make an impression on those who see it. It should look good no matter what size it is used for, from pens to billboards.

Chanin Walsh, creative director, Ampersand Design (www.ampersandesign .net) says, "Many people come to us for what we call 'phase 2' logos and web sites. We always wished we could have gotten to them earlier to keep them from putting out things that really did not represent them well. If cost is an issue, we recommend keeping things classy and simple and then actually budgeting to develop their brand identity."

Walsh continues, "Sometimes a homemade logo can do more damage than good. It's like holding out a billboard that says, 'I'm a new start-up business, and I am on a shoestring,' which is not the image most people want to project."

Look at other business logos, especially those in your industry and your competitors to get some inspiration. Graphic artists can help you design one, or you can use copyright-free art or even your own photos or line drawings. If you use a graphic artist, then you will have an original logo that you can trademark to guarantee it remains exclusively yours. A logo will become an important part of your business identity package. If it is well designed and true to your business image, it can be a dynamic marketing tool.

Bagging and Packaging

The packers at grocery stores used to ask you before they began packing your groceries, "Paper or plastic?" Now, however, mostly plastic bags are used, and stores' names and logos often are imprinted on them. Of course, if the bags are then reused to give an item to someone else, then that person gets to read the store's name, and so on. If you have items to sell, consider getting your own plastic or paper bags printed. If you sell pricey items, though, make sure your bags are classy. Putting them into inexpensive plastic bags hurts your image.

The same principle applies to having the proper packaging for any products you sell. You need to package your products so people will buy them. There are packaging experts to help you, or talk to a local graphic artist and your printer for more tips and feedback.

A package expert can inform you about current packaging trends, what your target market likes and dislikes, and help you find an affordable solution and also a vendor to supply you with the packaging for your business.

Nancy Cleary, a graphic artist and small publisher, creates unique marketing packages for clients (www.Box-Is.com). "If a picture is worth a thousand words, great packaging is worth a thousand dollars," says Cleary. "Whether you are packaging a product for sale or your ideas in a business proposal, a cohesive and creative presentation will establish immediate credibility. You have a nanosecond to grab, and keep, your viewers' attention—when you make a memorable impression with an iconic logo, an unforgettable tagline, or a fresh way to package and display your products you will have measurably more success."

Suggested Resources

Books

> *Design It Yourself Logos Letterheads and Business Cards: A Step-by-Step Guide* by Chuck Green (Gloucester, MA: Rockport Publishers, 2001). www.ideabook.com.

> *Silent Selling: Best Practices and Effective Strategies in Visual Marketing*, 3rd ed., by Judith Bell and Kate Ternus (New York: Fairchild Books, 2006).

Web Info

> http://packagingnewsyoucanuse.blogspot.com, blogs: "Packaging News You Can Use" and "Insights, Tips and Technologies on How to Package Products People Will Buy."

> www.Entrepreneur.com/howto, *Entrepreneur* magazine's free, online, how-to guide, "How to Create a Logo."

78. Marketing Messages

Publishing Promotional Newsletters

Newsletters, electronic newsletters (e-zines, see Method 87), magazines, and all your business literature can be included in your direct-mail marketing campaigns. Keeping in touch with your customers on a regular basis also helps you build a relationship with them. If you provide them with a free publication, print or online, it can inform your customer, promote repeat business, and attract potential customers. You can make it interactive and interesting by inviting customer questions and comments. Lesley Spencer Pyle, founder and president of HomeBasedWorkingMoms.com, says, "Our print newsletter and our e-newsletter have served as a great way to keep in touch with our members as well as market to prospective members. We have people who become members after subscribing to our free e-Newsletter."

If you have the knowledge but are a little rusty on your writing skills, you can hire a freelance editor to help you with the grammar and clarity.

Brochures and Booklets

Brochures are one of the most popular forms of marketing. They can be used as a direct marketing piece to generate leads by using a tear-off, mail-back postcard on your last brochure panel; to tell customers a little about the history of your business and your background; and most important, to highlight the benefits they will receive from buying your products or using your services. To save money, use your desktop publishing software to design and create a brochure using standard 8.5 × 11-inch paper that you can triple-fold and fit into a business-size envelope.

Know how you are planning to use your brochure: As a follow-up to a personal meeting or customer query? As an order form for orders or reorders? For information about the care of purchased products? To introduce your business to potential customers? Have a headline that asks a question and a photo or illustration on the front that makes it more interesting. Keep the wording simple, and make sure it looks professional. You can send it to members of groups to which you belong. Proofread it, especially your name, address, business e-mails, and any other important contact information. Put them in your media packets, too.

Booklets are an excellent way to provide customers with promotional content and more detailed information or tips. They can give instructions or be a follow-up to an offer for free information on a topic listed in one of your ads or direct-mail pieces and should be complete in structure. Focus on one topic and make it easy to read. Include illustrations and photos to make it interesting. You can produce the pages yourself, staple them together, and use a folded-over binding cover. Use a stronger paper for durability. Look over the selection at your nearest copy center or your printer. Use the booklets for free offers to entice new customers.

Postcards and Self-Mailers

Postcards have advantages over a direct-mail package, because they are almost always read, whereas many direct-mail packages are just thrown away unopened. The affordability of postcards enables you to send them out more often to your mailing list or regular customers. You can use them as reminders about your products or services, an announcement of an upcoming sale, for quick surveys, to provide some tips, and to generate additional sales inquiries.

One professional organizer sends out organizing tips for the Christmas holiday. Authors have their books' covers printed on postcards to mail to faithful readers or to hand out as large business cards. Keep the design simple and the message clear. Ask your postmaster what days of the week are best for mailing them, so they do not get lost in the heavy mail delivery days. If you cannot afford a larger direct mailing, postcards are an effective and economical alternative.

Self-mailers are another reasonably priced direct-mail method. They can include all the elements of a direct-mail package, but are a smaller version arranged to fit on one folded sheet of paper. As with the brochure, you can fold self-mailers into three or four panels, and designate each panel to present whatever benefits, offers, feedback, or information you want the recipients to know or respond to. Again, ask your printer for recommendations as to the weight of paper that will best withstand the mailing process.

Maximizing Business Cards

Business cards are essential little marketing tools that have helped launch many entrepreneurs' ventures. Here are some ideas to maximize their messages:

- Always have the essentials: your name and position, address, and all phone and fax numbers; e-mail addresses, logo, and a tagline or slogan if there is room. Place your photo on it if you are a professional consultant or speaker or in another business such as real estate in which you wish to be recognized by potential clients. Try not to clutter the business card too much, or your message will get lost in too many details. Consider your cards as an introduction to you and your business, a "ticket" or "invitation" to potential customers to hear more about what your business can do for them.
- Consider the weight of the cover stock, the finish, the print, the color(s), and design and how it reflects your business image. A professional consultant with a private practice could have a linen finish, with conservative lettering; while the two women clowns in the entertainment business had their clown faces put on their card and outlined it with brightly colored balloons.
- Use business cards as "mini" direct-mail promotions, including them in all your business correspondence, attaching them to your giveaways or products and self-mailers, or use them as a coupon. A mall kiosk that sells watches and batteries gives first-time customers a business card. Every time afterward, when these customers make a purchase there, their card is punched and after so many punches, they get a free watch battery.
- Christopher J. Brunner, of GreatFX Business Cards (www.greatfxbusinesscards .com), says, "Utilize the back side of your business cards for maximum marketing impact. Include a coupon or discount offer so that your client will

have a reason to keep and use your business card. A sale from one card could potentially pay for the entire stack."

If you need ideas for business card designs, look at your local printer's business-card catalog to see all the possibilities, and then use those formats as an inspiration to design your own customized card. You cannot physically carry a billboard along with you everywhere, but you can bring lots of your business cards to hand out and possibly reach more potential customers than one large, stationary billboard on a busy highway (see also Chapter 14, "Business Card Axioms").

Customized Sales Literature

Direct-mail considerations were discussed in Method 73. Here are some basic tips to make the components of a standard direct-mail package, envelope, sales letter, flyer, and a reply card more successful in prompting responses:

- *The envelope:* It is an important first step in your sales pitch, with the primary goal to have your recipients open and read what is inside. Make it eye-catching in color and in your wording. Tempt your prospects to open it with a question or notice of important information. Be careful of scare tactics in mimicking the look of official government or legal letters. Prospects can resent being fooled that way.
- *The sales letter:* Jeffrey Dobkin, direct mail and marketing expert says a sales letter should be included in every mailing package and that by doing so, you can increase your direct mail response by 30 to 40 percent. Some other tips: emphasize again (and again in all your customer correspondence) your business's benefits; make the letter personal between you and the recipients; encourage them to call and make it easy for them to respond with a toll-free number, reply card, prepaid reply envelope or postcard, and your e-mail address; at the end of your letter, include a P.S. (because most people read them) to highlight an offer, remind them of a new offer or product, or urge them to act. And last, mail often to your defined target market.

    Dobkin also advises, "You should *not* ask for an order in their mailing package. The *only* objective of their mailing package should be to generate a response: make people call for a *free* valuable booklet, sample, or more information. Then *you* answer the phone and verify interest or close the sale."
- *The flier (or flyer):* This is a sheet or small brochure that contains additional details about your product or service that your sales letter stated in its introduction. As mentioned about brochures, they should stand alone and expound more about the advantages your customers will get from using your business offerings. Endorsements and testimonials can sup-

port your benefits' statements. Fliers and brochures can also be used for additional promotional purposes such as in other mailings, at trade shows and conferences, in your press kits.

- *Reply cards:* can be individual or attached to your flier to be torn off and returned. Allow enough space for your recipients to write any information you have requested. To invite follow-up calls or requests for more information, have simple boxes that they can check off. If you provide their address on a peel-off sticker, it will be easier for them to place their address right on the reply card. Again, use card stock that can withstand mailing and check with your postmaster about mailing permits and required postage.

It may take sometime to come up with the best direct mailing method for your business, but it will be worth your time, money, and energy if your business thrives on the successful responses you receive.

Advertorials

When staff or freelance writers (not copywriters) write a feature about a business owner or professional for a newspaper or magazine, they have to be sure they do not make it sound like an "advertorial," or "infomercial"—a long written advertisement for that business owner—or the editors will reject their story as being biased. However, you can write your own advertorials to gain publicity, but realize you will have to *pay* for the space. If you look at newspapers, you can find examples of advertorials, often professionals writing advice in column formats, usually with their photos included.

Real estate agents may offer home-selling tips; chiropractors may offer health tips; and lawyers offer legal tips. If your information is valuable, you may receive prospect inquiries. Readers have favorite columnists, and if you can afford to offer regular advertorial columns, you may develop a faithful readership and eventually acquire paying clients. Approach editors of the publications that include a readership of your target markets to see if they offer this type of advertising, find out the costs, and give them some samples of your pieces for their review.

Logos and Slogans on Materials

You may have a great looking business logo and a catchy slogan, but if you do not use these tools to differentiate you from competitors, then you are not maximizing the market advantage these marketing tools can give to your business. Of course, you will want them on all your promotional correspondence, business cards, promotional products, and your ads and publicity strategies.

If you tout your excellent customer experience, however, and do not follow through, your logo and slogan will come to stand for falseness, and disgruntled customers will quickly spread negative word of mouth. The only way to stand out is to make your business images offer distinct benefits and consistently follow through on what you promise. Chapter 10 presents some additional ways to develop successful customer relationships.

Think carefully about the image you want your logos and slogans to convey to the world, where they are placed, and what values and benefits they represent for your target market (see also Method 33).

Customer Endorsements and Testimonials

Testimonials from satisfied customers are powerful tools in getting past prospects' skepticism. People expect you to be proud of your business and its offerings, but if you can get others who have used your services or products to publicly praise your business, it is very effective in persuading new customers to contact you.

An author of a how-to writing book suggests, "Get testimonials or endorsement from well-known people in the industry related to your business or book, or use remarks from satisfied clients' or customers' letters you may receive and include their comments in your marketing materials." Their statements can be strong selling points for your products or services, especially if you get someone as famous as this writer did when James A. Michener endorsed her book. How did she get the famous Michener to write a blurb for her book? She simply wrote him a letter asking him and included a copy of her manuscript.

You can do the same with someone famous, but having sincere customers' nice comments will also do very well in spreading the good word about your business. Some tips: Ask your customers for feedback after using your products or services as soon as possible. Get their permission to use them in your promotions and ask if they can be specific about the benefit(s) they liked best as to your pricing, service, quality, and so on. If they provide you with an endorsement or testimonial, always send them a thank-you note.

One word though: The FTC has regulations about misrepresenting information to consumers including the validity of testimonials and endorsements, so only include those statements that honestly came from people who purchased or have used your products or services (or in the author's case, read her book). If you claim an expert has endorsed your business offerings, the expert must be qualified in your industry to judge your product or service and have actually analyzed or used it. For more information, go to the FTC web site: www.ftc .gov/bcp/guides/endorse.htm.

Phone Messages (Tapes and Voice Mail)

As your business grows, you might consider making a telephone-hold marketing audiotape that can thank the person for calling and provide brief information about your company or additional products. Always provide the opportunity for the caller to leave a voice mail message or to contact you or a representative directly. Consult with your local telecommunications firm for its fees to provide you with the equipment, connections, and produced tape (see also Method 79 for more phone tips).

If worded well, voice mail messages can help turn prospects into paying customers. If you are not available when customers respond to your mailings or business cards, craft messages that sell. Here are some pointers:

- Make it approximately 30 seconds in length.
- Thank them for calling you and include your name, your business, the best times they can reach you again or times when you will be returning calls and any other ways they can get in touch with you.
- Include a statement about the benefits of your business.
- If there is time, inform them about any upcoming events or sales or present discounts.
- If possible, give them the option to speak to a live person. You can do this by hiring a virtual receptionist or answering service that can contact you immediately if needed.
- Keep your voice mail up-to-date. Do not say "Happy New Year," in your voice mail when it is June.

When you are leaving a message on a client's or business associate's voice mail:

- Agree to leave a message in a client's or customer's voice mailbox.
- Say briefly why you are calling and mention the names of any persons who referred you.
- Speak s-l-o-w-l-y! It is irritating to most recipients to have to repeatedly replay your message to understand it or to get a callback number. Leave your callback number at the beginning of your message and repeat it before you hang up.
- Let them know when you will be available to receive calls.
- If you do not hear from them in a reasonable amount of time, call them again. Messages can be accidentally deleted or garbled due to technological "glitches."

Practice your voice mail delivery so you sound professional and include all the important messages you wish to convey to prospect.

Remember, with all messages you must respond and stay in constant touch with those who have patronized your business. Superior marketing messages and campaigns are not only those that increase customer responses to your ads or publicity strategies. They are the messages that get customers to respond, to buy, to buy again, and refer you to others because they know they are getting products or the delivery of services that your competitors cannot provide.

Suggested Resources

Books

Design-It-Yourself: Graphic Workshop: The Step-by-Step Guide by Chuck Green (Gloucester, MA: Rockport Publishers, 2005), projects for logos, letterheads, businesses cards, newsletters, and web site design.

Direct Marketing Strategies by Jeffrey Dobkin (Merion Station, PA: Danielle Adams Publishing, 2006). www.dobkin.com.

Jeffrey Dobkin's Successful Low Cost Direct Marketing Methods, by Jeffrey Dobkin (Merion Station, PA: Danielle Adams Publishing, 2006). www .dobkin.com.

Marketing with Newsletters: How to Boost Sales, Add Members and Raise Funds with a Print, Fax, E-Mail, Web Site or Postcard Newsletter, 3rd ed., by Elaine Floyd (Ballwin, MO: EfG, 2003).

Web Info

www.Entrepreneur.com/howto, *Entrepreneur* magazine's free, online, how-to guide, "How to Create a Logo."

www.greatfxbusinesscards.com, GreatFX Business Cards; online print shop, business cards postcard printing.

www.sellingselling.com, Alan J. Zell, sales expert's site for selling tips, articles.

www.tipsbooklets.com, Tips Products International, articles, products about promotional booklets.

10

Grow with Smart Customer Relationship Management

Without customers, a business cannot exist; thus getting and *keeping* customers is not only essential to your profits, it is vital to the continued existence and future of your business. Chapter 10 presents methods to attract customers (even over larger competing businesses), foster your customers' loyalty, and reward them for repeat business and referrals.

Business experts talk these days about *customer relationship management* (CRM). It refers to all the methods, strategies, and technologies that businesses use to satisfy customers so that sales continue and increase. With foreign competition and big businesses offering customers much lower pricing than many small businesses can challenge, you can compete by offering a personal relationship with your customers that larger companies cannot duplicate. Successful CRM requires more than just smiling and saying thank you when your customers hand you money; it includes all of the following:

- First contact with customers through mailings, phone calls, or in-person meeting
- Responses to inquiries
- Sales
- Follow-ups
- Customer service
- Employees
- Ongoing follow-ups

Practicing customer relationship management requires your dedicated commitment to showing customers that you care about them and the quality of the work your business provides. There is also an economic factor. It takes less effort and money to satisfy existing customers than to prospect for new ones, a fact that will affect your profit margin and growth.

79. First Impressions *Are* Lasting

A majority of sales are not made when you first contact or meet a prospect; however, how your conduct impresses potential customers may later determine whether they buy your product or service. If it was a bad first impression, that person is likely to spread the word to others and affect their opinions of you before you *ever* approach them. One hundred years ago, people usually did not travel far to do business. Today, people travel and talk to one another the world over and are connected with technology in ways that our forebears never imagined. Act cordially, respectfully, and with confidence when you make an initial contact, and that good impression may travel around the world.

Business Phone Etiquette

Etiquette covers rules of conduct in certain situations. In this case, the rules focus on how to respond to phone calls from potential or faithful customers who have questions or concerns.

Conversation

The first priority is to have your phone system and technology in place so you can converse and handle customers adequately whether you work from home or a downtown office. You want a system that can handle the number of customers you presently have and that can be easily upgraded if responses to your business quickly increase. If you have a toll-free number and combine it with an automated voice-mail service, it can handle your customers' calls efficiently and professionally. Use a headset to free your hands so you can reach for materials or write or type information. Talk to phone service representatives for the options that best fit the needs of your business calls.

Here are some additional tips when discussing business with customers:

- Never interrupt them. Let there be a pause when they are finished speaking to make sure they have finished what they had to say.
- Use appropriate language. Watch your grammar and stay away from inappropriate slang terms.
- Avoid putting customers on hold unless it is an emergency. If a sibling fight breaks out or a background noise in your office suddenly starts, apologize to the customer and tell them you will get back to them in a few minutes.
- Try to answer the phone before it rings three times, or you may lose the caller.
- Be a good listener. This sounds simplistic, but many people do not actually *listen* to what customers are saying. To be sure you heard them correctly, repeat what they said back to them—"You mean . . ." or "You are saying . . ."—and the customer will correct you if you are wrong. If it is a

complaint, listen very closely; then write down the problem and what they want you to do to resolve the issue (see also Method 81).

- Do not tape callers' conversations or put them on a speakerphone without their permission. Check with your state's regulations regarding the taping of phone conversations.
- Always return calls as soon as possible and at the times the callers said they would be available.
- Let your customers hang up first, so you do not miss any of their questions or comments.

Again, maximize available phone system technology or hire a phone service or a virtual assistant so you can take advantage of voice-on-demand capabilities. These will permit you to record information about your products, services, or special offers, or provide the caller with additional options. Some services will enable you to send your voice-mail messages and audio recordings over the Internet or relay voice messages to your e-mail or text messaging on your cell phone. It is amazing how people can be reached almost anywhere in the world with today's technology.

What a Virtual Receptionist Can Do for You

Home business owners face an overload of daily business tasks, but you can free up time *and* present a memorable first impression to potential customers by hiring a virtual receptionist, a professionally trained *person* who answers your business calls when you cannot. A virtual receptionist (VR) is different from a virtual assistant (VA) in that a VR can schedule appointments and patch callers through to your cell phone, voice mail, or to another office. They can also forward detailed messages via fax, e-mail, text messaging, or by any communication you choose. Virtual assistants can do the same things, but they have a more collaborative relationship with clients and do many different tasks.

Virtual receptionists are ideal for companies that want to provide customers with personalized services or for businesses with virtual offices and whose employees work from home or frequently travel. Sole proprietors, partners, and spouses in business together find it a handy service whenever they are all away. Their businesses can stay "open" because virtual receptionists will always answer their phones.

Call centers that offer virtual receptionists, like AnswerPlus (www .answerplus.ca) of Canada, have a selection of customized applications. They can be used for business hours calls, after-hour calls, overflow calls when the owner is on the phone, or other specialized functions. No matter what the circumstances, all your callers will be greeted with a live voice, and by a person trained to follow a standard (scripted) answering technique, providing a professional consistency every time your business number is called and answered.

To use a virtual receptionist, all you need is a phone number (though a call center can supply that) and a plan with a *call forwarding* feature. Most home business owners already have a fax machine, cell phone with voice mail and/or text messaging, and a computer or mobile devices with access to e-mail—the technology that enables virtual receptionists to contact you anywhere in the world. Check in your local phone directories for call centers or teleservice companies near you to see what options they have available.

Faxes

E-mail business correspondence and solicitations have challenged the popularity of fax solicitations, though the Internet has enabled faxes to be sent through its lines, too. Depending on the phone system or teleservice you have hired, you can use a fax-on-demand option along with recording extensions. This enables callers to get order forms or other information by dialing in their fax numbers and hanging up. Their fax numbers will then be automatically dialed by the automated system that will deliver your stored fax with that specified recording.

To convey a professional image, your faxes should have large, bold print to ensure they are legible; be free of grammatical errors; be condensed to one sheet, if possible; and contain your name, address, e-mail address, and web site, and an opt-out number for those who no longer wish to receive your faxes. If you must have a cover sheet, use your logo, slogan, and some brief advertising message. Some companies also place a disclaimer on the bottom, in the event their fax is sent accidentally to the wrong number. It is best to get permission before you send information, and in your ads offer to fax more information to them on their request.

Broadcasting a large quantity of faxes without permission from the recipients is not always the best way to impress and get new customers. If you want to do a large fax broadcast, it might be less expensive and save you time to use a fax service. In addition to adhering to new FCC rules, you should keep in mind that businesspeople do not like to have sheets of unsolicited faxes in their trays or all over their office floors; or to be startled awake by a phone ringing at 4 A.M. in their home office.* (See also Method 78, "Phone Messages (Tapes and Voice Mail)" and Chapter 14, "Cold Calling Tips.")

Etiquette of Customer Approach

How you talk, dress, meet, and greet potential customers and other business owners can influence whether these people will want to do business with you or partner with you in entrepreneurial projects. A former English teacher with a

---

* As noted in Chapter 9, review the FCC's rules about fax solicitations, so that you are compliant with those guidelines in sending faxes for advertising purposes: Junk Fax Prevention Act of 2005 (FCC, www.fcc.gov).

students' tutoring business developed a spin-off venture for employees who had been promoted to management positions involving more contact with customers and other employees. The course focused on using correct grammar and on speaking in front of others. Using wrong or inappropriate language or slurs can hurt you and your business image.

Being courteous and considerate of other people's feelings and interests is just good manners—things like not smoking, eating, or chewing gum in front of someone; avoiding controversial topics; and being attentive when someone else is talking. These principles are usually learned in childhood and should be inherent in all of us. If you find this area difficult, you can hire customer service or etiquette specialists to help you acquire skills that welcome, not turn people away. Another possibility is to have staff handle the speeches or most of the contacts with customers.

Therein lies the challenge: How can you pitch your business to prospects or the media in a minute or less, without coming on too strong or boring them? Often referred to as one's *Elevator Pitch,* it is a short introduction about you, your business, and its benefits to customers. To get more a full 30 seconds of attention from prospective customers, focus on people's interests, state how your business can help them solve their problems, and say it with enthusiasm and in straightforward terms.

Instead of answering the typical question, "What is it that your business does?" with an "Oh, I am a professional organizer," Erin Gruver, of lifeStyle by Erin (www.lifestylebyerin.com) says, "I work with my clients to help them find creative ways to defeat chaos and clutter in their homes and offices." Kimberly Kardos-Bensing, an award-winning graphic artist and owner of Heirloom Occasions (www.heirloom-occasions.com) does not say, "I create custom invitations." She says instead, "I create conceptual works of art, each with a story to tell."

Figure out what you do for your customer and incorporate it into your elevator pitch. Then practice it in front of other business owners to get their suggestions and feedback. Finally, attend some meetings and actually use your pitch. If it is effective, the next question you may hear is one from a potential customer, "Do you have a business card?" or "Can I have more information?" or better, "When can we meet to discuss what your business has to offer?"

Additional Methods of Introducing Your Business

Participating in community events and charity benefits for nonprofit organizations teaching adult classes, and holding demonstrations are great ways to mix with people and provide opportunities for them to meet you and ask questions about your business. No matter how you meet prospects, devise a system—a notepad, handheld device, or other planner—to get potential buyers' names and contact information so you can get in touch with them later.

Another way is sending a letter of introduction to those names that have been referred to you or a smaller section of your target audience such as members of your business organization or group. Include the connection between you (membership in the same organization, or the name of the person who referred you), a brief description of your business's benefits, and your qualifications, along with an offer to talk or meet with them at their convenience. Include your contact information and a business card. Try to make it only one page in length.

If you need assistance, you can hire a professional writer or service that specializes in sales letters.

As mentioned in Chapter 14, "Cold Calling Tips," telemarketing works; it just takes practice. Follow-up calls to your mailings or requests for more information are important for turning inquiries into buyers. To pursue potential customers without pestering them, when you call, ask if it is a good time. If they say no, ask them if they would like for you to call back. As with the letter, let them know who referred you or remind them they wanted you to give them a call when you met them previously. Listen to their comments about business or your industry. One respondent told a writer, "You writers are all alike," in commenting about an unpleasant interview experience. In such situations, answer in a professional manner, stressing that is not how you do business. Know when to end the conversation, but thank them for their time and leave them with the open offer that you are always available if needed.

First impressions are important to convince people to patronize your business, but with basic manners and professional courtesy, you can convince prospective customers that you value their time and input, and hope to develop a future relationship.

Suggested Resources

Books

> *AMA Handbook for Customer Satisfaction: A Complete Guide to Research, Planning and Implementations* by Alan F. Dutka (Lincolnwood, IL: NTC Publishing Group, 1995).

> *Business Etiquette: 101 Ways to Conduct Business with Charm and Savvy* by Ann Marie Sabath (Franklin Lakes, NJ: Career Press, 2002).

> *The Business Style Handbook: An A-to-Z Guide for Writing on the Job with Tips from Communications Experts at the Fortune 500* by Helen Cunningham and Brenda Greene (New York: McGraw-Hill, 2002).

> *How to Build the [Your Name Here] Sales System* by Gill E. Wagner (CafePress, 2004). Order from www.honestselling.com.

> *How to Win Customers and Keep Them for Life: Revised and Updated for the Digital Age*, rev. ed., by Michael LeBoeuf (New York: Penguin Group, 2000).

> *Telephone Courtesy and Customer Service*, 3rd ed., by Lloyd C. Finch (Menlo Park, CA: Crisp Learning, 2000).

www.customerservicepoint.com, customer service articles, tips.

www.drnunley.com, site of marketing expert, Dr. Kevin Nunley; marketing ideas and articles such as "How to Boost Your Small Business With Powerful Telephone Techniques" and others.

www.sba.gov/starting_business/marketing/highimpact.html, "12 High-Impact Marketing Programs You Can Implement by Next Thursday," customer-centered marketing tips.

80. Staying Fresh

Trend Alerts: Fad or Not?

How many times do we wish that we had invested our money in some stock company whose prices were just pennies compared with what they are now? Some entrepreneurs just seem to have the knack for "catching that train before it leaves the station," as the saying goes. Recognizing a trend is one thing, but knowing how to profit from it for your business is another. You may wonder, who sold the first e-book?

How did Pierre Omidyar, the founder of eBay, think of starting that most successful online auction? Then, again, fads, like the "Pet Rock," of the 1970s, which was originated by Gary Dahl, are one-of-a-kind happenings that catch the attention of the public for a short time and then, just as quickly, go out of favor (though, usually not entirely).

Statistics show that small businesses weather trends better than fads. Trends are slower growing, usually generated by changes in population growth, politics, and technology. Trends appeal to large population segments, become a part of people's lives, and have much longer staying power than a fad, which is usually outlandish and impractical. Trends often run in cycles and may repeat every so often, or the nostalgia of that time will be brought back.

In terms of your customers, you do not have to immediately embrace every new idea, but you do have to be aware of changes and new ideas in your industry, and you must make changes as your customers begin to demand them or as you see your competitors taking advantage of new ideas and offering new benefits for customers. Assess trends and fads as they pertain to your business plan's long-range objectives. Do not rush out to get venture money just to keep with a trend. See how the market responds to it.

Stay alert for new niches and customer markets that may open up. Get customer feedback with surveys or samplings. Small businesses can only watch and look for clues to the right response if a fad or trend hits their sector.

Conducting surveys and listening to your customers when they repeatedly ask for a new product or service are ways that you can learn whether a trend may be on its way.

What You Read; What You See; What You Hear; What You Think; What You Attend

What are some good methods of tracking trends?

- *Keep up with the news:* Stay informed of the ongoing movements in your field and business by watching television business and investment shows; reading books and reports by trend specialists; reading industry trade and general business publications—national newspapers like *USA Today,* the *Wall Street Journal,* the *Philadelphia Inquirer,* and additional major city newspapers—and reading your local newspapers' business pages (see Suggested Resources later in this chapter; and also Chapter 14, "Reading for Business and Marketing Success").
- *Observe:* Take notice of how products and services are used and see if there is a growing frustration or problem that you could solve.
- *Listen:* Be attentive when your customers, families, friends, and business associates talk about their lives, needs, and problems, especially those age groups that fall into the range of your target customers. The needs and wants of baby boomers are different from those of Generation X.
- *Analyze:* To spot trends, you have to concentrate primarily on the social, economic, and political changes not just in your own neighborhood, but the world over. If you consistently try to find connections or tie-ins between the different areas you are studying, you may be up-front there with the trend experts and can prepare your business for changes in your customers' buying preferences.
- *Attend:* Never stop learning. Enroll in business or technology courses to upgrade your knowledge and skills; attend lectures by people in your industry at nearby colleges or universities. Attend trade shows to talk with those innovators of new products and systems.

Even if you think you have identified a new trend, analyze it thoroughly before making major investments for changes in your business. Do some test-marketing first of any new ideas. If you get a repeated good response, then consider going ahead to find ways your business can capitalize on this trend ahead of your competitors.

Analyze Competitors

To better serve your regular customers and attract new ones, you have to analyze what competitors do right and do wrong when it pertains to satisfying them. Chapter 4 discussed the importance of analyzing competitors when conducting your market research and when creating your business plan's objectives and goals. You can narrow that examination even further by assessing what they bring to their customers; and if there is a small niche of customers that they are not helping. You can produce baked goods for seniors but are your competitors making baked goods for their special health needs? Here are some ways to evaluate your competition's offerings:

- Examine their advertisements to see what products or services they are offering and the age group(s) they are targeting. Look at their promotional materials, pricing, and method of distribution to see whether you can offer something that they cannot or prefer not to provide.
- Send out direct mailings with response cards, offer to do some talks to target groups, and ask potential customers in person for ideas, or make some cold-calling phone calls to get feedback from people about what they wish a service or product like yours had.
- Look for stories and media coverage on your competitors to read what the owners and executives pride themselves on and where they hope to take their business.
- Just ask. Talk directly with your competitors to see if they receive calls for jobs or projects that they prefer not to do and that you could tackle instead.

How to Identify a New Market

If your business is profitable, you may be wondering why experts advise that you should always be looking for new markets. New competitors can move in next door or in the next town at any time, and with the global market expanding, new competitors can come from all over the world. If you do not look beyond your existing products and present customers, you risk your business becoming obsolete. Sales growth depends on identifying new market outlets for your services and products. Here are tips for identifying new markets:

- Review your previous market research and do new research to see how your target market has changed and if new sidelines have opened up.
- Look for population growth changes or new housing developments or new business openings in your neighborhood to identify new markets and mail or contact them with your promotional materials.
- Consider creating new products or services for your regular customers.
- Look for possible new markets outside your area, state, or country. Back at home again, hand out your promotional literature to those that you work with on a regular basis: your experts, printer, attorney, banker, consultants, and other professionals. Ask for their materials, so you can reciprocate and hand out their sales literature.

Developing a new market is similar to starting your business again: Revise your business plan and seek assistance from business experts like those at SCORE or Women's Centers or SBDCs or business incubators, so you can plan your new strategies for survival and growth (see also Method 98). Consider any steps carefully, so you will not extend your business more than you can manage in operation or with finance. Look for new markets, but at a pace that you can handle and afford.

Suggested Resources

Books

> *The Must-Have Customer: 7 Steps to Winning the Customer You Haven't Got* by Robert Gordman with Armin Brott (New York: Truman Talley Books, 2006).
>
> *Next: Trends for the Near Future* by Ira Matathia and Marian L. Salzman (New York: Overlook, 1999).

Organization

> The Trends Research Institute, www.trendsresearch.com, Gerald Celente, director; publishes *Trends Journal;* tracks many trend categories.

Web Info

> www.EntrepreneurialConnection.com, National Association for the Self-Employed (NASE), offers monthly microbusiness trends every month. Click on the "Trend Alert" tab at the top of the page.
>
> www.nowandnext.com, web site of What's Next, a bimonthly business intelligence report focusing on new ideas and trends.

81. The Care and Feeding of Devoted Customers

Satisfied customers are generally happy customers, whose word-of-mouth praise will help build a solid customer base for your business. They are your key to referrals and repeat business. Your friendliness and attitude toward pleasing your customers, as well as those of any employees should be the foundation of your customer service.

Offering the Best Customer Service

If you are just starting out, it is likely that your preliminary market research revealed just who your ideal customers should be. If you are already established and making money, you should know a bit more about your paying customers to serve them better: What is important to them? What are their main business or personal concerns? What *specifically* can your business offer that will make them remain your loyal patrons and not turn to your competitors?

Kelly Poelker, virtual assistant and president of Another 8 Hours, Inc. (www.Another8Hours.com), says, "The Golden Rule applied to business—treat your customers the way you want to be treated. Customer service plays a major role in making your business survive and thrive. Remember that it takes a lot more time, energy, and resources to gain a new client than to keep an existing one happy. In return, your client base will grow through referrals from satisfied customers. Word-of-mouth marketing from satisfied customers is the biggest compliment your business can get. Don't just be good at customer service—excel in it! It could mean the difference between a client choosing you over a competitor."

Customer service alone can be the deciding factor for people to choose your business over another one. Here are some tips for providing outstanding customer service:

- *Provide automated customer service:* There are four methods to handle customers' questions or prospects' queries when they cannot reach you or prefer to do the research on their own:
  1. Create a business web site that features your products or services and additional ways you can be contacted. Include your site's URL on all your correspondence, promotional materials, and in your advertising.
  2. Maximize the capabilities of voice mail, voice-mail services, or virtual receptionist (see Method 79). These are better than answering machines, because you can provide longer explanations, additional information, or current offers.
  3. Utilize fax-back programs. Commercial fax service companies can store your fax documents on their system and when your clients need to access those documents, you just type in a designated code and the service will make those documents immediately available.
  4. Use automated e-mail. When potential customers request more information or sign up for a free e-zine, you want to start out with a good relationship. The responding e-mail should sound like a person is writing and give the customer some idea of what information to expect in the future. You can even offer a discount coupon, a free electronic report, or some type of reward for contacting you.
- *Show care:* Personable treatment with respect and honesty is valued by everyone.
- *Be timely:* Respect customers' time. Responding in a timely manner is important to customers with busy lives.
- *Be current:* Keep up with new technologies to make customers' ordering, requests, and overall experience hassle-free.
- *Promise accuracy:* Provide information or execution that is thorough and correct. If you do not know, seek experts' help or be honest and refer your clients to others who have the answers.

- *Provide choices:* Most buyers like to have choices. You do not have to have a huge selection, but try to provide several options or packages of your products and services.
- *End positively:* End on a strong note with a little extra surprise for your customers, a little gift with a follow-up thank-you letter, or some other way that impresses your customers with your commitment to their satisfaction and that sets your business apart from others.

Even if you believe you are offering optimum customer service, there is always room for improvement. With today's increasing global markets, prospective customers have multiple companies from which to choose. If you understand from your target market's perspective how they want you to deliver your products or services, their loyalty and referrals should provide you with a solid and growing business for years to come.

Rewarding Customer Loyalty

Rewarding customers' repeat business is not as expensive as you might think. Here are suggestions:

- *Thank you, Thank you:* Sending a thank-you letter in the postal mail (preferred) to express your appreciation for customers' purchases or referrals shows customers that you care about them and not just the bottom line. With a letter in hand, they can recommend your services to someone else who is visiting them in their homes or in their offices. Others will think "Wow! That business owner really values customers." For a few moments of your time and a few cents for the card and postage, you could ensure continued repeat business and even more referrals.
- *On Time, On Budget:* Provide yourself with enough time to complete a project to meet customers' deadlines and with the pricing you estimated. If you are late or way over on your cost estimates, that may cause a ripple effect and make your customers also late with their commitments. If you start a project and see it is going to be late or more costly, tell your customers as early as possible so they can make adjustments or new contracts. No one likes unpleasant surprises. Those clients will look elsewhere in the future.
- *Respond Promptly:* With today's technology, voice mail, e-mails, and even letters can get lost. Thus, when customers contact you, acknowledge that you received their communication and that you will answer them at length as soon as you can.
- *Be financially faithful:* Give your customers their money's worth; and pay your bills on time.

Dr. Robert Sullivan, business expert and founder of the Small Business Advisor (www.isquare.com) says, "Stay Close to Your Customers. Remember how impressed you were when the auto dealership sent you a postcard on your car's birthday with an offer for a free car wash? How about the time the retail store sent you an e-mail asking how you were enjoying your last purchase and if there are any problems?"

"These businesses are 'staying close' to their customers. Remember that it takes much less effort to KEEP a customer than to GET a new customer! It makes good sense to figure out ways that you can reestablish contact with someone who has made a former purchase. Thanks to e-mail this is easy and inexpensive to do," says Sullivan.

Rewarding customers' loyalty need not be expensive and can add to your customers' continued faithfulness and to your profits (see also Methods 48 and 83).

Educating Your Customers

Today, we have access to so much information that it is overwhelming at times. Providing loyal or prospective customers with ongoing, free information related to your products or services and your industry can demonstrate that you care about them. Information that can help them save money and take better care of their purchases shows customer appreciation that will not be forgotten. You can provide helpful tips and instructions with miniseminars or demonstrations, postcards, or e-mail tips and electronic newsletters (e-zines). Provide outdoor cooking recipes for those who just purchased an outdoor grill; mail postcards with organizing tips for the holidays or moving; send e-mails for craft ideas using a special new modeling project, and other suggestions.

You know your product or service best and the benefits of its use. Do not assume your customer does, so give them news they can use to take full advantage of their purchases. The challenge here is to provide free information that will also lead to your clients' future business, but without the hard sell. Your objective then is to convey a business image that says your business is customer-centered and that you want to offer more to your customers than just selling something. It says you would like to develop an ongoing relationship even after customers buy from you.

Handling Customer Complaints

No matter what business you are in, you will not please all your customers all the time. It can be upsetting on an emotional basis because small business owners are the primary producers of their products or services and take complaints as a personal affront. You know, or at least you thought you were giving your customers the best of what you had to offer. Why, you ask, is someone not happy?

Here are ways to deal with unhappy customers:

- Try not to take complaints personally. Realize that customers do not really know you (unless they are friends or family members), and they are just expressing their dissatisfaction.
- Listen completely to the reasons for their complaints and then ask specific questions as to where there was a misunderstanding. Stay calm and

professional and avoid abusive language. On the other hand, you have the right not to be abused, either.

An irate customer was overheard in a chain store that sold phones and technology equipment, venting to its manager. He had sent her cell phone back for free repair twice, and now she was complaining of a tiny scratch on the side of the phone: "I hope Satan comes up and swallows you and takes you down with him into the depths of hell!" All because the young man could not, according to company policy, give her a new cell phone without a scratch.

- Ask how they wish their complaint resolved and see if you can reach a compromise. Sometimes, just acknowledging their dissatisfaction will help to defuse their anger or unhappiness. You can offer a partial or complete refund; a free coupon; or to redo the service, depending on what was in your business policies or contracts.

A woman was exhibiting one of her national products at a trade show when a person walked up and saw it, and said to her friend, "That," pointing to the product, "is terrible." She then walked away without saying what displeased her. The owner never had the opportunity to ask the details.

To prevent future complaints:

- Establish business policies for your refunds and guarantees.
- Have your lawyer review the details of any business contracts you are offered so you know your responsibilities and those of your client.
- Focus on customer service. Follow through with what you promised and always offer a little more than they expected.

If you give your customers the best possible service, reward them, and handle their dilemmas and complaints, your actions will directly affect your repeat business and the number of referrals you receive. Learn how to provide customer service effectively, and you should never have to worry about the success of your business.

Suggested Resources

Books

Building Customer Loyalty: 21 Essential Elements in Action by JoAnna Brandi (Dallas, TX: The Walk the Talk, 2001).

Complaint Management: The Heart of CRM by Bernd Stauss and Wolfgang Seidel (Stamford, CT: South-Western Educational Publications, 2005).

Customer Service Training 101 by Renee Evenson (New York: AMACON, 2005).

Relationship Marketing: New Strategies, Techniques and Technologies to Win the Customers You Want and Keep Them Forever by Ian H. Gordon (Hoboken, NJ: John Wiley & Sons, 1998).

Satisfaction: How Every Great Company Listens to the Voice of the Customer by Chris Denove and J. D. Power (New York: Penguin Group, 2006).

Web Info

www.customer-retention.com, "Customer Retention and Loyalty," site of JoAnna Brandi, customer service expert; articles, biweekly tips.

www.Entrepreneur.com/howto, *Entrepreneur* magazine's free, online, how-to guide, "How to Build a Stellar Customer Service Program."

www.score.org/guides.html, SCORE's 60-second guide, "Establishing Great Customer Service."

82. Customer Communication Tips

The basic principle of CRM is simple: Provide for your customers' needs and they will not go elsewhere. To ensure you are meeting their needs, you must establish a communicative relationship between them and yourself. Here are some ideas.

What to Ask Customers to Obtain Honest Evaluations

Sometimes we ask questions whose answers we dread or at least prefer not to hear. But when it pertains to customers, you want honest evaluations because you need to hear their opinions to satisfy them. The best time to survey customers is right after they have made a purchase from you. Include your customer surveys and questionnaires in your postal mailings or e-mail. Here is just a small sampling of the questions you can ask:

- What do you like or dislike about my products, services, customer service, or other?
- How did you find me? Did you hear of my business through ads? Referrals? Publicity? Other?
- Did you use any other businesses like mine before? If so, what did you like or dislike about them?
- How did we (your business) do in overall performance?
- What product or service would you like to see added?

You can encourage customers to respond to your surveys or questions by offering an incentive—a coupon, a small gift, or a discount toward a future purchase. Assess their answers for ways you can improve service, to avoid competitors' mistakes, and be more attuned to their preferences. Look at positive assessments, too. Be sure to repeat aspects of your business that your customers say they liked and emphasize those products or services in your ads. Software, online providers, and your created survey are all good routes for collecting your responses.

Frequent Communications

Stay in touch with customers by providing useful information through any communication modes you have available. If you do it on a regular basis, with a newsletter, e-zine, or postcard, customers will begin to look for these. If you have a blog or a message board in which customers can participate and offer suggestions to one another, they will be more likely to visit your web site often.

Whatever you send should be fairly short. People do not have time to sit and read pages and pages of an article. Keep your lines of communication easy and open. Place your customer service number on your business materials and web site so they can talk to you or a trained staff. Make it a policy to get back to all callers within 24 hours. Keeping customers' communication lines open will prevent frustrations and dissatisfaction from building up and will encourage them to stay with your business.

What Customers Do Not Say

Some customers will never complain to you because they do not have the time or they cannot find your contact information. They may continue to do business with you, but less frequently, until they can find another company that responds better to their needs. If you have not heard from customers lately, send a postcard or e-mail, or give them a call. They might have moved, changed their contact information, or just lost your business card in their clutter.

When you do reach them, ask if there is anything you can do for them, and if there is a reason you have not heard from them lately. It might be a perfectly legitimate reason (they were on vacation or handling a family matter), or it may be their opportunity to tell you what bothered them the last time they did business with you.

You may notice that your cash flow has decreased or that you are receiving fewer referrals. It may be an indication that you need to reevaluate your business offerings and service to see that it is 100 percent customer driven and that any staff you have also reflect your willingness-to-serve attitude. If your staff or receptionists are surly, will not make eye contact, or do not respond to customers, you will lose customers very quickly.

What Drives Customers Away

Here are some common business mistakes that drive customers away:

- Not returning calls or providing them with the information they requested. If there will be a delay, let them know and give them the option for a refund, a credit for a future purchase, or a backorder at a later date.
- Being discourteous. You and your staff should be polite over the phone, online, or in person. Think of your favorite department stores or the little shops you frequent. Is there a person there who makes a connection with customers, who actually makes eye contact with customers or smiles? Do you miss that person when he or she is not working that day? Great salespersons make prospects feel important as individuals.
- Never getting back to a customer or new prospect when they have a question or request.
- Not delivering what you said you would. If you cannot do or provide something, do not promise it in the first place.
- Not being concerned. If customers come to you for a service or product your business does not handle or make, they will appreciate your suggestions of others who can help them. And other business owners may refer potential customers back to you in the future.
- Not recognizing customers' loyalty. Thank-you notes, designating a "customer of the month," award, little gifts, and other tokens of appreciation make customers feel appreciated and welcome.

It is just common sense and courtesy. Treat your customers like you would want (and like) to be treated and your business will thrive (see also Chapter 14 "Connecting with Customers").

Suggested Resources

Books

The Arthur Andersen Guide to Talking with Your Customers, rev. ed., by Michael J. Wing and Arthur Andersen LLP (Dover, NH: Upstart Publishing, 1997).

How to Conduct Telephone Surveys by Linda B. Bourque, PhD and Eve P. Fielder (Newton, NH: Sage Publications, 2002).

How to Conduct Your Own Survey by Priscilla Salant and Don A. Dillman (New York: John Wiley & Sons, 1994).

Web Info

> www.eCustomerServiceWorld.com, Online Customer Service Associate Membership organization, timely articles, discounts on customer service books.

> www.surveystar.com, survey specialists, examples of demo surveys.

83. Additional Ideas for Showing Customer Appreciation

Notes and Greetings

You can have thank-you cards and greeting cards printed with your logo and illustrations on the front for a professional look, but always handwrite a little note inside to make your cards look more personal. Send greeting cards out not just during the winter season, but all seasons. Many business owners send out birthday and anniversary cards to their customers, or congratulatory cards whenever they read or hear about a customer receiving an award or recognition for their work or community involvement.

Personalized Gifts

Depending on your customers and your budget, you can give out personalized and promotional gift items to thank your customers throughout the year. Promotional product consultants can suggest what is appropriate for the status of your customers and estimate the price it should cost. Talk with your accountant, who can advise you what gifts are and are not deductible. Spend an appropriate amount on a gift—too much may appear as a bribe; too little may make you look cheap or insincere.

You can also show your appreciation by making a donation to your customers' favorite charity in their name, or if they are authors, giving copies of their books to their public library (see also Method 76 and Chapter 14, "Choosing the Best Promotional Product for Your Business").

Little Extras

Sometimes it is the little things we say or do that impress the most. You can provide your customers with extras such as a tiny bottle of cleaner when they buy your jewelry; or hand delivery (if geographically possible) of a product or service; or some other unexpected effort, for no extra charge. You will make customers feel special and slightly surprised that you would go one more step for them. They will be more likely to return again or give you a referral.

Without customers, you cannot have a business. Without *satisfied* customers, you cannot *stay* in business. Dedicate your business goals and objectives to pleasing your customers, getting lots of them, and most importantly, keeping them.

Suggested Resources

Books

Clued In: How to Keep Customers Coming Back Again and Again by Lewis Carbone (Upper Saddle River, NJ: Financial Times/Prentice Hall, 2004).

Customers for Life: How to Turn That One-Time Buyer into a Lifelong Customer, rev. ed., by Carl Sewell and Paul B. Brown (New York: Doubleday Books, 2002).

11

Grow with the Internet (It's *Still* the Wild, Wild Web): You Can Survive and Thrive Online

The "Dot-Com Bomb" discouraged many from starting Web businesses, but today many entrepreneurs are using the Internet to start solid, successful ventures. Most business owners, professionals, and other self-employed individuals have web sites to promote their ventures, no matter what kind of work they do. Potential customers expect it and even ask for it. Chapter 11 describes some Internet business promotion basics that you can use to establish your business presence on the Web.

84. Establish a World Wide Web Business Presence

Explore Your Best Web Business Presence Options

While there are numerous ways to market your business using the Internet, one of the best ways is to establish a business web site. Why? For the profit potential!

The Census Bureau of the Department of Commerce stated that the total e-commerce sales for 2005 were estimated at $86.3 billion, an increase of 24.6 percent from 2004. As more people become comfortable shopping online, they begin to use it in other ways. They can research and compare products and services between you and your competitors with pricing, products, or services, and the convenience in ordering. They can participate in online newsgroups to get opinions and referrals from participants for the best places to do online business, find information, or spread good or bad word of mouth about businesses with whom they have had dealings. They can go shopping around the world.

Statistics like these are reason for almost anyone with the entrepreneurial spirit to establish an online moneymaking site immediately, but web sites can range from very low-cost if you build your web site yourself to paying a Web designer thousands to set up a sophisticated site with audio, video capabilities, and more. The more preliminary research and planning you do before you take your business on the Internet or upgrade a present web site, the better will be your chances of success.

You need to go back to your original business plan and use it as a guide to plan the marketing strategies of either having a web site as part of your present venture or as your primary source of income. You should first decide why you want a web site and then plan your promotional activities based on that reason. Here are some of the most frequent uses for web sites and the different marketing strategies:

- *E-commerce or e-tailing:* An online store can sell anything and everything, from books and collectibles to gifts. Customers need easy and secure methods of transactions.
- *Informational:* These are community web sites like *i*Village.com, online publications, or sites like Blue SuitMom.com that present information for specific populations, genders, or industries. These owners market with their content that encourages visitors to return.
- *Professionals:* Consultants, business coaches, marketing experts, authors, and other self-employed individuals use their web sites to establish themselves as experts with their articles and ancillary products such as audiotapes, CDs, books, and such. They can post their schedules, appearances, business hours, rates, and other details for potential customers who want to make appointments or contact them.
- *Brick-and-mortar retail stores:* These stores have online web sites for potential customers to check their sales and latest products or items and to order through the mail.
- *Creative venturists:* Skilled craftspersons, artists and artisans, cartoonists, movie producers, comedians, photographers, freelance writers and authors (including bloggers), musicians and their groups, and others who produce unique creations use the Internet to reach larger markets and showcase their talents and to sell sideline products.
- *Technology and Business-to-Business:* These enterprises include computer and home/small office supplies, software and other technology, tech information, and Web-based services, design, hosting, marketing, maintenance, and others that need the Internet for personal and business reasons.
- *Media:* Newspapers, radio, television, and magazines and publications (print and online) offer the latest news online as a supplement and interactive opportunities for readers, viewers, and listeners.
- *Others:* Included here are combinations of all or some of the previously listed plus those of health, fitness, nonprofit and for-profit organizations,

business groups, communities, governments and their agencies, hobby enthusiasts, research, online auctions, and many other niche web sites.

The point of listing these categories of web sites is to determine what type you need to market your business and how simple or complex you want it to be. If you know what type of web site you want, you can plan its structure and content. If you have an informational web site, you will need to post regular content in the form of articles or e-zines. If you are selling products online, you will have to make ordering them easy and secure. And if you want an interactive site, you will have to provide online chats, teleclasses, message boards, and other attractions to encourage repeat visitors.

Create a Noteworthy URL and E-Mail Addresses

In establishing a noteworthy URL, you will want to choose a domain name that relates to you and your business and will help build recognition of your brand. If you have a registered name, XYZ Business, then, it makes sense to have XYZ.com (commercial ventures). Recently, new extensions have been added such as *store* (for e-commerce web sites), *biz* (for businesses), *info* (for information-based web sites), *nom* (for individuals) and others. These extensions are not widely known, however, and could confuse potential customers looking for your web site.

Some other tips in choosing a domain name: It should not be abbreviated, and should be easy to remember and pronounce such as http://www.JonesFruit.com instead of www.JnsFrt.com. Your entire URL (uniform resource locator) should have your name: www.yourdomainname.com and not http://www.theircompany/215453yourbusinessname if you were to lease space from another web site. For a few extra dollars a year, you might want also to purchase domain names that are close to yours and lead to your original site. This might occur if people try to phonetically type your business's name into the URL and misspell it. You do not need an additional site or hosting for these alternative domain names, and your hosting provider can easily connect these other false names to your actual business web site.

Your web site address and e-mail address should be connected to help build your online identity. The name portion of your e-mail address should be the same as your web site address such as you@yourdomainname.com, instead of the common you@yahoo.com or you@hotmail.com. A web provider can provide you with "e-mail forwarding" so that e-mails sent to you@yourdomainname.com can immediately be forwarded to you@yahoo.com or you@hotmail.com. Senders never know that you@yourdomainname.com is really you@yahoo.com or you@hotmail.com.

In addition, if a customer misspells or writes in some other word before the "@" (the user name), your web provider can still forward their e-mail message to you. For example, if they misspelled an e-mail to you such as me@yourdomainname .com, their e-mail would still be forwarded to you@yahoo.com or you

@hotmail.com, so those e-mail messages would not be returned or lost somewhere in cyberspace. This feature also permits you to create several specific e-mails like products@yourdomainname.com, orders@yourdomainname.com, or contact@yourdomainname.com, and have them all forwarded to you@yahoo.com or you@hotmail.com.

With these options, you can use your business domain name and its e-mail addresses before you construct a web site. They will enhance the professionalism of your business and enable you to start an online business relationship with existing and new customers.

Suggested Resources

Book

> *Essential Business Tactics for the Net*, 2nd ed., by Larry Chase and Eileen Shulock (Hoboken, NJ: John Wiley & Sons, 2001).

Web Info

> http://website101.com, WebSite 101, "Free Small Business Tutorials for E-commerce Entrepreneurs."
>
> www.Entrepreneur.com/howto, *Entrepreneur* magazine's free, online, how-to guide, "How to Start an E-Business."
>
> www.gigalaw.com, Internet legal news.
>
> www.sba.gov/training/courses.html, online courses, "Building Your web site" and "Managing the Digital Enterprise."
>
> www.selfstartersweeklytips.com, "Self-Starters Weekly Tips," Internet marketing strategies.

85. Web Business Plan and Construction Basics

Just as you created a business plan for your entire business, you should write a web business plan, with emphasis on the marketing aspect.° Also create a web budget. It will help you determine what designs and web hosting choices you can afford.

° To reassure prospective customers that their personal and financial information is private and secure, you can apply to the Better Business Bureau to follow their requirements to receive their BBB*OnLine* Reliability and BBB*OnLine* Privacy seals that you can post on your web site. Visit the BBB web site (www.bbb.org) for more information.

Plan

Having a plan early in your web site's development will give you an edge over your competitors.

A productive web site should help you reduce costs, increase your sales, or both. It should also help improve communications and services and strengthen relationships with the most important persons related to your business—your customers. Here are some web plan essentials:

- *Marketing:* Decide (1) how you will use your site to market your business; and then (2) how you will market your site to attract customers and convince them you can solve their problems or needs?
- *For customers:* Know your target market: their ages, the common interests that will draw them to your site, the technology they use, and their computer and Internet preferences. Your site must be created with a specific focus on its target users.
- *For your site's mechanics and purpose:* Know your mission or vision for your site. For the mechanics and operation: Know who is going to design and host it; how much money you will need for it to go online and then to maintain it monthly; the time you will have to devote to it; and how much technology, equipment, and skill you need to maintain it unless you plan to have a professional do it (see also Method 40).

Construction Basics

Once you have protected your domain name, then you must construct your site (unless you decide to "park" it for awhile until you are ready). To maximize your Web presence, your site should present a professional image, and the best way to do that is to hire a Web designer. Although you can do it yourself with software and templates, a skilled designer can incorporate your logo and business name into a polished web site and advise you about any extra features you might want to include.

Web Site Basics

- *Build it.* You can design it using web site creation software that came with your computer package; or if you know something about Web design, you can use Macromedia Dreamweaver (www.macromedia.com); or choose a web designer who is experienced in your industry or profession.
- *Choose a hosting company.* This decision should be based on your projected plans for your site's use:
  —If you want an uncomplicated site consisting of only a few pages of text and simple graphics, almost any company can host it, generally at less than $15 a month.

—If you plan to have a content-heavy site, you will need a dynamic site with server-side scripting and database usage.

—If you plan for your site to *be* your business as an e-commerce site with a catalog, shopping cart, and credit card processing capabilities, you can use e-commerce solutions from web-hosting companies like Microsoft's Web Hosting for Small Business with Commerce Manager or Yahoo Merchant Solutions, and others. They bundle site-building tools, catalog capabilities, shopping carts, payment, shipping services, and more. They may be more affordable in the long run than building a site yourself and having to obtain all those features.

To conduct e-commerce on your own, you will need shopping cart software like those listed in "Suggested Resources" for this section. They allow you to take credit cards and also offer marketing tools to help you track visitors, use e-mail marketing, database creation, surveys, and other promotional avenues for your site.

If your sales require you to get an Internet merchant account from your bank, ask your own bank or search for credit card processing companies and payment gateway account companies. You will need this service to verify your customers' credit card accounts and connect into your Internet merchant account. A more affordable way to start accepting online payments is to establish an account with an account-based system like PayPal (www.paypal.com). These systems charge a set amount for every transaction, and offer some additional services for businesses. (See also Chapter 5, "Establishing Payment Options.")

—If you are planning to have a site with potentially heavy traffic, you should consider dedicated hosting that provides you with your own server and dedicated bandwidth. You probably will not need this immediately, and you can upgrade to this option if your site's sales and participation become extensive.

- *Consider auction sites.* Many business owners, professional craftspersons, and entrepreneurs start selling through online auction sites like eBay to test their markets for their business offerings. Many small online users have gone on to open successful eBay Stores that permit them to sell from a fixed designation on eBay.
- *Operate and maintain your web site venture.* If possible, arrange to update it on your own as needed. If your web site actively involves your customers, you will be updating it often to meet their needs and requests for new information and products.

This is just a brief overview of some web site basics and options to consider in your commercial web site plan. It is best to take sufficient time to thoroughly research all the opportunities by meeting with several web designers or web hosting companies, and web site consultants for the best recommendations for your online presence and your budget.

Ask for feedback from associates, friends, and others who have web sites to see if you need to revise or refine it. After you launch your web site, keep an eye out for any niche that may open up as you go online. It might even be one that you did not envision and that could possibly be more profitable than the business for which your site was designed.

Once your web site is in operation, notify the media with a press release and put the URL on all your business and marketing materials, in all your media ads, and on taglines to your e-mails to help potential customers find your web site.

Suggested Resources

Books

> *GigaLaw Guide to Internet Law* by Doug Isenberg (New York: Random House, 2002).
>
> *How to Get Your Business on the Web: A Legal Guide to E-Commerce* by Fred Steingold (Berkeley, CA: Nolo Press, 2001). Book and CD-ROM.
>
> *Planning Your Internet Marketing Strategy: A Doctor Ebiz Guide* by Ralph F. Wilson (Hoboken, NJ: John Wiley & Sons, 2001). www.wilsonweb.com.

Software

Here are some popular shopping-cart software programs. Your trade industry, profession, or online entrepreneurs may suggest others:

> GoEcart.com, www.goecart.com
>
> KickStartCart.com, www.kickstartcart.com
>
> 1Shoppingcard.com, www.1shoppingcart.com
>
> ShopSite, Inc., www.shopsite.com

Web Info

Information sites and some Payment Gateway Account companies. Again, ask others in your trade or industry or business owners for their recommendations:

> http://sbdcnet.utsa.edu/sbic/e-com.htm#, free online E-Commerce Guide by the SBDC Net (SBA.gov related)
>
> http://provider.com/contracts.htm, advice about writing contracts for web designers, developers and programmers with links to legal advice, sample agreements, and real contracts used by web designers
>
> www.authorize.net, Authorize.Net

www.cybersource.com, CyberSource

www.Entrepreneur.com/howto, *Entrepreneur* magazine's free, online, how-to guides, "Taking Your Business Online"

www.verisign.com, VeriSign

86. Establish a Customer-Friendly Web Site

Customer Focus

A large factor in contributing to the success of your business web site is the interaction you offer your customers and site visitors. Knowing the profile and computer capabilities of those people most likely to come to your site will dictate what your web site must provide. In planning for optimum customer satisfaction, you should have answers for the following questions:

- Will local customers use your products or services, or can they be sold overseas (see also Method 89)?
- Will your customers expect your web site to be like those of your competitors?
- Will you be offering a unique product or service or web site, not readily available elsewhere?
- Are you selling your products, services, or information directly to retailers or to consumers?
- Can you use your web site to sell auxiliary products? Present new sidelines or components or improve service to regular or potential customers?

Improving Site Usability

The friendlier or easier you develop your site for customers, the more likely they are to visit, stay awhile, and trust to buy from you. Here are some user-friendly tips:

- Make sure your images and pages load quickly. The Internet is "instant," and too many complex graphics or other features will slow your visitors' viewing and try their patience. Provide a "skip intro," if you introduce your site with an active graphic or audio.
- Test your transactions' processes regularly, including new upgrades, to make sure customers do not have trouble with ordering or participating.
- Provide alternatives such as phone numbers or instant messaging that customers can use to talk to you or a live technical or customer representative.
- Test your site using different browsers to ensure all visitors can view your site correctly.

- Make searches on your site efficient and capable of handling misspelled entries.
- Keep current with the latest technology and new features you can use to make your site more welcoming. Use voice-mail services that can send messages to you over the Internet so you will not miss any customer inquiries.

Encouraging Return Visits

Depending on your budget, here are a few ways you can attract and develop faithful relationships with your customers and encourage them to return to your web site:

- Encourage feedback with message boards, surveys and polls, instant messaging, and e-mails. Ellen Parlapiano, coauthor and online partner with Patricia Cobe, says "Connect with your audience. The web can be a wonderful way to survey potential customers and clients, and conduct informal focus groups. Whenever we are brainstorming new Mompreneur® projects, we reach out to the mothers who visit the message boards at our web site, www.mompreneursonline.com. For example, before launching our new Mompreneur® Marketplace, we asked our community members what kinds of products, services, and features they'd like to see there. It's also important to keep the feedback coming. Constantly ask your target audience what you're doing well, and what they think you could do better."
- Provide free material in the form of news, survey results, posted articles, subscription e-zines, tips, blogs (see also Method 87), streaming audio or video, forums, shareware, and other methods for exchange of information. Replace your information regularly to ensure visitors come back for the latest items.
- Offer samples of items you sell (e.g., one class of a teleclass or course, books, or e-books) to encourage more customers to buy and participate.
- Encourage visitors to answer a short daily survey.
- Hide a graphic or another visual on your web site and offer a prize for the first person to locate it. It encourages visitors to go through your site's pages.
- Reward faithful customers by providing exclusive information just for them.
- Encourage customers to send in profiles or practical tips and choose one a week to feature on your site.

These are just a few ways you can make your web site more appealing and enticing to customers and prospects. Use the ones that are most effective in getting traffic and that please your visitors. If you focus on your target users and design your site with strong and easy usability, you are likely to attract a following and encourage them to become faithful visitors and faithful buyers.

Suggested Resources

Books

> *Designing Web Sites for Every Audience* by Ilise Benun, Designed by Lisa Buchanan (Cincinnati, OH: F&W Publications, 2003).
>
> *Mompreneurs® Online: Using the Internet to Build Work at Home Success* by Ellen Parlapiano and Patricia Cobe (New York: Penguin Group, 2001).

Web Info

> www.EzineQueen.com, Alexandria Brown's site with articles; program/ manual "Boost Business with Your Own E-zine."
>
> www.promoteyourself.com, business promotional ideas including Internet marketing.

87. Top Internet Marketing Methods for Your Business and Your Web Site

In addition to the methods you use to encourage repeat visits to your web site, you will want to think about attracting new prospects, following through with sales, conducting ongoing market research, and developing online marketing tactics for either your business or its web site, or both. Here are marketing and advertising avenues you may want to try.

Affiliates, Links, and More

- *Affiliate marketing* is a promotion that permits you to advertise your site on other web sites. You pay a commission to them if the posting leads to a sale for you. This can work reciprocally when you become an "affiliate partner," and sell another site's goods such as books on your site as well.
- *Back linking* is more of a friendly exchange of links to others' sites that you can offer as a list of resources related to your business, for example, or in articles that you write and post online.
- *Banners* are visual advertising bars posted on sites, often with animated features to attract prospects to click on them. You usually pay by the number of impressions. They can help to build your brand and can be expensive. They can add revenue if posted on your site.

- *E-mails* that are unsolicited should not be sent over the Internet. Use permission marketing to prospects who provide you with their e-mail addresses and request more information about your business offerings or ask for an electronic publication. To avoid having your e-mails deleted as spam, write the title or topic of the requested material in the subject line of the e-mail you are sending out. Check with your web hosting service for their recommendations for e-mail list management software.
- *Online classified ads* can be used for free on the thousands of sites that allow you to post your ad, and plenty of low-cost sites also are available. Disadvantages of posting free classified ads include the time it takes to post them to all the sites you want and the poor odds that anyone will even find your ad with so many others in competition.

  For any classified ad (print or online), include your keywords in your headline and then mention the benefits of your products or services to customers. Keep your ad copy concise and include a "call to action" for people to contact you in some way for more information.
- *Search engines' listings* can help make your web site known and easy to find by registering your site's address. Your goal here is to have your site appear near the top of their indexes. Use as many keywords as possible so the search engines pick up your site through various search topics. You can register your web site yourself:

  —By going to each search engine and submitting your site as instructed.

  —Purchasing and using search engine optimization (SEO) software like WebPosition®, www.webposition.com; Submit Wolf, www.submitwolf .com; or SoftSpider, http://beseen.net/softspider.

  —Using a submission service like Submit It! www.submit-it.com, which will charge you a fee for registering your site with a certain number of search engines.

  —Using free services like Quickregister, www.quickregister.net.

  You should also know the difference between a search engine and a directory: Search engines create their listings automatically with the use of "spiders" or "crawlers" that index+ your site based on the keywords and phrases you enter and index all the pages in your web site.
- *Pay-per-Click, (PPC),* is a form of search engine marketing (Search Engine Optimization—SEO) where you buy traffic from other web sites based on a fee per click. Banners ads, flash ads, and textual ads are all available. It is good for your advertising, because you only have to pay for actual traffic that your ads generate. Go to GoogleAdWords (https://adwords .google.com/select) for more information.
- *Directories* like Yahoo have individuals who review your site to decide if they will accept your site based on the description you submit manually. They give no promises that your site will be included.
- *Signatures* are the text messages that are automatically added to your message newsgroup and mail software programs. They can be easily set

up in Outlook or AOL or other commercial e-mail hosts. Jeff Zbar, writer and speaker on technology, entrepreneurship and home office topics (www.ChiefHomeOfficer.com) says that every e-mail that leaves your outbox can become a marketing tool that includes your Identity or alias (on the "From" line) you send your e-mails under, to the Subject line. Zbar's e-mails have an attached signature that is configured to move across your screen and up your screen. It really catches your attention!

Zbar says the other simple tool that is standard on every e-mail application is your "Signature" or Sig File, a message or graphic automatically embedded at the end of your outgoing e-mail messages. Zbar suggests you include the following in your sig file:

Your formal name (that way, you can close your actual message to the recipient informally with your first name or initials)

Your complete contact information, mailing address, phone/fax numbers

A brief mention of your area of expertise and link to your web site

A Tip of the Day, pithy message or another "leave-behind" that will make your sig more memorable

Zbar continues, "When building your sig, try to keep each line relatively short and about the same number of characters as the line(s) above and below it. This makes the sig a block of copy that's easy on the eye."

Zbar's Setting Up a Sig File

Jeff Zbar

To set up a sig file in Outlook, go to Tools, Options, and then Signatures. If you choose to place a simple text message in your e-mail, click the "Text" button at the bottom. Then type in your message. To include an image in your sig file, instead of clicking the "Text" button, click the "File" button, and Browse to select a file from the appropriate directory. When done, click "Apply" and "OK."

To set up a sig file in AOL, go to "Mail," then "Set Mail Signatures," then "Create Signatures." Give your sig a name, then type in your message. If you use both AOL and Outlook, copy the sig already created in AOL or Outlook and paste it into the signature field in the other. Then click "OK."

In Outlook and AOL, you can create different sig files for different outbound e-mails—depending on the recipient or marketing message you want to portray. You can edit text-based sigs even after they're placed in the outbound e-mail. Or you can delete them, if there's no need to include one (if you're sending an email to a family or friend).

Jeff Zbar is an author, speaker, and expert on entrepreneurship, telework, and all facets of working from home and the Chief Home Officer.com.

Web Writing—Articles, E-Zines, E-Reports, or E-Booklets

Writing informative pieces for your target market is effective in building your reputation as an expert and is appreciated by potential customers who can use your information to improve their lives or help their businesses succeed. Your writing will also lead to more frequent search engine listings and links from other web sites. E-zines can also be lead-ins to sell CDs, e-books, e-booklets (or offer as a free bonus), and other items to your customers. Write short and concise articles for the Web and if appropriate, add links with more information for your readers.

Blogs, Internet Talk Shows, and Pod Casts

Here are some ways you can market on the Internet:

- *Blogs* have only recently become very popular. They are "web logs" by amateur and professional journalists, experts, and businesspersons. Build a blog on www.Blogger.com (Google's free blogging service) or on your own to present new ideas or products, educate your customers, increase your listing on search engines, and enhance your image as expert in your field, and to encourage feedback and conversation between your customers.

  Aliza Sherman Risdahl (www.mediaegg.com) author of *The Everything Blogging Book* says, "A blog is a web site with a fresh twist—current postings that are time- and date-stamped and in reverse chronological order. If you are thinking of starting a blog, plan ahead, know your target audience, know your topic and make sure you have a lot of useful and interesting things to say. But make sure you also let your personality shine through," says Risdahl.

  She continues, "Blogs make great communications tools, but they require a time commitment and consistency to be effective. And don't create a blog in a vacuum. You need to market your blog both online and offline to attract attention."

- *Internet Talk Shows* are also a fairly recent innovation. On Jim Blasingame's site, Small Business Network, Inc. (www.smallbusinessadvocate.com), you can hear him interview many business experts and authors on his nationally syndicated weekday Radio/Internet talk show, *The Small Business Advocate*, one of the first to use on-demand audio streaming. Send press releases to hosts of such shows to be invited as a guest. Your customers can listen to your interview, and you can reach a large, worldwide audience.

  If you are thinking of starting your own show, keep in mind that it can be expensive and you will be competing against thousands of other Internet audio streams as well as the many terrestrial and satellite radio stations. For more information, About.com has an excellent series of topics on this topic. Visit: http://radio.about.com/cs/latestradionews/a/aa011804a.htm.

- A *pod cast,* or podcasting, uses simple recording technology to record advice or tips for your customers that they can download and listen to on their handheld devices. This marketing tool accomplishes much of what blogs and writing can do: foster customer communications; establish your expertise; and help increase your sales. For more information on how you can conduct podcasting for yourself and your business, visit the informative site, http://blog.podblaze.com.

After your site becomes active, enlist a traffic monitoring system for your site so you can analyze how many visitors are coming, how they are finding your site, the pages they are visiting the most, and whether these visits are leading to increased sales. Monitor responses often, to make your site more effective and appealing to your faithful and new customers. Do not forget to also use offline methods to send people to your web site such as press releases, talks, and other traditional marketing methods.

Netiquette and the Better Business Bureau's Code of Online Business Practices and Other Regulations

The Better Business Bureau (BBB) has a Code of Online Business Practices that is their guide to "business to customer" conduct in electronic commerce. You can read this document at www.bbbonline.org/reliability /code/code.asp.

The Council of Better Business Bureaus, Inc. has a web site, Children's Advertising Review Unit, www.caru.org, with guidelines for advertising to children: CARU's Self-Regulatory Guidelines for Children's Advertising to ensure advertising is truthful and appropriate for children. Read the document at the site.

In addition to this code, there are also regulations and guidelines about advertising in general that you can read at the Federal Trade Commission's site, www.FTC.gov (click on "Business," and then "Advertising Guidance" section).

There is also what is referred to as *Netiquette,* rules of ethical and procedural conduct that Internet users—both individuals and entrepreneurs—are expected to follow. These include avoiding inappropriate language, not sending out unsolicited e-mails, not forwarding deceptive or pyramid schemes, asking permission before sending e-mail attachments, not revealing others' e-mail addresses when you send out group messages, and other rules that deal with common courtesy and privacy. You want your online image to stand for respect and honesty.

Suggested Resources

Books

Complete Guide to Internet Publicity: Creating and Launching Successful Online Campaigns, 2nd ed., by Steve O'Keefe (New York: John Wiley & Sons, 2002).

The Everything Blogging Book: Publish Your Ideas, Get Feedback, And Create Your Own Worldwide Network by Aliza Sherman Risdahl (Holbrook, MA: Adams Publishing Group, 2006).

Guerrilla Marketing Online by Jay Conrad Levinson (New York: Houghton-Mifflin, 1995).

Naked Conversations: How Blogs Are Changing the Way Businesses Talk with Customers by Robert Scoble and Shel Israel (Hoboken, NJ: John Wiley & Sons, 2006).

101 Ways to Promote Your Web Site: Filled with Proven Internet Marketing Tips, Tools, Techniques, and Resources to Increase Your Web Site Traffic by Susan Sweeney (Gulf Breeze, FL: Maximum Press, 2006).

Podcasting: Do It Yourself Guide by Todd Cochrane (Hoboken, NJ: John Wiley & Sons, 2005).

The Ultimate Guide to Electronic Marketing for Small Business: Low-Cost/High Return Tools and Techniques That Really Work by Tom Antion (Hoboken, NJ: John Wiley & Sons, 2005).

Web Radio: Radio Production for Internet Streaming by Chris Priestman (Stoneham, MA: Focal Press, 2001).

Web Info

http://amarketingexpert.com/store, *Striking Internet Gold,* by Penny C. Sansevieri, a book on marketing and PR.

http://dir.webring.com/rw, Webring directory.

http://wdfm.com, *Web Digest for Marketers,* founder, Larry Chase; weekly e-newsletter.

www.adverblog.com, Adverblog, interesting visuals and discussion about advertising and online marketing.

www.marketingterms.com, Internet marketing and reference site; also index of best sites and articles.

www.mikes-marketing-tools.com, Excellent source for Internet marketing.

www.sfscore.com/business_toolbox.html, SCORE.org's Internet workbook, *How to Really Market on the Internet.* Also look for the "Internet Learning Tutor 103," a free, interactive course on how to market using web site, e-mail, and online advertising.

www.tipsbooklets.com, Paulette Ensign's consulting site with articles on how businesses can profit with electronic and hard copy tips booklets.

www.wilsonweb.com, Internet marketing expert, Ralph Wilson's "Web Marketing Today."

88. Network on the Net

The Internet has enabled business owners and entrepreneurs and consumers alike to engage in online meaningful (and sometimes meaningless) conversations, discussions, and forums. The more you provide practical and helpful information to your target audience, the more likely potential customers will go to your web site to investigate your services or products. Here are three more ways to reach those audiences.

Using Subscriptions to List-Serves and Usenet Newsgroups

All online discussion groups are free of charge, and open to anyone who wishes to participate. These electronic discussion groups are less structured and allow you to freely exchange information with others in your industry or profession, or with other entrepreneurs. You need a subscription to participate in Listservs, whose messages are sent as single messages or compiled as digests and are automatically mailed to your computer mailbox, like a daily newsletter.

Subscriptions to newsgroups are through Usenet, where you go to read messages posted on the Internet. Several days later, the messages are automatically deleted. Both types of discussion groups can be unmoderated or moderated for inappropriate postings. You cannot enter solicitations in these forums or you will be kicked out; however, if in providing information about the topics being discussed, you mention your web site or business and someone asks about it, you can explain about your business and any other details that a participant wants to know.

Webrings are a group of sites that are joined through similar interests that refer people to one another for free. Instead of browsing through major search engines, you can navigate from one to another. If you have a web site, you can form your own webring or join another for networking opportunities, information, and possible leads and referrals.

Additional Online Contacts

- *Announcement sites:* These sites provide news about the latest web sites, articles, and resources. These postings are only online for a short time, but they are archived so you can read them later.
- *Award sites:* You can enter your web site for consideration and possible recognition.

- *Directories:* Web directories exist in almost every category and link to other web sites in similar specialties. You have to register with them and have your site reviewed by an editor for inclusion. The media often peruse these directories to find people to interview for their reports or articles.
- *Partnering:* You can form strategic online alliances with other business owners to add value to your products or services and increase revenue-generating opportunities.
- *Contest and games:* Consider sponsoring monthly contests or games related to your business to attract new prospects to your site. These special events can sometimes create a media "buzz" or attention among Internet groups. Make sure you are following FTC guidelines regarding contests.

Chats

Chats (short for "Internet Relay Chat") are real-time online discussions. You can host these on your own site for visitors' feedback, to answer questions, and to encourage group discussion for solving problems, giving technical support, or providing leads and networking opportunities. You can also be a chat guest on other sites to talk on subjects of interest to prospective customers. Chats can help in promoting new books, products, or services you have launched.

You can also invite experts or leaders in your field to be chat guests. For those faithful customers who missed any chats, you can archive the transcripts. Most sites with chat capabilities and message boards have policies for chat conduct and do not permit blatant selling and solicitations, profanity, or potentially libelous statements. It is best to market yourself as an expert than to try to sell anything or lure people to your site. If they are interested in what you have to say, they will find your site, anyway. The cost and maintenance for chat capability, though, may be out of the range for new web site owners.

Again, the less static and more interactive your web site is, the more people will come to it and stay. Most web hosting companies offer maintenance packages so that you can update your site as needed. It is up to you to make your site unique and have it stand out from your competitors by keeping it current and constructive. People value their time so you want your site to be a worthwhile investment of that time. In return, you will earn their trust and loyal patronage.

Suggested Resources

Books

Exploring Web Marketing and Project Management Interactive Workbook by Donald Emerick, Susan Joyce, Kimberlee Round, and Kim Round (Upper Saddle River, NJ: Pearson Education, 2000).

101 Ways to Boost Your Web Traffic: Internet Marketing Made Easier, 3rd ed., by Thomas Wong (Union City, CA: Intesync, 2004).

89. Growing Globally

Import and Export Considerations

Even if your small business is located in a rural area, you can still consider global markets for your business as the Internet and trade programs open new markets every day around the world. According to the latest findings of the Bureau of Economic Analysis of the Department of Commerce, the United States is currently in a trade deficit of approximately $68.0 billion. Small businesses represent over 95 percent of U.S. exported goods, but only around 1.8 percent of all firms export goods and services. With advancements of technology and Internet enabling international hookups, the potential markets for small businesses in exporting are huge.

Because of the current deficit, the federal and state governments are encouraging small businesses to participate in exporting. The goal is to create new jobs and improve our country's trade balance. Government support for *importing* goods and services is usually more likely when there are joint ventures between businesses in different countries.

Just as in the U.S. market, the size of your business for exporting is not as important as discovering the appropriate business niche. Selling successfully overseas involves many of the same principles as running a successful business in the United States. Exporting also has many advantages for small businesses. These include increased growth, markets, and profits; tax advantages; added business offerings; and enhanced business image.

It will take a commitment and considerable effort on your part to develop export markets and take advantage of the resources available to you to sell on an international level. You will need to plan, conduct market research, and adapt to different methods in packaging, measurements (using the metric system), and other related factors.

Here are some export-import considerations from trade experts:

- *Do preliminary research.* Ask yourself if you have the right product, if there is competition and, if so, what is different about yours? Is there an untapped market niche? If you have been successful here, can you apply those same marketing strategies in another country?
- *Conduct market research.* Conducting market research on the country to which you are thinking of exporting is the key to exporting success. Ask basic questions such as, "Is English mandatory?" If you are selling software, does it have to be in German, French, and Chinese? Starting out, maybe you cannot do that, so you will only look at English-speaking markets—England, New Zealand, Australia (even though it is farther away than Mexico, it could be more expensive to translate your software into Spanish). Internationally, market research is a little bit tougher because you are dealing with foreign people and foreign markets, but the problems and issues are the same.

- *Determine costs.* If market research results show potential foreign markets, you then have to determine your extra trade costs such as tariffs, transportation, and so on. After figuring your costs, you then have to ask, "Can I still sell it at a profit?" Realize, too, your price for your product or services will vary according to each country and their population's ability to pay your prices.
- *Support and study the process.* You and your staff have to be committed to supporting the export process, and realize there is a learning curve in international trade. It takes time for you to learn about countries, how people buy things there, what kind of packaging works for them, and how to deal with cultural aspects. An important part of mastering the trade process is learning the requirements to complete the international transaction in terms of necessary documentation, shipping, payment mechanisms, compliance with export/import laws and regulations, and so on.

Finding Help

There are many resources that provide assistance for small and medium-sized businesses seeking to export. Here are the major ones (see also Method 52):

- *Federal programs:* The U.S. Small Business Administration (SBA) and U.S. Department of Commerce provide services that include export counseling, workshops and training seminars, publications, and financial assistance. You can find out about these programs and counseling at the following places:
  —*U.S. Export Assistance Centers:* www.sba.gov/oit/export/useac.html, EACs offer a full range of federal export programs and services under one roof.
  —*SCORE:* www.score.org, With over 400 locations, its volunteers provide free counseling, many with years of international business experience.
  —*Small Business Development Centers:* www.sba.gov/SBDC, The SBDCs vary in their export programs. Some have one person or a small group of experts that specialize in import/export assistance, while others are dedicated solely to international trade. Search online or call the SBA Info Locator (800-827-5722) for local SBDCs.
- *State:* Contact your state or (or Canadian province) for offices of international trade assistance or an export network.
- *Chambers of Commerce:* Consult city or town offices, or your county's economic development arm, to see if local trade offices or councils exist. Some chambers actively promote exports and provide training programs, counseling, referrals, trade missions, and publications.
- *International trade associations:* Many of these associations and other private organizations offer a wide range of services. Most conduct regular meetings with qualified speakers and provide networking opportunities with others involved in international trade.

- *Export management and export trading companies:* These companies serve as export sales intermediaries and representatives for manufacturers. Services include locating foreign buyers, promoting products, making export sales, providing documentation, and shipping products overseas.
- *Consulting firms:* Trade consultants can provide information on domestic and foreign trade regulations and overseas markets, and can assess overseas commercial and political risk. They often specialize in product lines and geographic areas. Some small law firms, accounting firms, or specialized marketing firms also provide international-trade consulting services.

No matter what the size of your business, international trade can benefit your venture, your customers, and your country's economy. Thousands of small companies already compete in the global market, why not yours?

Suggested Resources

Association

Federation of International Trade Associations (FTA), www.fita.org/webindex /index.html, web site has many resources for global business.

Books

Building an Import/Export Business, 3rd ed., by Kenneth D. Weiss (Hoboken, NJ: John Wiley & Sons, 2002).

Global Trade and Business Show Directory, United States IBP (Washington, DC: International Business Publications, 2004).

Federal Information (Additional)

Trade Information Center (TIC), www.export.gov/TIC, (800)-USA-TRADE, first stop for companies seeking export assistance and directs them to U.S. Export Assistance Centers located across the United States. TIC is part of (www.Export.gov), the portal to all export-related assistance and market information offered by the federal government.

www.AssessYourInternationalRisk.org, an SBA site that is designed to provide small businesses with information that will help them determine what insurable exposures they may encounter in doing business overseas.

www.sba.gov/gopher/Local-Information/Useacs, location of U.S. Export Assistance Centers (USEACs) that have international trade specialists from the U.S. Department of Commerce to consult with business owners and entrepreneurs interested in international commerce.

www.sba.gov/OIT/info/Guide-To-Exporting/index.html, "Breaking into the Trade Game," 3rd ed., a comprehensive guide to the export process and an indispensable handbook for new and experienced exporters.

www.sba.gov/training/courses.html, online courses, "International Trade."

Web Info

www.auerbach-intl.com, Auerbach International Inc./Translations Express™, translations services.

www.Entrepreneur.com/howto, *Entrepreneur* magazine's free, online, how-to guide, "How to Take Your Company Global."

www.worldtradepress.com, books on export-import.

Grow with Spin-Offs and New Product or Service Developments: How Many Ways to Diversify?

Chapter 12 focuses on evaluating and investigating the options of expanding your business through network marketing, licensing, or a franchise or business opportunity.

Large businesses and corporations have entire divisions for performing "R&D" (research and development) for new products or services. As an entrepreneur or small business owner, you can also profit from spin-offs, but you often have to overcome the obstacles of finding enough time and money to pursue new business avenues. Here are suggested strategies for discovering compatible products that will provide value and revenue-generating outlets for you and your business.

90. Creating New Products, Services, Methods, and Procedures

Why Diversify?

Diversification is important for your small business for several reasons:

- It can help increase your cash flow because of seasonal slowdowns or because you have reached a base line of customers at the present time, but operating costs are still the same or rising.
- You can reach new markets if a trend is fading or outsourcing, or a larger competitor is encroaching on your customer base.
- It can provide another source of income, while enabling you to cut back on a job that is becoming increasingly physically taxing.

- Customers will be pleased if you can offer them a service or product they have been requesting.
- You can work on perfecting a new sideline whenever you have time available (no set hours).
- If you decide to take on an aspect of your business that previously you subcontracted, you can gain greater control over your business offerings.
- Diversification enables you to do *cluster marketing*, which means offering potential customers a combination of two services or products (or a mix) so they can accomplish or buy more than one thing at a time (a hairdresser salon might offer its clients the opportunity to have manicures and pedicures).
- You can create it once, and then sell it an unlimited number of times.

Questions to Help You Find Something New

How can you find a new sideline? Sometimes it just happens because of a repeated customer demand for an added product or service, but you can also do some creative entrepreneurial thinking. Here are some questions to help you in your quest for a spin-off idea:

- What problem(s) do you often encounter in your business operations? Sometimes, we never try to improve something until we are forced to—the old cliché of "necessity is the mother of invention,"—so identify problems and look for solutions that help you or your customers.
- Anything that saves your customers time and money will be popular, so what new product or application or approach could help your customers (e.g., free delivery or installation of a product they buy)?
- Are you recognized as an expert in your field? If so, can you package your advice or get paid to talk about it or demonstrate?
- What related product or service from another company would sell well with your business offerings? Specialty cheesecakes from a woman's home food business for desserts in your catering service, for example? Professional pet groomers often sell pet care supplies or food to their clients. One professional groomer added a "dog wash" area so owners of large dog breeds could comfortably bathe their own pets. She also sold a selection of pet shampoos and grooming products.
- Again, what do your customers ask or wish for? Is there some innovation you can create that would answer their needs and that you can market as a one-of-a-kind product? Several professional organizers have solved organizing dilemmas for their clients with products they created and went on to sell these products to other clients.
- Is there someone else or a group of people with whom you can brainstorm ideas for solutions to a problem? A woman balloon decorator, who spe-

cialized in decorating for weddings, asked her husband about designing a freestanding and collapsible wood arbor that she could set up and decorate at wedding receptions. Using his woodworking skills, he built one that was so well designed they sold the pattern to other balloon decorators. If you have discovered something that will save colleagues time and money or is unique, others may be willing to pay you a good price for it.

If you want to diversify, you should take an innovative approach to every aspect of your business and be open to opportunities that could prove lucrative.

Diversification Basics: From R&D to Sales

As your business grows, new ideas or solutions will develop that you never envisioned in your original business plan. Rather than rush headlong into a major investment of money, first examine the practicability of your spin-off proposal. Here are some factors that will help you decide whether to add this spin-off to your business offerings:

- Talk to your board of advisors or a business coach, consultant, or legal expert for feedback, opinions, and impartial advice.
- Meet with business counselors at small and women's business development centers for their advice and for their referrals for any applicable government loans and guidance.
- Make some models (products) or some test runs of proposed services.
- Conduct more extensive market research: Determine your ideal markets, potential customers' needs, compare with your competitors, check out any licensing or regulations you must follow, and find out if and how to protect the intellectual property of your product or service.
- Look for sources of financing.
- Plan your distribution and marketing strategy.

Just as with starting a new business, it takes time to fully develop a new spin-off and get it ready to present to your customers, but taking time to adequately prepare your offering will help ensure its success.

Spin-Offs and Sidelines

Residual and passive income sources are closely related. With residual income, you receive regular payments for a lengthy period as a result of a single sale, such as with network marketing (home party companies) or affiliate participation, where you receive a commission for each sale. With passive income, you earn money without much exertion such as with real estate investments, a book (after it is written), affiliate web site programs, CDs, e-books, and other products you might have developed.

Inventions (Templates, Software, Patterns, Toys, Recipes, and Formulas)

Yes, you will see many inventors' products for sale on QVC and other home shopping channels, but most inventions come from people within an industry and are sold primarily within that industry. If you invent a new product or service in your business, you are more likely to sell it within your trade and professional industry. One neonatal nurse, for example, invented a special carrier for premature infants. The process to trademark and patent is costly and lengthy, but most Small Business Development Centers (www.sba.gov/SBDC) (see Additional Resources in the back of the book) have business experts who can advise you.

Franchises or Business Opportunities

Some business owners package their successful ventures and sell the idea and procedures (opportunities) to other entrepreneurs or develop a franchise in which buyers pay the owner fees to operate the business, following company procedures (see Method 94 for more information, resources).

Professional Speaker

Some successful business owners become highly sought-after speakers as they share their experiences with others at business and industry conferences and for various organizations and institutions. After 30 some years in the computer industry, Rochelle Balch (www.RochelleBalch.com) has become an internationally recognized public speaker. She still has her successful computer consulting business, but enjoys her speaking outlets.

Business Coaching

This is a kind of consulting service, but it is more of an ongoing, almost mentor relationship in which coaches meet with or phone their clients regularly to guide them through their marketing and operations. A woman who had a profitable promotional products business for 20 years now instructs others in ways to achieve success in her industry.

Consulting

Many persons who have experience, expertise, and credentials in a specific profession or industry consider becoming a consultant. In this competitive profession, most consultants start out on a part-time basis and build up a client base that eventually permits them to go full time. Successful consultants are good at identifying practical solutions to problems.

Informational and How-To Products

Included are many items based on entrepreneurs' expertise and skill such as video and audio products, live demonstrations, classes, books, radio, television. Many entrepreneurs create successful products by sharing their skills and know-how. They teach classes, teleclasses, or make videos and audio recordings, with some going on to have their own radio or television appearances. Some, like Jeannie Papadopoulos, sell their supplies. When she first started holding instructional workshops on window painting, her students could not find the paint and supplies, so she ordered the supplies for her students. As the popularity of her workshops grew, Papadopoulos hired a brush maker to fabricate her own line of brushes, perfectly matched to her paints and her window-painting specifications. She recently put her workshops on DVD and now is selling them from her web site as another of her business' sideline products.

SALE OF RELATED BUSINESS ITEMS

These include promotional products, supplies, parts, or additional services. Richard and Angela Hoy own the Writer's Market electronic newsletter, WritersWeekly.com and branched out to start a successful e-book publishing business for other writers.

JOINING FORCES

Join forces with other entrepreneurs to generate new income opportunities. Two professional organizers each have their own clients, but work together with local real estate agents to assist homeowners in rearranging their houses to appeal to prospective buyers.

FORM AN ASSOCIATION OR NETWORKING GROUP MEMBERSHIP

Trade associations and business groups were organized to provide support and information to members. One marketing consultant began a local business-networking group that meets monthly. She charges attendees a meeting fee and has had such good attendance that she plans to open additional regional chapters.

WEB SITE

As seen in Chapter 11, a web site is an excellent marketing tool for your business, but sometimes it *becomes* the business. Liz Folger, author of *Stay-at-Home Mom's Guide to Making Money* branched out into having a successful web site, BizyMoms.com, hosting live chats, and selling many business e-books by other authors.

GIFTS

The gift or toy industry presents a huge opportunity for you to market unique items, sometimes an outgrowth of your present business. A plastics company in Pennsylvania created a plastic parts building set that went worldwide in its popularity and became its main business.

CRAFTS, ART, DECOR

Skilled artists and craftspersons of one-of-a-kind creations often create smaller, more commercial pieces to bring in money to help support their unique pieces.

Many use former job skills to make their art. One former welder visits junk-yards to find scrap metal to weld into garden art pieces.

OTHER

Many times, a spin-off or sideline venture may just "happen," or evolve from your original business in unexpected ways. One man joined his father in his appliance business after college. For fun, he had one of his workers paint an old refrigerator and put it in the store window. Someone called up and bought it and a new sideline business was born of restoring old refrigerators and stoves. Another man, Butch, who had his own body shop, repaired an antique toy gas-powered car for a friend and started a sideline business restoring these cars for collectors. Using their entrepreneurial creativity (defined by Vadim Kotelnikov in Chapter 7), and the skills they already had, these two men launched into lucrative side businesses.

The moral here is that as a business owner, you should always keep an open mind about the directions your business could go, but again, do some preliminary market research to make sure your idea has a waiting market (see also Chapter 4).

Suggested Resources

Books

> *Rules for Revolutionaries: The Capitalist Manifesto for Creating and Marketing New Products and Services* by Guy Kawasaki and Michele Moreno (Toronto, Ontario: HarperCollins Canada, 2000).

> *Selling the Dream: How to Promote Your Product, Company, or Ideas—And Make a Difference: Using Everyday Evangelism* by Guy Kawasaki (New York: HarperCollins, 1992).

Web Info

> www.Entrepreneur.com/howto, *Entrepreneur* magazine's free, online, how-to guide, "How to Develop New Products or Services."

INVENTIONS

Association

> United Inventors Association of the United States of America, www.uiausa .org, a not-for-profit inventors' community center.

Book

> *What Every Inventor Needs to Know about Business & Taxes* by Stephen Fishman (Berkeley, CA: Nolo Press, 2005). Book and CD-ROM.

Web Info

www.mominventors.com, membership available; also books, information, resources for mothers interested in the invention process; online store of members' products.

www.Uventures.com, an online technology transfer marketplace.

PROFESSIONAL SPEAKER

Association

National Speakers Association, www.nsaspeaker.org

Book

Speaking Your Way to the Top: Making Powerful Business Presentations by Marjorie Brody (Boston, MA: Allyn & Bacon, 1997; see also Chapter 14, "Speaking Up for Your Business").

BUSINESS COACHING

Web Info

www.comprehensivecoachingu.com, Comprehensive Coaching U

CONSULTING

Book

Million Dollar Consulting™ Toolkit: Step-by-Step Guidance, Checklists, Templates and Samples from "The Million Dollar Consultant" by Alan Weiss (Hoboken, NJ: John Wiley & Sons, 2005).

INFORMATIONAL AND HOW-TO PRODUCTS

Book

Making Videos for Money: Planning and Producing Information Videos, Commercials, and Infomercials by Barry Hampe (New York: Owl Books, 1998).

SALE OF RELATED BUSINESS ITEMS

Book

Winning at New Products: Accelerating the Process from Idea to Launch, 3rd ed., by Robert G. Cooper (New York: Perseus Books Group, 2001).

JOINING FORCES

Book

Teaming Up: The Small Business Guide to Collaborating with Others to Boost Your Earnings and Expand Your Horizons by Paul and Sarah Edwards (Collingdale, PA: Diane Publishing, 1997).

Form an Association or Networking Group Membership

Book

> *The Best Home Businesses for the Twenty-First Century,* 3rd ed., by Paul and Sarah Edwards (Los Angeles: Jeremey Tarcher, 1999).

Web Site

Books

> *Design Your Own E-Shop: Creating & Promoting Successful Small Business Sites* by Molly Holzchlag (West Sussex, United Kingdom: AVA Publishing, 2004).

> *Stay-at-Home Mom's Guide to Making Money: How to Choose the Business That's Right for You Using the Skills and Interests You Already Have,* rev. ed., by Liz Folger (New York: Three Rivers Press, 2000).

Gifts

Book

> *The Toy and Game Inventor's Handbook: Everything You Need to Know to Pitch, License and Cash-In on Your Ideas* by Ronald O. Weingartner and Richard Levy (New York: Alpha, 2003).

Crafts, Art, and Decor

Magazine

> *The Crafts Report,* www.craftsreport.com, print magazine for professional artists and craftspersons.

91. Modifying Your Business's Offerings to Meet Your Customers' Expectations

While you are monitoring your competitors, they are also monitoring you with the same goal of creating similar products or services. That is why concentrating on customer service may be the deciding factor that makes people come to you instead of them. Emphasis on customer relationship management (CRM) is what can make your business stand out, and it may be a key factor in its survival.

Yes, customers are constantly looking for quality products and services and at competitive prices, but now they also evaluate your dealings with them before, during, and after your sales.

When you first start a business, an important element in your marketing plans is to develop a profile of your ideal customers, their likes, dislikes, and what they expect from your business. Your marketing strategies basically target these prospects, but as your customer base expands, you may need to consider modifying the marketing plan to include other customers, while remaining ready to adjust your business offerings to the changing needs of your faithful customers. The dilemma here is how to balance pleasing your existing customers while offering "new and improved" offerings to attract new business.

Your cash flow is an excellent measurement of customer satisfaction. Happy customers are the reason for revenues and profits. To keep them satisfied, you want to get a clear understanding of their needs and how they value your business. Here are methods, some old, some new, that you can use to ensure your current customers continue to be repeat customers:

- Use spot surveys with regular customers, to take a quick indicator of their customer satisfaction. You can mail surveys to a randomly selected group of people in your database; hand out questionnaires at trade shows, business shows, and conferences; or conduct a web-based survey. Spot surveys are also good opportunities to get feedback from prospects when you are considering expanding into another area with a new product or service.
- Make a phone call soon after customers buy your service or product to be sure they are still happy with their purchase, and then follow up with periodic phone calls to get opinions and feedback from persons who have purchased or used your business' offerings.
- Ask customers if they would like to be part of a focus group and meet from time to time to discuss their satisfaction level and make suggestions for improvement or changes.
- Conduct a concentrated survey of all your customers with a mailing or on your web site. Have specific questions to measure certain aspects of your business and service, make it brief, and easy to complete, and offer a little reward—a discount, a free report, or some other incentive—to encourage more responses.
- If possible, offer live Internet chats so customers can ask questions or give feedback.
- Monitor your competition to see what new innovations they are selling and if you should think of modifying also.

In the ever-changing world of business, customers' demands can change overnight, so your CRM should also be able to adapt. Listening to customers and understanding their needs and expectations, will keep them happy and that is what will make them want to come back to you (see also Method 80).

Suggested Resources

Book

Collaborative Customer Relationship Management: Taking CRM to the Next Level edited by Alexander H. Kracklauer, D. Quinn Mills, and Dirk Seifert (New York: Springer-Verlag, 2003).

Web Info

> www.Entrepreneur.com/howto, *Entrepreneur* magazine's free, online, how-to guides, "How to Invest in New Technology and Equipment" and "How to Tackle a New Market."

92. Does Your Business Need a Makeover?

In Chapter 10, you read some tips on how to stay up with current trends so your business would not go out of date. As you think of new products and spin-offs to bring in additional income, you might also want to think about updating other aspects of your business to make it more relevant to existing and new prospects. The following questions can help you determine if just parts of your business need redoing or if you need a complete makeover:

- How do customers view your present products and service? Do a poll or survey for your loyal customers, and a survey with the general population.
- Do they know your brand or image by sight or description? If the results of your survey show people have a different image than you thought your business projected, then you have to decide which one you want to emphasize and concentrate your marketing efforts there.
- Is your industry radically changing, similar to the way the computer made the typewriter obsolete, or are the changes more subtle? If it is a radical change, then you soon must find new income streams in your industry. An owner of a metal polishing company whose business shined vehicle metal bumpers and truck mirrors, lost his major business when car makers no longer made those shiny bumpers. He purchased a degreasing machine that his same customers needed for degreasing metal parts. He also discovered another customer, a foundry that needed metal products ground down and sanded. By using different belts on his machines, he could perform that task, and it eventually gave him more business than his regular customers.
- If you do a business makeover, is there a chance that you may lose your present, steady customers or can you update existing products and services and customer service so that you will still keep your loyal customers but attract new ones? You may have to educate your customers with workshops or demonstrations so they accept adaptations to your revised products or services.
- Is it time to update your technology for better customer communications, production, and efficiency? Change is constant, which is why you stay current with changes in your industry and customers' preferences (see Method 80). It is more affordable to change a little at a time, try new methods or introduce new products gradually, than to try to do it all at

once. Complete makeovers are dramatic, but your customers will be more accepting if it is not all at once.

Note, too, that many industries now are served by business coaches and entrepreneurial consultants who owned similar businesses like yours and are now advising others with their professional expertise to assist as professional mentors or advisors. Contact your networking associates for referrals or international business coaching organization. Check, too, with your local chapters of SCORE (www.score.org) who may also have volunteers who worked in similar enterprises as yours.

The world market and consumers are becoming more diverse, and so you will need to make over your business as your customers' needs dictate.

Suggested Resources

Association

Worldwide Association of Business Coaches, www.wabccoaches.com, information, referrals.

Book

Jump Start Your Business Brain: Ideas, Advice, and Insights for Immediate Marketing and Innovation Success by Doug Hall and Tom Peters (Cincinnati, OH: Emmis Books, 2006).

Web Info

www.1000ventures.com, e-coaching products, including business innovation.

93. Licensing Your Product or Service

An alternative to manufacturing a product or providing a unique service is to license, or give permission to someone to produce a product or service for which you own the patent, trademark, copyright, or trade secret. In return, you receive royalty payments. Novelty and clothing companies, for example, have licenses from the Disney corporation for the right to print their characters on many products. Software developers give licenses to computer companies to install their software on computers.

Licensing gives you an income, while taking advantage of another company's marketing muscle to market it. The disadvantage is that you may have no say how that company uses your product.

It will take some investment of time and money on your part to obtain the intellectual property (patent, trademark, copyright) that legally makes you the owner. Filing legal and application fees, building or creating prototypes, conducting market research to get potential customers' responses, and other activities involved in getting your product or service ready for sale, can be very expensive and take longer than you anticipated. At some point, you may have to seek investors or some other way to help you in financing development.

First and foremost, seek expert advice during the entire process. Consult with a patent and licensing attorney, preferably someone familiar with your business's industry, about licensing and rights agreements here in the United States and overseas. Talk also with consultants and ask other entrepreneurs who have gone through the licensing process for their recommendations.

To find companies that might be interested in licensing, look in your own industry by reading trade publications, attending trade shows, and tapping into your network contacts. Before signing any licensing agreement with a company, check the company's reputation and references, and have your lawyer explain fully all the terms in any proposed contract.

Licensing can lead to a very profitable spin-off, but as with your original business, write a plan with goals and then carefully assess each step along the way so that you do not sign away your rights to unscrupulous companies.

Suggested Resources

Books

How to License Your Million Dollar Idea: Everything You Need to Know to Turn a Simple Idea into a Million Dollar Payday, 2nd ed., by Harvey Reese (Hoboken, NJ: John Wiley & Sons, 2002).

Profit from Your Idea: How to Make Smart Licensing Deals, 5th ed., by Richard Stim (Berkeley, CA: Nolo Press, 2006). Book and CD-ROM.

Thomas Register of American Manufacturers, for finding companies to help produce prototypes, manufacture, or possibly license from you. It is available at most public libraries and at www.thomasregister.com.

94. Turning Your Venture into a Franchise, Business Opportunity, or Network Marketing

After a magazine featured her business, the owner of a home owners' referral service received so many requests for start-up information that she compiled her business guidelines into a manual and sold it as a business opportunity to others who wanted to start a similar service in their communities. Many entrepreneurs have become rich by packaging their businesses' operations into opportunities or franchises or network marketing (party plans, direct selling) that offer publications, training, and consultations.

However, not all businesses are suitable to expand into these opportunities, and there are laws and regulations you must follow if you take your business in these directions. Here is some basic information to consider if you are thinking about expanding into these opportunities.

Differences between an Opportunity and a Franchise

Generally, an owner starts a *business opportunity* by putting together an operational manual, business forms, and other materials and then sells the package to other entrepreneurs to get them started in the business. There may or may not be some ongoing support, but not as much as with franchises. The founder of the business opportunity usually offers some initial training and support, but after a certain amount of time, the buyers of the opportunity are on their own. There are no franchise fees. These are much smaller operations and more affordable than franchises.

A *franchise* is a business opportunity in which the franchisee pays a company (the franchisor) for the right to sell and distribute its products or services and uses its trademark and trade name. Franchisees pay an initial franchise fee, and there may or may not be ongoing royalty fees, advertising costs, or mandatory costs of purchasing the company's supplies to operate the franchise. A franchisee has to follow the company's procedures, and the total cost may reach thousands of dollars.

Network marketing or *multilevel marketing companies* are direct selling opportunities in which distributors purchase the rights from the business owner to market its products to customers within a given territory (though not always exclusive). Cosmetics, toys, baskets, and many other items are sold under well-known brand names. Two women who partnered in making craft items, sold most of their creations through their own home parties. Another woman used her credit cards and money borrowed from a relative to start a lingerie network marketing company that expanded to having sales distributors across the country.

Legalities

You should first consult with professionals—legal, financial, and management professionals and consulting firms that specialize in franchise or business opportunity development. There are laws and regulations that you must adhere to when offering your business to others in these forms. Attorneys will advise you about the pros and cons of this type of business structure and give you some idea of all the paperwork, time, and money that will be required.

Best Option for Your Business?

Paula Kay, owner of Ageless Checkers, Inc. (www.agelesscheckers.com) says, "When I started my home care agency for seniors, the reception was huge and an immediate success. My company recruited active retirees to provide cooking, cleaning, transportation, shopping, and companionship duties to homebound seniors. I quickly realized that older folks all over the country were in need of this sort of assistance . . . that didn't require medically trained workers, but people with compassion and common sense. The idea of a home business opportunity for new entrepreneurs came to me through my experience of achievement. I am delighted to share my success with others."

Kay is currently working on a second business opportunity that will combine her love of children and her desire to help build their self-esteem.

Here are ways to tell if you and your business are ready for expanding into an opportunity or network marketing:

- Your business should have a universal demand and a good profit potential for those purchasing it.
- You should have a successful business and marketing plan you can take to the bank.
- You should have previous work experience, training, or education in the industry so you understand the industry.
- You should have the necessary financing and commitment for this venture to make it succeed.

If you strongly believe other entrepreneurs can be as successful at running your business as you have been, then go ahead and investigate the possibility of growing your business into these opportunities. You may not become the next McDonald's restaurant, but the results may still be financially rewarding beyond anything you expected.

Suggested Resources

Association

International Franchise Association, www.franchise.org, sells industry-related books, publications; web site posts a section of answers to common franchise questions; "Franchising Basics," and a free, online introductory course to franchising.

Book

Mancuso's Small Business Basics: Start, Buy or Franchise Your Way to a Successful Business, 2nd ed., by Joseph R. Mancuso (Naperville, IL: Sourcebooks, 1997).

Web Info

www.Entrepreneur.com/howto, *Entrepreneur* magazine's free, online, how-to guide, "How to Franchise Your Business."

www.franchisetrade.com, franchise articles, including franchising your company.

95. Legal Basics of Expansion

As mentioned in Chapter 6, you need to have a list of experts on hand as you start, operate, and grow your business. If you are considering expanding your business, a lawyer will help you follow the laws, regulations, and licensing requirements, and protect your rights and liability as you take the steps of growth.°

Legal Concerns

Do not overlook these legal aspects of expanding your business. Lawyers and accountants can assist you in the following ways:

- *Collections and credit:* Providing legal documents and sometimes court involvement to collect money owed you, extend credit, and get credit.
- *Closing a business:* Supplying official notification and other matters needed to close a business.
- *Standard contracts:* Drawing up customized contracts and reviewing ones that are presented to you.
- *Disclosure:* Advising the wording that sellers have to tell buyers in sales and contracts.
- *Disclaimers and liability:* Writing the legal wording that releases the seller from liability for a buyer's use of a product or service.
- *Disputes:* Handling disagreements over expanding your business between partners, investors, and family matters.
- *Incorporation and legal structures:* Guiding owners, as their businesses grow, in how to turn their business into one of the corporation structures. (Incorporation has advantages, but it also requires more paperwork and accounting tasks.)

° These resources and definitions are not a substitute for seeking legal and accounting advice from attorneys and accountants and other business experts who specialize in these areas of business.

- *Investor agreements:* Writing the legal documents needed when business owners sell stock in their business and investors put money in their businesses.
- *Internet:* Starting an e-commerce web site, copyright issues, and many other issues that require legal counsel.
- *Employment laws, and human resources:* Advising business owners, when hiring employees, about the regulations covering benefits, discrimination, harassment, safety, termination, workers' compensation, and other related issues.
- *Immigration:* Explaining the required documentation and other procedures for hiring noncitizens of one's country.
- *International trade:* Protecting products and following international laws.
- *Intellectual property:* Advising how to protect your copyright, patent, or trademark.
- *Licensing:* See Method 93.
- *Real estate:* Advising buy-sell-rental agreements, which vary from location to location.
- *Retirement:* Advising you how to keep your business going after you retire and how to continue receiving income from it.
- *Taxes:* Advising how to do proper reporting and resolving disputes about deductions.

Choosing a Lawyer

If you are in business for yourself, chances are you will need a *business attorney* sooner or later, and it is better that you take the time to find one or several from which to choose *before* you have a legal concern. Here are general tips in making a selection:

- Get referrals and feedback from business associates for lawyers that they have used and also consult legal referral associations.
- Know the business areas in which they specialize and if they have any experience in your industry.
- Have an idea of their pricing, and if they work on retainers.
- Interview more than one attorney because you have to feel comfortable working with them.

You want an attorney who is competent; someone who will listen and enable you to be involved in your matters; who responds in a timely matter to your calls and business dealings; and who is fair and trustworthy. Choose all your experts carefully, because their advice can contribute largely to your business's failure or success (see also Method 54, "Suggested Resources").

Suggested Resources

Books

The Internet Legal Guide: Everything You Need to Know When Doing Business Online by Dennis M. Power (Hoboken, NJ: John Wiley & Sons, 2001).

Legal Guide for Starting & Running a Small Business, 9th ed., by Fred Steingold (Berkeley, CA: Nolo Press, 2006).

Web Info

http://smallbusiness.findlaw.com, FindLaw for Small Business, lawyer database, legal information.

Grow into the Future: How Far and Which Way Do You Want to Go?

Chapter 13 provides guidelines for evaluating your business in its present stage, tips for financing its growth, and suggestions for maintaining your enthusiasm. There are also questions for you to consider in deciding just how large you wish your business to grow and some ways to manage that growth.

Even though Chapter 12 discussed changes and new products, business experts caution new business owners from branching out too quickly. Instead, focus your marketing efforts and business development on one area until you have achieved major success. This chapter can help you in making essential decisions about your business's growth and future.

96. Recreating Your Work Space for Maximum Efficiency and Profit

There is a 1950 movie, *Cheaper by the Dozen* (Steve Martin starred in a remake), in which the father, played by Clifton Webb, was an efficiency expert, helping businesses be more efficient. The trouble was, he applied the same principles to family life with humorous results. After you have been operating your business for six months or a year, you might take a look at how well organized your marketing and operations are. Your aim is to be in control and aware of every component of your business Experts recommend ongoing periodic monitoring of your business' activities to ensure its operational efficiency.

Professional Organizers

Like many consultants, professional organizers specialize in different areas. They may be a lifesaver in getting rid of clutter and chaos and getting your business back on track. Erin Gruver, professional organizer, provides these tips for re-organizing your work space:

- Remember everyone is different so just because it works for "Jane" doesn't mean it will work for you.
- Remember to keep active files close to your desk—and reference files in a filing cabinet.
- Your workspace is prime real estate so be cautious about what you keep there. An overabundance of unimportant information will cause distraction and anxiety—when you work for yourself, focus is important.
- Make sure your filing cabinet is good quality. If you have to struggle to open the drawers—chances are you won't and the files will pile up on the floor.
- Go through all your reference files annually and determine if you still need them. If you are unsure what files you need for financial/tax or legal purposes, check with your accountant or an attorney.
- It is a general rule that 80 percent of files in a cabinet are never retrieved. So if you don't need them—recycle them. But don't forget to shred any confidential information.

"There are so many organizing systems out there—research them and determine which ones will work best for you," says Gruver.

Your Operations

You can always become more efficient in your overall business operations. If, as the saying goes, time is money, then using your time more wisely should also make you more money. Some suggestions:

- Hire an efficiency expert or business coach familiar with your industry. Sometimes you do not have to reinvent the wheel, you just have to avoid the same ruts. Just one of two tips from these experts could change your business operations and profits dramatically.
- Create directions for every facet of your business operations. Suppose your printer begins to print out your envelopes in red ink instead of black. It may take you an hour of reading the manual to identify the cause. If you can solve the malfunction on your own, write down the steps of how you fixed the red ink problem, so the next time it happens, you know what actions to take or whom to call. Keep a record of each marketing tactic you used to repeat the successful ones more often.
- Look to technology to simplify tasks such as new database software, an updated computer system, another phone line, or some other piece of equipment that will make completing your tasks easier and faster.
- Look for outside help. Hiring virtual assistants or receptionists, or independent contractors, as you can afford it, will let you concentrate on the core work that only you can perform.

These are just a few of the many ideas to make your business operate more efficiently. How your business is organized and operates is also guided by its type and the products or services you provide. Follow suggestions by experts in your industry and any experts you hire, and periodically evaluate how you can eliminate wasteful time and money.

Suggested Resources

Books

> *The E-Myth Revisited: Why Most Small Businesses Don't Work and What to Do about It* by Michael E. Gerber (New York: Collins, 1995).
>
> *The Organized Executive: A Program for Productivity—New Ways to Manage Time, Paper, People, and the Electronic Office,* rev. ed., by Stephanie Winston (New York: Warner Business Books, 2001).

Software

> ManagePro, www.performancesolutionstech.com, multipurpose management software.

97. Avoiding Business Burnout

Signs of Burnout

One young woman told me, "I absolutely love my business! I am up until 2 A.M. every night and can hardly wait until morning to start again." She certainly does not lack enthusiasm, but at this pace, she will eventually wear herself out and discover that she cannot do it all, or she will lose her enthusiasm and not want to do it any longer. Here are some signs of burnout and stress:

- You get recurring headaches caused by tense shoulder, neck, and back muscles.
- You have bouts of insomnia or wake up frequently in the middle of the night with butterflies in your stomach, thinking only about business matters.
- Your sense of humor deteriorates, and you feel constant fatigue. If you cannot laugh at yourself or situations sometimes, or enjoy your life, you could be headed toward serious depression.
- You catch frequent colds or the flu.
- You snap at your family or loved ones, or you are rude to your customers.

If you recognize these signs, get help, try some of the following renewing strategies, or in extreme cases, consider selling your business and starting something new.

Strategies to Fight Burnout

Sometimes just having a few practical tips and taking some planned steps are all that it takes to renew your enthusiasm for your business activities. Here are a few you might try:

- Hire a business coach to bounce off your fears and successes, and to help you stay on track.
- If you are a microbusiness owner, call, e-mail, or meet with other entrepreneurs, especially those who are your cheerleaders or mentors, to exchange ideas and relieve the stress of business for a short while.
- Stay healthy by spending time with your family, taking rests, eating right, and exercising regularly. If you do not take care of yourself, your relationships and then your business will suffer.
- Adjust your expectations. Set smaller goals that can help you achieve the larger objectives.
- Create incentives to reward yourself when you have tackled X number of business tasks or goals.
- If you enjoy writing your thoughts, keep a journal about your business. Nancy Cleary writes down creative ideas and keeps a daily log of her business's ups and downs to help her look back and see how far she has progressed with her company, Wyatt-MacKenzie Publishing, www.wymacpublishing.com.
- Attend an industry workshop or course to learn the newest trends and upgrade your skills.
- Permit yourself to have fun in your business. Allow yourself to have some projects that may not be as lucrative as others, but will bring you great satisfaction and joy.
- When you are ready, start making some cold calls. Write the script so you will not stumble over your words in your conversation, and set goals for how many calls you will make during each planned time period. In between, call some happy customers to ask how they are and if there is anything else with which you can assist them. Their feedback will be a boost to your morale and will give you a chance to help them again, if needed.
- Take a time-out. If possible, take a hiatus or cut back on stressful projects or your hours. Take a rest and a vacation.
- Join or form a laughter club! They can ease your stress and help you or your staff or associates achieve a new perspective on your business challenges and your lives.
- Use your business to volunteer for a nonprofit group or to help someone who really cannot afford your products or services. You will get that "warm and fuzzy" feeling and realize how blessed you are!

Take time to get your energy back and reenergize your enthusiasm and purpose. The more energy you have, the better you can provide the best products and services for your customers, and enjoy the business of doing it.

Suggested Resources

Books

> *Break Free from Burnout in 30 Days! Secrets of a Burnout Survivor* by Mary Lewis (Marketing Clinic, 2002).
>
> *Slack: Getting Past Burnout, Busywork, and the Myth of Total Efficiency* by Tom DeMarco (New York: Broadway Books, 2002).

Web Info

> www.score.org/guides.html, SCORE's 60-second guide, "Fighting Business Burnout."
>
> www.worldlaughter.com, information about joining or forming a laughter club.

98. Using Your Business Plan to Monitor Progress and Plan New Strategies

As your business grows, you may find it increasingly harder to monitor chores, workers, and outside help. Reviewing your business plan will help you select the right focus of your energies and money and the direction in which to take your business.

Evaluating Your Business's Growth History

Whenever you are thinking about taking steps to expand your business, you should first assess your business in its present state. Do you just need to make your business more efficient or do you need to tackle new markets because of changing trends? The best way to evaluate your business's accomplishments is to review your business plan.

Using your plan, here are important facets of your business that will help in your decision to expand:

- Your business plan's financial section can assist you in making a breakeven analysis and determining a sales projection forecast. One of the main concerns of small business owners is present cash flow. How much is owed to you by clients or customers (accounts receivable), and how much do you owe for goods and services you have received (accounts payable)? Your cash flow should show that you have enough to pay your bills on time and continue your marketing efforts to bring in new customers. If not, you will have to cut back on expenses, hold off making more purchases, or seek additional financing.
- Evaluate your market plan and the marketing methods that had the greatest success; plan to repeat those methods, and make it a goal to try some new ones.

- Look at customers' polls, surveys, or comments to see how they evaluate your product or service and what improvements you might make or added benefits you could offer.
- Review your mission statement to see if your business is heading in the direction you originally envisioned. If it is not on that path, then ask yourself, "Is this a good thing in that I have found new, more profitable marketing directions, or is it a bad thing and I am going off in too many directions?"

Your business plan is a guide, a blueprint that will tell you where you are and where you want to go. Use it to help in all your business decisions.

Are You There Yet? Ready-to-Grow Indicators

- You start thinking about exploring additional markets.
- You find yourself spending more time on administrative tasks than production and innovation.
- You are running out of space for your office and production needs.
- You are getting more demands for products or services than you can handle.
- Your accountant says your business is on sound financial ground and ready for expansion.
- You are ready both mentally and physically to tackle the challenge of business growth.

Modifying Your Business Plan

Your business plan is a management device to check the ongoing progress of your business. As it grows, you may have to modify or revise the plan to find the income sources you need. Here are tips to keep your plan a working business management tool:

- Look for dangers that could sabotage your success such as going in too many directions at once, overextending your credit, and forgetting your loyal customers. Take steps to prevent these risks from occurring.
- Make note of your business successes and the actions that made them happen. Make them a new priority in your plan.
- If you plan to get funding for expansion, work with your accountant or financial planner to try to get adequate funds for your new plan, plus a little extra to provide for unexpected costs, but not so much that you will go too deeply into debt.

- Decide if your market plan can be applied to your expansion plans or if you need to revise your tactics or hire a marketing consultant to help you plan the next phase of your business.
- As with your original plan, conduct market research for your new plan and offerings before you start on the expansion tips. Your research may reveal that at present, it is better to stay with your current market and possibly try to undertake your plan in the future when your finances are firmer or the potential will be worth the expense of development.

If you did not do so in your original business plan, you can rewrite it to establish some estimated timelines and signposts to better gauge your progress and identify obstacles so that you can avoid them. Remember, this is not the only time you will modify your plan. You should revise and modify it as often as your business's changing circumstances dictate (see also Method 40).

Incubate Your Business

If you have a home-based business or are working out of a tiny space and your business is showing indications of rapid growth, you may want to consider having your business become involved with a business incubator. The Small Business Administration says studies reveal that legitimate incubators can increase their tenant companies' chances of success by as much as 80 percent to 93 percent compared with 20 percent in the general economy. One woman who owned a family business creating homemade hot sauces used a local incubator to get her sauces distributed across the country and compete against foreign competition.

For-profit and not-for-profit incubators are supported partly by government or grant funding. Their purpose is to help established businesses take the next step in growth so they can contribute jobs and strengthen the local economy where they are located. The accepted businesses are usually housed in one building, allowing for more affordable rents, with the added benefits of shared business management and support services, office support staff, and conference and meeting rooms.

You have to apply and be accepted for your business to be included in an incubator. This involves providing a business plan, presenting financial statements, and fulfilling other prerequisites. Business incubators can include small ventures from an assortment of industries or specialize, like those fostering food businesses and e-commerce companies. To find out if your business qualifies for this assistance, you can search the web site of the National Business Incubation Association (www.nbia.org) or contact your nearest Small Business Development Center: www.sba.gov/SBDC.

Suggested Resources

Book

Incubators: A Realist's Guide to the World's New Business Accelerators by Colin Barrow (Hoboken, NJ: John Wiley & Sons, 2001).

99. Obtaining a Loan (for Expansion)

In Chapter 5, Methods 45 and 46 basic and creative start-up financing resources were discussed. You can use most, if not all, the resources listed in that chapter to finance your expansion plans.

Best Sources

If your sales indicate there is a potential market to support your future growth, it is an indication that your business is a good candidate for an expansion loan. Banks, investors, state agencies, the SBA, venture capitalists, and other lenders are more likely to grant you a loan because your sales indicators support the belief that you can repay it. When seeking expansion money, the other principles of borrowing money apply as well: Have low personal and business debts, have a detailed business plan showing sales projections, and demonstrate that you have the requisite experience and knowledge (this is also true for any employees). Lenders want assurance that you and any supporting staff or partners are experienced and competent in your field.

Here are additional resources for getting money to expand or start a new project, especially if your business is larger than a one-person small business:

- Small Business Innovation Research (SBIR) grants are meant to encourage technology development among small businesses in conjunction with the federal government's needs. As mentioned, the SBA does not give grants to entrepreneurs to start businesses. For more information, go to the U.S. Small Business Administration's web site, www.sba.gov/SBIR.
- People who invest their own monies in small businesses with growth potential are called *angel investors*. They generally invest in small companies for as much, if not more, satisfaction in helping entrepreneurs grow their businesses as they do for getting a return on their investments. Some you may know, depending on whom you ask among your friends, family, acquaintances, and business associates; there may be others you do not know but who seek out companies in which to invest their money.
- Other options for midsize businesses are employee stock ownership plans (ESOPs), in which you sell shares of your business to employees; Small Corporate Offering Registrations (SCORs) that permit you to raise money by issuing stock directly to the public without the assistance of an underwriter; and direct public offerings (DPOs), another method that permits you to sell stocks directly to the public. These fund-raising stock options require the assistance of legal and financial experts, and your small business may or may not be ready to qualify for these avenues. Talk to other entrepreneurs who funded their businesses with these options for information about their experiences, and ask if they can share any tips and referrals of experts or companies that assisted them.

One of the best ways to finance your growth is through your business's earnings and efficient operations. It is simpler and you remain in control of your business as opposed to meeting the demands of investors, lending institutions, public holdings, and angels, who—at some point—will all try to dictate how you should operate your business or even require an actual percentage of your business.

Venture Capital

Venture capital (VC) is the financial investment in new or existing firms that exhibit the potential for extensive growth. Venture capitalists can give large loans to young companies, primarily those that they consider to have a potential for rapid growth. Interest on VC loans can be expensive and may require exchanging an interest in your company to get the loan. Statistics show that only a small percentage of companies receive VC funding, and it is used primarily for expansion and not start-ups.

Venture Capitalists Can Make Up Several Types of Firms

- *Private independent firms* have no affiliations with any other financial institutions.
- *Affiliate or subsidiary firms* make investments in behalf of banks, insurance companies, outside investors, and the parent firm's clients; or they are "direct investors" or "corporate venture investors," subsidiaries of nonfinancial, industrial corporations making investments on behalf of the parent.
- *Angel Groups* are informal or formal private (wealthy) investor groups that help fund businesses too small to attract professional venture capital. Angels do not usually require a large piece of your company in exchange for their money like VCs.
- *Government-affiliated investment programs* help companies locally, statewide, or federally; venture capital firms may augment their own funds with federal funds and leverage their investment in qualified investing companies.
- *Small Business Investment Companies (SBICs)* are venture capital firms licensed by the U.S. Small Business Administration (SBA) to provide either long-term debt or equity financing to qualified small businesses. There are now several SBICs that are SBA-backed women-owned venture capital companies (see Suggested Resources). However, these loans are for already-established businesses in later stages.

Before approaching a venture capital firm, you should consult with financial experts who can assist you in evaluating if your business is a good candidate for venture capital financing.

Whatever financing sources you seek, do the research beforehand to find the best financing match for your business. You should find it easier, however, to get financing for an established business over a start-up.

Suggested Resources

Books

The Directory of Venture Capital & Private Equity Firms, 2006: Domestic & International, edited by Richard Gottlieb and Laura Mars-Proietti (Millerton, NY: Grey House Publishing, 2006). Find in public or university libraries.

The Handbook of Financing Growth: Strategies and Capital Structure by Kenneth H. Marks, Larry E. Robbins, Gonzalo Fernandez, and John P. Funkhouser (Hoboken, NJ: John Wiley & Sons, 2005).

How Your Company Can Raise Money to Grow & Go Public by Robert Paul Turner, Megan Hughes, and Garrett Sutton (Reno, NV: Success DNA, 2001).

Streetwise Financing the Small Business: Raise Money for Your Business at Any Stage of Growth by Charles H. Green (Holbrook, MA: Adams Media Corp., 2003).

Web Info

www.Entrepreneur.com/howto, *Entrepreneur* magazine's free, online, how-to guide, "How to Seek Expansion Financing."

VENTURE CAPITAL (SOME OF MANY)

Web Info

www.businessfinance.com, Business funding comprehensive resource site.

www.capitalacrossamerica.org, capital across America is a Small Business Investment Company (SBIC), licensed by the Small Business Administration (SBA).

www.financingforwomen.com, small business financing resources.

www.sba.gov/starting_business/financing/loanpackage.html, SBA article, "How to Prepare a Loan Package."

100. Managing Growth over the Long Haul

Managing your business growth will be an ongoing challenge, but following your business and market plan and being determined to succeed will have a large impact on your success. Not everyone wants a huge business, and these entrepreneurs are very comfortable with their company's present size. There may be a time, however, when you will want to pass your business on as a legacy or sell it and retire or move on to yet another venture. Here are guidelines for taking your business wherever you wish to go with it.

Is There a Limit to Growth?

Your business's continued growth depends on factors such as the finances that were just discussed, ability to manage, and the continuing available customer base for your products or services. Not every business owner wants a multibusiness or the largest business in his or her area or nation. Making more money does not necessarily follow automatically if you expand your business. The extra costs for production, distribution, hiring, or subcontracting employees or other companies, as well as the time you invest, can quickly eat up any extra money your expanded business might bring in.

Statistics demonstrate that if you stay focused on your core products and services, and your specific successful niche, your business is more likely to be successful. Branching out too quickly may distract you from the original product lines that helped brand your business and make it an initial success, and your business may even go under. This advice may seem to contradict the discussion in Chapter 12 about business spin-offs. But many sidelines resemble the original products, and the process to expand is not as costly as starting from scratch with a new product.

You can still explore new markets, but never forget what your best seller is, and who your best customers are. Get professional advice, weigh all the pros and cons, and start your expansion steps only when you are ready. Jane Mitchell concentrated on her specialty cheesecakes. She will make birthday cakes and other special cakes for custom orders, but she says she likes the pace and the fact that she is known in her area for having the best-tasting cheesecakes and does not want to lose that reputation or her customers, who are willing to pay her for those scrumptious desserts.

Is There a Time to Sell?

There may be a time you want to sell your business, pass it along to family, or close it. Selling your business may be a way for you to finance your retirement or another venture. If you pass it along to family, you may still be able to work as an advisor or part-time employee, but closing it may be best if your market has completely disappeared or you have no interest in seeing it in someone else's hands.

Business experts recommend that you begin to plan an exit strategy when you write your business plan *before* you even launch your business. A well-planned exit strategy will help make the transition easier whether you sell, bequeath, or close the business. You can review the strategy whenever you periodically revise your business plan.

If you are expecting to pass your business on to your children, it makes sense to have them help you in the business from an early age. One car dealer with several dealerships made each of his sons and daughters work in the business as a salesperson and in other positions while they were going to college, so they would be ready to carry it on if they wanted to in the future. Of course, family members may not want to carry on the business, so you might consider hiring a business advisor to help them or you in making contingency plans to sell it. It is also imperative to consult with an attorney for the necessary contracts, wills, or other documents that will pass your business along.

There are brokers who can do this for you, or you can do it yourself, with legal help. It makes sense that your business will bring a higher price if it is profitable, is well managed, has an existing customer base, and has good projected sales forecasts. It may be more difficult to sell a services business, especially if you are the primary provider of those services. What you are selling then is your customer base, and sometimes the new owner will not give the same customer service that you did or your regular customers do not want or like the new owner, and your loyal customers may leave and go elsewhere.

You may have to close your business if your family members have no interest in your business, the economy is poor, the market has disappeared for your business, or your business is too far in debt. No matter what your exit strategy, you should seek professional counsel from a lawyer and an accountant to help you through each phase.

When you market and grow your business from the start, you are actually planning for its and your future. It is something to keep in mind from the day you get your first customer.

Keys for Success: Some Final Survive-and-Thrive Marketing Tips

- *Go with your plan.* Set up from the start and give your marketing tactics a chance to succeed. Do not withdraw too soon. Sometimes it may take a year for results with advertising strategies.
- *Try a marketing mix of a combination of strategies.* Abby Marks Beale says that as a sole proprietor of her speaking and training business, The Corporate Educator (www.TheCorporateEducator.com), many people ask how she gets business. "I wish I could say to do 'this one thing and you will get all the business you want," says Beale. "There is no exact formula. Instead, I believe that if you throw enough stuff against the wall, something's gotta stick, which means I try every avenue and see what works well. Of the 30 or more strategies I have used, the best ones for me thus far are to do a great job when I am speaking or training, keeping in touch with 'subscribed fans' through a monthly e-newsletter and religiously following up with interested meeting planners," she says.

- *Do not be stingy with your market plan's budget.* You can spend carefully and wisely, but you still will have to pay something toward advertising and promotions.
- *Say thanks but no thanks to clients or customers who are dragging you down.* Erin, the professional organizer, says, "Decide what parameters you have for the clients you want to work with. For example, I want to work with clients that respect my time and value my services and ideas. I only want to work with clients that are as invested in their project and goals as I am. Don't waste your valuable time and energy working with clients that don't measure up. So if they don't make the grade—cut them loose!"
- *Make supplying your loyal customers' needs a priority in your business.* Thank them for their business and keep them happy by staying in touch with them as you would any friend. As the cliché states, "You can't have too many friends," in this case happy customers.
- *Marketing is constant.* Never stop. Marketing is the lifeblood of your business. If you stop or become stagnant, so will your business's "circulation" and ability to reach new customers or keep your faithful ones.

Marketing is not that difficult, and there are more than just these 100+ ways to get customers. It is important to be fair, have fun, and market constantly because your business cannot survive or thrive without it.

Suggested Resources

Books

Bigger Isn't Always Better: The New Mindset for Real Business Growth by Robert M. Tomasko (New York: AMACON, 2006).

Deciding to Sell Your Business: The Key to Wealth and Freedom by Ned Minor (Denver, CO: Deciding to Sell, LLC, 2003).

The Essential Guide to Managing Small Business Growth by Peter Wilson and Sue Bates (Hoboken, NJ: John Wiley & Sons, 2003).

The Future of Work: How the New Order of Business Will Shape Your Organization, Your Management Style and Your Life by Thomas W. Malone (Boston: Harvard Business School Press, 2004).

Web Info

www.Entrepreneur.com/howto, *Entrepreneur* magazine's free, online, how-to guide, "Exit Strategies for Your Business."

Ongoing Growth: Additional Practical Tips for Maintaining and Sustaining Your Business

A common trait among entrepreneurs is that they are persistent in their quest to achieve business success. They never stop asking questions and learning. Here are 25 additional suggestions based on chapters in this book. They provide advice for continuing and increasing your personal business acumen and your profits.

IDEAS TO HELP YOUR BUSINESS GROW AND SURVIVE

1. Beating Global Markets

Many large companies that once subcontracted smaller businesses to do projects are now outsourcing those jobs to overseas companies whose employees work for less. Here are some suggestions to help your business stand out from the foreign competition:

- Conduct market research to find services or products that foreign companies cannot provide your clients.
- Meet with regular or prospective clients to present the benefits of your business such as custom-designed products or services for their *specific* needs, identification of problems before a crisis develops, and the ability and flexibility to provide immediate assistance to solve unexpected emergencies.

- Supply your clients with outstanding quality services and relationships, and let them know *their* bottom line is a priority of yours.
- Become a source of valuable market information. Provide your clients with ongoing current information and tips in their industry through newsletters, e-zines, postcards, and reports—all to help your *clients* have an edge over *their* competitors.

Concentrate on these factors and your clients will want to keep close by and not "wander" abroad!

Suggested Resources

Books

> *Marketing Services: Competing through Quality* by Leonard L. Berry (Glencoe, IL: Free Press, 1991).
>
> *The Small-Mart Revolution: How Local Businesses Are Beating the Global Competition* by Michael H. Shuman (San Francisco: Berrett-Koehler Publishers, 2006).

2. Business Card Axioms

Business cards are an important marketing tool in promoting your business. Think of them as tiny "billboards," that can have a visual and memorable impact on potential customers. Here are some axioms or ideas for maximizing their marketing potential (see also Method 78 for more tips).

- Always hand out more than one card at a time, urging the recipient, "If you know of anyone else who can use my products or services, please feel free to give them one, too."
- Have your card printed with notches that can fit most popular desktop business card holders.
- Carry cards with you at all times and in an easily accessible place like a shirt pocket.
- If you are exhibiting at a trade show, place your cards where they can be easily picked up by attendees.
- Hand out your cards face down, so people will turn them over to read your name.
- Have magnetic backing on some of your cards, especially if you are a provider of emergency services such as a computer consultant or professional counselor; regular customers can then place the cards on their appliances and not have to look for your contact number.

- Post them (with permission) on community bulletin boards in grocery stores, Laundromats, restaurants, and other public places that have bulletin boards for this purpose.
- Include cards with every product order or invoice or in business correspondence.
- If you have several customer types, print your cards to highlight the benefits that fit each one's needs.
- Ask other entrepreneurs for innovative ways they market their cards. Look at their cards to get ideas that you can incorporate into yours.

Courtesy tip: Before handing out your card to prospective customers or networking associates, show interest in *their* problems or interests, or their businesses by asking questions and listening. When they ask you about yours, you can give them your 30-second pitch and wait to see if they show further interest and ask for your card. You do not want to come across as a hard sell, but rather as someone who is truly interested in what they have to say. There are many other ways to use your cards to help increase your marketing power. Many business owners have old cards sitting in their offices. This should never happen if you make it a priority to hand some out each day.

Suggested Resource

Book

> *Identity Solutions: How to Create Effective Brands with Letterheads, Logos and Business Cards* by Cheryl Cullen and Amy Schell (Cincinnati, Ohio: HOW Design Books, 2003).

3. Business Identity Package

One of the first steps you want to take when starting a business is to create a *business identity package*. Experts you might consult for this step include a professional namer (like Marcia Yudkin, www.namedatlast.com) if you have not already chosen a name; a graphic artist or designer for a logo, or designs; a quality printer of business materials; a marketing consultant; and a lawyer if you want to get a trademark for your name and identity.

Your business identity package can include business cards, order forms, stationery, labels, and invoices preprinted with your company name, address, logo, web site design; display equipment; catalog sheet; uniforms, vehicles, product shape, color, and anything else that is visual and represents your business. Your identity should be dynamic and consistent and should communicate to your customers who you are and what you or your product can do for them. It will help develop your brand—what differentiates you and your business from your competitors.

Knowing your target market and why those customers would want to buy your products or services will help guide you in this identity. The owner of a children's party business will have a fun and colorful identity to appeal to the children, while an accountant's or financial advisor's identity will be more sedate and professional in its materials, as clients would expect.

Study other businesses to see what they use and to help you select what you want your identity package to communicate to your potential customers.

Suggested Resources

Book

> *Designing Identity: Graphic Design as a Business Strategy* by Marc English (Gloucester, MA: Rockport Publishers, 2000).

Web Info

Online articles about business identity:

> www.signalfireproductions.com/business.htm, Signalfire Productions' "What is Business Identity?"

> www.money.howstuffworks.com/biz-identity.htm, "How Business Identity Works" by Lee Ann Obringer, comprehensive article with resources.

4. Business-to-Business Marketing Tips

If your target customers are for-profit firms, government agencies, and non-profit organizations, or business-to-business (B2B), here are some tips for finding possible clients:

- Join local and national business and trade associations for networking and referrals.
- Attend industry trade shows, conferences, and seminars to stay current with industry advancements and to meet prospective business owners.
- Join forces with owners of like or compatible businesses to handle larger jobs, promote referrals, and barter services.
- Please your current customers, but search for new ones, so you will have a constant flow of work and profits.
- Develop a specialized market niche to meet the needs of small businesses that larger competitors bypass.
- If you qualify as a minority or woman-owned business, contact a local Small Business Development Center (www.SBA.gov/SBDC) to have your business certified for participation in government contracts.

- Contribute articles to small business publications to establish yourself as an expert in your field.
- Offer to speak to community or business groups on a topic related to their organization.

Once you obtain your first B2B clients, build working relationships with them to gain their trust by proving you can consistently do an adequate job, on time, and according to budget, so they will hire you for future projects.

Suggested Resource

Book

Hope Is Not a Strategy: The 6 Keys to Winning the Complex Sale by Rick Page (New York: McGraw-Hill, 2003).

5. Choosing the Best Promotional Products for Your Business (see also Method 76)

We all have them: pens, magnets, coffee mugs, T-shirts, and other assorted items with the names of businesses or professionals imprinted on them, given out by businesses and professionals to help promote their companies or services. There are many promotional products catalogs from which you can choose articles for a wide range of prices. With so many objects available, how do you choose the ones that will best fit your budget and have the most promotional impact for your business? Here are some suggestions from promotional product experts:

- Give products that are of value. Stay away from those plastic items that look like they came out of a machine for a quarter.
- Give products to potential customers who have expressed interest in or who are looking for services or products like yours. Examples are people you meet and talk to at your trade show booth, or those who attend your classes or seminars or ask you to send them some information.
- Choose products that paying customers will keep handy so they can call you first when they want to repeat their purchases.
- Products should relate to your business. Mouse pads from computer businesses, pet brushes from animal groomers, "to do" reminder magnets from professional organizers are examples of items that customers will find useful and that will remind them of the business owner who distributed the gift.
- Find products that are tasteful, unique to your industry, and reflect positively on your business.

To ensure you choose the best giveaway for your potential customers, consult with an experienced promotional products distributor. Ask other business owners for referrals or visit the web site of the industry's association, the Promotional Products Association International, to find a distributor near to you.

Suggested Resource

Association

Promotional Products Association International, www.ppa.org, industry association and membership referrals.

6. Cold-Calling Tips

Cold-calling—contacting potential customers by calling (or visiting) unannounced, to inform them of your business products or services—may be one of your least favorite tasks. It can, however, be an effective method for reaching potential customers. Here are some tips to help you make these calls:

- *Have a targeted list.* Do not just randomly pick out names from a business directory. Some preliminary research about the company or person you are calling will help you slant your sales pitch to potential customers who can best use your product or service. Garner likely customers' names from attending trade shows, referrals, or association meetings.
- *Do the math.* Before you start your calling campaign, break down your business figures to determine how many new customers you should get or products you should sell that month, so you can make enough calls to get one new paying customer or sell X number of items.
- *Practice what you want to say* and have your business information ready if your caller has questions.
- *Keep track of your calls.* Write down whom you called, the date and time, and the person's response. Make a note if this was the wrong time, wrong person, wrong extension, or any other incorrect information so you will not make the same mistake twice. Jot down positive notes as well, so you will not be discouraged.
- *Make special note of those who were not ready to buy, but expressed interest,* so you can make periodic follow-up calls.
- *Make the most of your call.* You have less than 30 seconds to grab your prospects' attention, so make sure you mention how your services or products offer them a unique benefit.

- *Do not waste your prospect's time with personal greetings or chitchat.* Get right to the point of your call.
- *If a prospect asks a question about your products or services, answer the question instead of continuing your sales pitch.* If prospects ask for more information, ask if you can send them sales literature or samples, and then follow through. If they ask about your prices, go ahead and give them some basic price quotes.
- *Smile when you talk;* it will put you more at ease, and you will project friendliness.
- *Schedule a time each day to make your calls,* so you will get into the habit.
- *Consider hiring a sales assistant, a virtual assistant, or trading cold calls with another business owner,* if you really, really, hate making these calls or need assistance.

You may never be comfortable making cold calls, but if you continue to do so in a professional manner, it might prove to be one of the most successful marketing methods for your business. No one knows more about your business than you!

Suggested Resources

Books

> *Conquering Cold-Calling Fear Before and After the Sale* by Don Surath (Fort Bragg, CA: Cypress House, 2003).
>
> *Red-Hot Cold Call Selling: Prospecting Techniques That Really Pay Off,* 2nd ed., by Paul S. Goldner (New York: AMACON, 2006).

7. Competing against the Big Guys

If you try to be a David against a Goliath, you will need more than a slingshot to compete (other than the "Divine Intervention" assistance that David received). It would probably take far greater financial and distribution resources than you have now to succeed on the big guys' level. However, you can make your business appear larger than it is and offer benefits to potential customers that larger companies cannot provide. Here are a few suggestions:

To Appear Larger

- Hire a virtual receptionist company to answer your phones and take messages 24 hours a day, giving the impression that your company is capable of large-scale projects.
- Use all top-quality promotional materials and mailings, as though you are a big company with a large advertising budget.

To Beat the Big Guys

- Provide fine-tuned, custom-based services and products.
- Serve smaller niche markets that larger companies prefer not to handle or do not handle well.
- Encourage referrals from professionals whose clients are in your target market. Their endorsement will give you credibility over competitors.
- Add value to your products or services like free delivery or installation so you do not have to lower your prices to compete with bigger companies.
- Add specialty products that complement your business and are not carried by bigger stores.
- Invite experts to speak or hold in-store seminars about the products or services you sell.
- Dedicate your business to helping one or more nonprofit organizations and sponsor events. People will see you on a personal basis and see that you care about your community.
- Send letters or e-mails to regular customers with offers or information tailored just for them.

Be proud you are small in the way that you can better serve the needs of your customers, and highlight those reasons in your advertising and publicity campaigns. People just want the best service or product that solves their problems and if you do that in a timely manner with excellent customer service, they will not care how large your company is.

Suggested Resources

Books

> *Think Big, Act Small: How America's Best Performing Companies Keep the Start-Up Spirit Alive* by Jason Jennings (New York: Portfolio, 2005).
>
> *Up against the Wal-Marts: How your Business Can Prosper in the Shadow of the Retail Giants,* 2nd ed., by Don Taylor and Jeanne Smalling Archer (New York: AMACON, 2005).

8. Connecting with Customers

As discussed in Method 81, to better serve your customers, you must communicate effectively. How you respond to your customers as unique individuals demonstrates that you can relate to and understand them. It is all part of fostering customer service, satisfaction, and loyalty. Here are ways to overcome barriers that can stand between you and good customer relationships:

- *Terminology:* Use terms with which your customers are familiar. The more knowledgeable customers are about your industry, the more technical terms you can use in your conversations. If they are novices, you can either briefly define the terms when you mention them or avoid using them altogether. Include a "Frequently Asked Questions" (FAQs) section on your web site or in a printed pamphlet that you give to potential customers who ask for more information and to customers who purchase your products or services. *Under no circumstances* should you ever talk down or use a patronizing tone to your customer. No one wants to feel stupid!
- *Tone:* Be positive and upbeat, but not to the point of being overfriendly or you will come across as being false.
- *Friendliness:* You want to be serious about the quality of your business's goods or services, but intersperse your conversations with a bit of pleasantry about common interests such as sports, family, pets, or other "safe" topics of conversation. This can help customers feel you relate to them better, and they will be more at ease dealing with you.
- *Ethnicity:* We live in a global economy, so if your regular customers are not native to your country, you might take some time to learn some of their language's common words and phrases or popular customs to demonstrate you value our world's cultural diversity.
- *Age:* The ages of your customers will dictate their life's goals and influence their purchasing decisions. Familiarizing yourself with what an age group considers important at certain times in their lives will help you better understand their needs and how to serve them.
- *Regional differences:* If you did not grow up in the community in which your business is located, take time to acclimate yourself to your customers' attitudes and the ways they conduct business, so you will not offend them in some way or be surprised at how you are treated in conducting business.

If you treat all your customers with respect and strive to find commonly shared interests, you can establish not only good rapport but quite possibly, long-lasting (and profitable) business relationships and even personal friendships.

Suggested Resource

Book

Communicating with Customers by Patrick Forsyth (London: Orion, 1999).

9. Consider the Worst-Case Scenarios and Plan for Them

Rochelle Balch (www.rbbalch.com) author of *C-E-O & M-O-M* and *Brag Your Way to Success,* is the owner of a successful computer consulting business. She has weathered major fluctuations in business and recommends business owners consider worst-case scenarios and plan for them. Two other women had a thriving antique business until a major fire destroyed several blocks of their small town, including the building that housed their shop.

How do you prepare for downtimes, shifts in customer markets, thefts, and minor and major disasters? Method 21 mentioned the most important things to have covered: insurance to protect your business property, yourself, and your family; safeguards against security threats; and careful compliance with legal and regulatory concerns. Here are some steps that can help you prepare for the worst:

- *Diversify:* Try not to have just one or two large clients. What happens if that customer goes elsewhere? Expand your marketing campaigns to strive for a balance of both large and small markets, and build up your business with several revenue streams to ensure you will have a steady income.
- *Disasters:* Make a recovery plan in the event of fire, flood, earthquake, or hurricane (like Katrina); take precautions to protect costly equipment and back up valuable files like customers' and suppliers' information. Have uninterruptible power supply (UPS) technology to have time to save your computer files in the event of power failures. Talk to a computer consultant for advice of what to back up and not.
- *Insurance:* Reread your insurance policies and ask specific questions of your agents about what is and what is not covered.
- *Security:* Take precautions to protect your business or office space, your equipment, and your customer information from physical and identity theft.
- *Legal:* Ignorance is not a good defense should you be fined or sued for something related to your business. If you have a food-related business, for example, licensing, permits, and inspections are involved. Every industry has legalities. Learn what you can and cannot do to prevent actions against you.
- *Keep your list of experts and their contact information in a safe place so you will not waste time trying to get in touch with them.*

If the worst *does* happen, it will still set you back, but not as far as if you were completely unprepared. Rochelle Balch expanded her consulting business by finding a new market of potential customers, and the two women with the antique business were able to rent in the same town and with their insurance money (they were certainly glad they had it), found antiques to open their doors again. To survive and thrive, hope for the best, but prepare for the worst.

Suggested Resources

Books

Brag Your Way to Success: The Guidebook to Self-Promotion by Rochelle Balch (Gendale, AZ: RB Balch & Associates, 2001). www.rbbalch.com.

Business Security: Over 50 Ways to Protect Your Business! by T. A. Brown (Las Vegas, NV: Crary Publications, 2004).

The Buyer's Guide to Business Insurance by Don Bury and Larry Heischman (Irvine, CA: Entrepreneur Press, 1997). Book and disks.

C-E-O & M-O-M, Same Time, Same Place, rev. ed., by Rochelle Balch (Gendale, AZ: RB Balch & Associates, 1997). www.rbbalch.com.

Contingency Planning and Disaster Recovery: A Small Business Guide by Donna R. Childs and Stefan Dietrich (Hoboken, NJ: John Wiley & Sons, 2002).

The Entrepreneur's Guide to Business Law, 2nd ed., by Constance E. Bagley and Craig E. Dauchy (Stamford, CT: South-Western, 2002).

Government

U.S. Small Business Administration, www.sba.gov/DISASTER, you may be eligible for loans if you are in a declared disaster zone and your business has suffered related damage.

10. Create Marketing Budget Worksheets

As your marketing strategies develop, you need to record each one's cost and response. A good way to do this is to create your own template or fill-in budget or cash flow worksheet. Then use it to record the advertisers or organizations, expenses, and other important details of each marketing activity used so you can evaluate its effectiveness and refer to it whenever you need to review or repeat the same method. Have a separate sheet or page for each activity.

You might include the following information on such a worksheet:

- *Name of the advertiser or method:* Example: ABC newspaper or XYZ Run-for-a Cause (nonprofit).
- *Size of ad or how you participated:* Example: 2 column by 6; or press release announcing your business is seeking donations for every mile you run and all proceeds will go to the Run.
- *Fees:* List amounts that you paid for ad placement, copywriting, graphic design, and production.

- *Expenses:* List amounts that you paid for delivery, audiovisual tapes, photos, printing, and miscellaneous expenses.
- *Results:* Track and analyze responses and sales relative to paid ads. List comments or leads gained from your publicity in participating in a cause. Use this cause to help with your promotions (photos of you running or with the beneficiaries of this cause).

Store this information in easy-to-find computer or paper files that you can access for future reference. Use whatever filing system or chart that works best for you.

Keeping careful records of what you spend and the results will prevent you from wasting time and money on unproductive marketing pursuits.

There are numerous accounting ledgers and software programs; here are some aids for creating a marketing budget worksheet.

Suggested Resources

Electronic Manual

"Marketing Budget Toolkit" sold by Marketing Acumen, www.marketingacumen .com.

Software

Marketing Plan Pro, Marketing Expense Budget, by Palo Alto Software, Inc., www.paloalto.com.

Web Info

http://office.microsoft.com/en-us/templates/default.aspx, Microsoft Office online templates. Click on "Marketing Budget Plan."

11. Essential Bookkeeping and Record Keeping

Bookkeeping and record keeping are not the favorite tasks of many small business owners who would rather concentrate on the creative and production aspects of their ventures. However, setting up a financial record-keeping system can help organize your business transactions, give you ongoing financial reports, keep track of inventory, and save you time and money.

Here are tips on setting up a bookkeeping system for your business:

- Learn the basics of business bookkeeping. Enroll in adult education classes or courses at local business schools or community colleges. Learn the terminology—accounts receivable and payable, double-entry account-ing, and other recording terms.

- Talk to your accountant and ask other entrepreneurs and small busi-ness owners (especially those in similar businesses or the same in-dustry as you) what systems and accounting software they use and recommend.
- If your business needs a software program tailored for its specific needs, then you may have to turn to what is called a VAR—value-added reseller. If you decide to go this route (usually more expensive), arrange for a soft-ware demonstration and make sure the company will provide you with ongoing support for these more complicated programs.

A good system will help you check your business's development, prepare your financial reports, make note of your deductible business expenses, record all the sources (deposits) of money coming into your business (important to the IRS), and help prepare and support your tax return entries.

Having a good organized bookkeeping and record-keeping system in place also gives you a command of your business's present cash flow. Knowing your fi-nancial status at any moment will help you decide which steps you can or can-not afford to take next to achieve your goals and keep your business solvent while still delivering profits to your bottom line.

Suggested Resources

Books

> *Keeping the Books: Basic Record Keeping & Accounting for the Small Busi-ness,* 5th ed., by Linda Pinson (Chicago: Dearborn Financial, 2001).

> *Minding Her Own Business: The Self-Employed Woman's Guide to Taxes and Record Keeping,* 4th ed., by Jan Zobel (Naperville, IL: Sourcebooks, 2005).

Software

Two examples of the many existing business accounting software products:

> Peachtree, www.peachtree.com, line of accounting products.

> QuickBooks, www.intuit.com, accounting and tax products.

12. Follow-Ups: How Many Times?

In any new business start-up, finding and keeping those first customers is one of the biggest obstacles a new business owner has to overcome. Even if your pro-motional methods have generated a good response from potential customers, it does not always result in their purchasing your services or products. New business owners, especially, wonder how many times they should respond to new contacts before taking them off their list of potential customers. You may fear that you will harass these people, but you do not want them to forget about your business either.

An experienced business owner suggests, "Typically, a person has to hear or see something seven times before it registers to them that this may be something of value to them. I would suggest this general rule of contact: seven times. If there is phone contact and they still express no interest at that time, ask if you may call them back at such and such time. This way you are getting their permission, which helps eliminate your feeling that you are pestering them. Do not stop the contact until they tell you to stop. Always give them the option and everyone wins!"

Another experienced entrepreneur suggests, "I think one follow-up call and one newsletter is fine. If you think this is not enough, try increasing the newsletter mailings to two, as some people need to be prodded more than others. See if the returns from that second mailing equal the cost and time of sending it."

Still another business owner adds, "Yes there is a difference between being an easy quitter, a good marketer, and a pest. Each potential client will draw the line at a different point, so find the common ground with which you both are the most comfortable."

Some final tips:

- Send questionnaires and offer an introductory consultation or a free gift to all who respond.
- Call and schedule a convenient time for a phone interview or a meeting with clients in person (if you live in their area) to ascertain what their needs may be.

After you receive their feedback or meet with them, evaluate your customers' responses and answers to your questions, so you can market the benefit of your services or products to these potential customers, based on your solutions to their problems and needs.

Make customer contact a *daily* task. You need to have conversations with potential customers as often as your workload permits, because if you only concentrate on your present customers, your business will never grow and may even backslide. Set weekly goals for how many calls or contacts you will make. Remember, too, in your new or follow-up contacts, that customers buy results, so help them see the benefit of hiring your services or using your products to improve their lives or their own ventures (see also Method 79, "Etiquette of Customer Approach").

Suggested Resources

Books

> *Getting Business to Come to You: A Complete Do-It-Yourself Guide to Attracting All the Business You Can Enjoy,* 2nd ed., by Paul and Sarah Edwards and Laura Clampitt Douglas (New York: Penguin Group, 1998).

> *Think like Your Customer: A Winning Strategy to Maximize Sales by Understanding and Influencing How and Why Your Customers Buy* by Bill Stinnett (New York: Mc-Graw Hill, 2004).

13. Looking "Big"

You may be a small company or business, but you do not have to act small. Many million-dollar businesses operate from home offices without clients ever realizing it. The secret is all in how you conduct business. Here are some ideas to look like bigger companies, but better:

- *Act big in terms of meeting and greeting potential customers.* Look and act professional, and make everything connected to your business mimic larger businesses' operations, including your correspondence, phone conversations, ordering and delivery, and more. For example, you can contract with call centers for virtual receptionists who can handle customer communications 24/7 if needed.
- *Make your business's identity look big.* Nancy Cleary, graphic designer and owner of a small publishing business (www.wymacpublishing.com), says, "Find a designer with branding experience to capture your ideas and provide professional graphics for online and real world cross-promotion. As you contribute your expertise to numerous venues, and receive verbal and visual credit, you'll appear 'big' by appearing often in your market. Your brand equity goes up as your familiar slogan, logo, book cover, or voice emerges everywhere—and customers, and the media, will notice."
- *Mimic marketing tactics of big companies.* Try to capture the dynamics of their ads, for example, but on a smaller, more affordable scale.
- *Use handheld devices.* Stay organized with application service providers (ASPs) such as HotOffice.com. The ASPs use an Intranet tool to offer an instant online office that enables you to connect to associates, customers, and vendors from any location. You can share documents, send and receive e-mail, have online conferences, and provide additional applications that will save you money and increase your efficiency. Find additional ASPs listed at www.aspstreet.com, a portal and search engine.

- *Use a professional-sounding address for your business.* If it sounds like it is on a country road (unless you are selling country-style items), use a post office box or a mailbox service company.
- *Inc. your business.* When you are established, consider upgrading your business from a sole proprietorship to a corporation. There are many methods for incorporating, so consult with your legal and business experts for a suitable structure. There is more paperwork involved, so some business owners choose the alternative and apply for a DBA ("Doing business as," taking a fictitious business name).
- *Operate like the big guys.* Take credit card payments or have an 800-number for ordering or inquiries.
- *Have a professional office.* If you work out of your home, rent or barter office space from business associates or arrange to meet clients at their offices.

The more professional your business looks, the better your prospects will be. With these suggestions and others, other companies will perceive that your business is just the right size for the large projects they have in mind. Then it is up to you not only to complete their work to their satisfaction, but also to do it beyond their expectations, so they will not care what your size is (see also Method 33, and "Competing against the Big Guys," this chapter).

Suggested Resources

Book

> *Differentiate or Die: Survival in Our Era of Killer Competition* by Jack Trout and Steve Rivkin (Hoboken, NJ: John Wiley & Sons, 2001).

Virtual Reception Service

AnswerPlus, www.answerplus.ca.

14. Marketing Mistakes to Avoid

A characteristic of entrepreneurs is that they are not afraid of making a mistake; they learn from it and continue on to make their business a success. Here are some marketing mistakes you want to avoid:

- *Trying to reach too many types of potential customers.* Using your market research as a guide, concentrate your marketing efforts on one targeted group at a time for their feedback and response to your promotions, pricing, and your business offerings.

- *Marketing only when business is down.* Marketing is an ongoing group of promotions that you need to do during both good and bad times to ensure a steady maintenance and growth of your business.
- *Being reluctant to try new ways of marketing.* If you do not try new marketing strategies, you may miss an untapped and lucrative group of paying customers.
- *Forgetting your loyal customers.* No one likes being taken for granted, so remember to keep in touch with faithful customers with mailings, e-mails, offers, and other demonstrations of your appreciation for their patronage.
- *Not creating a marketing budget and allocating how much to spend.* How and where you spend money for advertising and promotional activities is an integral part of your marketing plan. Review your overall business plan and its objectives and financial projections to set up an affordable marketing budget that provides for those marketing campaigns that will match your business goals.

Suggested Resource

Book

Marketing Mistakes, rev. ed., by Robert F. Hartley (Hoboken, NJ: John Wiley & Sons, 2005).

15. Handling Business Disagreements*

You are owed money by customers or vendors; the business owner with whom you are doing work trade says your barter work for them is not of equal value with what they are providing you and now you owe them cash; your partner wants to take the business in a direction that you oppose; or a client owing you money assumes you will discount the bill because he knows you want his future business.

There are several ways to try to settle a business dispute:

- *Negotiate.* Call, write, visit, or send e-mail messages to find out how the other side views the problem and how they would like to see it resolved. Let them know your position and ask if you can both come up with an acceptable compromise. It is important to act professional and unemotional and stay away from name-calling or blaming.
- *Have a third party be a mediator.* Hire or ask an expert who is acceptable to you both to act as a nonbiased individual, whose decision is nonbinding.

---

* These are only tips for general information and in no way constitute legal advice.

The expert assists you both in reaching a joint agreement. If you cannot resolve your dispute, then you both can pursue other options.

- *Ask for binding arbitration.* In this case, a third party examines the facts and stances of you and the other party. Usually, the arbitrator's decision cannot be appealed. This method can be costly, but not as expensive as going before a judge or having a trial.
- *Litigate.* This last option is the most expensive; it involves lawyers and judges and possibly juries who will negotiate to reach an agreement, or decide if you or the other person is in the right.

When in doubt, consult with a qualified attorney who is knowledgeable in business or in the area concerning the conflict. To avoid future conflicts, have your lawyer prepare a standard business contract for your use and always have your attorney review any contract that another party asks you to sign.

Suggested Resources

Kit

The Small Business Start-Up Kit: A Step-by-Step Legal Guide, 4th ed., by Peri H. Pakroo (Berkeley, CA: Nolo Press, 2006). Book and CD-ROM.

Software

Quicken Legal Business Pro 2007, www.nolo.com, contracts, letters.

16. How to Increase Back-End Sales

Back-End sales are follow-up sales to customers who have previously purchased your products or services. These buying customers can provide you with significant business profits if you know how to approach them. Here are some suggestions:

- Create a product or service closely related to your customers' original purchase. Many authors sell electronic reports, CDs, and audiotapes related to their books that often cost as much as or more than the original product. With this possibility in mind, plan a back-end marketing strategy. For example, if you are a retailer selling hiking boots, suggest that the buyer might also need shoe wax or a weather-resistant polish.
- Use database software for regular contact and to assist you in sending a prewritten message over the Internet or through the postal mail immediately after a customer purchases an item or uses your service.
- When you are ready to start selling a new product or service, first send a prerelease offer to your mailing list to bring in quick cash and receive feedback about the pricing and quality of the new offering.

- Because we live in a transient society, make sure you send offers of any sales on such items to your mailing list customers.
- To save on costs, consider joining with other business owners in marketing your back-end sales products together if the products or services complement one another.

If you do not follow up after customers make a sale, business experts say you risk losing 70 to 90 percent of your potential profits to competitors. Back-end sales are essential to your business survival and future growth (see also Chapter 12).

Suggested Resource

Book

Complete Idiot's Guide to Direct Marketing by Robert Bly (New York: Alpha Books, 2001).

17. Marketing in Tough Times

If you own a business for a number of years, you will inevitably experience its financial ups and downs, sometimes because potential customers are turning to new trends in your industry and sometimes because the economic times have taken a downward turn. Here are positive actions you can take to boost your profits during these periods:

- Reconnect with your customers. Call or mail them a note asking how you can help them. If you show sincere interest in helping them find solutions to their problems, they will appreciate that you care about them.
- Position your business as a problem solver. From customer surveys and feedback, carefully evaluate their responses and let them know how your product or service can specifically solve the problems they specified.
- Get to know your customers' interests and their community and family involvement, and send them interesting or helpful information. Send notes and congratulatory cards to customers when they or family members receive an award or public recognition. It lets them know you are interested in them as individuals.
- Give that extra effort for repeat and new sales. Announce with a press release or direct mailings, extra or more convenient hours, free pickup and delivery, or a new service or product and follow up on every lead or inquiry.
- Highlight your expertise by offering to give a talk at a customer's group or organization or send out a regular newsletter with practical tips your customers can use.

If you are trying to survive in tough economic times, chances are so are your customers, so the more effort you use to stay connected, the more likely your customers will trust and like you. They will feel they are getting more for their money than buying from your competitors: someone who cares about them—you!

Suggested Resource

Book

Guerrilla Marketing during Tough Times by Jay Conrad Levinson (Long Island, NY: Morgan James Publishing, 2005).

20. Monitoring Market Goals with a Marketing Calendar

When you create a market plan, the goals you set should be reasonable and attainable, especially in terms of an achievable time or date. A good way to see if you are achieving marketing goals is to create a marketing calendar. This will make your marketing tasks more manageable and provide you with time lines and dates to schedule the start of a specific marketing activity. With a marketing calendar giving you date deadlines, you can plan the steps leading up to the date set, allowing you ample time to be ready.

Your calendar is an "at-a-glance" overview of specific marketing activities you are planning or have planned, and provides constancy with your marketing efforts. You can add stars or some other rating symbol beside each activity to designate its effectiveness in generating customer response or sale. You can elaborate further in a written summary about each activity on a marketing budget sheet (see previous section). Your marketing calendar can help you improve and grow a successful business.

Suggested Resources

Book

Guerrilla Retailing: Unconventional Ways to Make Big Profits from Your Retail Business by Jay Conrad Levinson, Elly Valas, and Orvel Ray Wilson, CSP (Herndon, VA: Guerrilla Group Press, 2004).

Web Info

http://marketing.about.com/od/marketingworksheets, You can download a marketing calendar template at About.com's "Marketing Tools and Help."

19. Radio Interview Tips

If you place an ad in a promotional directory like *Radio-TV Interview Report* (www.rtir.com), say for your book that was just released, you might receive as many as 40 requests for radio interviews from around the country. Radio is fun because you can do interviews from home, and in jeans. Here are some tips for a successful interview:

- Ask the directory for an editorial schedule so your ad will be in an issue that focuses on topics related to your book.
- When producers call for an interview, they may suggest the angle of the interview, or you can suggest one. Ask them where they are located and who their listeners are, so you can speak to that audience. I have had live radio interviews from Florida to North Dakota (the friendliest station).
- Once you have decided on a topic, offer to send a set of suggested questions and a review copy of your book if they have requested it. Have answers written out for you and the interviewer. But, have other resources at hand, because during radio time, interviewers may ask questions that are different from the ones you sent.
- When you and the producer have set the time for the interview, confirm it with a follow-up e-mail or letter or call the day before.
- About 20 minutes before the time of the interview, find a quiet space to talk and mute all other surrounding phones, oven timers, and send the children and pets out to play.
- During the interview, be upbeat, positive, and keep your answers short. Smile when you talk, and it will come through in your voice. Listen carefully to the questions to make sure you answer them correctly. Pause before you answer a question and speak slowly so you will not talk too fast to be understood. Nervousness tends to make us talk faster than normal.
- Offer listeners a free tip sheet and give them a web site or address where they can write for more information.
- No two radio stations or interviewers are the same, so relax and talk to your audience as though they were sitting right next to you. One of my wildest interviews was for a morning radio program in Florida. The two DJs spoke most of the time about an alligator loose in a housing development. It was a bit difficult to talk seriously about home business topics around that, but I did get a few points across.
- Even if an interview is scheduled for a half hour, the intermittent breaks and commercials will make it much shorter than that, so make sure the questions you submit are the main ones you want to cover and be sure to mention that your sheet is available free to listeners.

- When the interview is finished, the interviewers usually just hang up. Sometimes producers will stay on and thank you, but not always.
- Always thank the interviewer on air for having you as a guest and send a thank-you note afterward. Do not forget to request a tape of the interview.

You may get some response or an increase in sales as a result of your interview, but there probably will not be a rush to the bookstore or your web site. Remember, the more your name and your business's name are out there, the more opportunities will open up for you.

Suggested Resource

Book

> *101 Media and Marketing Tips for the Sole Proprietor* by Nanette Miner (Bristol, CT: BVC Publishing, 1998).

20. Reading for Business and Marketing Success

What you read can be worthwhile for both you and your customers. Here are a few publications that can be found in major bookstores and online.

BUSINESS MAGAZINES

First are the national business ownership-oriented magazines. These include *Entrepreneur* magazine (www.entrepreneur.com), and those with general business-related management and ownership information like *BusinessWeek* (www.businessweek.com), *Business 2.0* magazine (www.business2.com), *Money* magazine (http://money.cnn.com/magazines/moneymag), *Smart Money* (www.Smartmoney.com), and *PROFIT* magazine (www.PROFITguide.com) for Canada's entrepreneurs. Most of these publications have corresponding web sites with helpful articles for small business owners.

SMALL AND HOME-BASED BUSINESS MAGAZINES

Those hoping to start a new home-based business and those looking to expand an existing one make up the audience targeted by most home-based and small business publications in print and online. These include *Home Business Magazine* (www.HomeBusinessMag.com), *Fortune Small Business* (www.fsb.com), and *Small Business Opportunities* (www.sbomag.com).

WOMEN AND MINORITY PUBLICATIONS

These publications focus on the unique entrepreneurial challenges of their readership. These include *Black Enterprise* (www.blackenterprise.com), *Enterprising Women* (www.enterprisingwomen.com), *Hispanic Business* magazine

(www.hispanicbusiness.com), and *Minority Business Entrepreneur* (www.mbemag
.com), for minority and women business owners.

ORGANIZATION AND INDUSTRY PUBLICATIONS

Almost every professional organization and trade industry association has one
or more publications—newsletters, journals, e-zines, and magazines—that it
sends to its membership. The National Association for the Self-Employed
(NASE) publishes *Self-Employed* magazine and the industry of promotional
products has their magazine, *Successful Promotions*, as do others like the Small
Publishers Association of North America (www.SPANnet.org) and the National
Mail Order Association (www.nmoa.org). Reading publications like these is especially helpful to stay current with marketing strategies and to find marketing
tips and listings.

Regional and local business journals are also available, such as *Small Business
News* (www.sbn-online.com/splash.asp) or the *San Francisco Business Times*
(www.bizjournals.com/sanfrancisco).

NEWSPAPERS

If your business deals with corporate customers, a woman business owner
recommends reading a business newspaper like the *Wall Street Journal*
(www.wsj.com) to which she subscribes. "It helps you stay abreast of national
business and consumer trends," she says, "Plus you can relate the articles to
your customers' needs and help you stay a leader in your field." Most other national and major city newspapers, such as *USA Today* (www.usatoday.com) or
the *New York Times* (www.nytimes.com), also have business sections.

Your city and local papers provide important content: annual business editions; community news, which can give you tips on competitors and prospective
customers; and information about state and local laws that may affect your
business.

ONLINE PUBLICATIONS

You can choose among countless online publications that are comprehensive
such as *CanadaOne Magazine* (www.canadaone.com): a free online magazine
for small businesses in Canada, with hundreds of articles, business profiles, and
reviews, or *The Online Magazine for Work at Home Moms* (www.WAHM
.com). You also can subscribe to business and/or marketing e-zines like Joan
Stewart's *Publicity Hound* (www.publicityhound.com) or Dr. Ralph F. Wilson's
(www.WilsonWeb.com) *Web Marketing Today*.

With so many excellent sources of print and online business and marketing
information, you can easily be overwhelmed trying to decide which ones to
read. Only *you*, however, can determine the publications that are most beneficial to you and your customers. Before you subscribe to any of them, browse
the Internet, visit your local library, or buy or borrow several sample copies of

publications that interest you to get a better idea of their contents and slants. As a busy entrepreneur, you may not be inclined to (or feel you have enough minutes to spare) to read all or even some of these suggested sources, but make no mistake, your competitors will!

Suggested Resource

Web Info

> www.gebbieinc.com, Gebbie Press, Inc., offers an online source of more than 24,000 media listings, including business and marketing publications.

21. Speaking Up for Your Business

You may think back to those days of dreaded oral book reports that you had to give in school but learning how to be an effective speaker can be a boost to your business and become a possible lucrative sideline. Here are several tips for becoming a dynamic and well-paid speaker:

- Know your audience and why they came to hear you. Introduce yourself to members before your talk, so you will see some friendly faces.
- Dress professionally and appropriately for your audience.
- Know the purposes of your talk: to inform and to entertain. Provide useful information. Practice often.
- Use frequent eye contact. Speak clearly and with enthusiasm and passion. Vary your voice's inflection to keep your audience's interest.
- Open with an anecdotal problem and close your talk with its solution. Know when to stop! Remember "KISS" (Keep It Short and Simple).
- Keep the audience interested and involved in your talk by having them participate. Ask them to raise their hands to answer your questions or have them interact with one another.
- Leave time for audience questions and interaction. Distribute handouts that summarize your presentation and list meaningful resources. Include your business contact information and order forms for any products you are selling.

Suggested Resources

Books

> *101 Secrets of Highly Effective Speakers,* 3rd ed., by Caryl Rae Krannich (Manassas Park, VA: Impact Publications, 2004).
>
> *Speak and Grow Rich,* rev. ed., by Dottie Walters and Lilly Walters (New York: Prentice Hall Press, 1997).

CD

Susan Harrow's CD, *Sell Yourself without Selling Your Soul: Self-Esteem from the Inside Out,* www.prsecretstore.com/cd-selfesteem.html, 2005 Fresno Women's Conference, including presentation tips.

22. Staying Fit and "Weight-Less"*

Starting and growing a business may be hazardous to your waistline and overall health if you are not careful. The long hours it takes to get a business off the ground or running may force you to cut back on exercise, or you may find yourself continually snacking to alleviate stress or boredom, or you may do all of these, resulting in an unwelcome weight gain of 5 or 10 pounds or more.

Here are some commonsense tips from health and fitness experts to help you keep your weight down and your fitness level up:†

- *Find a professional.* There are many experts who can help you plan an individualized diet and exercise program that will benefit you the most while suiting your preferences and lifestyle. Visit professional organizations' web sites like those of the American Council on Exercise (www .acefitness.org) to search databases, or the site of the American Dietetic Association (www.eatright.org) to find food and nutrition professionals.
- *When possible, combine business errands and exercise.* Walk to get office supplies or as you talk on your portable or cellular phone; ride a stationery bike while you read your mail; or invite another entrepreneur or a customer for a game of tennis and afterward have a business power lunch (low-cal, of course).
- *Plan your meals.* Persons who plan their meals and snacks tend to lose weight and eat healthier than those who just grab whatever food is nearby when they are hungry. A licensed nutritionist can assist you in planning a healthy and delicious food regimen that will help you keep your weight down and your energy level up.
- *Make exercise a regular habit.* Skip the cinnamon bun and coffee break and instead schedule short, regular exercise breaks during your workday to dance, stretch, run up and down steps, jump rope, walk your dog, or choose any other activity that gets your heart pumping and *that you*

---

* Health experts recommend you *always* check with your physician *before* you embark on any exercise and diet program.

† Parts of this section were previously published in the October 2003 issue of *Home Business Magazine,* an international publication for the growing and dynamic home-based business market. Available on newsstands, in bookstores and chain stores, and via subscriptions ($15.00 for one year, six issues). Visit www.homebusinessmag.com.

enjoy. Encourage your family to join you in these activities. Exercise clears your mind and also improves your mood.

- *Drink plenty of water.* Stay hydrated and do not overload on caffeine or sugar-laden drinks that can add tenseness or empty calories.
- *Take the time to prepare and sit down to enjoy your meals.* It is also a good opportunity to eat and converse with your family.
- *Eat breakfast.* People who skip their morning meal compensate by overeating later in the day.
- *Set up your own fitness corner.* For inclement weather or for a quick exercise break, set up an area in or near your home office with a few free weights and one or two of your favorite pieces of fitness equipment. Find free or low-cost apparatus at garage sales.
- *Try to avoid eating and working at the same time.* You want to be aware of what and how much you are eating.
- *Keep a log.* Journal daily what you eat and when and how long you exercise, especially as you begin your program so you can monitor your progress. Reward yourself each week for sticking to your plan.

Be patient and do not set your expectations too high. It takes time and persistence to acquire a healthier lifestyle, but the results will be worth it. Not only will you look and feel better, but you will also have a noticeable increase in stamina and energy for running your successful business and for all the other important things in your life.

Suggested Resources

Web Info

www.pueblo.gsa.gov, Federal Citizen Information Center, click on "Health" and view the "Exercise & Diet" section of available publications.

www.shapeup.org, Shape Up America! a nonprofit organization founded by former U.S. Surgeon General, Dr. C. Everett Koop, committed to educating the public about the importance of health and weight and offering such educational guides as *Healthy Weight, Healthy Living; Fitting Fitness In, Eating Smart, On Your Way to Fitness,* and *99 Tips for Family Fitness Fun.*

23. Summer Marketing Tips

Summer is a hectic time for most of us. Previous schedules are turned upside down when school-age kids are on vacation and need things to do and places to go. We spend more time doing outdoor activities, going on long or short vacation trips, and participating in other special events. We may find ourselves exhausted attempting to deal with all this rush—not to mention trying to maintain and market our businesses during these often-slower months.

How can you get your customers' attention when they, too, are preoccupied with their own seasonal activities? Consider these marketing tips and tricks:

- *Offer a "summer special" promotion.* Joanne, an independent branch advisor for a popular home decor, network-marketing business, says the company sponsors a favorite program this time every year, with part of the proceeds going to breast cancer research. She says, "Not everyone goes on vacation, so this program gives customers the incentive and opportunity to still have a festive time by hosting a party."
- *Introduce and test a new product or service.* Bert says the summer months were always her slowest time with her home-based antiques business until she added lace curtains and pottery. She says, it was a good time to introduce her new items. "The curtains brought in my regular customers and often vacationing friends who were visiting with them, and though the pottery was well liked, the curtains did so well that I became a successful distributor for the company that made them."
- Advertise in local and regional travel brochures and guides that are supplied free to resort hotels, bed-and-breakfasts, restaurants, and so on. Do not forget to add your seasonal and regular business hours, contact information, and directions or a map so visitors can locate you.
- *Participate in community events.* Look for outdoor markets, fairs, festivals, "old-towne" days, and other community events where you can have a table or booth for advertising opportunities.
- *Give Promotional Products.* Give away free samples, tips booklets, and other products with your business contact information printed or attached to them at these community affairs.
- *Offer summer hours.* Use a summer schedule that may be more convenient to your customers.
- *Check out possible leads while on vacation.* If you and your family go on vacation, research beforehand the places you will be visiting. While there, call on others in your line of business for networking ideas and possible leads for new markets.
- *Look into nonprofit opportunities.* Donate your products or volunteer your services to a charity auction or event such as a hospital lawn fete for free publicity while helping a worthy cause. For example, donate T-shirts with your logo for all the participants in a community fun run.

Michelle, who owns a desktop publishing business, says she cuts back in her marketing activities to spend more time with her family. "I do, however, take time in the summer to plan my market strategy so I can be prepared to resume it, full force, when the kids go back to school." Thus, try or plan one of these marketing ideas, but do not forget to enjoy the fun that summer brings, too!

Suggested Resources

Books

> *Brand Hijack: Marketing without Marketing* by Alex Wipperfurth (New York: Portfolio, 2005).
>
> *Fool-Proof Marketing: 15 Winning Methods for Selling Any Product or Service in Any Economy* by Robert W. Bly (Hoboken, NJ: John Wiley & Sons, 2002).

24. Time to Turn Away Business

If you are an independent contractor, a professional consultant, or produce a product, there are times when it is a smart business move to turn away business. Here are some of those instances:

- When a larger corporation demands your exclusive time or production. Large orders or projects and their promised money may at first be exciting and promising; however, if the demands of larger businesses will take so much time that you cannot handle your other faithful customers, or have time to market to new ones, then you face the danger of being controlled by those larger companies in terms of pricing, payment arrangements, or even the quality of your offerings. Besides, if you have no other customers or clients, what is going to happen to your business if these larger companies decide to go elsewhere? In addition to this risk, you face the possibility of jeopardizing your independent contractor status according to the IRS.
- If a client asks you to do a job for "the publicity" and no payment, but with promises of future paying projects. "Promises" are not cash in your bank account!
- When you have to spend a substantial amount of money and time for this project, with no offer of financial support from the client.
- When you do not know the company or the representative, yet the firm places a large order for your product or craft. Business owners, craftspersons, and artisans may be susceptible to scam artists who place large orders from foreign countries or with bogus credit cards. Always ask for references to call and check, but do your own research on the background of such companies to ensure they are legitimate.
- When considering selling your product to a catalog or on a home shopping channel. Before you approach such outlets, consider whether you can produce the amount required in the stipulated time, how the produc-

tion process may be affected, and whether the quality of your products will remain the same. One crafter had a popular item chosen for a holiday catalog. She ended up working day and night, and asking friends and family to help out in her assembly line so she could meet her deadline for production, packaging, and delivery. In her case, she opted not to be included in the next catalog. She preferred creating and selling at a rate she could produce and still have a good income.

- When it just does not "feel" right. There are times in business dealings when you are tempted to say yes to an arrangement, but it does not feel right for going ahead. A man called a businesswoman with the offer of making an information commercial ("infomercial") for her company and gave the names of others who successfully sold their wares this way. The woman turned him down because (1) she never heard of him, (2) he promised she would make lots of money, and (3), she decided that an infomercial would hurt her business image. Listen to your gut instincts.

- Ask your business mentors, your "board of directors," for their suggestions. If their overwhelming consensus is to back away, then it may be best to heed their advice, especially if they have had experience in this area, good and bad.

When you have said no, be done with it. Do not dwell on what might have been, if only you had said yes. It is better to control your marketing and distribution in ways that you feel are best for your business, and not according to what someone else is attempting to talk you into. Be true to yourself; be true to the mission of your venture.

Suggested Resource

Book

> *What No One Ever Tells You about Starting Your Own Business: Real-Life Start-Up Advice from 101 Successful Entrepreneurs (What No One Ever Tells You About Starting Your Own Business)*, 2nd ed., by Jan Norman (Chicago: Kaplan Business, 2004).

25. Write a Dynamic Company Profile

Your press kit and portfolio should include a company profile. You can use it for introductions to an audience, for media interviews, for prospective clients, and for financing purposes. It is also useful to provide background for potential networking partners, new employees, and interns. Here are tips for composing a dynamic profile:

- Your first few sentences should include a description and highlight the features that make your business unique. Include a "hook" or an interesting anecdote—why you started your business, a special process you use to create your products, a "rags to riches" story, or anything else that would interest an editor or reporter. If you include statistics about your industry, they can be a good lead-in to why your business is important in today's economy.
- Profile your typical customers and their needs, and give specific examples such as before-and-after scenarios showing how your business's offerings have benefited them. Provide some projections of your target market's growth.
- Tell who you are, where you came from, what you did, and any awards or recognition received by you or your company.
- Provide a financial picture of your business's growth and its projected objectives.
- Include your business contact information, your web site, phone numbers, and e-mail addresses.
- Include all this information on one page. Media persons love copy that is succinct.
- Have copies of photos, color and black and white, of you and your business—its storefront, its web site, or a product or service. The media love to include photos with features.
- Have the profile packaged in a folder and on quality paper to present a professional image, and have several of them with mailing envelopes should you need to send them on short notice.
- If you need some assistance in composing your business profile, you can hire a freelance writer to write it or to proofread it for errors and overall readability.

Once you have this profile, you can elaborate on it for annual reports; insert parts of it in your brochures and other promotional materials; post highlights of it on your "About Us" web site page; and use it for additional opportunities to promote you and your business. Keep it on file so you can update it periodically. A dynamic profile can make a terrific first impression and propel your business to further success.

Suggested Resources

Web Info

www.allisonbliss.com/resources.htm#advertising, "Create a Company Profile or Bio," online tool offered for sale by marketing expert, Allison Bliss.

www.whatspossible.com, *Success Strategies Guide: 10 Keys for Success for Small Business Owners* by Denise O' Berry, e-book.

Glossary

The following list is a selection of marketing and business terms in general use.

The 80/20 rule or principle is attributed to Vilfredo Pareto, an Italian economist, meaning, in terms of marketing, that 80 percent of your business comes from approximately 20 percent of your customers.

Accounting period is a regular period of time, such as a quarter or year, for which a financial statement is produced for a business.

Accounts payable is the money owed by your business for goods and services you received.

Accounts receivable is the money owed you by customers for your goods or services.

Accrual basis is the financial record keeping in which income is recorded when it is earned and expenses are recorded when incurred.

Ad Allowance is the contribution of money by the vendor toward the cost of advertising.

Advertising is the use of publication or media ads, direct mailings, Internet e-mails, brochures, signs, promotional products, commercials, or other displays to get your service (or product) noticed by your regular or potential customers.

Agent is a person who is paid a commission by you to carry out the sale of your products or services to your customers. Agents include brokers, manufacturers, and commission representatives (sometimes referred to as "reps").

Amortization is the reduction of debt through installment payments.

Appreciation is an increase in the value of property.

Assets include all the items of value (tangible or intangible) owned by a person or corporation.

Audit is a formal review and confirmation of financial accounts and records.

Back-end sales are follow-up sales to customers who have previously purchased your products or services (see Chapter 14).

Back link, also referred to as an "inbound link," is a type of Internet URL address exchange that automatically links one web site to another. You will often see back links in articles when they refer to a person, business, organization, or agency that has a current web site. When you click on that reference, it will take you directly to the mentioned subject's web site.

Balance sheet is a financial description showing the assets, liabilities, and a business owner's net worth in a business as of a given date.

Bandwidth is the speed at which information is transferred over networks of the Internet.

Barter is the exchanging of goods or business services without the use of money.

Baud is the speed at which computer modems can transmit data. Baud speed is registered in BPS or bits per second.

Benefits are the features of your products or services that meet the needs of your target customers. Benefits help differentiate you from competitors.

Bid pricing is the estimating of all the expenses involved in finishing a project, then adding your profit margin to arrive at the total cost it will take you to complete the project as specified in contract terms.

Blog is a Web log or journal updated daily or regularly on the Internet by an individual (the "Blogger") or by web sites that focus on specific topics.

Blog branding is writing a blog about your services or products to inform and attract potential customers.

Boilerplate is the legal language, often labeled the "fine print," that states the details in a business contract or agreement.

Brand is a symbol, name, or other recognizable designation that differentiates a company. Quality, customer service, pricing, and other ways that your product or service has affected your customers can affect whether your business's brand is seen as a positive or a negative.

Breakeven point is the dollar amount your business must make so that your sales income equals your total costs. From this point, you can determine the prices you must charge for your products or services so that your business will make a profit.

Brokering is the marketing of other people's talents or products and taking a fee. Examples: literary, sports, and talent agenting.

Browsers are software programs such as Netscape or Microsoft Internet Explorer that enable you to read and navigate the HTML Internet documents so you can "search" or "browse" for information.

Business blogging is a Web log or Blog, an online marketing tool used by a business to build a better relationship with its customers by providing value with meaningful information, build trust, encourage customers' participation, and improve communications.

Business image is the overall impression that your business presents to customers.

Business interruption insurance is a type of insurance that covers a business's continuing expenses, such as taxes and payroll, as well as loss of net profit.

Business opportunity is a business venture sold by a companies or entrepreneurs who wish to expand their company or sell their idea to others who want to start a business. A business opportunity usually is a "package" complete with a manual, business forms, and sometimes the equipment. Customer support may or may not be included. Be sure to research opportunities before you invest any money to make sure they are legitimate and not scams. Ask for references.

Business plan is a written description and strategic plan that includes a definition of the business's products and/or services, financial strategies, organization, summation of overhead, start-up and operating costs, potential markets, and the people involved in making the business operate and succeed.

Buzz marketing means to gather a group of volunteers willing to try your product or service, and then talk about their user experience to acquaintances. Their talk or "buzz" will encourage potential customers to try your business offerings.

Capital is the worth of a person's assets; or a business's net worth—the assets minus the liabilities.

Cash flow is the amount of money coming into your business from its sales, and amount of money going out to pay business expenses. Business owners work with their financial experts to regularly monitor their cash flows and to estimate *projected cash flows* to ensure the owner's business has adequate funds coming in to meet its expenses and to show a profit after it pays those expenses.

Certified lenders are banks that are certified by the SBA to participate in the SBA's guaranteed loan program. The banks agree to the SBA's conditions and in return the SBA agrees to process any guaranteed loan application within three business days. SBA district offices can provide you with lists of certified banks in your area.

C&F is a commercial designation that means the stated value of a shipment of goods includes all costs and freight involved in shipping the goods to their destination.

Cluster Marketing is the combining of two services or products (or a mix) to offer to potential customers so they can accomplish more than one thing at a time.

COD stands for collect (or cash) on delivery. It means payment must be made for goods when they are received or delivered.

Cold calling is an unannounced sales call or visitation to potential customers to inform them about your services or products.

Collateral security is what a borrower gives to a lender to guarantee a loan. Examples are property, vehicles, equipment, securities, and other items of value.

Community marketing is the formation of online publications and communities to develop ongoing members' relationships.

Consulting is the undertaking of working on a variety of projects simultaneously, often for different clients, and on separate premises from the client companies. Examples: project management and organizational consulting.

Consumables are items used up or "consumed" when equipment operates, such as cartridges for photocopiers or printers.

Contingency Fees are payments to persons only if they successfully complete assigned jobs.

Contracting is taking on work within an organization for a period of time as an independent contractor or subcontractor without receiving employee benefits. Examples: computer programming, editing, graphic design.

Corporation is a legal business structure that recognizes the owner(s) as a separate entity. There are several forms such as C-corporations, S-corporations, nonprofit corporations (see also sole proprietorship, partnership, and LLC).

Cost is the total of the fixed and variable expenses (costs to you) to manufacture or offer your product or service to your customers.

Credit is the power or ability to obtain goods in exchange for a pledge to pay later.

Current Liabilities are business debts that are due and payable within the next 12 months.

DBA "Doing Business As" is used with a fictitious name under which the business owner(s) will operate.

Debt Financing is borrowing money that is to be repaid over a period of time, usually with interest (short- or long-term).

Deficit is a business's net loss due to expenditures exceeding income, or the excess of liabilities over assets.

Demographics are statistics that provide information about a group of people such as their ages, gender, income level, occupation, education levels, nationality, and race. The U.S. Department of Labor www.dol.gov and the U.S. Census Bureau www.census.gov are two of our federal government's largest provider of these statistics.

Depreciation is a deduction that can be written off the value of property (e.g., office equipment—but not land because it is not expendable) over a period of time. Check with your accountant for the latest updates on home business tax deductions.

Direct Costs are those costs that can be traced and designated directly to a specific product, such as the cost of wax in decorative candles.

Direct Loan is the financial assistance provided through the lending of federal monies for a specified period of time, with a reasonable expectation of repayment. Such loans may or may not require interest payments.

Direct Marketing includes the mailing of promotional materials, in-person selling, and other business-to-potential customers sales methods that business owners use to persuade their targeted population to buy their products or services.

Distributor is a wholesaler who has purchased the rights to market one company's goods (usually not numerous companies' products as an independent sales representative would do) to customers within a given territory—though not always exclusive. You are in business for yourself and set your own hours.

Double-entry accounting is an accounting system in which the left-side entries (*debits*) are balanced by an equal total of all the right-side entries (*credits*). Credits or debits can be applied to any general ledger account, whether it is an expense, asset, liability, income, or capital.

Download is the transferring of files to your computer from another computer.

Due diligence is the concern that a reasonable person uses under the circumstances to avoid harm to other persons or their property; analysis, research.

Employer Identification Number (EIN) is a number assigned to a business from the IRS that is to be shown on all business tax returns, documents, and statements. Many sole proprietors and independent contractors use their Social Security numbers. Contact your local IRS office and consult with your accountant for more information.

Enterprise is another term for a business or venture.

Equity financing is the money contributed to the firm by the owner(s) and investors.

Evergreen (marketing) strategy is a lead developer such as a listing in the telephone directory's business section; or a Chamber's directory. People who need your products or services seek you, and your ad is "always" there.

Expense is money spent for services or products.

FAQ stands for "Frequently Asked Questions." It is often listed on Internet sites to help supply answers to common questions on a certain topic or subject.

Firewall is a type of computer programming that is used for security so that a network user can see through the firewall into the Internet, but other Internet users cannot see through the firewall into your network. Businesses who sell products or services over the Internet use firewalls to protect customers' private information (e.g., credit card numbers used for ordering).

Fiscal Year is any 12-month calendar year used by a business or a government agency as an accounting period.

Fixed expenses are those expenses that generally do not change from month to month (rent, insurance, interests on loans, etc.).

"Flaming" is having your electronic mailbox (e-mail) swamped with hate mail in reprisal for breaking the unwritten rules of Internet etiquette, such as sending out many spam e-mails or unwanted sales posts.

Four Ps are the parts of the marketing mix that you can manage to get the attention of potential customers: product, price (the perceived value of your business offerings), place (your delivery), and promotion (your advertising and publicity).

Franchise is a business operated with a standardized format and recognized products or services. With a business contract, you pay the owner of the franchise (franchisor) for the right to sell the franchise's product or service within a certain area.

Franchisee is the licensee, the person who pays a royalty and often a franchise fee for the right to sell and distribute the franchisor's products and use its trade name or trademark.

Franchisor is the owner of a franchise, also called the licensor, who sells his or her trade name and business system to franchisees.

Freelancers are persons who work independently and are paid fees for their services. They may work at their homes or at their customers' locations. Freelancers include writers, graphic designers, consultants, job trainers, desktop publishers, software developers, and other independent professionals.

Frequency refers to the number of times your target market is shown your advertisement.

Fulfillment is the operation of receiving orders and shipping and tracking goods sold through direct marketing.

Fusion marketing is the linking of your business's promotional efforts to those of a related or nearby business.

General ledger is the primary record of the expenses, income, assets, and liabilities of a business.

General partnerships are business structures in which the partners share equally in risks, rewards, and the rights of control. Partnerships can be formal with written agreements or informal with no written agreements. Only general partnerships, however, are generally eligible for bank loans.

Gross income usually pertains to a business's income before deductions.

Gross profit is the result of subtracting the cost of services or goods sold from sales.

Guarantor is often referred to as the "cosigner" and is a person who agrees to pay a loan if the borrower cannot (defaults).

Guerrilla marketing is the term originated by marketing expert, author, Jay Conrad Levinson (www.gmarketing.com). It means using a variety of original methods to market effectively and economically.

Home page is the page your Internet browser loads at start-up and is also often the name given to the first web site document that is shown when you visit a new web site or follow a link.

HTML stands for Hypertext Markup Language; it is the standard format for creating documents and pages on the Internet, the World Wide Web.

Hyperlink (often shortened to "link") refers to a listing of one web site's URL on another site's page; a user can click on the link to move immediately to an entirely different web site, usually to obtain related information.

Income is the money you have received for your products or services. It can also refer to investment returns.

Income statement is a financial accounting showing the profit or loss of your business within a specified period.

Integrated marketing is the joint use of two or more marketing strategies to sell a service or product.

Internet is a cooperatively run and globally distributed collection of computer networks that was started about 20 years ago as a government-funded project to set up communications in the event of a nationwide nuclear attack. It has since been adopted around the world by businesses, organizations, and individuals to promote commerce and exchange information. The Internet exchanges information via a common set of rules for exchanging data and is referred to as "the Information Superhighway."

Internet service provider is the company that provides access to the Internet.

Intranet is a communications and productivity tool that utilizes standard Internet protocols and technologies (TCP/IP, HTTP, and HTML, search engines, and such) within a company or organization.

JPEG is a Web graphics format used to display photographs and artwork on the Web (it was developed by the Joint Photographic Experts Group).

Lead Time is the preparation time a business owner estimates it will take to implement a new product or service (research, market testing).

Liability in relation to accounting, means a commitment to another party and the amounts to be paid to others.

Lien is the legal right to hold or sell property of another for purposes of getting payment for money owned.

Line of credit is given when a lender agrees to permit a borrower to draw a prespecified amount on an as-needed basis from an account.

Liquid Assets are assets (stocks, precious metals, other) that can be readily changed into cash.

Liquidation is the act of selling the assets of a business to pay off debts.

LLC stands for limited liability corporation. It is a legal structure that provides personal liability protection to the business owner and costs less to form and maintain than corporations.

Logo is the recognizable, exclusive image that is identified with a business and is owned by that business.

Marketing includes the research, positioning, pricing, promotions, analysis, advertising, publicity, and all other activities involved in the buying and selling of a product or service.

Market niche is a defined group of customers who are particularly suited for your product or service. Your business fulfills their needs when other businesses are usually concentrating on larger groups.

Market potential is the determination of the most likely customer who might purchase your product or service.

Media outlets are the newspapers, magazines, television and radio stations, billboards, and other places where you can purchase commercial space and time to advertise.

Mission statement declares your business's purpose and the reason for its presence. It can stay relevant for a long time.

Net profit is the result obtained when expenses are subtracted from revenues.

Networking is a process of building and maintaining working relationships through direct, personal contact. Virtual networking is the same thing, except that it involves using the Internet.

Niche refers to a small segment of a population of potential customers.

A one-person enterprise pertains to working on one's own, usually at home. Examples: computer repair and servicing, bookkeeping, crafts, and many other self-employment ventures.

Overhead includes all the nonlabor expenses that a business needs to operate.

Partnering or work sharing is the process of obtaining a contract as an individual or small business and sharing a portion of the work with another individual or group in a one-time effort.

Partnership (general) is the alliance of two or more persons as co-owners of a business-for-profit.

Passive income is money you earn without much exertion such as real estate investments or packaged products you have created.

Passive marketing is a type of marketing strategy such as on-the-shelf directories that will work for you when your attention is drawn elsewhere (see Method 74).

Percentage Fee is a payment made to a person who makes a sale such as real estate agents or literary agents.

Permission marketing generally refers to e-mail and opt-in sections on your web site inviting people to voluntarily enter their e-mails or home/business addresses to receive more information about your business offerings or to subscribe to an electronic newsletter.

Personal financial history is a record of your borrowings and repayments, plus a listing of your personal assets and liabilities (extremely important to a lender when you are applying for a business loan).

Pixel is the smallest element of a display that can be assigned a color. The higher the number of pixels (from Picture and Element), the better the picture resolution, in a digital camera. The more expensive cameras have *megapixel resolution*—support for images with at least a million pixels.

Place refers to all the actions it takes to distribute your products or services to your customers.

Plug-in is a feature that can be added to a browser enabling you to receive the multimedia features of certain Web pages.

Podcast is a web broadcast of video or audio files available to download or subscribe to on the Internet.

Podcasting is the Internet delivery of video or audio files like music or radio programs using RSS (Rich Site Summary) or Atom syndication (both XML-based Web content) that can be downloaded to personal computers or hand-held devices.

Position is how your target market or your prospects perceive you or your business. The positioning statement is what you would like the brand image to be.

Positioning statement describes how you wish your business to be perceived and what marketing strategies you conduct to fashion and maintain it. It is a plan for brand development.

Price is the selling price per unit customers pay for your product or service.

Principal is the remainder of what is owed on a loan, without the interest.

Product refers to the items, services, or ideas your business provides to your customers.

Profit and loss statement is a report of a business's operations for specified periods. The bottom line reveals the owner's net profit or loss.

Pro forma is a financial planning statement that projects the future performance of a business.

Promotion includes ongoing sales and advertising campaigns designed to catch the attention of and motivate your target customers to purchase your product or service.

Publicity is getting coverage in the media. You generally do not have control over what is written or said about you or your business or other matters related to you.

Public Relations encompasses all the promotional activities that a professional, business owner, company, or organization participates in to enhance its public image and purpose.

Pyramids are illegal business scams in which a few people at the top make money from many people who are at the bottom of the list and who generally lose their initial (and often substantial) investment. Many pyramids are disguised and tout themselves as legitimate multilevel marketing companies (MLMs).

Receivables is the money owed to your business by its customers.

R&D stands for "research and development" in the quest for new products or services that a business can offer its customers.

Research abuse as defined by the Marketing Research Association, is "sugging," and "frugging," two mistreatments of the research process, and are never used by legitimate companies conducting market or opinion research (www.mra-net.org/resources/abuse.cfm). *Sugging* is claiming to be conducting a survey for market research when really trying to sell something. *Frugging* is claiming to be taking a research poll or survey when really trying to raise money.

Residual income is the system of ongoing, regular payments that you receive as a result of a single sale.

Retainer is a payment made to business experts or consultants in either one or regular payments to ensure their availability if their expertise is needed.

ROI stands for "return on investment," and is a basic cost-benefit analysis to assess how much it costs you in money to carry out the action.

RSS stands for *Rich Site Summary* and is a type of XML format used for the delivery of Internet content.

Sales are income-generating activities designed to attract potential buyers from a target market to make purchases based on highlighting the business's benefits and pricing.

"Sandwich Generation" is the age group of population that is responsible for their older parents and relatives as well as for their children and even grandchildren.

SASE is an abbreviation for self-addressed, stamped (first-class) envelope. *LSASE* means a long, business-size, self-addressed, stamped envelope. This is often used for a return reply to a query or request for information (used by professional, freelance writers).

Scam is an illegal business opportunity that promises quick profits. Many today offer lucrative work-from-home schemes. Check their references or inquire at the Better Business Bureau, Federal Trade Commission, and The National Fraud Information Center.

Seasonality refers to business buying patterns affected by weather seasons (businesses affected by the outdoors) and holidays (Christmas, Mother's Day).

Segmentation is how a business targets its marketing efforts to people or businesses that are most likely to buy its products or services.

Silent advertising includes images or trademarks identifying a business, organization, or individual that are exhibited on signs, in media advertisements, on promotional products, and on other materials.

Slogans are phrases that business owners use to advertise their products or services for advertising and business identity purposes.

Small Business Incubator is an association of small businesses usually housed in one building to share building facilities, staff, and other business services that a small business could not afford on its own. Many home businesses join incubators if their business needs to expand out of its home location.

SOHO is an acronym for "Small Office/Home Office" and generally stands for a small business operating out of a home or small office suite with one to five employees. Often these SOHO enterprises consist of consulting, professional practices, and other service-type businesses.

Sole proprietor is a legal form of business ownership in which the business is owned and controlled by one person. One's name can be used in the business or it can operate under a fictitious name (DBA). The owner is fully liable and personal assets are not protected from lawsuits.

Spam is the promoting or sending unwanted solicitations or materials to unknown users or to user groups on the Internet.

Spreadsheet refers to a numerical data table consisting of columns and rows related by formulas. It is used by businesses for tracking customer profiles and other business data.

Tagline is a statement or motto that succinctly defines or represents an organization's mission.

Talent pooling is the formation of a group of self-employed people with different talents to win a contract that none of them could handle on their own. Examples: film production and large publication projects.

Target market consists of the potential customers to whom you are directing your marketing activities.

Tax number is also called your *sales tax number.* It is given to a business by your state revenue department enabling you to purchase goods and products wholesale without paying sales tax. You also need this number to go to wholesale shows and also exhibit your goods there. Contact your local state legislator's office for the address of your state government's office.

Telecommuter is an employee who works from home, one or more days a week, for a company, using technology and communications equipment (telecommunications) to complete the assigned work. The telecommuter usually meets periodically at the employer's location for meetings and consultations.

Time Study is an analysis of how much money you need to make an hour to cover your overhead and operating costs, your time, and your desired profit margin.

Upload is the transmitting of a file from your computer to another.

URL (Uniform Resource Locator) stands for the address notation that points to a particular document or site on the World Wide Web.

Usenet is the system that disburses to a multitude of newsgroups all over the Internet.

Variable costs are costs that change as a result of the production output of your goods or services (shipping, materials, labor).

Venture capital is the financial investment in new or existing firms that exhibit the potential for extensive growth.

Viral marketing is using the Internet's power of large groups of people to spread marketing messages as fast as possible to everyone possible.

Vision statement describes what an organization strives to be in the future, its direction.

Waybill is the document sent along with shipped products that explains the shipment's costs and route.

Webcast is using web technologies to distribute live or delayed sound or video broadcasts.

Webinar is an online seminar that may include audio and video clips as part of its presentation.

Word-of-mouth marketing (WOM) is the concentrated effort to encourage customers and your networking partners to refer your business to other potential customers.

Working capital is the money that is available for your business's daily operations.

World Wide Web, aka "the Web," is a collection of millions of computers on the Internet that contain information and multimedia (sound, graphics, animation, etc.) that have been put in a single format called HTML (hypertext markup language), though it is no longer the only language.

Suggested Resources

Book

> *Dictionary of Marketing Terms*, 3rd ed., by Betsy-Ann Toffler and Jane Imber (Hauppauge, NY: Barron's Educational Series, 2000).

Web Info

> www.knowthis.com/general/terms.htm, KnowThis! Sources for marketing definitions.

> www.managementhelp.org, "Free Management Library" including definitions of all aspects of marketing developed by Carter McNamara, MBA, PhD, Authenticity Consulting, LLC.

> www.marketingpower.com/mg-dictionary.php, American Marketing Association's *Dictionary of Marketing Terms*.

> www.sticky-marketing.net/glossary/index.htm, Sticky Marketing, exchange of marketing information; site includes a glossary.

> www.sba.gov/library/sbaglossary.html, U.S. SBA glossary of business terms.

Additional Resources

Associations* and Organizations

Business

National Association for the Self-Employed (NASE), www.nase.org, offers health insurance and other benefits to members, also offers "Micro Business Advice" on its site.

National Association of Women Business Owners (NAWBO), www.nawbo .org, national organization for women business owners with chapters in many major U.S. cities.

National Small Business Association, www.nsba.biz, a volunteer-led organization, 70+ years old; advocate for state and federal policies benefiting small businesses.

U.S. Women's Chamber of Commerce, www.uswomenschamber.com, an advocacy group supporting women's economic and leadership issues; member conferences, virtual meetings, and teleconferences on related business topics.

Industry and Trade

Associations on the Net†, www.ipl.org/div/aon, the Internet Public Library lists Internet sites providing information about a wide variety of professional and trade associations and other groups.

Encyclopedia of Associations by Gale Group, www.gale.com, found in libraries' reference sections and lists many industry associations.

---

* These represent only a *small listing* of the many existing business and marketing resources available on the Internet and offline. Search for ones in your industry that best serve the needs of you and your business and those that are recommended by your network of business associates, professionals, and experts.

† Many trade associations are nonprofit and do not have the staff to handle queries or provide start-up information. Whenever contacting them via postal mail, always include a self-addressed, stamped envelope (SASE).

Marketing Resource Center, www.marketingsource.com, sells a directory of associations, mailing lists, and other products; site also includes a library of links to many articles on both traditional and Internet marketing strategies and techniques.

State and local chamber chapters of the U.S. Chamber of Commerce, free business tools and resources, www.ChamberBiz.com, www.uschamber.com.

Marketing

American Marketing Association, www.marketingpower.com, professional industry, publications, web site has free guides on marketing topics.

National Mail Order Association, www.nmoa.org, industry organization providing resources for companies involved in direct marketing.

Books

Management and Growth

Bootstrapper's Success Secrets by Kimberly Stanséll (Franklin Lakes, NJ: Career Press, 1997).

Business Know-How: An Operational Guide for Home-Based and Micro-Sized Businesses with Limited Budgets by Janet Attard (Holbrook, MA: Adams Media Corp., 1999).

How to Run a Thriving Business: Strategies for Success and Satisfaction by Ralph Warner (Berkeley, CA: Nolo Press, 2004).

Women's Home-Based Business Book of Answers: 78 Important Questions Answered by Top Women Business Leaders by Maria Bailey (New York: Crown Publishing Group, 2001).

Marketing

According to Kotler—The World's Foremost Authority on Marketing Answers Your Questions by Philip Kotler (New York: AMACON, 2005).

Entrepreneur Magazine's Ultimate Small Business Marketing Guide: Over 1,500 Great Marketing Tricks That Will Drive Your Business through the Roof by James Stephenson (Irvine, CA: Entrepreneur Press, 2003).

Fool-Proof Marketing: 15 Winning Methods for Selling Any Product or Service in Any Economy by Robert W. Bly (Hoboken, NJ: John Wiley & Sons, 2002).

Getting Business to Come to You: A Complete Do-It-Yourself Guide to Attracting All the Business You Can Handle, 2nd ed., by Paul and Sarah Edwards and Laura Clampitt Douglas (New York: Penguin Group, 1998).

The Give to Get Marketing Solution by Joe Gracia (Watertown, WI: Give to Get Marketing, 2005). www.givetogetmarketing.com.

Homemade Money, Bringing in the Bucks! A Business Management and Marketing Bible for Home-Business Owners, Self-Employed Individuals, and Web Entrepreneurs Working from Home Base by Barbara Brabec (Lanham, MD: M. Evans, 2003). www.barbarabrabec.com.

Marketing for the Home-Based Business, 2nd ed., by Jeff Davidson (Holbrook, MA: Adams Media Corporation, 1999).

101 Ways to Market Your Business by Andrew Griffiths (Australia: Allen & Unwin Pty., 2001).

101 Ways to Promote Yourself: Tricks of the Trade for Taking Charge of Your Own Success by Raleigh Pinskey (New York: HarperCollins, 1999).

The Portable MBA in Marketing, 2nd ed., by Charles D. Schewe and Alexander Hiam (Hoboken, NJ: John Wiley & Sons, 1998).

Sell Yourself without Selling Your Soul: A Woman's Guide to Promoting Herself, Her Business, Her Product, or Her Cause with Integrity and Spirit by Susan Harrow (New York: HarperCollins, 2003). www.prsecrets.com.

Small Business Marketing for Dummies, 2nd ed., by Barbara Findlay Schenck (Hoboken, NJ: John Wiley & Sons, 2005).

What Clients Love: A Field Guide to Growing Your Business by Harry Beckwith (New York: Warner Books, 2003).

Business Start-Up and Management Resources

Government: Federal Agencies Helpful to Business and Commerce

Consumer Product Safety Commission (CPSC), www.cpsc.gov, offers guidelines for product safety requirements.

Federal Trade Commission (FTC), www.ftc.gov, regulations for advertising, franchising, and other business operational guidelines.

U.S. Census Bureau (CB), www.census.gov, statistics and demographics for information and research.

U.S. Department of Agriculture (USDA), www.usda.gov, offers publications on selling to the USDA. Publications and programs on entrepreneurship are also available through county extension offices nationwide.

U.S. Department of Commerce (DOC), www.commerce.gov, DOC's Business Assistance Center provides listings of business opportunities available in the federal government. This service also will refer businesses to different programs and services in the DOC and other federal agencies.

U.S. Department of Labor (DOL), www.dol.gov, publications on compliance with labor laws; statistics; information on Veterans' Employment and Training Service (VETS); and Women's Bureau.

U.S. Department of Treasury, Internal Revenue Service (IRS), www.irs.gov, offers information on tax requirements for small businesses.

U.S. Environmental Protection Agency (EPA), www.epa.gov, offers many publications designed to help small businesses understand how they can comply with EPA regulations.

U.S. Food and Drug Administration (FDA), www.fda.gov, offers information on packaging and labeling requirements for food and food-related products.

Government Publications with Information for Entrepreneurs

The Consumer Information Catalog, Federal Citizen Information Center, www.pueblo.gsa.gov, "Small Business," with topics such as "Spotting Business Scams," "Small Business Resource Guide," "Buying a Franchise," and more. Read online or order complete catalog: (888) 878-3256.

SBA business publications on many topics, www.sba.gov/library/pubs.html.

Government: State

Check with your local state representative or senator or your state's or province's web site for manuals published by your state that provide start-up information, and the state departments that handle industry and business regulations and registrations:

Starting and Operating a Business in . . . (a series of books written for each U.S. state) by Michael D. Jenkins, PSI Research (Central Point, OR). Search for one at your local public library or bookstore.

WEB INFO

www.sba.gov/hotlist/license.html, Internet links to each state's business licensing department.

SBA: Information for Business Start-Up and Management

FirstGov.gov, www.firstgov.gov, government portal; click on "Businesses and Nonprofits."

Service Corps of Retired Executives (SCORE), www.score.org, offer free counseling and low-cost seminars. They are women and men who were former successful business executives and now volunteer to help women and men start and grow enterprises. Go to their site to find the office nearest to you.

U.S. Department of Labor's Office of Disability Employment Policy, www.dol.gov/odep, employment and entrepreneurship programs.

U.S. Small Business Administration's Small Business Development Centers (SBDCs), www.sba.gov/SBDC, work in conjunction with the business departments of universities and also offer ongoing free or low-cost business counseling and seminars.

Veterans Business Outreach Centers (VBOCs), visit www.sba.gov/VETS, offers business information and counseling to veterans interested in small business ownership and service-disabled veteran entrepreneurs.

Women's Business Development Centers (WBDCs), www.onlinewbc.gov /wbc.pdf, exist across the United States and its territories and are specifically set up to help women start and manage businesses, and also offer free or low-cost seminars and business counseling. Search the web site for offices nearest to you.

WEB INFO

wwww.DisabilityInfo.gov, "An Online Resource for Americans with Disabilities."

www.irs.gov/businesses/small/index.html, the Internal Revenue's page, "Small Business and Self-Employed One-Stop Resource" of tax information about starting, operating, or closing a business.

www.MindYourOwnBiz.org, youth entrepreneurship web site sponsored by the SBA and Junior Achievement Worldwide.

www.sba.gov/training/courses.html, free online SBA start-up, marketing, and management courses.

www.sba.gov/women, SBA's "My Biz" section for Women's Business Programs.

Marketing Experts

See the Contributors section for other marketing experts:

http://wdfm.com, *Web Digest for Marketers,* founder, Larry Chase, e-zine.

www.actionplan.com/books.html, "Action Plan Marketing," site of Robert Middleton, marketing consultant; site lists his recommendations of other marketing experts' books on "positioning," "packaging," "promotion," "persuasion," and "performance."

www.dobkin.com, web site of Jeffrey Dobkin, direct marketing specialist, articles, books.

www.FrugalMarketing.com, by Shel Horowitz, excellent money-saving tips.

www.gmarketing.com. Jay Conrad Levinson, "The Father of Guerrilla Marketing" books.

www.ideabook.com, site of designer Chuck Green offering marketing ideas, tips, techniques, and related articles, resources.

www.marketing-mentor.com, founded by self-promotion guru, Ilise Benun.

www.marketingsherpa.com, Anne Holland's Marketing Sherpa, a marketing research firm (not a news organization) and publisher of case studies, benchmark data, and how-to best practices for professional marketers.

www.promoteyourself.com, Raleigh Pinskey, books, articles, consulting, speaking, promotional programs, and ideas.

www.publicityhound.com, Joan Stewart, publicity expert; excellent articles, e-books, e-zine.

www.sethgodin.com/purple, Seth Godin, author of *Purple Cow* (excellent marketing book).

www.wilsonweb.com, Ralph Wilson's "Web Marketing Today."

www.yudkin.com, site of marketing expert, author, Marcia Yudkin; marketing and publicity topics.

Publications, Business

Online

bizjournals, www.bizjournals.com, business journals published around the country.

Bizpreneur News, www.smallbizpreneurs.com, a free, semimonthly e-newsletter that offers small business owners and entrepreneurs valuable information about managing and marketing their ventures, providing good customer service, increasing sales, and developing their web presence, in addition to providing education on legal issues, taxes and finances, and related topics. To subscribe, please visit www.smallbizpreneurs.com.

Print*

Black Enterprise, www.blackenterprise.com, focuses on African American businesspeople.

---

* Search also on your favorite search engine for additional industry and trade publications.

Entrepreneur magazine, www.Entrepreneur.com, focuses on entrepreneurs, business owners, and self-employed individuals. Site has many articles, how-to guides, and tools.

Enterprising Women, www.enterprisingwomen.com, features for women business owners.

Hispanic Business magazine, www.hispanicbusiness.com, focuses on issues for Hispanic business leaders, owners, and entrepreneurs.

Home Business Magazine, www.HomeBusinessMag.com, focuses on home-business ideas, opportunities, management.

Inc. magazine, www.inc.com, online site has free how-to business guides; www.inc.com/guides, topics for small business management.

Minority Business Entrepreneur, www.mbemag.com, for minority and women business owners.

PROFIT magazine, www.PROFITguide.com, for Canada's entrepreneurs.

Small Business Opportunities, www.SBOmag.com, business ideas, management articles.

REFERENCE

Gale's Directory of Publications and Broadcast Media (Detroit, MI: Gale Research). Lists most trade magazines. www.gale.com.

Television

Small Business Television, www.sbtv.com, television on the Internet, has Money, Marketing, Management channels.

Web Info

Marketing

http://marketing.about.com, marketing section of About.com with articles and ongoing marketing information.

www.MarketingTerms.com, "Internet marketing reference and index of the best sites and articles."

www.MarketingPrinciples.com, advanced marketing consultants, online marketing resource site, many articles and topics.

www.MarketingProfs.com, an online publishing company with articles, newsletter, seminars; excellent exchange of marketing information from "professionals and professors."

Online Courses, Free

www.HP.com, Hewlett-Packard's free online courses for the home and home office consumer.

www.Microsoft.com/smallbusiness/hub.mspx, Microsoft Small Business Center, resources, sales and marketing solutions, articles, online courses, webcasts, and more.

www.SBA.gov/training/courses.html, SBA free business courses including, "Marketing & Advertising," "E-Commerce," "Planning Tools," and others; also Webinars.

Small Business and General Information Portals

http://directory.google.com/Top/Business/Small_Business/Resources, business resource directory.

www.AllBusiness.com, all business, many home/small business articles, including a "Marketing and Sales" section; business guides.

www.BizOffice.com/library, "Small and Home Based Business Library"; alphabetized card catalog, "M" topics include market research, strategies, and other related information.

www.BusinessKnowHow.com, Small Business/Home Business Resources, free newsletter, blog.

www.ChiefHomeOfficer.com, Jeff Zbar's blog and information site for entrepreneurs, virtual officers, small and home-based business owners, telecommuters, road warriors, and other independent workers.

www.Entrepreneur.com, *Entrepreneur* magazine's site, offers free, online, how-to guides on business and marketing topics.

www.Eventuring.org, Kauffman Foundation's resource site for entrepreneurs, including a large section, "Sales and Marketing."

www.FindArticles.com, articles from publications; subjects are organized by major categories.

www.Lowe.org, Edward Lowe Foundation, offers "Entrepreneur's Resource Center" with business information.

www.MomsMakingMoney.org, work-at-home information and business marketing ideas, e-newsletter, teleclasses.

www.Office.com, business-to-business company offering links and information for small businesses.

www.Score.org/guides.html, SCORE's free 60-second guides on business, marketing topics.

www.SmallBusinessAdvocate.com, Jim Blasingame's web site, business information, e-zine.

www.Toolkit.cch.com, Business Owner's Toolkit, business-related articles including marketing.

Miscellaneous

Business Forms

"Small & Home-Based Business Forms," by BizOffice.com, www.bizoffice .com/business_forms/index.html (see also Viking Office Products for forms).

Tax Terms, www.taxgaga.com/pages/c-taxresources/dir-glossary.html, glossary of tax terms by Tax Gaga.com.

Persons with Disabilities

ASSOCIATIONS

Disabled Businessperson Association, www.disabledbusiness.com.

BOOKS

No More Job Interviews! Self-Employment Strategies for People with Disabilities by Alice Weiss Doyel (Augustine, FL: Training Resource Network, 2000). www.trninc.com.

Unlikely Entrepreneurs: A Complete Guide to Business Start-Ups for People with Disabilities and Chronic Health Conditions by Roseanne Herzog (Traverse City: North Peak Publishing, 1999).

DIRECTORY

The Boulevard, www.blvd.com, a resource directory of products and services for those with physical challenges, the elderly, caregivers, and health care professionals.

EXPOS

Abilities EXPO, www.abilitiesexpo.com, products and services in designated U.S. cities.

World Congress & Exposition on Disabilities, www.wcdexpo.com, products and services.

AbleLink Technologies, www.ablelinktech.com, technology fostering independence for individuals with intellectual disabilities.

Dynavox Systems LLC, www.dynavoxsys.com, speech output devices and technology.

Supplies, Office

Write or visit the web sites for their latest catalogs:

Dick Blick Art Materials, www.dickblick.com, catalog of all types of art supplies.

Lefty's Corner, www.leftyscorner.com, sells office and writing supplies and other items for left-handers.

Quill Monthly Office Products Catalog, www.quill.com, office supplies.

Viking Office Products, www.vikingop.com, all types of office products; on-line site has a "Business Resource Center," including various downloadable forms used in business.

Canadian Resources

Association

Canadian Women's Business Network, www.cdnbizwomen.com, Women Business Owners of Canada.

Business Services

Canada/British Columbia Business Services, www.smallbusinessbc.ca, provides timely and accurate business-related information, referrals on federal and provincial government programs, services, and regulations.

Government

Canada Business Service Centers, www.cbsc.org, provides a wide range of information on government services, programs, and regulations and answers questions about starting a new business or improving an existing one.

Publications

Canadian Business magazine, www.canadianbusiness.com, online site of print publication.

SoHo Business Report, www.sohobusinessreport.com (formerly *Home Business Report*), quarterly print publication of business information and resources for Canadian entrepreneurs.

Web Info

http://strategis.ic.gc.ca, *Strategis,* produced by Industry Canada, a department of the federal government; a valuable resource of information for consumers and businesses; includes information and guides on starting, financing a business, exporting, and other pertinent issues of having a business in Canada.

About the Author

Priscilla Y. Huff is a freelance business writer and author of the best-selling *101 Best Home-Based Businesses for Women,* third edition (New York: Random House 2002), *A Self-Employed Woman's Guide to Launching a Home-Based Business,* and other related books specializing in topics about small and home-based businesses and women's entrepreneurship. For the past 20 years, she has written numerous articles and columns on these subjects for such print publications as *Home Business Magazine, Home Business Journal, Income Opportunities, Small Business Opportunities, Pennsylvania Magazine,* and other publications and has been quoted in *Forbes,* the *New York Times,* the *Savannah Business Journal,* and other major print, radio, and TV media.

She was a home business expert and columnist for *i*Village.com and www.BizyMoms.com and is currently a columnist for Home-Based Working Moms (www.HBWM.com), MomsMakingMoney.org, and SmallBizpreneur's Network (www.smallbizpreneurs.com). She has also contributed business articles and tips to Corel Corporation's OfficeCommunity.com, Fortune Small Business (online, www.fsb.com), HomeStore.com, WomensForum.com, WomensEnews.org, www.MomsBusinessMagazine.com, www.BlueSuitMom, www.Committment.com, www.SmallBusinessAdvocate.com, and other business and Web and print publications. Her business, LITTLE HOUSE Writing & Publishing, offers business information, consulting, and research services, as well as e-books and other publications.

About the Foreword Author

Patricia C. Gallagher is a mother of four. She has an MBA and is an entrepreneur and small-press publisher, the author of seven books, and a professional speaker. She was a former account executive (industry consultant) for AT&T national accounts. When her second daughter was born, Gallagher resigned from her account executive position at AT&T and started her own at-home child care business. Based on this venture and her experiences, she went on to write the successful books, *Start Your Own At-Home Child Care Business*, second revised edition (St Louis, MO: Mosby, 1995) and *So You Want to Open a Profitable Day Care Center* (St Louis, MO: Mosby, 1995).

Gallagher also self-syndicates two columns: "A View from Main Street," a reflection of her lessons learned in life, based on personal and friends' experiences and from her book, *The Gift of Changing Yourself: Daily Reflections for Women in Transition* (Worcester, PA: Young Sparrow Press, 2004) and "Mom-Cent$," money-saving tips and advice for parents, a sideline of her self-published book, *Raising Happy Kids on a Reasonable Budget*.

Her books and columns helped her start a small publishing business, Young Sparrow Press, and her "team of angels" business, www.TeamofAngelsHelpMe .com. She is a professional feature speaker at entrepreneur conferences and for various nonprofit groups and organizations. She recently launched a campaign for peace in the world by personally distributing 50,000 yellow team of angels pins attached to laminated bookmarks that were inscribed with a new poem, "A Team of Angels for Peace in Our World." You can find Patricia Gallagher at www.teamofangels.com.

Contributors

The following entrepreneurs, business owners, and experts graciously shared their business and marketing expertise with you:

Janeen R. Adil, author of *Children and Adults*, www.janeenadil.com.

Maria T. Bailey, author, radio talk show host, nationally known speaker, and the foremost authority on marketing to moms, BSM Media (www.bsmmedia.com), Mom Talk Radio (www.momtalkradio.com), and Publisher of *Today's Blue Suit Mom* magazine.

Rochelle Balch, computer consultant, professional speaker, and author of *C-E-O & M-O-M* and *Brag Your Way to Success*, www.rbbalch.com.

Abby Marks Beale, corporate productivity specialist, helps busy professionals work smarter, faster, and just plain better; author of *10 Days to Faster Reading* and *Success Skills: Strategies for Study and Lifelong Learning*, www.TheCorporateEducator.com.

Jeanette R. Benway, professional speaker and inventor of the Cozy Rosie, www.cozyrosie.com.

Peter Bowerman, professional copywriter, business coach, and author of *The Well-Fed Writer, The Well-Fed Writer: Back For Seconds,* and *The Well-Fed Self-Publisher,* www.wellfedwriter.com.

Christopher J. Brunner, GreatFX Business Cards, www.greatfxbusinesscards.com.

Peggi Clauhs, owner of The Cooking Cottage at Cedar Spring Farms, Sellersville, Pennsylvania, www.thecookingcottage.org.

Nancy Cleary, graphic design, BFA; founder and CEO of Wyatt-MacKenzie Publishing, Inc., www.wymacpublishing.com.

Debra M. Cohen, president, Home Remedies® of NY, Inc.; Homeowner Referral Network (HRN) Business; www.homereferralbiz.com.

Nancy Collamer, career counselor and Founder of www.jobsandmoms.com.

Jeffrey Dobkin, direct marketing specialist and author of "Jeffrey Dobkin's Successful Low Cost Direct Marketing Methods" and "Direct Marketing Strategies," www.dobkin.com.

Diana Ennen, publisher of the fiction thriller *Sledgehammer*, marketing specialist, and author of *Virtual Assistant—The Series: Become a Highly Successful, Sought After VA*, www.virtualwordpublishing.com.

Mike Ference, originator of the term, *Microwaveable Marketing* and Ference Marketing & Communications, www.ferencemarketing.com.

Joan Fisler, certified divorce financial analyst and financial advisor.

Patricia C. Gallagher, author, marketing expert, professional speaker, and owner of Young Sparrow Press, www.teamofangels.com.

Maria Gracia, owner of Get Organized Now! and author of the *Finally Organized, Finally Free* book series, www.getorganizednow.com.

Erin Gruver, professional organizer and owner of lifeStyle, www.lifestylebyerin.com.

Susan Harrow, media coach, marketing strategist, and author of *Sell Yourself without Selling Your Soul*, www.prsecrets.com and www.prsecrets.com/publicityblog.html.

Allen Hart, founder of Christian Work at Home Dads, www.CWAHD.com.

Jill Hart, founder of Christian Work at Home Moms, host of CWAHM Talk Radio, www.CWAHM.com.

Richard Henderson, publisher of *Home Business Magazine*, an international publication available on newsstands, in major bookstores, and via subscriptions. Visit www.homebusinessmag.com for more information.

Richard and Angela Hoy, owners of BookLocker, http://www.booklocker.com; WritersWeekly, http://www.writersweekly.com.

Kimberly Kardos-Bensing, graphic designer, creative director of Heirloom, conceptual designs and invitations, www.heirloom-occasions.com.

Paula Kay, owner of Ageless Checkers, Inc., www.agelesscheckers.com.

Kathy J. Kobliski, founder and president of Silent Partner Advertising; author of *Advertising without an Agency Made Easy*, www.silentpartneradvertising.com.

Vadim Kotelnikov, inventor, author, and founder of Ten3 Business e-Coach, www.1000ventures.com.

Jodie Lynn, award-winning, internationally syndicated family/health columnist and radio personality; author of *Syndication Secrets: What No One Will Tell You!* and *Mom CEO (Chief Everything Officer): Having, Doing, and Surviving*

It All! radio host of *Inside Parenting Success;* syndicated column: Parent to Parent, www.parenttoparent.com.

Nancy Mills, creator of the Spirited Woman Approach to Life, community-based Web PR specialist, www.TheSpiritedWoman.com.

Denise O'Berry, small business expert and author of *Small Business Cash Flow: Strategies for Making Your Business a Financial Success,* www.cashflowtruth.com.

Jeannie Papadopoulos, twenty-nine year professional in Signage and Window Painting. Owner, creator of Window Jeannie, Inc. (www.windowjeannie .com; http://windowjeannie.ca/); author of *How to Paint Windows.* Creator, Window Painting Workshop© "The Hidden Career;" and full line of Window Jeannie products for window painters. Training; paints, brushes, and supplies.

Ellen Parlapiano, writer, speaker, consultant, and coauthor of *Mompreneurs®: A Mother's Practical Step-by-Step Guide to Work-at-Home Success,* revised edition, and *Mompreneurs® Online,* www.mompreneursonline.com.

Raleigh Pinskey, Raleigh Communications, visibility success coach, speaker, and author of the international best-selling *101 Ways to Promote Yourself: Tricks of the Trade for Taking Charge of Your Own Success,* and 40+ CDs, books, MP3s, and DVDs specializing in getting your brand in front of your target market over and over again, www.PromoteYourself.com.

Kelly Poelker, master virtual assistant and president of Another 8 Hours, Inc., www.Another8Hours.com; author of *Virtual Assistant: The Series: Become a Highly Successful, Sought After VA,* third edition, www.VA-TheSeries.com.

Lesley Spencer Pyle, MSc, author of *The Work-at-Home Workbook;* founder and president of HBWM.com Inc. and Home-Based Working Moms, www.HBWM.com.

Aliza Sherman Risdahl, Web pioneer, author of *The Everything Blogging Book,* www.mediaegg.com.

Penny C. Sansevieri, publicist, freelance writer, instructor, and author of *From Book to Bestseller, Get Published Today,* and *Striking Internet Gold;* CEO of Author Marketing Experts, Inc., www.amarketingexpert.com.

John D. Schulte, author of *Direct Marketing Toolkit,* available through the National Mail Order Association (NMOA); president and chairman of NMOA, www.nmoa.org, information line: (612) 788-4197.

Janet Crenshaw Smith, president of Ivy Planning Group LLC, www.ivygroupllc .com, celebrating 15 years of excellence and recognized by *Black Enterprise, Working Woman,* and *USA Today.*

Joan Stewart, publicity expert and publisher of *The Publicity Hound's Tips of the Week* e-zine, www.PublicityHound.com.

Robert Sullivan, PhD, small business expert and author of *The Small Business Start-Up Guide,* third edition; owner of the Small Business Advisor, www.isquare.com.

Chanin Walsh, creative director of Ampersand Design, Inc., www.ampersandesign .net.

Debbie Williams, professional organizer and author of *Common Sense Organizing,* www.OrganizedTimes.com.

Valerie Young, dreamer in residence; information and inspiration to find one's life mission and live it, www.ChangingCourse.com.

Jeff Zbar, writer and speaker on technology, entrepreneurship, home officing, telework, and work/life balance, www.chiefhomeofficer.com.

Jan Zobel, EA, Bay Area tax professional (enrolled agent), specializing in working with self-employed people for nearly 30 years; author of *Minding Her Own Business: The Self-Employed Woman's Essential Guide to Taxes and Financial Records.* www.JanZtax.com.

Index

A

Accounting software, 287
Action, in advertising, 194
Address, mailing, 290
Address Verification Software (AVS), 101
Adil, Janeen R., 53
Advertising, 178–204
  ad structure, 183–184
  in alternative publications, 138
  classified, 185–186, 234
  direct mail, 178–182, 200–201
  directories, 184–185
  importance of, 19, 72
  key codes, 189–190
  marketing messages, 197–204
  miscellaneous visual tactics, 193–197
  multilingual-global, 185
  peak seasons, 184
  promotional products, 192–193
  rates, 186–188
  regulations, 237
  tips, 183–189
  tracking responses, 189–191
  word-of-mouth, 102, 146–147
Advertising auction, 188
Advertorials, 201, 303
Advisory board, 125–126, 303
Affiliate firms, as venture capitalists, 270
Affiliate marketing, 233
AFL-CIO, 5–6
Age, in communication, 283
Agency discount, advertising, 186
American Council on Exercise, 299
American Dietetic Association, 299
American Marketing Association, 79
Angel investors, 269, 270

Announcement web sites, 239
AnswerPlus, 207
AOL, setting up sig files in, 235
Application service providers, 289
Arbitration, binding, 292
Art, as spin-off venture, 249–250, 252
Articles, writing, 161–163, 173, 236, 279
Associations, 82, 96, 249, 252
Attention-getters, 138
Attorneys, choosing, 260
Auction sites, 229
Audiotapes, producing, 292
Automated customer service, 215
AVS (Address Verification Software), 101
Awards, 94–95, 159–160, 239

B

Back-end sales, 292–293
Back linking, 233
Backups, data, 65
Bags, for advertising, 196
Bailey, Maria T., 146, 162, 171–172
Balance, finding, 52–53
Balch, Rochelle, 4–5, 159, 160, 248,
  283–284
Bank loans, 91–92
Banners, 233
Bartering, 103–104, 187
Beale, Abby Marks, 273
Benefits of your business, highlighting,
  141–142
Bensing, Kimberly, 48
Benway, Jeanette R., 165–166
Better Business Bureau (BBB), 41, 227,
  237

Big, looking, 281, 289–290
Billboards, 194
Binding arbitration, 292
Black Enterprise, 296
Blasingame, Jim, 236
Blogs, 161–163, 201, 236
Board of directors, 125–126, 303
Bookkeeping, 62, 286–287
Booklets, 173–176, 198, 236
Books, writing, 173, 174–175
Bowerman, Peter, 145, 175, 181
Branding, 47–50
Breakeven analysis, 98, 266
Brochures, 198
Brunner, Christopher J., 199–200
Budget, 274, 285–286, 291
Budget marketing, 141–144
Burnout, 264–266
Business:
    cards, 199–200, 276–277
    climate, 4–5
    coaches, 123–124, 248, 251, 263, 265
    failure rate, 8
    ideas, 33–37
    identity package, 277–278, 289
    image, 46–47, 140–141
    incubators, 73, 268
    magazines, 296
    makeovers, 254–255
    management and start-up courses,
        14–15
    Matchmaking, 119
    names, 29–32
    operations:
        documenting, 263
        efficiency of, 263–264
    opportunities, 248, 256–259
    owners' groups, 109–112
    plans:
        creating, 71–73
        implementing, 73–74
        importance of, 17
        modifying, 267–268
        reviewing, 266–267
    support services, 129
Business plan, components of, 71–72
Business 2.0, 296

Business-to-business marketing, 225,
    278–279
BusinessWeek, 296
Buying a business, 40–41
Buying service, advertising, 187

C

Call centers, 207–208, 289
Call forwarding, 208
Canada Business Service Centres
    (CBSCs), 118
CanadaOne Magazine, 297
Canadian government resources, 118
CareerBuilder.com, 6
Cash flow, 19–20, 104–107, 266
Catalog sales, 302–303
CDs, producing, 174, 292
Cell phones, 69, 70, 194
Center for Women's Business Research, 6
Certified Development Company/504
    Loan Program, 89–90
Chambers of commerce, 242
ChangingCourse.com, 7
Charity auctions and donations, 170
Chats (Internet Relay Chat), 240, 253
Checks, for customer payments, 101
Children, 7, 42, 59, 273. *See also* Family
Children's Advertising Review Unit, 237
Classes, teaching, 170–171
Classified ads, 185–186, 234
Clauhs, Peggi, 153
Cleary, Nancy, 29, 48–49, 155–156, 197,
    265, 289
Closing your business, 259, 273
Cluster marketing, 246
Coaches, business, 123–124, 248, 251,
    263, 265
Cobe, Patricia, 232
Code of Online Business Practices, 237
Cohen, Debra M., 126, 141–142, 149
Cold calls, 265, 280–281
Collaborating with other entrepreneurs,
    133–134, 249, 251
Collamer, Nancy, 156, 173
Collections, 102–103, 259

Columns, writing, 161, 201
Commercial photographers, 158–159
Communication, 61–62, 219–222, 282–283
Company profiles, 303–304
Competitors:
analyzing, 72, 212–213
foreign companies as, 275–276
larger companies as, 281–282
as market research resource, 77
monitoring, 253
price comparisons with, 97
as promotion resource, 134
staying ahead of, 16
Complaints, customer, 217–218
Computer equipment, 64–65, 69–70
Computer networks, 66
Conferences, 122
Consultants, 131, 243
Consulting, as spin-off venture, 248, 251
Contests, 94–95, 159–160, 169, 240
Contracts:
for bartering, 104
government, 118–120, 278
legal concerns, 259
negotiating, 132
preparing, 33
and pricing, 99
reviewing, 33
Cooperative extension services, 118
Cooperative marketing, 134, 181
Copywriting, 143, 181
Corporate sponsors, as financing source, 95
Corporations, 32–33, 259, 290
Costs, 97–98
Council of Better Business Bureaus, Inc., 237
Count-Me-In for Women's Economic Independence, 96
Crafts, as spin-off venture, 249–250, 252
Crafts Report, The, 133, 161
Creative financing, 94–96
Creative marketing, 136–140
Creative venturists, 225
Creativity, entrepreneurial, 136
Credit, 100, 102, 259

Credit bureaus, 92–93
Credit cards, 90–91, 100–101
Customer relationship management (CRM), 205–223
communication tips, 219–222
customer appreciation, 222–223
customer service, 214–219
defined, 205
first impressions, 206–211
staying fresh, 211–214
Customers:
appreciation of, 222–223
communicating with, 219–222, 282–283
complaints from, 217–218
contact information system, 209, 292
dissatisfied customers, 220–221
educating, 217
endorsements and testimonials from, 202
etiquette of customer approach, 208–209
evaluations from, 219–220
payment options, 100–103
referrals from, 102, 146–147
rewarding, 102, 146–147, 216–217, 219
surveys of, 219–220, 253, 267, 293
too many, 13
Customer satisfaction, 220–221, 252–254
Customer service, 22, 214–219

D

Dahl, Gary, 211
Data backups, 65
Debit cards, 91
Debt, 4, 74
Decor, as spin-off venture, 249–250, 252
Demonstrations, giving, 170–171
Digital photography, 158
Direct mail advertising, 178–182, 200–201
Directories:
advertising in, 184–185
Internet, 234, 240
Directors, board of, 125–126, 303

Direct public offerings (DPOs), 269
Direct response wording, 181
Disabilities, entrepreneurs with, 66–67,
    68, 114–115
Disasters, 284
Disclaimers, 259
Disclosure, 259
Discounts:
    for advertising, 186–187
    customer, 102
Disputes, handling, 259, 291–292
Diversification, 245–261
    business makeovers, 254–255
    customer satisfaction, 252–254
    franchises, business opportunities, and
        network marketing, 256–259
    importance of, 245–246
    legal concerns, 259–261
    licensing, 255–256
    as risk management, 284
    spin-off ventures, 245–252, 246–250
Divorce service business, 45–46
Dobkin, Jeffrey, 10, 180, 200
Documenting business operations, 263
Doing business as (DBA), 30, 290
Domain names, choosing, 226
Donovan, Jim, 173
Door hangers, 196
DVDs, producing, 174

E

Early payment (advertising discount),
    187
eBay, 211, 229
E-booklets, 236
E-books, 173–174
E-commerce, 224, 225, 229
Economy, 4–5
Editors, 150–151
Educating customers, 217
800 phone numbers, 193–194
Electronic booklets, 236
Electronic books, 173–174
Electronic newsletters, 197–198
Electronic reports, 236, 292
Elevator Pitch, 209, 277

E-mail:
    automated, 215
    creating address, 226
    forwarding, 226–227
    managing, 55
    for marketing, 234
    signature files, 234–235
    while traveling, 69–70
Employee leasing companies, 129
Employees, 126–130
    family and friends as, 128–129
    hiring, 126–127
    incentives and feedback, 127–128
    other options, 129
    with special needs, 129
    virtual assistants, 129–130, 263
Employee stock ownership plans
    (ESOPs), 269
Employer Identification Number (EIN),
    33
Employment laws, 260
Endorsements, customer, 202
Ennen, Diana, 162–163
Enterprising Women, 296
Entrepreneur, 296
Entrepreneurial creativity, 136
Entrepreneurs:
    with disabilities, 66–67, 68, 114–115
    motivations of, 3–7
    statistics, 1–2
    success factors, 8–9
Envelopes, 200
Equipment:
    computer, 64–65, 69–70
    leasing, 58
    office, 20, 57–58, 61
E-reports, 236, 292
Ergonomics, 58–59
E-tailing, 224, 225, 229
Ethernet, 66
Ethics, marketing, 12
Ethnicity, and communication, 283
Etiquette of customer approach, 208–209
Evaluations from customers, 219–220
Excitement factor, 137
Exercise, 299–300
Exhibiting at trade shows, 176–177, 276
Exit strategy, 272–273

Expansion loans, 269, 270–271
Expert, establishing yourself as, 171–172
Expert contacts, 15, 20, 122–124, 284
Exporting, 241–244
E-zines, 236

F

Factoring, 95
Fads, 211
Failure, fear of, 8, 26–27
Failure rate, business, 8
Fair Credit Reporting Act, 92–93
Family:
    as employees, 128–129
    as financing source, 95
    involving in business, 21, 42–43
    needs of, 3–4, 5
Faxes, 193, 208, 215
Fear of failure, 8, 26–27
Fear of success, 27
Federal Communications Commission
    (FCC), 193, 208
Federal government resources, 88–89,
    116–118, 119. *See also specific*
    agencies
Federal Trade Commission (FTC), 41,
    184, 202, 237, 240
Feedback, 127–128, 219–220
Fees, in ads, 184
Ference, Mike, 110–112
Fillers, 164
Finances, controlling, 62, 74
Financial Planning Association, 123
Financing, 87–96
    bank loans, 91–92
    creative, 94–96
    credit cards, 90–91
    for expansion, 13–14, 267, 269–271
    government loans, 88–90, 93
    grants, 90, 93, 269
    preliminary considerations, 87–88
Financing plans, customer, 100
First impressions, 206–211
Fisler, Joan, 44–46
Fitness, physical, 299–300
504 Loan Program, 89–90

Fixed costs, 97–98
Flexible hours, 3–4, 5
Flyers, 200–201
Focus, lack of, 24
Focus groups, 253
Folger, Liz, 249
Follow-me services, 70
Follow-ups, 287–289
Fortune Small Business, 296
Franchises, 248, 256–259
FreedomVoice, 130
Friendliness, 283
Friends:
    as employees, 128–129
    as financing source, 95
    involving in business, 42–43
Funding. *See* Financing
Furniture, office, 20, 57–58, 61

G

Gallagher, Patricia C.:
    corporate sponsors, 95
    creative marketing, 23
    establishing yourself as an expert, 171
    involving children in business, 42
    library presentations, 116
    stickers, 193
    TV talk shows, 167–168
    vehicle signage, 195
Gifts:
    promotional, 192–193, 222, 279–280,
        301
    as spin-off venture, 249, 252
Global markets, beating, 275–276
Goals, marketing campaign, 82
Godin, Seth, 10–11
Google AdWords, 234
Google Alerts, 163
GovCommerce.net, 119
Government-affiliated investment
    programs, 270
Government contracts, 118–120, 278
Government loans, 88–90, 93
Government Marketing Assistance
    Program, 119
Government resources, 88–90, 115–119

Gracia, Maria, 62
Grants, 90, 93, 269
Graphic Artists Guild, 82, 97
Graphics, 183, 289
Greeting Card Association, 121
Greeting cards, 192, 222
Growth, 13–14, 16–17, 267, 271–274
Gruver, Erin, 44, 124, 209, 262–263, 274

H

Handheld devices, 69, 70, 289
Hardware, computer, 64
Harrow, Susan, 166
Hart, Allen, 128–129
Hart, Jill, 42
Headlines, ad, 183
Health insurance, 5–6
Henderson, Richard, 21
Hewlett-Packard courses, 21
Hiring employees, 126–127
Hispanic Business, 296–297
Hobby versus business, 39–40
Holidays, 172, 192
Home-based business magazines, 296
Home-Based Working Moms, 167
Home Business Magazine, 296, 299
Home offices, 56–57. *See also* Offices
Home shopping channel sales, 302–303
Hooks, 149–150, 153
HotOffice.com, 289
How-to products, 173–174, 248–249, 251
Hoy, Angela, 85, 249
Hoy, Richard, 85, 249

I

Illustrations, in ads, 183
Impasse, overcoming, 53–54
Importing, 241–244
Income, residual versus passive, 247
Incorporation, 32–33, 259, 290
Incubators, 73, 268

Independent contractors, 131–133, 263
Independent service organizations (ISOs), 101
Industry associations, 82, 121
Industry pricing recommendations, 97
Industry publications, 297
Infomercials, 201, 303
Informational products, as spin-off venture, 248–249, 251
Installment payment plans, 100, 102
Insurance, 5–6, 143, 284
Intellectual property, 248, 255–256, 260
Internal Revenue Service (IRS). *See also* Taxes
  bartering, 104
  financial information, 89
  hobby versus business, 39–40
  independent contractors, 131
  resources, 118
International ads, 185
International trade, 185, 241–244, 260
International trade associations, 242
Internet, 224–244. *See also* Web sites
  access to, 64–65, 69–70, 143
  directories, 234, 240
  establishing presence on, 224–227
  international trade, 241–244
  legal concerns, 260
  marketing methods, 233–239
  merchant accounts, 229
  networking on, 239–240
  talk shows, 236–237
Internet Relay Chat, 240, 253
Interns, 129, 143
Introduction, letters of, 209–210
Inventions, 248, 250–251
Inventory management, 27–28
Investor agreements, 260
Invoices, 102, 103

J

Job security, 4–5
Journal keeping, 52, 55, 265, 300
Junk Fax Prevention Act, 193, 208

K

Kardos-Bensing, Kimberly, 46, 209
Kay, Paula, 258
Key codes, 189–190
Knowledge, acquiring, 14–16
Kobliski, Kathy J., 72
Kotelnikov, Vadim, 136

L

Laptop computers, 65, 69–70
Larger companies, competing against, 281–282
Laughter clubs, 265
Lawn signs, 195–196
Lawyers, choosing, 260
Leads, following up on, 23
Leads groups, 21
Lead Small Business Development Centers, 117. *See also* Small Business Development Centers (SBDCs)
Leasing:
  employees, 129
  equipment, 58
  office space, 59–60
Legal issues, 259–261, 284
Legal structure of business, 32–33
Letters of introduction, 209–210
Letters to editors, 163–164
Liability, 259
Library resources, 115–116
Licensing, 255–256
Listening skills, 114, 206–207
Listserves, 239
Litigation, 292
Loans:
  bank, 91–92
  for expansion, 269, 270–271
  government, 88–90, 93
  for women entrepreneurs, 90
Local area networks (LANs), 66
Local government resources, 89–90, 115–116, 118
Logos, 140, 183, 196, 201–202
Long-range plans, as success factor, 9

Loyalty, as success factor, 9
Lynn, Jodie, 161

M

Magazines, 161–163, 187, 201, 296–297
Magnetic business cards, 276
Mail, managing, 55
Mailing lists, 179–180
Mail order rate, 186
Makeovers, business, 254–255
Manning, Robert D., 90
Marketing:
  budget, 141–144, 285–286, 291
  business-to-business, 225, 278–279
  calendar, 294
  campaigns, 81–82
  consultants, 124
  defined, 10
  ethics, 12
  goals, 82
  importance of, 23–24
  interns, 143
  messages, 197–204
  mistakes to avoid, 290–291
  mix, 80
  objectives, 81
  strategies, 80, 82
  support group, 108–109
  in tough times, 293–294
Market plan:
  budget for, 274
  creating, 78–81
  defined, 11
  evaluating, 84–85, 266, 268
  importance of, 18–19
Market research, 75–78
  for dealing with foreign competition, 275
  for diversification, 247
  for expansion, 268
  for exporting, 241
  features of, 18
  importance of, 17–18
  studying trends, 16
Maturity, and success, 8
McClennan, Winnie, 153

McDonald's restaurants, 25
Mechanical Dimensions (advertising sizes), 186–187
Media attention, 149–150, 165–166
MediaBids, 188
Media Buying Specialists, 187
Media contacts, 150–151, 154
Media kits, 151–152. *See also* Press kits
Mediators, 291–292
Media training, 165–168
Media web sites, 225
Meetings over meals, 110
Mentors, 124–125, 303
Microsoft Outlook, setting up sig files in, 235
Microsoft's Web Hosting for Small Business with Commerce Manager, 229
Microwavable Marketing, 111–112
Mills, Nancy, 42–43
Minority Business Entrepreneur, 297
Minority entrepreneurs, 2, 278, 296–297
Mission statement, 9, 72, 79–80, 267
Mitchell, Jane, 272
Mobile technology, 69–70
Mom-Writers Publishing Cooperative, 155–156
Money, 296
Money orders, 101
Multilevel marketing companies, 256–259
Multilingual-global ads, 185
Multiple businesses, 38–39
Multiple insertions (advertising discount), 187
Music, in advertising, 194

N

Names, business, 29–32
National Association for the Self-Employed, 121, 297
National Association of Professional Organizers, 123
National Association of Women Business Owners, 121
National Business Incubation Association, 73

National Fraud Information Center, 41
National Mail Order Association, 187, 188, 297
National Writer's Union, 121
Negotiation, 291
Netiquette, 237
Networking, 8, 113–114, 144–145, 239–240
Networking groups, as spin-off venture, 249, 252
Network marketing, 256–259
New markets, identifying, 213–214
Newsgroups, 239
Newsletters, 102, 111, 197–198, 288, 293
Newspapers, 161–163, 187, 201, 297
New York Times, 297
Niche market, 10, 43–46
Nominations, for contests and awards, 159–160
Nonprofit opportunities, 169, 301

O

O'Berry, Denise, 18, 105
Objectives, for marketing campaign, 81
Office Business Center Association International, 59, 60
Offices:
    alternative spaces, 59–60
    ergonomics and safety, 58–59
    furniture and equipment, 20, 57–58, 61
    layout, 57
    location, 56–57, 290
    reorganizing, 262–263
    setting up, 56–61
Office supplies, 58
Office support services, 129
Omidyar, Pierre, 211
Online classified ads, 234
Online discussion groups, 239
Online Magazine for Work at Home Moms, The, 297
Online payment services, 101
Online publications, 297
Open houses, 113
Organization and industry publications, 297

Organizers, professional, 62, 262–263
Outlook, setting up sig files in, 235
Overspending, 20, 91

P

Packaging, product, 196–197
Pagers, 69, 70
Panel discussions, 171
Papadopoulos, Jeannie, 138–139, 174,
    194–195, 249
Paperwork, controlling, 62
Parlapiano, Ellen, 232
Partner financing, 95–96
Partnering, on Internet, 240
Partnerships, 32, 133, 135
Part-time businesses, 37–38, 94
Part-time jobs, 94
Passing business on to your children, 7,
    273
Passive income, 247
Patents, 248, 255–256
Payment options, customer, 100–103
Payne, Vicki, 174
PayPal, 229
Pay-per-Click (PPC), 234
Pay raises, 4
Pensions, 5
"People time," controlling, 61
Permission marketing, 234
Pets, limiting access to office, 59
Phone etiquette, 206–208
Phone messages, 202–203
Phone numbers, 193–194
Photos, 158–159, 183
Physical fitness, 299–300
Pinskey, Raleigh, 146
Placement, in marketing strategy, 80
Podcasting, 66, 237
Poelker, Kelly, 129–130, 215
Political service, 112
Portfolios, 142–143
Positioning, in marketing strategy, 80
Postage technology, 67, 68–69
Postcards, 102, 198–199
Prerelease offers, 292
Presentations, making, 170

Press kits, 157–159, 166. *See also* Media
    kits
Press releases, 153–157, 165–166
Pricing, 22–23, 80, 82–83, 96–100
Prioritizing, 52
Privacy, on web sites, 227
Private independent firms, as venture
    capitalists, 270
Procrastination, 53–54
Product-based businesses, 36
Products:
    licensing, 255–256
    in marketing strategy, 80
    packaging for, 196–197
    updating, 25–26
Professional employer organizations
    (PEOs), 129
Professionals, web sites for, 225
PROFIT, 296
Promotion, in marketing strategy, 80
Promotional products, 192–193, 222,
    279–280, 301
Promotional Products Association
    International, 121, 280
Promotion pieces, writing, 160–165
PRO-Net, 119
Publications:
    alternative publications, 138
    recommended, 296–298
Publicity, 148–153
Publicity Hound, 297
Pyle, Lesley Spencer, 138, 170, 171,
    197–198

Q

Quality, as success factor, 8–9
Questionnaires, 219–220, 253, 288

R

Radio programs, 166, 167, 295–296
Raises, pay, 4
Raising prices, 98–99
Rate sheets, 99
Ready-to-grow indicators, 267

Real estate, 260
Record keeping, 62, 286–287
Referrals, 102, 146–147
Regional differences, in communication, 283
Remnant space, 186–187
Renting office space, 59–60
Reply cards, 201
Reporters, 150–151
Residual income, 247
Retail sales, 36
Retail store web sites, 225
Retirement plans, 5
Return on investment (ROI), 190–191
Rewarding customers, 102, 146–147, 216–217, 219
Riddle, John, 172
Risdahl, Aliza Sherman, 193, 236
Risk management, 24–25, 283–285
Rockefeller, John D., 94
Rural Business-Cooperative Service, 89

S

Sales:
  back-end, 292–293
  catalog, 302–303
  of related business items, 249, 251
  retail, 36
  wholesale, 36
Sales letters, 200
Sales literature, 200–201
Sales projections, 72, 266
Sandwich board signs, 195
San Francisco Business Times, 297
Sansevieri, Penny C., 174–175
SBA. *See* U.S. Small Business Administration (SBA)
SBDCs. *See* Small Business Development Centers (SBDCs)
Scent, in advertising, 194
Schell, Orville, 166
Scholarships, establishing, 170
Schulte, John D., 186–188, 189–190
SCORE. *See* Service Corps of Retired Executives (SCORE)
Search engine optimization, 234

Seasonal parties or festivals, 113
Self-doubt, 53
Self-employed. *See* Entrepreneurs
Self-Employed magazine, 297
Self-mailers, 199
Self-publishing, 175
Selling your business, 272–273
Seminars, 15, 170–171
Senior citizens, as employees, 129
Service-based businesses, 36
Service Corps of Retired Executives (SCORE):
  business makeovers, 255
  business plans, 73
  entrepreneurs with disabilities, 67
  exporting, 242
  financing, 89
  resources, 117
  seminars and counseling, 15
Services:
  licensing, 255–256
  updating, 25–26
Shopping cart software, 229, 230
Signature files, 234–235
Signs, 195–196
Skills, acquiring, 14–16
Slogans, 201–202
Small and home-based business magazines, 296
Small Business Development Centers (SBDCs):
  business plans, 73
  entrepreneurs with disabilities, 67, 115
  exporting, 242
  financing, 88
  government contracts, 119, 278
  international business, 185
  management assistance, 117
  seminars and counseling, 15
  trademarks and patents, 248
Small Business Innovation Research (SBIR), 269
Small Business Investment Companies (SBICs), 89, 270
Small Business News, 297
Small Business Opportunities, 296
Small business statistics, 2

Small Corporate Offering Registrations (SCORs), 269
Small Publishers Association of North America, 297
Smart Money, 296
Smith, Janet Crenshaw, 192
Software, 64, 65, 229, 230, 287
Sole proprietors, 32, 33
Sounds, in ads, 183
Speakers, professional, 248, 251, 279, 293, 298–299
Special events and outreach ideas, 169–173
Spot surveys, 253
State government resources, 89–90, 116, 119, 242
Stewart, Joan, 151, 297
Stickers, for advertising, 193
Stock options, 269
Strategies, marketing campaign, 82
Subcontracting, 131–133, 263
Submission service, search engine, 234
Subsidiary firms, as venture capitalists, 270
Success, fear of, 27
Success factors, 8–9
Successful Promotions, 297
Sullivan, Robert, 119, 216–217
Summer marketing tips, 300–302
Supplier-vendor-customer financing, 95
Supplies, office, 58
Surveys, customer, 219–220, 253, 267, 293

T

Taglines, 30, 31
Taste, in advertising, 194
Taxes, 26, 104, 260. *See also* Internal Revenue Service (IRS)
Tax ID numbers, 33
Technology, 64–69
  and efficiency, 263
  for entrepreneurs with disabilities, 66–67, 68
  equipment, 64–65
  use of, 21–22

for virtual meetings, 65–66
web sites, 225
Teleclasses, 66
Teleconferencing, 66
Telemarketing, 210
Telephone directories, advertising in, 185
Telephone etiquette, 206–208
Telephone messages, 202–203
Telephone numbers, 193–194
Television, 167–168
Terminology, in customer communication, 283
Territorial government resources, 119
Testimonials, customer, 202
Test mailings, 180
Test-marketing, 84
Thank-you letters, 216, 222
30-second pitch, 209, 277
Thomas Register of American Manufacturers, 76, 77
Time management:
  principles, 51–54
  time-wasting activities, 54–56
  tips, 61–64
Tip sheets, 164, 295
Toll-free phone numbers, 193–194
Tone, in communication, 283
Touch, in advertising, 194
Trademarks, 248, 255–256
Trade shows, 176–177, 276
Travel, and mobile technology, 69–70
Trends, tracking, 16, 211–212
Tribal Business Information Centers (TBICs), 117
Turning away business, 302–303
TV, 167–168

U

Uniform resource locator (URL), 226
Uninterruptible power supply (UPS) devices, 65
U.S. Department of Agriculture, 89
U.S. Department of Labor, Office of Disability Employment Policy, 115
U.S. Export Assistance Centers, 117, 242

U.S. Small Business Administration
(SBA):
business plans, 73
Certified Development Company 504
Loan Program, 89–90
courses, 21
entrepreneurial resources, 116–118
entrepreneurs with disabilities, 67
exporting, 242
financing, 89–90
library, 117
loans, 88, 89–90, 93
Office of Technology, 118
Office of Veterans Business
Development, 67
Office of Women's Business
Ownership, 89, 117–118
seminars and counseling, 15
venture capital, 270
USA Today, 297
Usenet newsgroups, 239

V

Value-added resellers (VARs), 287
Vanity phone numbers, 194
Variable costs, 98
Vehicle signage, 195
Venture capital, 270
Videoconferencing, 66
Videos, producing, 174
Virtual assistants, 129–130, 263
Virtual meetings, 65–66
Virtual receptionists, 207–208, 215, 263,
281, 289
Virus protection software, 65
Voice mail, 202–203, 207, 215
Volunteering, 171, 265

W

Wages, 3, 4
Wall Street Journal, 297
Walsh, Chanin, 196
Warranties, 102

Web conferencing service, 66
Web hosting, 228–229
Web Hosting for Small Business with
Commerce Manager, 229
Web Marketing Today, 297
Web plans, 228
Webrings, 239
Web sites:
articles on, 161–163
categories, 225–226
columns on, 161, 201
constructing, 228–230
customer-friendly, 231–233
for customer service, 215
planning, 228
as spin-off venture, 249, 252
uses, 224–226
Web writing, 236
Weight control, 299–300
Wholesale sales, 36
Williams, Debbie, 172
Wilson, Ralph F., 297
Window painting, 138–139, 194–195,
249
Wireless technologies, 66, 70
WomenBiz.gov, 119
Women entrepreneurs:
government contracts, 278
publications for, 296–297
specialty loans, 90
statistics, 1–2
Women's Business Centers:
government contracts, 119
resources, 117–118
Women's Business Development
Centers:
business plans, 73
entrepreneurs with disabilities, 67
financing, 89, 90
seminars and counseling, 15
Women's Yellow Pages, 185
Word-of-mouth advertising, 102,
146–147
Work-for-trade, 103–104, 187
Work hours, 3–4, 5, 99
Worksheets, marketing budget,
285–286

Work space. *See* Offices
Worst-case scenarios, 283–285
Writer's Market, 97, 162, 164, 174
Writing:
    articles, 161–163, 173, 236, 279
    books, 173, 174–175
    columns, 161, 201
    how-to publications, 173–174
    promotion pieces, 160–165
    Web writing, 236
Wyatt-MacKenzie Publishing, Inc.,
    155–156

Y

Yahoo Merchant Solutions, 229
Yellow Pages, 185
Young, Valerie, 7
Yudkin, Marcia, 277

Z

Zbar, Jeff, 235
Zobel, Jan, 26